THREE EXCITING

The Store	*1995 Tours*
A BRAND NEW retail store sellling a wide range of aviation books, telescopes, binoculars, plastic model kits scale model airliners in fact everything **aviation associated**	A full range of European and United States tours offering the highest standards in organisation, transportation and accommodation

CURRENT TITLES

UNITED STATES MILITARY AIRCRAFT SERIAL BATCHES 1960-1993
A5 format ISBN 0 947755 11X (order code AA01) price £5.50
A handy pocket reference covering all USAF, US Army, USN\USMC and USCG serials allocated since 1960. Extensive notes on cancelled and Foreign Sales batches.

USMIL - UNITED STATES MILITARY AIRCRAFT SERIALS
A5 format ISBN 0 947755 13 6 (order code AA03) price £12.50
Undoubtedly THE book for the serious military enthusiast. and now in its sixth edition. So popular has the current title been that it was reprinted late last year. It covers all current USAF, US Army, USN and USCG aircraft with a section listing NASA, FAA and other Government agencies. A section records AMARC residents, as well current units and bases worldwide handling US military aircraft.

TRANSPORT AIRCRAFT of the CIS A5 format ISBN 0 947755 14 4 (order code AA04) price £9.50
Certainly not the first book on this subject, but surely the most thorough, comprehensive and effective presentation of the absolute plethora of information now emerging from the former Soviet Union. The book is divided into THREE distinct sections. The first is a listing in ICAO civil code order of current aircraft, subdivided by operator and type. Secondly is a full production record of all major former Soviet transport aircraft types, showing construction and\or build number, sub-type, and all registrations\serials chronologically listed. Finally, the third section is a cross-reference of all known serial\registration allocations. This book is a MUST for Soviet enthusiasts.

WORLDMIL - World Military Aircraft Serials A5 format ISBN 0 947755 16 0 (order code AA06) price £12.50
A companion volume to USMIL and EUROMIL, probably the most comprehensive listing of the remaining air forces of the World not covered by the other two titles.

BCAR - British Civil Aircraft Registers PART II (Out of Sequence)
A5 format ISBN 0 947755 18 7 (order code AA08) price £6.50
As well as listing in a clear, easy to read format all Out of Sequence allocations, all In-Sequence allocations since G-BNAA are also listed. This updates the numerous so called complete registers published at the time. Later this year Aviation Associates will produce its own version of the 1919-1985 section of the British Register.

TITLES IN PREPARATION

OLDMIL - OBSOLETE & PRESERVED MILITARY AIRCRAFT SERIALS - PART I
A5 format ISBN 0 947755 20 9 (order code AA10) price £12.50

EUROMIL - EUROPEAN MILITARY AIRCRAFT SERIALS
A5 format ISBN 0 947755 24 1 (order code AA14) price £12.50)

A further eight publication are planned

For FULL information on THE JOURNAL, THE STORE or 1995 AVIATION TOURS write today to:

Aviation Associates Ltd. P.O. Box 3201,.London E7 8RJ.

Plus a full POST FREE mail order service for all our own publications as well as all major publishers. Write for brochure.

AVIATION ASSOCIATES

NOW YOU HAVE PURCHASED MILITARY AIRCRAFT MARKINGS WHY NOT EXPAND YOUR KNOWLEDGE WITH THE 'TAHS' RANGE OF SPECIALIST BOOKS FOR THE ENTHUSIAST, HISTORIAN OR SPOTTER?

AIRBAND RADIOS
We specialise in top quality airband radios. Usually available from stock are the YUPITERU range of radios, ie the VT125-II, VT-225, MVT7000 and the MVT-7100.

AIRLINES 95
The 13th edition available late March is the established spotters favourite for coverage of the world's airline fleet listing. Every airline in the world where aircraft from light twin to wide bodies are operated. 170 countries, 1,700 airlines, over 25,000 registrations. Each aircraft is listed with registration, type, c/n, p/i, and where applicable line and fleet number and name. Available as Comb Bound (ie metal lay flat binding at just **£8.95** or in a loose leaf binder at **£11.95**.

AIRPORT MOVEMENTS
Is a monthly magazine published and distributed by THE AVIATION HOBBY SHOP. AIRPORT MOVEMENTS gives airport movements on a regular basis for the following airports: Heathrow, Gatwick, Stansted, Luton, Birmingham, Shannon, Bournemouth, Bristol, Cardiff, East Midlands, Jersey, Northolt, Southampton, Southend as well as foreign airport reports on a space available basis. Average monthly page content is around 28. AIRPORT MOVEMENTS is available around the 15th to the 20 of the month from a number of different outlets in the South of England, the Midlands and the Manchester area at a price of 75p per copy. However, should you wish to have a regular standing order for this publication to be despatched hot from the press we will be more than happy to place your name on our regular mailing list. To have you own copy of AIRPORT MOVEMENTS sent to you each month costs £1 per copy and this includes first-class mail delivery in the UK. You can subscribe for three, six or 12 months. To receive a free sample copy of our choice send a stamped 9inx6in envelope.

TURBO PROP AIRLINER PRODUCTION LIST
Now available the second edition of Turbo Prop Airliners Production List gives full production and service histories of EVERY WESTERN - BUILT TURBOPROP AIRLINER to enter service since 1948. Each aircraft is listed by manufacturer and type in construction number sequence. Each individual entry then lists line number (where applicable), sub-type, and first flight date where known. The entry then goes on to list every registration carried by the airframe, owners and delivery dates, leases, crash or withdrawal from service dates and any other relevant information. There is a complete cross reference of registration to c/n for every type covered. This publication is available in two formats:–Soft-back in card covers with sewn binding at **£10.95** or in a dark green loose-leaf binder at **£13.95**.

WORLD AIRLINE FLEET NEWS
Published monthly, World Airline Fleet News is dedicated to the ever changing and exciting world of airlines and airliners–reporting new airlines, new and used airliner transactions, livery changes and much more. Unrivalled photographic coverage on a worldwide basis is complimented by the generous use of colour. Each issue contains approximately 50 illustrations with around 30 in colour. World Airline Fleet News is produced on quality gloss art paper for the best photographic reproduction. Sample issue **£3.25**.

World Airline Colours–Volume 1
This long awaited revised edition of volume 1 of World Airline Colours is now available. Features 148 colour pictures and informative text. Price **£13.95**

The Vital Guide to Commercial Aircraft & Airliners
A concise and highly detailed reference work to the most important commercial aircraft and airliners in operation today. Also included is a special guide to 100 of the world's most significant airlines. 300 superb up-to-the-minute colour photographs illustrate a range of types from around the globe, making this an indispensible guide to all those who need to know about civil aircraft today. Price **£9.95**.

Soviet Transports
A Production list of Russian-built airliners. Listed by type and place of manufacture, it also includes all registrations, constructors numbers, operators, leases, dates and names. Price **£10.95**.

Airlines Coding & Airports Decoding
The three and four-letter codes of almost 15,000 airport, airfields and airstrips sorted on name, three-letter code and four-code. The two- and three-letter codes of more than 3,500 airlines and aviation related companies sorted on name, two-letter code, three-letter code and callsign. Price **£10.95**.

Callsign 95–The Civil & Military Aviation Callsign Directory
The most comprehensive callsign directory available for aircraft and radio enthusiasts, containing over 7,000 civil and military callsigns. The civil directory lists alphabetically almost 3,000 callsigns in current use with airlines, governments, handling agents and other operators around the world. The military section contains well over 4,000 current and historical tactical callsigns, noted over the past decade. Information contained within this section includes, Callsign, Aircraft type, Air-Arm, Code, Unit, base, plus other relevant information. Price **£7.95**.

95 JET & PROP JET – NEW LAY-FLAT EDITION
The only standard reference for the total world-wide corporate fleet identification. Available again by popular demand – in one pocket-sized book. More than 7,700 Jets and 8,600 Projects listed with registration marks, construction numbers and owner identification. Over 250 different models and model derivatives and 43 manufacturers from 143 countries. **Available now £10.95**.

HEATHROW AIRPORT SUMMER TIMETABLES 1995
Lists arrivals/departure times, fight numbers, departure points, period of operation and arrival/departure terminal. Also included are airport decode, airline flight designator decode, radio frequencies and airport layout maps. **AVAILABLE APRIL, PRICE £3.95.**

FREE CATALOGUES
All our goods are listed in our two free catalogues. Catalogue 1 books, postcards, colour slides and airband radios. Catalogue 2: plastic kits, decals and modelling accessories. Write, ring or fax for your free copy today.

We are just 10 minutes drive from Heathrow Airport, just off the M4/M25 motorways. Bus U3 operates between Heathrow Central and West Drayton BR station, two minutes walk from the shop. *All major credit cards accepted. 24hr 'Ansaphone' service.*

The Aviation Hobby Shop

(Dept MAM), 4 HORTON PARADE, HORTON ROAD, WEST DRAYTON, MIDDLESEX UB7 8EA
Tel: 01895 442123   Fax: 01895 421412

Military Aircraft Markings '95

Ian Allan abc

Peter R. March

IAN ALLAN Publishing

Contents

Photographs by Peter R. March (PRM) unless otherwise credited

This sixteenth edition published 1995

ISBN 0 7110 2341 7

All rights reserved. No part of this book may be
reproduced or transmitted in any form or by any
means, electronic or mechanical, including photo-
copying, recording, or by any information storage
and retrieval system, without permission from the
Publisher in writing.

© Ian Allan Ltd 1995

Published by Ian Allan Ltd
and printed by Ian Allan Printing Ltd
Coombelands House, Addlestone, Surrey KT15 1HY

Front cover:
A Sea Harrier FRS1 of 800 NAS positions itself for landing on HMS *Invincible. Denis J. Calvert*

Rear cover, top:
Eurofighter 2000 (DA2). *BAe Defence*

Rear cover, bottom:
Hawker Hunter GA11 XF3000. *PRM*

Introduction

This sixteenth edition of *abc Military Aircraft Markings*, a companion to *abc Civil Aircraft Markings*, again sets out to list in alphabetical and numerical order all the aircraft which carry a United Kingdom military serial, and which are based, or might be seen, in the UK. The term *aircraft* used here covers powered, manned aeroplanes, helicopters, airships and gliders. Included are all the current Royal Air Force, Royal Navy, Army Air Corps, Ministry of Defence (Procurement Executive), Defence Research Agency, Test & manufacturers' test aircraft and civilian-owned aircraft with military markings.

Aircraft withdrawn from operational use but which are retained in the UK for ground training purposes or otherwise preserved by the Services and in museums and collections are listed. The serials of some incomplete aircraft have been included, such as the cockpit sections of machines displayed by the RAF Exhibition Flight, aircraft used by airfield fire sections and for service battle damage repair training (BDRT), together with significant parts of aircraft held by preservation groups and societies. Where only part of the aircraft fuselage remains the abbreviation <ff> for front fuselage/cockpit section or <rf> for rear fuselage is shown after the type. Many of these aircraft are allocated, and sometimes wear, a secondary identity, such as an RAF Support Command 'M' maintenance number. These numbers are listed against those aircraft to which they have been allocated.

A serial 'missing' is either because it was never issued as it formed part of a 'black-out block', or because the aircraft is written off, scrapped, sold, abroad or allocated an alternative marking. Aircraft used as targets on MoD ranges to which access is restricted, and un-manned target drones, are omitted, as are UK military aircraft that have been permanently grounded overseas and unlikely to return to Britain.

In the main, the serials listed are those markings presently displayed on the aircraft. Aircraft which bear a false serial are quoted in *italic type*. Very often these serials are carried by replicas, which are denoted by <R> after the type. The manufacturer and aircraft type are given, together with recent alternative, previous, secondary or civil identity shown in round brackets. Complete records of multiple previous identities are only included where space permits. The operating unit and its based location, along with any known unit and base code markings in square brackets, are given as accurately as possible. The unit markings are normally carried boldly on the sides of the fuselage or on the aircraft's fin. In the case of RAF and AAC machines currently in service, they are usually one or two letters or numbers, while the RN continues to use a well-established system of three-figure codes between 000 and 999 together with a fin letter code denoting the aircraft's operational base. RN squadrons, units and bases are allocated blocks of numbers from which individual aircraft codes are issued. To help identification of RN bases and landing platforms on ships, a list of tail-letter codes with their appropriate name, helicopter code number, ship pennant number and type of vessel, is included; as is a helicopter code number/ships' tail-letter code grid cross-reference.

Codes change, for example when aircraft move between units, and therefore the markings currently painted on a particular aircraft might not be those shown in this edition because of subsequent events. The effect of the Government's on-going Defence Cost Studies and its implementation through the RAF's Front Line First reductions and re-organisation accounts for the large number of changes in this edition. In particular the closure of Chivenor, Scampton, Finningley and Wyton will have a major effect through 1995 and 1996. Those airframes which may not appear in the next edition because of sale, accident, etc, have their fates, where known, given in italic type in the *locations* column.

The Irish Army Air Corps fleet is listed, together with the serials of other overseas air arms whose aircraft might be seen visiting the UK from time to time. The serial numbers are as usually presented on the individual machine or as they are normally identified. Where possible, the aircraft's base and operating unit have been shown.

USAF, US Army and US Navy aircraft based in the UK and in Western Europe, and of types which regularly visit the UK from the USA, are each listed in separate sections by aircraft type. The serial number actually displayed on the aircraft is shown in full, with additional Fiscal Year (FY) or full serial information also provided. Where appropriate, details of the operating wing, squadron allocation and base are added. The USAF is, like the RAF, continuing a major reorganisation which is producing new unit titles, many squadron changes and the closure of bases worldwide. Only details that concern changes effected by December 1994 are shown.

Veteran and Vintage aircraft which carry overseas military markings but which are based in the UK have been separately listed showing their principal means of identification.

Information shown is believed to be correct at 31 January 1995, and significant changes can be monitored through the monthly 'Military Markings' column in *Aircraft Illustrated*.

Acknowledgements

The compiler again wishes to thank the many people who have taken trouble to send comments, criticism and other useful information following the publication of the previous editions of *abc Military Aircraft Markings*. In particular the following correspondents: P. F. Burton, B. Dunnell, G. Fraser, H. W. Gandy, A.Helden, I.Logan, P.- J. Martin, A.P. March, M. K. Thompson and P. Wiggins.

This compilation has relied heavily on the publications of the following aviation groups and societies: *Air North, British Aviation Review* (British Aviation Research Group), Macclesfield Historical Aviation Society, *North-West Air News* (Air Britain, Merseyside Branch), *Osprey* (Solent Aviation Society), *Prestwick Airport Letter* (Prestwick Airport Aviation Group), *Scottish Air News* (Central Scotland Aviation Group) *Stansted Aviation Newsletter* (The Stansted Aviation Society), *Ulster Airmail* (Ulster Aviation Society) and the *Valley Air News* (Valley Aviation Society).

This fully revised edition of *abc Military Aircraft Markings* would not have been possible without considerable research and collation by Howard Curtis and checking by Wal Gandy, to who I am indebted.

PRM   **January 1995**

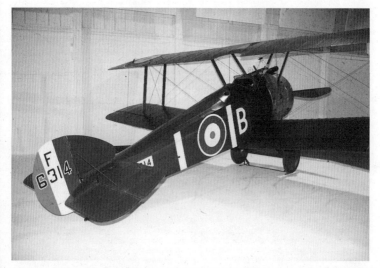

Sopwith Camel F6314 is exhibited in the RAF Museum at Hendon. *PRM*

Abbreviations

AAC	Army Air Corps
A&AEE	Aircraft & Armament Evaluation Establishment
AAS	Aeromedical Airlift Squadron
ABS	Air Base Squadron
ACC	Air Combat Command
ACCGS	Air Cadets Central Gliding School
ACCS	Airborne Command and Control Squadron
ACW	Airborne Control Wing
AEF	Air Experience Flight
AES	Air Engineering School
AEW	Airborne Early Warning
AFRES	Air Force Reserve
AFSC	Air Force System Command
AG	Airlift Group
AGA	Academia General de Air
AIU	Accident Investigation Unit
AkG	Aufklärürngsgeschwader (Reconnaissance Wing)
ALS	Airlift Squadron
AMC	Air Mobility Command
AMD-BA	Avions Marcel Dassault-Breguet Aviation
AMG	Aircraft Maintenance Group
AMS	Air Movements School
AMW	Air Mobility Wing
ANG	Air National Guard
APS	Aircraft Preservation Society
ARS	Air Refuelling Squadron
ARW	Air Refuelling Wing
ARWS	Advanced Rotary Wing Squadron
ASF	Aircraft Servicing Flight
AS&RU	Aircraft Salvage and Repair Unit
ATC	Air Training Corps
ATCC	Air Traffic Control Centre
AvCo	Aviation Company
Avn	Aviation
AW	Airlift Wing
AW	Armstrong Whitworth Aircraft
AW&CS	Airborne Warning & Control Squadron
BAC	British Aircraft Corporation
BAe	British Aerospace PLC
BAOR	British Army of the Rhine
BAPC	British Aviation Preservation Council
Batt	Battalion
BATUS	British Army Training Unit Support
BBMF	Battle of Britain Memorial Flight
BDRF	Battle Damage Repair Flight
BDRT	Battle Damage Repair Training
Be	Beech
Bf	Bayerische Flugzeugwerke
BFWF	Basic Fixed Wing Flight
BG	Bomber Group
BGA	British Gliding & Soaring Association
BILP	Bitveni Letecky Pluk (Attack Regiment)
BP	Boulton & Paul
BS	Bomber Squadron
B-V	Boeing-Vertol
BW	Bomber Wing
CAC	Commonwealth Aircraft Corporation
CARG	Cotswold Aircraft Restoration Group
CASA	Construcciones Aeronautics SA
Cav	Cavalry
CBAS	Commando Brigade Air Squadron
CC	County Council
CCF	Combined Cadet Force
CDE	Chemical Defence Establishment
CEAM	Centre d'Expérimentation Aériennes Militaires
CEV	Centre d'Essais en Vol
CFS	Central Flying School
CGMF	Central Glider Maintenance Flight
CIFAS	Centre d'Instruction des Forces Aériennes Stratégiques

CinC	Commander in Chief
CITAC	Centre d'Instruction Tactique
Co	Company/County
CSDE	Central Servicing Development Establishment
CT	College of Technology
CTE	Central Training Establishment
CTTS	Civilian Technical Training School
CV	Chance-Vought
D-BD	Dassault-Breguet Dornier
Det	Detachment
DH	de Havilland
DHC	de Havilland Canada
DRA	Defence Research Agency
DTI	Department of Trade and Industry
EAP	European Aircraft Project
EB	Escadre de Bombardment
EC	Escadre de Chasse
ECS	Electronic Countermeasures Squadron
EDA	Escadre de Detection Aéroportée
EdC	Escadre de Convoyage
EE	English Electric/Escadrille Electronique
EHI	European Helicopter Industries
EL	Escadre de Liaison
EMA	East Midlands Airport
EMVO	Elementaire Militaire Vlieg Opleiding
EoN	Elliot's of Newbury
EP&TU	Exhibition, Production & Transportation Unit
ER	Escadre de Reconnaissance
ERV	Escadre de Ravitaillement en Vol
Esc	Escuadron (Squadron)
Esk	Eskadrille (Squadron)
ET	Escadre de Transport
ETE	Escadron de Transport et Entrainment
ETOM	Escadron de Transport Outre Mer
ETPS	Empire Test Pilots' School
ETS	Engineering Training School
FAA	Fleet Air Arm/Federal Aviation Administration
FACF	Forward Air Control Flight
FBS	Flugbereitschaftstaffel
FBW	Fly by wire
FC	Forskokcentralen
FE	Further Education
FETC	Fire and Emergency Training Centre
ff	Front fuselage
FG	Fighter Group
FH	Fairchild-Hiller
FI	Falkland Islands
FLGFFB	Fliegerlehrgruppe Furstenfeldbruck
Flt	Flight
FMA	Fabrica Militar de Aviones
FONA	Flag Officer Naval Aviation
FRADU	Fleet Requirements and Air Direction Unit
FRA	FR Aviation
FS	Fighter Squadron
FSCTE	Fire School Central Training Establishment
FTS	Flying Training School
Fw	Focke Wulf
FW	Fighter Wing
FY	Fiscal Year
F3 OCU	Tornado F3 Operational Conversion Unit
GAL	General Aircraft Ltd
GAM	Groupe Aerien Mixte
GD	General Dynamics
GE	Groupement Ecole
GEC	General Electric Company
GHL	Groupe d'Helicopteres Legeres
GI	Ground Instruction/Groupement d'Instruction

7

HC	Helicopter Combat Support Sqn
HFR	Heeresfliegerregiment (Corps transport regiment)
HFWS	Heeresflieger Waffenschule
Hkp Div	Helikopterdivisionen
HMS	Her Majesty's Ship
HOCU	Harrier OCU
HP	Handley-Page
HQ	Headquarters
HS	Hawker Siddeley
HSF	Harrier Servicing Flight
IAF	Israeli Air Force
IAM	Institute of Aviation Medicine
IHM	International Helicopter Museum
IWM	Imperial War Museum
JATE	Joint Air Transport Establishment
JbG	Jagd Bomber Geschwader (Fighter Bomber Wing)
JG	Jagd Geschwader (Fighter Wing)
LSP	Letecky Slosky Pluk
LTG	Luft Transport Geschwader (Air Transport Wing)
LTV	Ling-Temco-Vought
LVG	Luftwaffen Versorgungs Geschwader (Air Force Maintenance Wing)
MARPAT	Maritime Patrouillegroep
McD	McDonnell Douglas
Med	Medical
MFG	Marine Flieger Geschwader (Naval Air Wing)
MH	Max Holste
MIB	Military Intelligence Battalion
MiG	Mikoyan-Gurevich
MoD(PE)	Ministry of Defence (Procurement Executive)
Mod	Modified
MR	Maritime Reconnaissance
MRF	Meteorological Research Flight
MS	Morane-Saulnier
MU	Maintenance Unit
NA	North American
NACDS	Naval Air Command Driving School
NAEWF	NATO Airborne Early Warning Force
NAF	Naval Air Facility
NASU	Naval Air Support Unit
NE	North-East
NI	Northern Ireland
NMSU	Nimrod Major Servicing Unit
NYARC	North Yorks Aircraft Restoration Centre
OCU	Operational Conversion Unit
OEU	Operation Evaluation Unit
PRU	Photographic Reconnaissance Unit
R	Replica
RAeS	Royal Aeronautical Society
RAF	Royal Aircraft Factory/Royal Air Force
RAFC	Royal Air Force College
RAFM	Royal Air Force Museum
RAFGSA	Royal Air Force Gliding and Soaring Association
RAOC	Royal Army Ordnance Corps
RCAF	Royal Canadian Air Force
RE	Royal Engineers
Regt	Regiment
REME	Royal Electrical & Mechanical Engineers
rf	Rear fuselage
RM	Royal Marines
RMC of S	Royal Military College of Science
RN	Royal Navy
RNAS	Royal Naval Air Station
RNAW	Royal Naval Aircraft Workshop
RNAY	Royal Naval Aircraft Yard
RNEC	Royal Naval Engineering College
RNGSA	Royal Navy Gliding and Soaring Association
ROF	Royal Ordnance Factory
RQS	Rescue Squadron
R-R	Rolls-Royce
RS	Reid & Sigrist/Reconnaissance Squadron
RSV	Reparto Sperimentale Volo
RW	Reconnaissance Wing
SA	Scottish Aviation
Saab	Svenska Aeroplan Aktieboleg
SAE	School of Aircraft Engineering
SAH	School of Air Handling
SAL	Scottish Aviation Limited
SAOEU	Strike/Attack Operational Evaluation Unit
SAR	Search and Rescue
Saro	Saunders-Roe
SARTU	Search and Rescue Training Unit
SCW	Sea Control Wing
SEPECAT	Société Européenne de Production de l'avion Ecole de Combat et d'Appui Tactique
SHAPE	Supreme Headquarters Allied Forces Europe
SIF	Servicing Instruction Flight
SKTU	Sea King Training Unit
Skv	Skvadron
SLP	Stihaci Letecky Plus (Fighter Regiment)
Sm	Smaldeel (Squadron)
SNCAN	Société Nationale de Constructions Aéronautiques du Nord
SOES	Station Operation & Engineering Squadron
SOG	Special Operations Group
SOS	Special Operations Squadron
SoTT	School of Technical Training
SOW	Special Operations Wing
SPAD	Société Pour les Appareils Deperdussin
Sqn	Squadron
SSF	Station Servicing Flight
T&EE	Test & Evaluation Establishment
TGp	Test Group
TMTS	Trade Management Training School
TS	Test Squadron
TsAGI	Tsentral'ny Aerogidrodinamicheski Instut (Central Aero & Hydrodynamics Institute)
TSLw	Technische Schule der Luftwaffe
TTTE	Tri-national Tornado Training Establishment
TW	Test Wing
UAS	University Air Squadron
UK	United Kingdom
UKAEA	United Kingdom Atomic Energy Authority
UNFICYP	United Nations' Forces in Cyprus
US	United States
USAF	United States Air Force
USAFE	United States Air Forces in Europe
USAREUR	US Army Europe
USEUCOM	United States European Command
USN	United States Navy
VGS	Volunteer Gliding School
VMGR	Marine Aerial Refuelling/Transport Squadron
VMGRT	Marine Aerial Refuelling/Transport Training Squadron
VQ	Fleet Air Reconnaissance Squadron
VR	Fleet Logistic Support Squadron
VS	Vickers-Supermarine
Wg	Wing
WLT	Weapons Loading Training
WRS	Weather Reconnaissance Squadron
WS	Westland
WTD	Wehrtechnische Dienstelle
WW2	World War II
ZDLP	Zmiesany Dopravny Letecky Pluk (Mixed Transport Aviation Regiment)

8

A Guide to the Location of Operational Bases in the UK

This section is to assist the reader to locate the places in the United Kingdom where operational military aircraft are based. The term *aircraft* also includes helicopters and gliders.

The alphabetical order listing gives each location in relation to its county and to its nearest classified road(s) (*by* means adjoining; *of* means proximate to), together with its approximate direction and mileage from the centre of a nearby major town, city or specific motorway junction.

Some civil airports are included where active military units are also based, but **excluded** are MoD sites with non-operational aircraft (eg *gate guardians*), the bases of privately-owned civil aircraft which wear military markings and museums.

User	Base name	County/Region	Location	Distance/direction from (town)
T&EE	Aberporth	Dyfed	N of A487	6m ENE of Cardigan
USAF	Alconbury	Cambridgeshire	E by A1/A14	4m NW of Huntingdon
RAF	Aldergrove/Belfast Airport	Co Antrim	W by A26	13m W of Belfast
RAF	Arbroath	Tayside	E by A933	2m NW of Arbroath
RAF	Benson	Oxfordshire	E by A423	1m NE of Wallingford
A&AEE	Boscombe Down	Wiltshire	S by A303, W of A338	6m N of Salisbury
RAF	Boulmer	Northumberland	E of B1339	4m E of Alnwick
RAF	Brize Norton	Oxfordshire	W of A4095	5m SW of Witney
RAF	Cambridge Airport/ Teversham	Cambridgeshire	S by A1303	2m E of Cambridge
RAF	Catterick	Yorkshire North	E by A1	7m WNW of Northallerton
RAF	Challock	Kent	S from A252	2m E of Charing
RAF	Chivenor	Devon	S of A361	4m WNW of Barnstaple
RAF	Colerne	Wiltshire	S of A420, E of Fosse Way	5m NE of Bath
RAF	Coltishall	Norfolk	W of B1150	9m NNE of Norwich
RAF	Coningsby	Lincolnshire	S of A153, W by B1192	10m NW of Boston
RAF	Cosford	Shropshire	W of A41, N of A464	9m WNW of Wolverhampton
RAF	Cottesmore	Leicestershire	W of A1, N of B668	9m NW of Stamford
RAF	Cranwell	Lincolnshire	N by A17, S by B1429	5m WNW of Sleaford
RNAS	Culdrose	Cornwall	E by A3083	1m SE of Helston
AAC	Dishforth	Yorkshire North	E by A1	4m E of Ripon
BAe	Dunsfold	Surrey	W of A281, S of B2130	9m S of Guildford
RAF	Exeter Airport	Devon	S by A30	4m ENE of Exeter
BAe	Filton	Avon	E by M5 jn 17, W by A38	4m N of Bristol
RAF	Finningley	Yorkshire South	W of A614, S of B1396	6m ESE of Doncaster
RNAY	Fleetlands	Hampshire	E by A32	2m SE of Fareham
RAF	Glasgow Airport	Strathclyde	N by M8 jn 28	7m W of city
RAF	Halton	Buckinghamshire	N of A4011, S of B4544	4m ESE of Aylesbury
RAF	Henlow	Bedfordshire	E of A600, W of A6001	1m SW of Henlow
RAF	Honington	Suffolk	E of A134, W of A1088	6m S of Thetford
RAF	Hullavington	Wiltshire	W by A429	1m N of M4 jn 17
RAF	Kenley	Greater London	W of A22	1m W of Warlingham
RAF	Kinloss	Grampian	E of B9011, N of B9089	3m NE of Forres
RAF	Kirknewton	Lothian	E by B7031, N by A70	8m SW of Edinburgh
USAF	Lakenheath	Suffolk	W by A1065	8m W of Thetford
RAF	Leconfield	Humberside	E by A164	2m N of Beverley
RAF	Leeming	Yorkshire North	E by A1	5m SW of Northallerton
RAF	Leuchars	Fife	E of A919	7m SE of Dundee
RAF	Linton-on-Ouse	Yorkshire North	E of B6265	10m NW of York
RAF	Little Rissington	Gloucestershire	W of A424	4m S of Stow-on-the-Wold
T&EE	Llanbedr	Gwynedd	W of A496	7m NNW of Barmouth
RAF	Lossiemouth	Grampian	W of B9135, S of B9040	4m N of Elgin
RAF	Lyneham	Wiltshire	W of A3102, S of A420	10m WSW of Swindon
DRA	Machrihanish	Strathclyde	W of A83	3m W of Campeltown
RAF	Manston	Kent	N by A253	3m W of Ramsgate
RAF	Marham	Norfolk	N by A1122	6m W of Swaffham
AAC	Middle Wallop	Hampshire	S by A343	6m SW of Andover
USAF	Mildenhall	Suffolk	S by A1101	9m NNE of Newmarket
AAC	Netheravon	Wiltshire	E of A345	5m N of Amesbury
RAF	Newton	Nottinghamshire	N of A52, W of A46	7m E of Nottingham
RAF	Northolt	Greater London	N by A40	3m E of M40 jn 1
RAF	Odiham	Hampshire	E of A32	2m SW of M3 jn 5
RNAS	Portland	Dorset	E by A354	3m S of Weymouth
RN	Predannack	Cornwall	W by A3083	7m S of Helston
RN	Prestwick Airport	Strathclyde	E by A79	3m N of Ayr

9

UK Operational Bases — continued

User	Base name	County/Region	Location	Distance/direction from (town)
RAF	St Athan	South Glamorgan	N of B4265	13m WSW of Cardiff
RAF	St Mawgan/Newquay Airport	Cornwall	N of A3059	4m ENE of Newquay
RAF	Samlesbury	Lancashire	N by A677, S by A59	3m E of M6 jn 31
RAF	Scampton	Lincolnshire	W by A15	6m N of Lincoln
RAF	Sealand	Clwyd	W by A550	6m WNW of Chester
RAF	Shawbury	Shropshire	W of B5063	7m NNE of Shrewsbury
RAF	South Cerney	Gloucestershire	W by A419	3m SE of Cirencester
RAF	Swansea Airport/ Fairwood Common	West Glamorgan	W by A4118	6m W of Swansea
RAF	Swanton Morley	Norfolk	W of B1147	4m NNE of Dereham
RAF/ Shorts	Sydenham/ Belfast City Airport	Co Down	W by A2	2m E of city
RAF	Ternhill	Shropshire	SW by A41	3m SW of Market Drayton
AAC	Topcliffe	Yorkshire North	E of A167, W of A168	3m SW of Thirsk
RAF	Turnhouse/Edinburgh Airport	Lothian	N of A8, E of M8 J2	6m W of Edinburgh
RAF	Upavon	Wiltshire	S by A342	14m WNW of Andover
RAF	Valley	Gwynedd	S of A5 on Anglesey	5m SE of Holyhead
RAF	Waddington	Lincolnshire	E by A607, W by A15	5m S of Lincoln
BAe	Warton	Lancashire	S by A584	8m SE of Blackpool
AAC	Wattisham	Suffolk	N of B1078	5m SSW of Stowmarket
T&EE	West Freugh	Dumfries & Galloway	S by A757, W by A715	5m SE of Stranraer
RAF	Weston-on-the-Green	Oxfordshire	E by A43	9m N of Oxford
RAF	Wethersfield	Essex	E from B1053	5m NW of Braintree
RAF	Wittering	Cambridgeshire	W by A1, N of A47	3m S of Stamford
RAF	Woodvale	Merseyside	W by A565	5m SSW of Southport
RAF	Wyton	Cambridgeshire	E of A141, N of B1090	3m NE of Huntingdon
WS	Yeovil	Somerset	N of A30, S of A3088	1m W of Yeovil
RNAS	Yeovilton	Somerset	S by B3151, S of A303	5m N of Yeovil

British Military Aircraft Serials

The Committee of Imperial Defence through its Air Committee introduced a standardised system of numbering aircraft in November 1912. The Air Department of the Admiralty was allocated the first batch 1-200 and used these to cover aircraft already in use and those on order. The Army was issued with the next block from 201-800, which included the number 304 which was given to the Cody Biplane now preserved in the Science Museum. By the outbreak of World War 1 the Royal Navy was on its second batch of serials 801-1600 and this system continued with alternating allocations between the Army and Navy until 1916 when number 10000, a Royal Flying Corps BE2C, was reached.

It was decided not to continue with five digit numbers but instead to start again from 1, prefixing RFC aircraft with the letter A and RNAS aircraft with the prefix N. The RFC allocations commenced with A1 an FE2D and before the end of the year had reached A9999 an Armstrong Whitworth FK8. The next group commenced with B1 and continued in logical sequence through the C, D, E and F prefixes. G was used on a limited basis to identify captured German aircraft, while H was the last block of wartime-ordered aircraft. To avoid confusion I was not used, so the new postwar machines were allocated serials in the J range. A further minor change was made in the serial numbering system in August 1929 when it was decided to maintain four numerals after the prefix letter, thus omitting numbers 1 to 999. The new K series therefore commenced at K1000, which was allocated to an AW Atlas.

The Naval N prefix was not used in such a logical way. Blocks of numbers were allocated for specific types of aircraft such as seaplanes or flying-boats. By the late 1920s the sequence had largely been used up and a new series using the prefix S was commenced. In 1930 separate naval allocations were stopped and subsequent serials were issued in the 'military' range which had by this time reached the K series. A further change in the pattern of allocations came in the L range. Commencing with L7272 numbers were issued in blocks with smaller blocks of serials between not used. These were known as blackout blocks. It would appear that this policy is being reintroduced at the present time. As M had already been used as a suffix for Maintenance Command instructional airframes it was not used as a prefix. Although N had previously been used for naval aircraft it was used again for serials allocated from 1937.

With the build-up to World War 2 the rate of allocations quickly accelerated and the prefix R was being used when war was declared. The letters O and Q were not allotted, and nor was S which had been used up to S1865 for naval aircraft before integration into the RAF series. By 1940 the serial Z9999 had been reached, as part of a blackout block, with the letters U and Y not used to avoid confusion. The option to recommence serial allocation at A1000 was not taken up; instead it was decided to use an alphabetical two-letter prefix with three numerals running from 100 to 999. Thus AA100 was allocated to a Blenheim IV.

This two-letter, three-numeral serial system which started in 1940 continues today with the current issue being in the later part of the ZH range. The letters C, I, O, Q, U and Y were, with the exception of NC, not used. For various reasons the following letter combinations were not issued: DA, DB, DH, EA, GA to GZ, HA, HT, JE, JH, JJ, KR to KT, MR, NW, NZ, SA to SK, SV, TN, TR and VE. The first postwar serials issued were in the VP range while the end of the WZs had been reached by the Korean War. At the current rate of issue the Z range will last well into the next century.

Note: Whilst every effort has been made to ensure the accuracy of this publication, no part of the contents has been obtained from official sources. The compiler will be pleased to continue to receive comments, corrections and further information for inclusion in subsequent editions of *Military Aircraft Markings* and the monthly up-date of additions and amendments that is published in *Aircraft Illustrated*. Please send your information to Military Aircraft Markings, PO Box 46, Westbury-on-Trym, Bristol BS9 1TF; or fax to 0117 968 3928.

Shuttleworth Collection's Miles Magister P6382. *PRM*

British Military Aircraft Markings

A serial in *italics* denotes that it is not the genuine marking for that airframe.

Serial	Type (other identity) [code]	Owner/operator, location or fate	Notes
164	Bleriot Type XI (BAPC 106/9209M)	RAF Museum, Hendon	
168	Sopwith Tabloid Scout <R> (G-BFDE)	RAF Museum, Hendon	
304	Cody Biplane (BAPC 62)	Science Museum, South Kensington	
433	Bleriot Type XXVII (BAPC 107/ 9202M)	RAF Museum, Hendon	
687	RAF BE2b <R> (BAPC 181)	RAF Museum, Hendon	
1197	Bleriot XI <R> (G-BPVE)	Privately owned, Booker	
1701	RAF BE2c <R> (BAPC 117)	Brooklands Museum, Weybridge	
2345	Vickers FB5 Gunbus <R> (G-ATVP)	RAF Museum, Hendon	
2699	RAF BE2c	Imperial War Museum, Lambeth	
3066	Caudron GIII (G-AETA/9203M)	RAF Museum, Hendon	
5492	Sopwith LC-1T Triplane <R> (G-PENY)	Privately owned, stored Ballymoney	
5894	DH2 <R> (G-BFVH) [FB2]	Wessex Aviation & Transport, Chalmington	
5964	DH2 <R> (BAPC 112)	Museum of Army Flying, Middle Wallop	
6232	RAF BE2c <R> (BAPC 41)	RAF, stored St Athan	
8359	Short 184 <ff>	FAA Museum, RNAS Yeovilton	
A301	Morane BB (frame)	RAF Museum, Hendon	
A1325	RAF BE2e (G-BVGR)	Privately owned, Rye	
A1742	Bristol Scout D <R> (BAPC 38)	The Aircraft Restoration Co, Duxford	
A4850	RAF SE5 <R> (BAPC 176)	South Yorkshire Aviation Museum, Firbeck	
A7317	Sopwith Pup <R> (BAPC 179)	Midland Air Museum, Coventry	
A8226	Sopwith 1½ Strutter <R> (G-BIDW)	RAF Museum, Hendon	
B415	AFEE 10/42 Rotabuggy <R> (BAPC 163)	Museum of Army Flying, Middle Wallop	
B1807	Sopwith Pup (G-EAVX) [A7]	Privately owned, Keynsham, Avon	
B2458	Sopwith F1 Camel <R> (G-BPOB) [R]	Painted as F542, 1993	
B4863	Eberhardt SE5E (G-BLXT) [G]	Sold to the USA, May 1994	
B6291	Sopwith F1 Camel (G-ASOP)	Sold to the USA, May 1994	
B6401	Sopwith F1 Camel <R> (G-AWYY/C1701)	FAA Museum, RNAS Yeovilton	
B7270	Sopwith F1 Camel <R> (G-BFCZ)	Brooklands Museum, Weybridge	
B9708	Sopwith 1½ Strutter <R>	Macclesfield Historical Av Soc	
C1904	RAF SE5A <R> (G-PFAP) [Z]	Privately owned, Syerston	
C3011	Phoenix Currie Super Wot (G-SWOT) [S]	Privately owned, Breighton	
C4451	Avro 504J <R> (BAPC 210)	Southampton Hall of Aviation	
C4912	Bristol M1C <R> (BAPC 135)	Northern Aeroplane Workshops	
C4940	Bristol M1C <R>	Bygone Times Warehouse, Euxton, Lancs	
C4994	Bristol M1C <R> (G-BLWM)	RAF Museum, Hendon	
C9533	RAF SE5A <R> (G-BUWE) [M]	Privately owned, Boscombe Down	
D2700	RAF SE5A <R> (BAPC 208)	Tangmere Military Aviation Museum	
D3419	Sopwith F1 Camel <R> (BAPC 59)	RAF, stored St Athan	
D5329	Sopwith F5 Dolphin	RAF Museum Store, Cardington	
D7560	Avro 504K	Museum of Army Flying, Middle Wallop	
D7889	Bristol F2B Fighter (G-AANM/ BAPC 166)	Privately owned, St Leonards-on-Sea	
D8084	Bristol F2B Fighter (G-ACAA/ F4516) [S]	The Fighter Collection, Duxford	
D8096	Bristol F2B Fighter (G-AEPH) [D]	The Shuttleworth Collection, Old Warden	
D8781	Avro 504K <R> (G-ECKE)	Privately owned, Cambridge	
E373	Avro 504K <R> (BAPC 178)	Privately owned, Eccleston, Lancs	
E449	Avro 504K (G-EBJE/9205M)	RAF Museum, Hendon	
E2466	Bristol F2B Fighter (BAPC 165) [I]	RAF Museum, Hendon	

Notes	Serial	Type (other identity) [code]	Owner/operator, location or fate
	E2581	Bristol F2B Fighter	Imperial War Museum, Duxford
	F141	RAF SE5A <R> (G-SEVA) [G]	Privately owned, Boscombe Down
	F344	Avro 504K <R>	RAF Museum Store, Henlow
	F542	Sopwith F1 Camel <R> (G-BPOB)	Privately owned, Booker
	F760	SE5A Microlight <R> [A]	Privately owned, Redhill
	F904	RAF SE5A (G-EBIA)	The Shuttleworth Collection, Old Warden
	F938	RAF SE5A (G-EBIC/9208M)	RAF Museum, Hendon
	F943	RAF SE5A <R> (G-BIHF) [S]	Privately owned, White Waltham
	F943	RAF SE5A <R> (G-BKDT)	Yorkshire Air Museum, Elvington
	F1010	Airco DH9A [C]	RAF Museum, Hendon
	F3556	RAF RE8	Imperial War Museum, Duxford
	F4013	Sopwith F1 Camel <R>	Privately owned, Coventry
	F5447	RAF SE5A <R> (G-BKER) [N]	Privately owned, Cumbernauld
	F5459	RAF SE5A <R> (BAPC 142) [11-Y]	
	F5459	RAF SE5A <R> (G-INNY) [Y]	Privately owned, Old Sarum
	F6314	Sopwith F1 Camel (9206M) [B]	RAF Museum, Hendon
	F8010	RAF SE5A <R> (G-BDWJ) [Z]	Privately owned, Graveley
	F8614	Vickers Vimy <R> (G-AWAU)	RAF Museum, Hendon
	H1968	Avro 504K <R> (BAPC 42)	RAF, stored St Athan
	H2311	Avro 504K (G-ABAA)	Gr Manchester Mus of Science & Industry
	H3426	Hawker Hurricane <R> (BAPC 68)	Midland Air Museum, stored Coventry
	H5199	Avro 504K (BK892/3118M/ G-ACNB/G-ADEV)	The Shuttleworth Collection, Old Warden
	J7326	DH Humming Bird (G-EBQP)	Privately owned, Bishops Stortford
	J8067	Westland Pterodactyl 1a	Science Museum, South Kensington
	J9941	Hawker Hart 2 (G-ABMR)	RAF Museum, Hendon
	K1786	Hawker Tomtit (G-AFTA)	The Shuttleworth Collection, Old Warden
	K2050	Isaacs Fury II (G-ASCM)	Privately owned, Brize Norton
	K2059	Isaacs Fury II (G-PFAR)	Privately owned, Dunkeswell
	K2075	Isaacs Fury II (G-BEER)	Privately owned, Sturgate
	K2227	Bristol Bulldog IIA (G-ABBB) (wreck)	Skysport Engineering, Biggleswade
	K2567	DH Tiger Moth (DE306/7035M/ G-MOTH)	Privately owned, Chalmington Manor
	K2571	DH Tiger Moth <R>	Privately owned, RAF Hereford
	K2572	DH Tiger Moth (NM129/G-AOZH)	Privately owned, Shoreham
	K2572	DH Tiger Moth <R>	The Aeroplane Collection, Hooton Park
	K3215	Avro Tutor (G-AHSA)	The Shuttleworth Collection, Old Warden
	K3584	DH Queen Bee (BAPC 186)	Re-marked as LF789
	K3661	Hawker Nimrod II (G-BURZ)	Privately owned, Rye
	K3731	Isaacs Fury <R> (G-RODI)	Privately owned, Hailsham
	K4232	Avro Rota I (SE-AZB)	RAF Museum, Hendon
	K4235	Avro Rota I (G-AHMJ)	The Shuttleworth Collection, Old Warden
	K4972	Hawker Hart Trainer IIA (1764M)	RAF Cosford Aerospace Museum
	K5054	Supermarine Spitfire <R> (BAPC 190)	Repainted as EN398
	K5054	Supermarine Spitfire <R> (BAPC 214)	The Spitfire Society, stored Southampton
	K5054	Supermarine Spitfire <R> (G-BRDV)	Privately owned, Hullavington
	K5414	Hawker Hind (G-AENP/BAPC 78) [XV]	The Shuttleworth Collection, Old Warden
	K5600	Hawker Audax I (2015M/G-BVVI)	Aero Vintage, Paddock Wood
	K6035	Westland Wallace II (2365M)	RAF Museum, Hendon
	K7271	Hawker Fury II <R> (BAPC 148)	Tangmere Military Aviation Museum
	K8042	Gloster Gladiator II (8372M)	RAF Museum, Hendon
	K8203	Hawker Demon I (G-BTVE/2292M)	Privately owned, Hatch
	K9926	VS Spitfire I <R> (BAPC 217) [JH-C]	RAF Bentley Priory, on display
	K9942	VS Spitfire IA (8383M) [SD-V]	RAF Museum, Hendon
	L1070	VS Spitfire I <R> (BAPC 227) [XT-A]	RAF Turnhouse, on display
	L1096	VS Spitfire <R> (BAPC 229) [PR-O]	Painted as MJ832
	L1592	Hawker Hurricane I [KW-Z]	Science Museum, South Kensington
	L1592	Hawker Hurricane I <R> (BAPC 63) [KW-Z]	Kent Battle of Britain Museum, Hawkinge
	L1679	Hawker Hurricane I <R> [JX-G]	Tangmere Military Aviation Museum

Serial	Type (other identity) [code]	Owner/operator, location or fate	Notes
L1710	Hawker Hurricane I <R> (BAPC 219) [AL-D]	RAF Biggin Hill, on display	
L2301	VS Walrus I (G-AIZG)	FAA Museum, RNAS Yeovilton	
L2940	Blackburn Skua I	FAA Museum, RNAS Yeovilton	
L5343	Fairey Battle I [VO-S]	RAF Museum, Hendon	
L6906	Miles Magister I (G-AKKY/T9841/ BAPC 44)	Museum of Berkshire Aviation, Woodley	
L7775	Vickers Wellington IA (fuselage)	Privately owned, Moreton-in-Marsh	
L8756	Bristol Bolingbroke IVT (RCAF 10001) [XD-E]	RAF Museum, Hendon	
N248	Supermarine S6A	Southampton Hall of Aviation	
N546	Wright Quadruplane 1 <R> (BAPC 164)	Southampton Hall of Aviation	
N1671	Boulton Paul Defiant I (8370M) [EW-D]	RAF Museum, Hendon	
N1854	Fairey Fulmar II (G-AIBE)	FAA Museum, RNAS Yeovilton	
N2078	Sopwith Baby (8214/8215)	FAA Museum, RNAS Yeovilton	
N2276	Gloster Sea Gladiator II (N5903) [H]	The Fighter Collection, Duxford	
N2308	Gloster Gladiator I (L8032/ G-AMRK) [HP-B]	The Shuttleworth Collection, Old Warden	
N2980	Vickers Wellington IA [R]	Brooklands Museum, Weybridge	
N3194	VS Spitfire I <R> (BAPC 220) [GR-Z]	RAF Biggin Hill, on display	
N3289	VS Spitfire I <R> (BAPC 65) [QV-K]	Kent Battle of Britain Museum, Hawkinge	
N3313	VS Spitfire <R> (BAPC 69) [BO-D]	Kent Battle of Britain Museum, Hawkinge	
N4389	Fairey Albacore [4M] (N4172)	FAA Museum, RNAS Yeovilton	
N4877	Avro Anson (G-AMDA) [VX-F]	Imperial War Museum, Duxford	
N5182	Sopwith Pup <R> (G-APUP/ 9213M)	RAF Museum, Hendon	
N5195	Sopwith Pup (G-ABOX)	Museum of Army Flying, Middle Wallop	
N5419	Bristol Scout D <R> (N5419)	Bristol Aircraft Collection, Banwell	
N5492	Sopwith Triplane <R> (BAPC 111)	The Fighter Collection, Duxford	
N5628	Gloster Gladiator II	RAF Museum, Hendon	
N5912	Sopwith Triplane (8385M)	RAF Museum, Hendon	
N6004	Short Stirling I	RAeS Medway Branch, Rochester	
N6037	DH Tiger Moth II (T6037/G-ANNB)	Privately owned, Carlisle (rebuild)	
N6181	Sopwith Pup (G-EBKY)	The Shuttleworth Collection, Old Warden	
N6290	Sopwith Triplane <R> (G-BOCK)	The Shuttleworth Collection, Old Warden	
N6452	Sopwith Pup <R> (G-BIAU)	FAA Museum, RNAS Yeovilton	
N6466	DH Tiger Moth (G-ANKZ)	Privately owned, Barton	
N6720	DH Tiger Moth (7014M) [RUO-B]	No 1940 Sqn ATC, Levenshulme	
N6797	DH Tiger Moth (G-ANEH)	Privately owned, Chilbolton	
N6812	Sopwith F1 Camel	Imperial War Museum, Lambeth	
N6847	DH Tiger Moth (G-APAL)	Privately owned, Little Gransden	
N6848	DH Tiger Moth (G-BALX)	Privately owned, Headcorn	
N6965	DH Tiger Moth (G-AJTW) [FL-J]	Privately owned, Tibenham	
N6985	DH Tiger Moth (G-AHMN)	AAC Historic Aircraft Flt, Middle Wallop	
N9191	DH Tiger Moth (G-ALND)	Privately owned, Shobdon	
N9192	DH Tiger Moth (G-BSTJ) [RCO-N]	Privately owned, Sywell	
N9389	DH Tiger Moth (G-ANJA)	Privately owned, Shipmeadow, Suffolk	
N9899	Supermarine Southampton I	RAF Museum Restoration Centre, Cardington	
P1344	HP Hampden I (9175M) [PL-K]	RAF Museum Restoration Centre, Cardington	
P1344	HP Hampden I <rf> (parts Hereford L6012)	RAF Museum, Hendon	
P2617	Hawker Hurricane I (8373M) [AF-A]	RAF Museum, Hendon	
P2793	Hawker Hurricane I <R> [SD-M]	Privately owned, Malton	
P2902	Hawker Hurricane I (G-ROBT)	Privately owned, Billingshurst	
P3059	Hawker Hurricane I <R> (BAPC 64) [SD-N]	Kent Battle of Britain Museum, Hawkinge	
P3175	Hawker Hurricane I (wreck)	RAF Museum, Hendon	
P3386	Hawker Hurricane I <R> (BAPC 218) [FT-A]	RAF Bentley Priory, on display	
P3395	Hawker Hurricane IV (KX829) [JX-B]	Birmingham Mus of Science & Technology	
P3554	Hawker Hurricane I (composite)	The Air Defence Collection, Salisbury	
P4139	Fairey Swordfish II (HS618) [5H]	FAA Museum, RNAS Yeovilton	

Notes	Serial	Type (other identity) [code]	Owner/operator, location or fate
	P5865	CCF Harvard 4 (G-BKCK) [LE-W]	Privately owned, North Weald
	P6382	Miles M.14A Hawk Trainer 3 (G-AJRS) [C]	The Shuttleworth Collection, Old Warden
	P7350	VS Spitfire IIA (G-AWIJ) [RN-S]	RAF BBMF, Coningsby
	P7540	VS Spitfire IIA [DU-W]	Dumfries & Galloway Av'n Mus, Tinwald Downs
	P8140	VS Spitfire II <R> (BAPC 71) [ZF-K]	Norfolk & Suffolk Av'n Museum, Flixton
	P8448	VS Spitfire II <R> (BAPC 225) [UM-D]	RAF Swanton Morley, on display
	P9444	VS Spitfire IA [RN-D]	Science Museum, South Kensington
	R1914	Miles Magister (G-AHUJ)	Privately owned, Strathallan
	R4897	DH Tiger Moth II (G-ERTY)	Privately owned, Hamstreet
	R4907	DH Tiger Moth II (G-ANCS)	Privately owned, Wreningham, Norfolk
	R5250	DH Tiger Moth II (G-AODT)	Privately owned, Tibenham
	R5868	Avro Lancaster I (7325M) [PO-S]	RAF Museum, Hendon
	R6915	VS Spitfire I	Imperial War Museum, Lambeth
	R9125	Westland Lysander III (8377M) [LX-L]	RAF Museum, Hendon
	R9371	HP Halifax II <ff>	Cotswold Aircraft Rest'n Group, Innsworth
	S1287	Fairey Flycatcher <R> (G-BEYB) [5]	Privately owned, Stockbridge
	S1579	Hawker Nimrod I <R> (G-BBVO) [571]	Privately owned, Dunkeswell
	S1595	Supermarine S6B	Science Museum, South Kensington
	T5298	Bristol Beaufighter <ff>	Midland Air Museum, Coventry
	T5424	DH Tiger Moth II (G-AJOA)	Privately owned, Chiseldon
	T5672	DH Tiger Moth II (G-ALRI)	Privately owned, Chalmington
	T5854	DH Tiger Moth II (G-ANKK)	Privately owned, Halfpenny Green (rebuild)
	T5879	DH Tiger Moth II (G-AXBW)	Privately owned, Tongham
	T5968	DH Tiger Moth II (G-ANNN)	Privately owned, Hollybush
	T6099	DH Tiger Moth II (G-AOGR)	Privately owned, Clacton
	T6256	DH Tiger Moth II	Privately owned, Cranfield
	T6269	DH Tiger Moth II (G-AMOU)	Sold to Thailand, 1993
	T6296	DH Tiger Moth II (8387M)	RAF Museum, Hendon
	T6313	DH Tiger Moth II (G-AHVU)	Privately owned, Liphook
	T6818	DH Tiger Moth II (G-ANKT) [91]	The Shuttleworth Collection, Old Warden
	T6991	DH Tiger Moth II (G-ANOR/DE694)	Privately owned, Paddock Wood
	T7109	DH Tiger Moth II (G-AOIM)	Privately owned, Shobdon
	T7230	DH Tiger Moth II (G-AFVE)	Privately owned, Biggin Hill
	T7281	DH Tiger Moth II (G-ARTL)	Privately owned, Egton, nr Whitby
	T7404	DH Tiger Moth II (G-ANMV)	Privately owned, Booker
	T7471	DH Tiger Moth II (G-AJHU)	Privately owned, Compton Abbas
	T7793	DH Tiger Moth II (G-ANKV)	Privately owned, Croydon, on display
	T7909	DH Tiger Moth II (G-ANON)	Privately owned, Sherburn-in-Elmet
	T8191	DH Tiger Moth II	Privately owned
	T9707	Miles Magister I (G-AKKR/8378M/T9708)	Gtr Manchester Museum of Science & Industry
	T9738	Miles Magister I (G-AKAT)	Sold to France as F-AZOR, 1994
	V1075	Miles Magister I (G-AKPF)	Privately owned, Shoreham
	V3388	Airspeed Oxford I (G-AHTW)	Imperial War Museum, Duxford
	V6028	Bristol Bolingbroke IVT (G-MKIV) [GB-D] <rf>	British Aerial Museum, Duxford
	V7350	Hawker Hurricane I (fuselage)	Brenzett Aeronautical Museum
	V7467	Hawker Hurricane I <R> (BAPC 223) [LE-D]	RAF Coltishall, on display
	V7767	Hawker Hurricane I <R> (BAPC 72)	Privately owned, Sopley, Hants
	V9281	WS Lysander IIIA (G-BCWL) [RU-M]	Wessex Aviation & Transport, Henstridge
	V9441	WS Lysander IIIA (G-AZWT) [AR-A]	Privately owned, stored Strathallan
	V9673	WS Lysander IIIA (V9300/G-LIZY) [MA-J]	Imperial War Museum, Duxford
	W1048	HP Halifax II (8465M) [TL-S]	RAF Museum, Hendon
	W2718	VS Walrus I (G-RNLI)	Privately owned, Micheldever
	W4041	Gloster E28/39 [G]	Science Museum, South Kensington

Serial	Type (other identity) [code]	Owner/operator, location or fate	Notes
W4050	DH Mosquito	Mosquito Aircraft Museum, London Colney	
W5856	Fairey Swordfish IV (G-BMGC) [A2A]	RN Historic Flight, Yeovilton	
W9385	DH Hornet Moth (G-ADND) [YG-L]	The Shuttleworth Collection, Old Warden	
X4277	VS Spitfire LF.XVIe (TB382/ 7244M) [XT-M]	RAF EP&TU, St Athan	
X4474	VS Spitfire LF.XVIe (TE311/ 7241M) [QV-I]	RAF EP&TU, St Athan	
X4590	VS Spitfire I (8384M) [PR-F]	RAF Museum, Hendon	
X7688	Bristol Beaufighter I (3858M/ G-DINT)	Privately owned, Hatch	
Z2033	Fairey Firefly I (G-ASTL) [275]	Imperial War Museum, Duxford	
Z5027	Hawker Hurricane IIB	Privately owned, Audley End	
Z5053	Hawker Hurricane IIB	Historic Flying, Audley End	
Z5722	Bristol Bolingbroke IVT (G-BPIV) [WM-Z]	British Aerial Museum, Duxford	
Z7015	Hawker Sea Hurricane IB (G-BKTH) [7-L]	The Shuttleworth Collection, Duxford	
Z7197	Percival Proctor III (G-AKZN/ 8380M)	RAF Museum, Hendon	
Z7381	Hawker Hurricane XII (G-HURI) [XR-T]	The Fighter Collection, Duxford	
AA908	VS Spitfire Vb <R> (BAPC 230) [UM-W]	Eden Camp Theme Park, Malton	
AB130	VS Spitfire Va (parts)	Privately owned, Ludham	
AB910	VS Spitfire Vb [AE-H]	RAF BBMF, Coningsby	
AD540	VS Spitfire Vb (wreck)	Dumfries and Galloway Av'n Museum	
AE436	HP Hampden I (parts)	Lincolnshire Av'n Heritage Centre, E Kirkby	
AE977	Hawker Sea Hurricane IB (G-TWTD)	Privately owned, Milden	
AL246	Grumman Martlet I	FAA Museum, RNAS Yeovilton	
AM561	Lockheed Hudson V (parts)	Cornwall Aero Park, Helston	
AP506	Cierva C30A (G-ACWM)	IHM,Weston-super-Mare	
AP507	Cierva C30A (G-ACWP) [KX-P]	Science Museum, South Kensington	
AR213	VS Spitfire Ia (G-AIST) [PR-D]	Privately owned, Booker	
AR501	VS Spitfire LF.Vc (G-AWII) (NN-A]	The Shuttleworth Collection, Old Warden	
AR614	VS Spitfire Vc (5378M/7555M/ G-BUWA)	Privately owned, Audley End	
BB807	DH Tiger Moth (G-ADWO)	Southampton Hall of Aviation	
BE417	Hawker Hurricane XIIb (G-HURR) [AE-K]	Privately owned, Brooklands	
BE421	Hawker Hurricane IIc <R> (BAPC 205) [XP-G]	RAF Museum, Hendon	
BH229	Hawker Hurricane IIb	Sold to New Zealand, February 1994	
BL370	VS Spitfire Vb	Privately owned, Oxford	
BL614	VS Spitfire Vb (4354M) [ZD-F]	Gr Manchester Mus of Science &Industry	
BL628	VS Spitfire Vb (G-BTTN)	Privately owned, Thruxton	
BL655	VS Spitfire Vb (wreck)	Lincolnshire Aviation Heritage Centre, East Kirkby	
BL924	VS Spitfire Vb <R> [AZ-G]	Tangmere Military Aviation Museum	
BM597	VS Spitfire Vb (5718M/G-MKVB) [PR-O]	Privately owned, Audley End	
BN230	Hawker Hurricane IIc (LF751/5466M)[FT-A]	RAF Manston, Memorial Pavilion	
BR600	VS Spitfire IX <R> (BAPC 222) [SH-V]	RAF Uxbridge, on display	
BR600	VS Spitfire IX <R> (BAPC 224) [JP-A]	Ambassador Hotel, Norwich	
BW853	Hawker Sea Hurricane XII (G-BRKE)	Privately owned, Milden	
BW881	Hawker Sea Hurricane XII	Privately owned, Milden	
DD931	Bristol Beaufort VIII (9131M) [L]	RAF Museum, Hendon	
DE208	DH Tiger Moth II (G-AGYU)	Privately owned, Ronaldsway	
DE363	DH Tiger Moth II (G-ANFC)	Military Aircrft Pres Grp, Hadfield, Derbys	
DE623	DH Tiger Moth II (G-ANFI)	Privately owned, Shobdon	
DE673	DH Tiger Moth II (6948M/G-ADNZ)	Privately owned, Hampton	
DE970	DH Tiger Moth II (G-AOBJ)	Privately owned, Cardiff	

Notes	Serial	Type (other identity) [code]	Owner/operator, location or fate
	DE992	DH Tiger Moth II (G-AXXV)	Privately owned, Membury
	DF128	DH Tiger Moth II (G-AOJJ) [RCO-U]	Privately owned, Abingdon
	DF155	DH Tiger Moth II (G-ANFV)	Privately owned, Shempston Fm, Lossiemouth
	DF198	DH Tiger Moth II (G-BBRB)	Privately owned, Biggin Hill
	DG202	Gloster F9/40 (5758M) [G]	RAF Cosford Aerospace Museum
	DG590	Miles Hawk Major (8379M/G-ADMW)	RAF Museum/Skysport Engineering Hatch
	DP872	Fairey Barracuda II (fuselage)	FAA Museum, stored Yeovilton
	DR393	Hawker Hurricane IIa (P3351)	*Sold to New Zealand, February 1994*
	DR613	FW Wicko GM1 (G-AFJB)	Privately owned, stored Berkswell
	DV372	Avro Lancaster I <ff>	Imperial War Museum, Lambeth
	EE416	Gloster Meteor F3 <ff>	Science Museum, Wroughton
	EE425	Gloster Meteor F3 <ff>	Rebel Air Museum, Earls Colne
	EE531	Gloster Meteor F4 (7090M)	Midland Air Museum, Coventry
	EE549	Gloster Meteor F4 (7008M)	Tangmere Military Aviation Museum
	EF545	VS Spitfire Vc <ff>	Privately owned, High Wycombe
	EJ693	Hawker Tempest V [SA-J]	*Sold to the USA as N7027E, 1992*
	EM720	DH Tiger Moth II (G-AXAN)	Privately owned, Little Gransden
	EM727	DH Tiger Moth II (G-AOXN)	Privately owned, Yeovil
	EM903	DH Tiger Moth II (G-APBI)	Privately owned, Halstead
	EN224	VS Spitfire F.XII (G-FXII)	Privately owned, Newport Pagnell
	EN343	VS Spitfire PR.XI <R>(BAPC 226)	RAF Benson, on display
	EN398	VS Spitfire F.IX <R> (BAPC 190) [JE-J]	Privately owned, Cannock, Staffs
	EP120	VS Spitfire Vb (5377M/8070M/G-LFVB)	The Fighter Collection, Audley End
	EX976	NA Harvard III	FAA Museum, RNAS Yeovilton
	EZ259	NA Harvard III (G-BMJW)	Privately owned, Wakefield
	EZ407	NA Harvard III	RN Historic Flight, stored Lee-on-Solent
	FB226	Bonsall Mustang <R> (G-BDWM) [MT-A]	Privately owned, Gamston
	FE695	NA Harvard IIB (G-BTXI)	The Fighter Collection, Duxford
	FE905	NA Harvard IIB (LN-BNM)	RAF Museum, Hendon
	FE992	NA Harvard IIB (G-BDAM) [KT]	Privately owned, Duxford
	FH153	NA Harvard IIB (G-BBHK) [GW-A]	Privately owned, stored Cardiff
	FM118	Avro Lancaster B.X <ff>	Privately owned, Gosport, Hants
	FR870	Curtiss Kittyhawk IV (NL1009N) [GA-S]	*Sold as F-AZPI by July 1994*
	FR886	Piper L-4J Cub (G-BDMS)	Privately owned, Netley, Hants
	FS728	NA Harvard IIB (G-BAFM) [F]	Privately owned, Denham
	FS890	NA Harvard IIB (7554M)	A&AEE, stored Boscombe Down
	FT239	NA Harvard IV (G-BIWX)	Privately owned, North Weald
	FT323	NA Harvard III (FAP.1513)	Privately owned, Cranfield
	FT375	NA Harvard IIB [5]	MoD(PE), A&AEE Boscombe Down
	FT391	NA Harvard IIB (G-AZBN)	Privately owned, Shoreham
	FX301	NA Harvard IIB (EX915/G-JUDI)	Privately owned, Bryngwyn Bach, Clwyd
	FX360	NA Harvard IIB (KF435)	Booker Aircraft Museum
	FX442	NA Harvard IIB [TO-M]	Privately owned, South Gorley, Hants
	FX760	Curtiss Kittyhawk IV (9150M) [GA-?]	RAF Museum, Hendon
	HB275	Beech C-45 Expeditor II (G-BKGM)	Privately owned, North Weald
	HB751	Fairchild Argus III (G-BCBL)	Privately owned, Little Gransden
	HH379	GAL48 Hotspur II <rf>	Museum of Army Flying, Middle Wallop
	HH982	Taylorcraft Plus D (LB312/G-AHXE)	Privately owned, Shoreham
	HJ711	DH Mosquito NF.II [VI-C]	Night Fighter Preservation Tm, Elvington
	HM354	Percival Proctor III (G-ANPP)	Privately owned, Stansted
	HM580	Cierva C-30A (G-ACUU)	Imperial War Museum, Duxford
	HS503	Fairey Swordfish IV (BAPC 108)	RAF Cosford Aerospace Museum, stored
	JR505	Hawker Typhoon IB <ff>	Privately owned, Coventry
	JV482	Grumman Wildcat V	Ulster Aviation Society, Langford Lodge
	KB889	Avro Lancaster X (G-LANC) [NA-I]	Imperial War Museum, Duxford
	KB976	Avro Lancaster X (G-BCOH)	Aces High, North Weald
	KB994	Avro Lancaster X (G-BVBP)	Aces High, North Weald
	KD431	CV Corsair IV [E2-M]	FAA Museum, RNAS Yeovilton
	KE209	Grumman Hellcat II	FAA Museum, RNAS Yeovilton

Serial	Type (other identity) [code]	Owner/operator, location or fate	Notes
KE418	Hawker Tempest <rf>	RAF Museum Store, Cardington	
KF183	NA Harvard IIB [3]	MoD(PE) A&AEE Boscombe Down	
KF388	NA Harvard IIB <ff>	Privately owned, Bournemouth	
KF435	NA Harvard IIB <rf>	Privately owned, Ottershaw	
KF487	NA Harvard IIB	British Aerial Museum, Duxford, spares use	
KF532	NA Harvard IIB <ff>	Newark Air Museum, Winthorpe	
KG374	Douglas Dakota IV (KN645/8355M) [YS]	RAF Cosford Aerospace Museum	
KG391	Douglas C-47A Dakota (G-BVOL) [AG]	Privately owned, Coventry	
KJ351	Airspeed Horsa II (TL659/BAPC 80) [23]	Museum of Army Flying, Middle Wallop	
KK995	Sikorsky Hoverfly I [E]	RAF Museum, Hendon	
KL161	NA Mitchell II (N88972) [VO-B]	The Fighter Collection, Duxford	
KN448	Douglas Dakota C4 <ff>	Science Museum, South Kensington	
KN751	Consolidated Liberator C.VI [F]	RAF Cosford Aerospace Museum	
KP208	Douglas Dakota IV [YS]	Airborne Forces Museum, Aldershot	
KZ191	Hawker Hurricane IV (frame only)	Privately owned, North Weald	
KZ321	Hawker Hurricane IV (G-HURY) (frame only)	The Fighter Collection, Duxford	
LA198	VS Spitfire F21 (7118M) [RAI-G]	RAF, stored St Athan	
LA226	VS Spitfire F21 (7119M)	RAF, stored At Athan	
LA255	VS Spitfire F21 (6490M) [JX-U]	RAF No 1 Sqn, Wittering (preserved)	
LA546	VS Seafire F46 <ff>	Privately owned, Newport Pagnell	
LB294	Taylorcraft Plus D (G-AHWJ)	Museum of Army Flying, Whitchurch	
LB312	Taylorcraft Plus D (G-AHXE)	Painted as HH982, June 1994	
LB375	Taylorcraft Plus D (G-AHGW)	Privately owned, Edge Hill	
LF363	Hawker Hurricane IIc	RAF, Audley End (on rebuild)	
LF738	Hawker Hurricane IIc (5405M)	RAF, RAeS Medway Branch, Rochester	
LF789	DH Queen Bee (BAPC 186)	Mosquito Aircraft Museum, London Colney	
LF858	DH Queen Bee (G-BLUZ)	Privately owned, Hatch	
LH208	Airspeed Horsa I (8596M) (parts only)	Museum of Army Flying, Middle Wallop	
LS326	Fairey Swordfish II (G-AJVH) [L2]	RN Historic Flight, RNAS Yeovilton	
LV907	HP Halifax III (HR792) [NP-F]	Yorkshire Air Museum, Elvington	
LZ551	DH Vampire [P]	FAA Museum, RNAS Yeovilton	
LZ766	Percival Proctor III (G-ALCK)	Imperial War Museum, Duxford	
LZ842	VS Spitfire IX (remains)	Privately owned, Battle, Sussex	
MF628	Vickers Wellington T10 (9210M)	RAF Museum, Hendon	
MH434	VS Spitfire LF.IXc (G-ASJV) [ZD-B]	The Old Flying Machine Company, Duxford	
MH486	VS Spitfire LF.IX <R> (BAPC 206) [FF-A]	RAF Museum, Hendon	
MH603	VS Spitfire IX	Sold to the USA, 1992	
MH777	VS Spitfire IX <R> (BAPC 221) [RF-N]	RAF Northolt, on display	
MJ627	VS Spitfire T.IX (G-BMSB) [9G-P]	Privately owned, Baginton	
MJ730	VS Spitfire HF.IXe (G-HFIX) [GZ-?]	Privately owned, Staverton	
MJ751	VS Spitfire IX <R> (BAPC 209) [DU-V]	D-Day Museum, Shoreham Airport	
MJ832	VS Spitfire <R> (BAPC 229) [DN-Y]	RAF Digby, on display	
MK356	VS Spitfire IX (5690M)	RAF BBMF, St Athan	
MK805	VS Spitfire LF.IX <R> [SH-B]	Privately owned, Lowestoft	
MK912	VS Spitfire LF.IXe (G-BRRA) [MN-P]	Privately owned, Paddock Wood	
ML407	VS Spitfire T.IX (G-LFIX) [NL-D]	Privately owned, Duxford	
ML417	VS Spitfire LF.IXe (G-BJSG) [2I-T]	The Fighter Collection, Duxford	
ML427	VS Spitfire IX (6457M) [I-ST]	Birmingham Museum of Science & Industry	
ML796	Short Sunderland V	Imperial War Museum, Duxford	
ML824	Short Sunderland V [NS-Z]	RAF Museum, Hendon	
MN235	Hawker Typhoon IB	RAF Museum, Hendon	
MP425	Airspeed Oxford I (G-AITB) [G]	RAF Museum, Hendon	
MT438	Auster III (G-AREI)	Privately owned, Middle Wallop	
MT847	VS Spitfire FR.XIVe (6960M) [AX-H]	RAF Cosford Aerospace Museum	
MT928	VS Spitfire HF.VIII (G-BKMI/MV154) [ZX-M]	Privately owned, East Midlands Airport	
MV262	VS Spitfire FR.XIV (G-CCVV)	Privately owned, Booker	

Notes	Serial	Type (other identity) [code]	Owner/operator, location or fate
	MV293	VS Spitfire FR.XIV (G-SPIT) [OI-C]	The Fighter Collection, Duxford
	MW376	Hawker Tempest II (G-BSHW)	Privately owned, Audley End
	MW401	Hawker Tempest II (G-PEST)	Privately owned, Brooklands
	MW404	Hawker Tempest II (IAF HA557)	Privately owned
MW467	VS Spitfire V <R> (BAPC 202)	Privately owned, Llanbedr
	MW758	Hawker Tempest II (IAF HA580)	Privately owned
	MW763	Hawker Tempest II (G-TEMT)	Privately owned, Brooklands
MW800	Hawker Tempest II (G-BSHW/ MW376) [HF-V]	Privately owned, Spanhoe Lodge
	NF370	Fairey Swordfish III	Imperial War Museum, Duxford
	NF389	Fairey Swordfish III [D]	RN Historic Flight, at BAe Brough
	NH799	VS Spitfire FR.XIV (G-BUZU) [AP-V]	*Sold to New Zealand as ZK-XIV, Feb 1994*
	NJ673	Auster 5D (G-AOCR)	Privately owned, Wellesbourne Mountford
	NJ695	Auster 4 (G-AJXV)	Privately owned, Tollerton
	NJ703	Auster 5 (G-AKPI)	Privately owned, Croft, Lincs
NJ719	Auster 5 (TW385/G-ANFU)	Privately owned, Newcastle
NL750	DH Tiger Moth II (T7997/G-AOBH)	Privately owned, Benington
	NL846	DH Tiger Moth II (F-BGEQ)	Brooklands Museum, Chessington (rebuild)
	NL985	DH Tiger Moth I (7015M)	Privately owned, Sywell
	NM181	DH Tiger Moth I (G-AZGZ)	Privately owned, Rush Green
	NP181	Percival Proctor IV (G-AOAR)	Privately owned, Biggin Hill
	NP184	Percival Proctor IV (G-ANYP) [K]	Privately owned, Chatteris
	NP294	Percival Proctor IV [SM-T]	Lincolnshire Av'n Heritage Centre, E Kirkby
	NP303	Percival Proctor IV (G-ANZJ)	Privately owned, Byfleet, Surrey
	NV778	Hawker Tempest TT5 (8386M)	RAFM Restoration Centre, Cardington
	NX534	Auster III (G-BUDL)	Privately owned, Middle Wallop
	NX611	Avro Lancaster B.VII (8375M/ G-ASXX) [LE-C]	Lincolnshire Av'n Heritage Centre, E Kirkby
	PA474	Avro Lancaster B.I [WS-J]	RAF BBMF, Coningsby
	PK624	VS Spitfire F22 (8072M) [RAU-T]	The Fighter Collection, Duxford
	PK664	VS Spitfire F22 (7759M) [V6-B]	RAF, stored St Athan
	PK683	VS Spitfire F24 (7150M)	Southampton Hall of Aviation
	PK724	VS Spitfire F24 (7288M)	RAF Museum, Hendon
	PL344	VS Spitfire LF.IXe (G-IXCC)	Privately owned, Booker
	PL965	VS Spitfire PR.XI (G-MKXI) [R]	The Fighter Collection, Duxford
	PL983	VS Spitfire PR.XI (G-PRXI)	*Sold to the USA, November 1992*
	PM631	VS Spitfire PR.XIX [N]	RAF BBMF, Coningsby
	PM651	VS Spitfire PR.XIX (7758M) [X]	RAF, stored St Athan
	PN323	HP Halifax VII <ff>	Imperial War Museum, Lambeth
	PP566	Fairey Firefly I (fuselage)	South Yorkshire Av'n Museum, Firbeck
	PP972	VS Seafire L.IIIc (G-BUAR) [6M-D]	Privately owned, East Midlands Airport
PR536	Hawker Tempest II (IAF HA457) [OQ-H]	RAF Museum, Hendon
	PS853	VS Spitfire PR.XIX [C]	Privately owned
	PS915	VS Spitfire PR.XIX (7548M/ 7711M) [P]	RAF BBMF, Coningsby
	PT462	VS Spitfire T.IX (G-CTIX)	*Sold to USA as N462JC, July 1994*
	PV202	VS Spitfire T.IX (G-TRIX) [VZ-M]	Privately owned, Duxford
	PZ865	Hawker Hurricane IIc (G-AMAU) [J]	RAF BBMF, Coningsby
	RA848	Slingsby Cadet TX1	The Aeroplane Collection, stored Wigan
	RA854	Slingsby Cadet TX1	The Aeroplane Collection, stored Wigan
	RA897	Slingsby Cadet TX1	Newark Air Museum store, Hucknall
	RD253	Bristol Beaufighter TF.X (7931M)	RAF Museum, Hendon
	RF342	Avro Lincoln B.II (G-29-1/G-APRJ)	Aces High, North Weald
	RF398	Avro Lincoln B.II (8376M)	RAF Cosford Aerospace Museum
RG333	Miles Messenger IIA (G-AIEK)	Privately owned, Felton, Bristol
RG333	Miles Messenger IIA (G-AKEZ)	Privately owned, Chelmsford
	RH377	Miles Messenger 4A (G-ALAH)	Privately owned, Stretton, Cheshire
	RH746	Bristol Brigand TF1	North-East Aircraft Museum, Usworth
	RL962	DH Dominie II (G-AHED)	RAF Museum Store, Cardington
	RM221	Percival Proctor IV (G-ANXR)	Privately owned, Biggin Hill
RN218	Isaacs Spitfire <R> (G-BBJI) [N]	Privately owned, Langham
	RR232	VS Spitfire HF.IXc (G-BRSF)	Privately owned, Lancing, Sussex
	RR299	DH Mosquito T.III (G-ASKH) [HT-E]	British Aerospace, Hawarden
	RT486	Auster 5 (G-AJGJ) [PF-A]	Privately owned, Old Sarum
	RT520	Auster 5 (G-ALYB)	South Yorkshire Av'n Museum, Firbeck

Serial	Type (other identity) [code]	Owner/operator, location or fate	Notes
RW382	VS Spitfire LF.XVIe (7245M/ 8075M/G-XVIA)	*Sold to the USA, Spring 1994*	
RW386	VS Spitfire LF.XVIe (6944M/ G-BXVI)	*Sold to the USA, 1992*	
RW388	VS Spitfire LF.XVIe (6946M) [U4-U]	Stoke-on-Trent City Museum, Hanley	
RW393	VS Spitfire LF.XVIe (7293M) [XT-A]	RAF, stored St Athan	
RX168	VS Seafire L.IIIc	Privately owned, High Wycombe	
SL542	VS Spitfire LF.XVIe (8390M) [4M-N]	*Sold to USA as N2289J, May 94*	
SL674	VS Spitfire LF.IX (8392M) [RAS-H]	RAF, stored St Athan	
SM520	VS Spitfire LF.IX	Privately owned, Audley End	
SM832	VS Spitfire F.XIV (G-WWII)	The Fighter Collection, Duxford	
SM845	VS Spitfire FR.XVIII (G-BUOS)	Privately owned, Audley End	
SX137	VS Seafire F.XVII	FAA Museum, RNAS Yeovilton	
SX300	VS Seafire F.XVII	Privately owned, Warwick	
SX336	VS Seafire F.XVII (G-BRMG)	Privately owned, Twyford, Bucks	
TA122	DH Mosquito FB.VI [UP-G]	Mosquito Aircraft Museum, London Colney	
TA634	DH Mosquito TT35 (G-AWJV) [8K-K]	Mosquito Aircraft Museum, London Colney	
TA639	DH Mosquito TT35 (7806M) [AZ-E]	RAF Cosford Aerospace Museum	
TA719	DH Mosquito TT35 (G-ASKC)	Imperial War Museum, Duxford	
TA805	VS Spitfire IX (remains)	Privately owned, Sandown, IOW	
TB252	VS Spitfire LF.XVIe (G-XVIE) [GW-H]	Privately owned, Audley End	
TB752	VS Spitfire LF.XVIe (8086M) [KH-Z]	RAF Manston, Memorial Pavilion	
TB885	VS Spitfire LF.XVIe	Shoreham Aircraft Preservation Society	
TD248	VS Spitfire LF.XVIe (7246M/ G-OXVI) [D]	Privately owned, Earls Colne	
TE184	VS Spitfire LF.XVIe (6850M/ G-MXVI)	Privately owned, Duxford	
TE462	VS Spitfire LF.XVIe (7243M)	Royal Scottish Mus'm of Flight, E Fortune	
TE476	VS Spitfire LF.XVIe (G-XVIB)	*Sold to USA as N476TE*	
TE566	VS Spitfire HF.IXb (G-BLCK) [DU-A]	Privately owned, Audley End	
TG263	Saro SR.A1 (G-12-1) [P]	Southampton Hall of Aviation	
TG511	HP Hastings C1 (8554M)	RAF Cosford Aerospace Museum	
TG517	HP Hastings T5	Newark Air Museum, Winthorpe	
TG528	HP Hastings C1A	Imperial War Museum, Duxford	
TJ118	DH Mosquito TT35 <ff>	Mosquito Aircraft Museum, stored	
TJ138	DH Mosquito B35 (7607M) [VO-L]	RAF Museum, Hendon	
TJ343	Auster 5 (G-AJXC)	Privately owned, stored Hook	
TJ398	Auster 5 (BAPC 70)	Aircraft Pres'n Soc ofScotland, E Fortune	
TJ569	Auster 5 (G-AKOW)	Museum of Army Flying, Middle Wallop	
TJ672	Auster 5 (G-ANIJ)	Privately owned, RAF Swanton Morley	
TJ704	Beagle A.61 Terrier 2 (G-ASCD) [JA]	Yorkshire Air Museum, Elvington	
TJ707	Auster 5 (frame)	Air Service Training, Perth	
TK718	GAL Hamilcar I	Royal Tank Museum, Bovington	
TK777	GAL Hamilcar I (fuselage)	Museum of Army Flying, Middle Wallop	
TL615	Airspeed Horsa II	Robertsbridge Aviation Society	
TP367	VS Spitfire XVIII	Privately owned, Hatch	
TS291	Slingsby Cadet TX1 (BGA 852)	Royal Scottish Mus'm of Flight, E Fortune	
TS423	Douglas Dakota C3 (G-DAKS)	Aces High Ltd, North Weald	
TS798	Avro York C1 (G-AGNV)	RAF Cosford Aerospace Museum	
TV959	DH Mosquito T.III [AF-V]	The Fighter Collection, stored Duxford	
TV959	DH Mosquito T.III <R>	Privately owned, Heald Green, Cheshire	
TW384	Auster 5 (G-ANHZ)	Privately owned, Headcorn	
TW439	Auster 5 (G-ANRP)	Privately owned, Exeter	
TW448	Auster 5 (G-ANLU)	Privately owned, Hedge End	
TW462	Beagle A.61 Terrier 1 (G-ARLO)	Privately owned, Chandlers Ford, Hants	
TW467	Auster 5 (G-ANIE) [ROD-F]	Privately owned, Middle Wallop	
TW511	Auster 5 (G-APAF)	Privately owned, North Cotes	
TW536	Auster AOP.6 (7704M/G-BNGE) [TS-V]	Privately owned, Middle Wallop	
TW591	Auster 6A (G-ARIH) [N]	Privately owned, Abbots Bromley	
TW641	Beagle A.61 Terrier 2 (G-ATDN)	Privately owned, Biggin Hill	
TX183	Avro Anson C19 (G-BSMF)	Privately owned, Arbroath	

Notes	Serial	Type (other identity) [code]	Owner/operator, location or fate
	TX213	Avro Anson C19 (G-AWRS)	North-East Aircraft Museum, Usworth
	TX214	Avro Anson C19 (7817M)	RAF Cosford Aerospace Museum
	TX226	Avro Anson C19 (7865M)	Imperial War Museum, Duxford
	TX228	Avro Anson C19	City of Norwich Aviation Museum
	TX235	Avro Anson C19	Caernarfon Air World
	VD165	Slingsby T7 Kite (BGA 400)	Privately owned, Dunstable
	VF301	DH Vampire F1 (7060M) [RAL-B]	Midland Air Museum, Coventry
	VF512	Auster 6A (G-ARRX) [PF-M]	Privately owned, White Waltham
	VF516	Beagle A.61 Terrier 2 (G-ASMZ) [T]	Privately owned, Crediton
	VF526	Auster 6A (G-ARXU) [T]	Privately owned, Middle Wallop
	VF548	Beagle A.61 Terrier 1 (G-ASEG)	Privately owned, Dunkeswell
	VH127	Fairey Firefly TT4 [200/R]	FAA Museum, stored RNAS Yeovilton
	VL348	Avro Anson C19 (G-AVVO)	Newark Air Museum, Winthorpe
	VL349	Avro Anson C19 (G-AWSA)	Norfolk & Suffolk Aviation Mus'm, Flixton
	VM325	Avro Anson C19	Midland Air Museum, Coventry
	VM360	Avro Anson C19 (G-APHV)	Royal Scottish Mus'm of Flight, E Fortune
VM791	Slingsby Cadet TX3 (XA312/ 8876M)	No 135 Sqn ATC,RAF Kenley
	VN148	Grunau Baby IIb (BAPC 33/ BGA2400)	Privately owned, Dunstable
	VN485	VS Spitfire F24 (7326M)	Imperial War Museum, Duxford
	VP293	Avro Shackleton T4 <ff>	Privately owned, Coventry
	VP519	Avro Anson C19 (G-AVVR)<ff>	The Aeroplane Collection, Hooton Park
	VP952	DH Devon C2 (8820M)	RAF Cosford Aerospace Museum
	VP955	DH Devon C2 (G-DVON)	Privately owned, Old Sarum
	VP957	DH Devon C2 (8822M) <ff>	No 1137 Sqn ATC, Belfast
	VP959	DH Devon C2 [L]	Privately owned
	VP967	DH Devon C2 (G-KOOL)	East Surrey Technical College, Redhill
	VP968	DH Devon C2	A&AEE Boscombe Down, derelict
	VP971	DH Devon C2 (8824M)	FSCTE, RAF Manston
	VP975	DH Devon C2 [M]	Science Museum, Wroughton
	VP976	DH Devon C2 (8784M)	*Burned at Northolt by October 1992*
	VP977	DH Devon C2 (G-ALTS)	*Burned at West Freugh by December 1993*
	VP978	DH Devon C2 (8553M)	RAF Brize Norton, instructional use
	VP981	DH Devon C2	RAF, stored Coningsby
	VR137	Westland Wyvern TF1	FAA Museum, RNAS Yeovilton
	VR192	Percival Prentice T1 (G-APIT)	SWWAPS, Lasham
	VR249	Percival Prentice T1 (G-APIY) [FA-EL]	Newark Air Museum, Winthorpe
	VR259	Percival Prentice T1 (G-APJB)	Privately owned, Coventry
	VR930	Hawker Sea Fury FB11 (8382M)	RN Historic Flight, Brough
	VS356	Percival Prentice T1 (G-AOLU)	Privately owned, Stonehaven
	VS517	Avro Anson T20	RN, stored Lee-on-Solent
	VS562	Avro Anson T21 (8012M)	Maes Artro Craft Village, Llanbedr
	VS610	Percival Prentice T1 (G-AOKL) [K-L]	Privately owned, Nayland
	VS623	Percival Prentice T1 (G-AOKZ) [KQ-F]	Midland Air Museum, Coventry
	VT260	Gloster Meteor F4 (8813M) [67]	Imperial War Museum, stored Duxford
VT409	Fairey Firefly AS5 (mostly WD889)	North-East Aircraft Museum, Usworth
	VT812	DH Vampire F3 (7200M) [N]	RAF Museum, Hendon
	VT935	Boulton Paul P111A (VT769)	Midland Air Museum, Coventry
	VT987	Auster AOP6 (G-BKXP)	Privately owned, Little Gransden, Cambs
	VV106	Supermarine 510 (7175M)	FAA Museum, stored Wroughton
	VV217	DH Vampire FB5 (7323M)	North-East Aircraft Museum, Usworth
	VV901	Avro Anson T21	Yorkshire Air Museum, Elvington
	VW453	Gloster Meteor T7 (8703M) [Z]	RAF Innsworth, on display
	VW985	Auster AOP6 (G-ASEF)	Privately owned, Upper Arncott, Oxon
	VX118	Auster AOP6 (G-ASNB)	Privately owned, Kingston Deverill
VX147	Alon A2 Aircoupe (G-AVIL)	Privately owned, Headcorn
	VX185	EE Canberra B(I)8 (7631M) <ff>	Science Museum, Wroughton
	VX250	DH Sea Hornet 21 [48] <rf>	Mosquito Aircraft Museum, London Colney
	VX272	Hawker P1052 (7174M)	FAA Museum, stored Wroughton
	VX275	Slingsby Sedbergh TX1 (8884M/ BGA 572)	RAF Museum Restoration Centre, Cardington
	VX461	DH Vampire FB5 (7646M)	RAF Cosford Aerospace Museum, stored
	VX573	Vickers Valetta C2 (8389M)	RAF Cosford Aerospace Museum, stored
	VX577	Vickers Valetta C2	North-East Aircraft Museum, Usworth
	VX580	Vickers Valetta C2	Norfolk & Suffolk Av'n Museum, Flixton
	VX595	WS51 Dragonfly HR1 [29]	Gosport Aviation Society, HMS *Sultan*
	VX653	Hawker Sea Fury FB11 (G-BUCM)	The Fighter Collection, Duxford
	VX665	Hawker Sea Fury FB11 <rf>	RN Historic Flight, at BAe Brough

Serial	Type (other identity) [code]	Owner/operator, location or fate	Notes
VX926	Auster T7 (G-ASKJ)	Privately owned, Little Gransden	
VZ304	DH Vampire FB6 (G-MKVI) [A-T]	Vintage Aircraft Team, Bruntingthorpe	
VZ345	Hawker Sea Fury T20S	RN Historic Flight, Brough (on rebuild)	
VZ462	Gloster Meteor F8	SWWAPS, stored Lasham	
VZ467	Gloster Meteor F8 (G-METE)	Privately owned, Biggin Hill	
VZ477	Gloster Meteor F8 (7741M) <ff>	Midland Air Museum, Coventry	
VZ608	Gloster Meteor FR9	Newark Air Museum, Winthorpe	
VZ634	Gloster Meteor T7 (8657M)	Newark Air Museum, Winthorpe	
VZ638	Gloster Meteor T7 (G-JETM) [HF]	Privately owned, Charlwood, Surrey	
VZ728	RS4 Desford Trainer (G-AGOS)	Snibston Discovery Park, stored Coalville	
VZ962	WS51 Dragonfly HR1 [904]	IHM, Weston-super-Mare	
VZ965	WS51 Dragonfly HR5	FAA Museum, at RNAS Culdrose	
WA473	VS Attacker F1 [102/J]	FAA Museum, stored RNAS Yeovilton	
WA576	Bristol Sycamore 3 (7900M/ G-ALSS)	Dumfries & Galloway Av'n Mus, Tinwald Downs	
WA577	Bristol Sycamore 3 (7718M/ G-ALST)	North-East Aircraft Museum, Usworth	
WA591	Gloster Meteor T7 (7917M) [W]	Meteor Flight, stored Yatesbury	
WA630	Gloster Meteor T7 [69] <ff>	Robertsbridge Aviation Museum, Mayfield	
WA634	Gloster Meteor T7/8	RAF Cosford Aerospace Museum	
WA638	Gloster Meteor T7	Martin Baker Aircraft, Chalgrove	
WA662	Gloster Meteor T7	South Yorkshire Aviation Museum, Firbeck	
WA984	Gloster Meteor F8 [A]	Tangmere Military Aviation Museum	
WB188	Hawker Hunter F3 (7154M)	Tangmere Military Aviation Museum	
WB271	Fairey Firefly AS5 [204/R]	RN Historic Flight, RNAS Yeovilton	
WB440	Fairey Firefly AS6 <ff>	South Yorkshire Aviation Museum, Firbeck	
WB491	Avro Ashton 2 (TS897/G-AJJW) <ff>	Avro Aircraft Rest' Society, BAe Woodford	
WB550	DH Chipmunk T10 [D]	RAF No 6 AEF, Benson	
WB556	DH Chipmunk T10	RAFGSA, Bicester	
WB560	DH Chipmunk T10	RAF No 4 AEF, Exeter	
WB565	DH Chipmunk T10 [X]	AAC BFWF, Middle Wallop	
WB567	DH Chipmunk T10	RAF No 12 AEF, Turnhouse	
WB569	DH Chipmunk T10 [R]	RAF No 5 AEF, Cambridge	
WB571	DH Chipmunk T10 (G-AOSF) [34]	Privately owned,	
WB575	DH Chipmunk T10 [907]	Privately owned	
WB584	DH Chipmunk T10 (7706M) <ff>	No 327 Sqn ATC, Kilmarnock	
WB585	DH Chipmunk T10 (G-AOSY) [RCU-X]	Privately owned, Blackbushe	
WB586	DH Chipmunk T10 [A]	RAF No 6 AEF, Benson	
WB588	DH Chipmunk T10 (G-AOTD) [D]	Privately owned, Biggin Hill	
WB615	DH Chipmunk T10 [E]	AAC BFWF, Middle Wallop	
WB624	DH Chipmunk T10 <ff>	South Yorkshire Air Museum, Firbeck	
WB626	DH Chipmunk T10 <ff>	Privately owned, Swanton Morley	
WB627	DH Chipmunk T10 [N]	RAF No 5 AEF, Cambridge	
WB645	DH Chipmunk T10	RAFGSA, Bicester, spares use	
WB647	DH Chipmunk T10 [R]	AAC BFWF, Middle Wallop	
WB652	DH Chipmunk T10 [V]	RAF No 5 AEF, Cambridge	
WB654	DH Chipmunk T10 [T]	AAC BFWF, Middle Wallop	
WB657	DH Chipmunk T10 [908]	RN, stored Yeovilton	
WB660	DH Chipmunk T10 (G-ARMB)	Privately owned, Shipdham	
WB670	DH Chipmunk T10 (8361M) <ff>	No 1312 Sqn ATC, Southend	
WB671	DH Chipmunk T10 [910]	Privately owned	
WB685	DH Chipmunk T10 <ff>	North-East Aircraft Museum, Usworth	
WB693	DH Chipmunk T10 [S]	AAC BFWF, Middle Wallop	
WB697	DH Chipmunk T10 [95]	RAF No 10 AEF, Woodvale	
WB702	DH Chipmunk T10 (G-AOFE)	Privately owned, Goodwood	
WB703	DH Chipmunk T10 (G-ARMC)	Privately owned, White Waltham	
WB739	DH Chipmunk T10 [8]	RAF No 8 AEF, Shawbury	
WB754	DH Chipmunk T10 [H]	AAC BFWF, Middle Wallop	
WB758	DH Chipmunk T10 (7729M) [P]	Privately owned, Torbay	
WB763	DH Chipmunk T10 (G-BBMR) [14]	Privately owned, Ottershaw	
WB922	Slingsby T21B	Privately owned, stored Rufforth	
WB981	Slingsby T21B (BGA3238)	Privately owned, Aston Down	
WD286	DH Chipmunk T10 (G-BBND) [J]	Privately owned, Bourn	
WD288	DH Chipmunk T10 (G-AOSO) [38]	Privately owned, Charlton Park, Wilts	
WD289	DH Chipmunk T10 [E]	RAF No 3 AEF, Colerne	
WD292	DH Chipmunk T10 (G-BCRX)	Privately owned, Old Sarum	
WD293	DH Chipmunk T10 (7645M) <ff>	No 1367 Sqn ATC, Caerleon	
WD305	DH Chipmunk T10 (G-ARGG)	Privately owned, Coventry	

Notes	Serial	Type (other identity) [code]	Owner/operator, location or fate
	WD310	DH Chipmunk T10 [B]	RAF No 3 AEF, Colerne
	WD318	DH Chipmunk T10 (8207M) <ff>	RAF Halton
	WD325	DH Chipmunk T10 [N]	AAC BFWF, Middle Wallop
	WD331	DH Chipmunk T10 [J]	RAF No 6 AEF, Benson
WD355	DH Chipmunk T10 (WD335) <ff>	No 1955 Sqn ATC, Wells, Somerset
	WD356	DH Chipmunk T10 (7625M)	Privately owned, St Ives, Cambridgeshire
	WD363	DH Chipmunk T10 (G-BCIH) [5]	Privately owned, Andrewsfield
	WD370	DH Chipmunk T10 <ff>	No 176 Sqn ATC, Hove
	WD373	DH Chipmunk T10 [12]	RAF No 2 AEF, Bournemouth
	WD374	DH Chipmunk T10 [903]	Privately owned
	WD377	DH Chipmunk T10	Dumfries & Galloway Av'n Mus, Tinwald Downs
WD379	DH Chipmunk T10 (WB696/ G-APLO) [K]	Privately owned, Jersey
	WD386	DH Chipmunk T10 <ff>	Vintage Aircraft Team, Cranfield
	WD388	DH Chipmunk T10 (G-BDIC)	Privately owned, Woodvale
	WD390	DH Chipmunk T10 [68]	RAF No 9 AEF, Finningley
	WD413	Avro Anson T21 (7881M/G-BFIR)	Privately owned, Lee-on-Solent
	WD646	Gloster Meteor TT20 (8189M) [R]	Privately owned, North Weald
	WD686	Gloster Meteor NF11	Muckleburgh Collection, Weybourne
	WD790	Gloster Meteor NF11 (8743M)<ff>	North-East Aircraft Museum, Usworth
	WD931	EE Canberra B2 <ff>	RAF Cosford Aerospace Museum
	WD935	EE Canberra B2 (8440M) <ff>	Privately owned, Bridgnorth
	WD954	EE Canberra B2 <ff>	Privately owned, Romford, Essex
	WD955	EE Canberra T17A [EM]	RAF Wyton
	WE113	EE Canberra T4 <ff>	Privately owned, Woodhurst, Cambridgeshire
	WE122	EE Canberra TT18 [845] <ff>	Blyth Valley Aviation Collection, Walpole
	WE139	EE Canberra PR3 (8369M)	RAF Museum, Hendon
	WE168	EE Canberra PR3 (8049M) <ff>	Privately owned, Colchester
	WE173	EE Canberra PR3 (8740M) <ff>	Privately owned, Stock, Essex
	WE188	EE Canberra T4	Solway Aviation Society, Carlisle
	WE192	EE Canberra T4 <ff>	
WE402	DH Venom FB50 (G-VENI)	Privately owned, Bournemouth
	WE569	Auster T7 (G-ASAJ)	Privately owned, Middle Wallop
	WE600	Auster T7(mod) (7602M)	RAF Cosford Aerospace Museum
	WE925	Gloster Meteor F8	Classic Jet Aircraft Group, Loughborough
	WE982	Slingsby Prefect TX1 (8781M)	RAF Cosford Aerospace Museum
	WE990	Slingsby Prefect TX1 (BGA 2583)	Privately owned, RAF Swanton Morley
	WF118	Percival Sea Prince T1 (G-DACA)	Privately owned, Charlwood, Surrey
	WF122	Percival Sea Prince T1 [575/CU]	Flambards Village Theme Park, Helston
	WF125	Percival Sea Prince T1 [576]	RN Predannack Fire School
	WF128	Percival Sea Prince T1 (8611M)	Norfolk & Suffolk Aviation Museum, Flixton
	WF137	Percival Sea Prince C1	SWWAPS, Lasham
	WF225	Hawker Sea Hawk F1 [CU]	RNAS Culdrose, at main gate
	WF259	Hawker Sea Hawk F2 [171/A]	Royal Scottish Mus'm of Flight, E Fortune
	WF369	Vickers Varsity T1 [F]	Newark Air Museum, Winthorpe
	WF372	Vickers Varsity T1 [A]	Brooklands Museum, Weybridge
	WF376	Vickers Varsity T1	Bristol Airport Fire Section
	WF408	Vickers Varsity T1 (8395M)	RAF Northolt, for ground instruction
	WF410	Vickers Varsity T1 [F]	Brunel Technical College, Lulsgate
	WF643	Gloster Meteor F8 [X]	Norfolk & Suffolk Aviation Museum, Flixton
WF714	Gloster Meteor F8 (WK914)	The Old Flying Machine Co, Duxford
	WF784	Gloster Meteor T7 (7895M)	RAF Quedgeley, at main gate
	WF825	Gloster Meteor T7 (8359M) [A]	Avon Aviation Museum, stored Yatesbury
	WF877	Gloster Meteor T7 (G-BPOA)	39 Restoration Group, North Weald
	WF890	EE Canberra T17 [EJ]	*Scrapped at Wyton, 1993*
	WF911	EE Canberra B2 <ff>	Pennine Aviation Museum, store
	WF916	EE Canberra T17 [EL]	RAF Wyton
	WF922	EE Canberra PR3	Midland Air Museum, Coventry
	WG300	DH Chipmunk T10 <ff>	RAFGSA, Bicester
	WG303	DH Chipmunk T10 (8208M) <ff>	RAFGSA, Bicester
	WG307	DH Chipmunk T10 (G-BCYJ)	Privately owned, Shempston Fm, Lossiemouth
	WG308	DH Chipmunk T10 [71]	RAF No 7 AEF, Newton
	WG316	DH Chipmunk T10 (G-BCAH)	Privately owned, Shoreham
	WG321	DH Chipmunk T10 [G]	AAC BFWF, Middle Wallop
	WG323	DH Chipmunk T10 [F]	AAC BFWF, Middle Wallop

Serial	Type (other identity) [code]	Owner/operator, location or fate	Notes
WG348	DH Chipmunk T10 (G-BBMV)	Privately owned, Moulton St Mary	
WG350	DH Chipmunk T10 (G-BPAL)	Privately owned, Popham	
WG362	DH Chipmunk T10 (8437M/8630M) <ff>		
WG403	DH Chipmunk T10 [O] (wreck)	AAC, Middle Wallop, spares use	
WG407	DH Chipmunk T10 [67]	RAF No 9 AEF, Finningley	
WG418	DH Chipmunk T10 (8209M/G-ATDY) <ff>	RAF No 10 AEF, Woodvale	
WG419	DH Chipmunk T10 (8206M) <ff>	No 1053 Sqn ATC, Armthorpe	
WG422	DH Chipmunk T10 (8394M/G-BFAX) [116]	Privately owned, Duxford	
WG430	DH Chipmunk T10 [3]	RAF No 1 AEF, Manston	
WG432	DH Chipmunk T10 [L]	AAC BFWF, Middle Wallop	
WG458	DH Chipmunk T10 [B]	RAF No 4 AEF, Exeter	
WG463	DH Chipmunk T10 (8363M/G-ATDX) <ff>	No 188 Sqn ATC, Ipswich	
WG465	DH Chipmunk T10 (G-BCEY)	Privately owned, White Waltham	
WG466	DH Chipmunk T10	*To German Historic Museum, July 1994*	
WG469	DH Chipmunk T10 [72]	RAF No 7 AEF, Newton	
WG471	DH Chipmunk T10 (8210M) <ff>	No 301 Sqn ATC, Bury St Edmunds	
WG472	DH Chipmunk T10 (G-AOTY)	Privately owned, Netherthorpe	
WG477	DH Chipmunk T10 (8362M/G-ATDP) <ff>	No 281 Sqn ATC, Birkdale	
WG478	DH Chipmunk T10	RAF, stored Shawbury	
WG479	DH Chipmunk T10 [F]	RAF No 3 AEF, Colerne	
WG480	DH Chipmunk T10 [D]	RAF No 7 AEF, Newton	
WG486	DH Chipmunk T10	RAF	
WG511	Avro Shackleton T4 (fuselage)	Flambards Village Theme Park, Helston	
WG718	WS51 Dragonfly HR3 [934]	Privately owned,	
WG719	WS51 Dragonfly HR5 (G-BRMA) [902]	IHM, Weston-super-Mare	
WG724	WS51 Dragonfly HR5 [932]	North-East Aircraft Museum, Usworth	
WG751	WS51 Dragonfly HR5	Privately owned, Ramsgreave, Lancs	
WG754	WS51 Dragonfly HR3 (WG725/7703M) [912/CU]	Flambards Village Theme Park, Helston	
WG760	EE P1A (7755M)	RAF Cosford Aerospace Museum	
WG763	EE P1A (7816M)	Gtr Manchester Mus'm of Science & Industry	
WG768	Short SB5 (8005M)	RAF Cosford Aerospace Museum	
WG774	BAC 221	Science Museum, RNAS Yeovilton	
WG777	Fairey FD2 (7986M)	RAF Cosford Aerospace Museum	
WG789	EE Canberra B2/6 <ff>	Privately owned, Mendlesham, Suffolk	
WH132	Gloster Meteor T7 (7906M) [J]	No 276 Sqn ATC, Chelmsford	
WH166	Gloster Meteor T7 (8052M)	Privately owned, Birlingham, Worcs	
WH291	Gloster Meteor F8	SWWAPS, Lasham	
WH301	Gloster Meteor F8 (7930M) [T]	RAF Museum, Hendon	
WH364	Gloster Meteor F8 (8169M)	Avon Aviation Museum, stored Yatesbury	
WH453	Gloster Meteor D16 [L]	MoD(PE), stored T&EE Llanbedr	
WH646	EE Canberra T17A [EG]	RAF Wyton, Fire Section	
WH657	EE Canberra B2	Brenzett Aeronautical Museum	
WH665	EE Canberra T17 (8763M) [J]	BAe Filton, Fire Section	
WH699	EE Canberra B2T (WJ637/8755M)	RAFC Cranwell, Trenchard Hall on display	
WH724	EE Canberra T19 <ff>	*Scrapped at Shawbury*	
WH725	EE Canberra B2	Imperial War Museum, Duxford	
WH734	EE Canberra TT18	MoD(PE) T&EE, Llanbedr	
WH740	EE Canberra T17 (8762M) [K]	East Midlands Airport Aero Park	
WH773	EE Canberra PR7 (8696M)	Privately owned, Charlwood, Surrey	
WH774	EE Canberra PR7 (fuselage)	*Scrapped at Farnborough, 1994*	
WH775	EE Canberra PR7 (8128M/8868M) <ff>	Privately owned, Bruntingthorpe	
WH779	EE Canberra PR7 [BP]	RAF No 39 (1 PRU) Sqn, Marham	
WH780	EE Canberra T22 <ff>	Privately owned, Stock, Essex	
WH780	EE Canberra T22 (minus cockpit)	RAF St Athan, Fire Section	
WH791	EE Canberra PR7 (8165M/8176M/8187M)	RAF Cottesmore, at main gate	
WH796	EE Canberra PR7 <ff>	Privately owned, Stock, Essex	
WH797	EE Canberra T22 <ff>	Privately owned, Stock, Essex	
WH797	EE Canberra T22 (minus cockpit)	RAF St Athan, Fire Section	
WH801	EE Canberra T22 <ff>	Privately owned, Stock, Essex	
WH803	EE Canberra T22 <ff>	Privately owned, Stock, Essex	
WH840	EE Canberra T4 (8350M) <ff>	Privately owned, Flixton	
WH846	EE Canberra T4	Yorkshire Air Museum, Elvington	

Notes	Serial	Type (other identity) [code]	Owner/operator, location or fate
	WH849	EE Canberra T4 [BE]	RAF St Athan, stored
	WH850	EE Canberra T4<ff>	Macclesfield Historical Av'n Soc, Barton
	WH854	EE Canberra T4 <ff>	Martin Baker Aircraft, Chalgrove
	WH863	EE Canberra T17 (8693M) <ff>	Newark Air Museum, Winthorpe
	WH876	EE Canberra B2 (mod)	MoD(PE), T&EE Aberporth, instructional use
	WH887	EE Canberra TT18 [847]	MoD(PE) stored, T&EE Llanbedr
	WH902	EE Canberra T17A [EK]	RAF Wyton
	WH903	EE Canberra B2 (5854M) <ff>	Yorkshire Air Museum, Elvington
	WH904	EE Canberra T19 [04]	Newark Air Museum, Winthorpe
	WH946	EE Canberra B6(mod)(8185M)<ff>	Privately owned, Tetney, Grimsby
	WH952	EE Canberra B6	Royal Arsenal, Woolwich
	WH953	EE Canberra B6(mod)	MoD(PE), Farnborough, wfu
	WH957	EE Canberra E15 (8869M) <ff>	Lincolnshire Aviation Museum, East Kirkby
	WH960	EE Canberra B15 (8344M) <ff>	Privately owned, Bruntingthorpe
	WH964	EE Canberra E15 (8870M) <ff>	Privately owned, Bruntingthorpe
	WH981	EE Canberra E15 [CN]	*Scrapped at Wyton, September 1993*
	WH984	EE Canberra B15 (8101M) <ff>	Privately owned, Bruntingthorpe
	WH991	WS51 Dragonfly HR3	Privately owned, Storwood, East Yorks
	WJ231	Hawker Sea Fury FB11 (WE726) [115/O]	FAA Museum, Yeovilton
	WJ237	WAR Sea Fury <R> (G-BLTG) [113/O]	Privately owned, Langham
	WJ358	Auster AOP6 (G-ARYD)	Museum of Army Flying, stored Middle Wallop
	WJ565	EE Canberra T17 (8871M) <ff>	Privately owned, Bruntingthorpe
	WJ567	EE Canberra B2 <ff>	Privately owned, Houghton, Cambs
	WJ574	EE Canberra TT18 [844]	*Sold as N77844, February 1994*
	WJ576	EE Canberra T17	Wales Aircraft Museum, Cardiff
	WJ603	EE canberra B2 (8664M) <ff>	Privately owned, Stock, Essex
	WJ607	EE Canberra T17A [EB]	Privately owned
	WJ614	EE Canberra TT18 [846]	*Sold to USA AS N76765*
	WJ629	EE Canberra TT18 (8747M) [845]	*Scrapped at Chivenor, March 1994*
	WJ630	EE Canberra T17 [ED]	RAF, stored Wyton
	WJ633	EE Canberra T17A [EF]	RAF Wyton
	WJ636	EE Canberra TT18 [CX]	RAF Wyton, Fire Section
	WJ639	EE Canberra TT18 [39]	North-East Aircraft Museum, Usworth
	WJ640	EE Canberra B2 <ff>	Privately owned, Guildford
	WJ676	EE Canberra B2 (7796M) <ff>	Privately owned, Guildford
	WJ677	EE Canberra B2 <ff>	RNAS Culdrose, Fire Section
	WJ680	EE Canberra TT18 (G-BURM) [CT]	Privately owned, Wyton
	WJ717	EE Canberra TT18 (9052M)	RAF CTTS, St Athan
	WJ721	EE Canberra TT18 [21]	Pennine Aviation Museum, Bacup
	WJ731	EE Canberra B2T [BK]	*Scrapped at Wyton, February 1994*
	WJ756	EE Canberra E15 [BB]	*Scrapped at Wyton, February 1994*
	WJ775	EE Canberra B6 (8581M) [J] (fuselage)	FSCTE, RAF Manston
	WJ815	EE Canberra PR7 (8729M)	*Burnt at Coningsby*
	WJ817	EE Canberra PR7 (8695M) [FU2]	*Scrapped at Wyton*
	WJ821	EE Canberra PR7 (8668M)	Bassingbourn, on display
	WJ861	EE Canberra T4 [BF]	*Scrapped at St Athan, February 1994*
	WJ863	EE Canberra T4 <ff>	Cambridge Airport Fire Section
	WJ865	EE Canberra T4	MoD(PE), stored Farnborough
	WJ866	EE Canberra T4 [BL]	RAF No 39(1 PRU) Sqn, Marham
	WJ872	EE Canberra T4 (8492M) <ff>	No 327 Sqn ATC, Kilmarnock
	WJ874	EE Canberra T4 [BM]	RAF No 39 (1 PRU) Sqn, Marham
	WJ876	EE Canberra T4 <ff>	
	WJ880	EE Canberra T4 (8491M) <ff>	Dumfries & Galloway Av'n Mus, Tinwald Downs
	WJ893	Vickers Varsity T1	T&EE Aberporth Fire Section
	WJ903	Vickers Varsity T1 [C] <ff>	Dumfries & Galloway Av'n Mus, Tinwald Downs
	WJ944	Vickers Varsity T1	*Painted as RNZAF NZ233, 1993*
	WJ945	Vickers Varsity T1 (G-BEDV) [21]	Imperial War Museum, Duxford
	WJ975	EE Canberra T19 [S]	Bomber County Aviation Museum, Hemswell
	WJ981	EE Canberra T17A [EN]	Privately owned
	WJ986	EE Canberra T17 [EP]	RAF Wyton, Fire Section
	WJ992	EE Canberra T4	FR Aviation, Bournemouth
	WK102	EE Canberra T17 (8780M) <ff>	Privately owned, Welshpool
	WK111	EE Canberra T17 [EA]	*Scrapped at Wyton, February 1994*

Serial	Type (other identity) [code]	Owner/operator, location or fate	Notes
WK118	EE Canberra TT18 <ff>	Privately owned, Worcester	
WK119	EE Canberra B2 <ff>	RAF Wyton, Fire Section	
WK122	EE Canberra TT18 [22]	Flambards Village Theme Park, Helston	
WK124	EE Canberra TT18 (9093M) [CR]	FSCTE, RAF Manston	
WK126	EE Canberra TT18 [843]	*Sold to USA as N2138J*	
WK127	EE Canberra TT18 (8985M) <ff>	Air Scouts, Bassingbourn	
WK128	EE Canberra B2	MoD(PE) T&EE, Llanbedr	
WK142	EE Canberra TT18 [848]	*Sold to USA as N76764*	
WK143	EE Canberra B2	T&EE Llanbedr Fire Section	
WK144	EE Canberra B2 (8689M) <ff>	Privately owned, Stock, Essex	
WK162	EE Canberra B2 (8887M) [CA]	*Scrapped at Wyton, 1993*	
WK163	EE Canberra B6	MoD(PE), Farnborough, wfu	
WK198	VS Swift F4 (7428M) (fuselage)	North-East Aircraft Museum, Usworth	
WK275	VS Swift F4	Privately owned, Upper Hill, nr Leominster	
WK277	VS Swift FR5 (7719M) [N]	Newark Air Museum, Winthorpe	
WK281	VS Swift FR5 (7712M) [S]	Tangmere Military Aviation Museum	
WK511	DH Chipmunk T10 (G-BVBT) [905]	Kennet Aviation, Cranfield	
WK512	DH Chipmunk T10 [A]	AAC BFWF, Middle Wallop	
WK517	DH Chipmunk T10 [84]	RAF No 11 AEF, Leeming	
WK518	DH Chipmunk T10	RAF BBMF, Coningsby	
WK522	DH Chipmunk T10 (G-BCOU)	Privately owned, High Easter	
WK549	DH Chipmunk T10 (G-BTWF) [Y]	Privately owned, Rufforth	
WK550	DH Chipmunk T10	RAF No 8 AEF, Shawbury	
WK554	DH Chipmunk T10 [4]	RAF No 1 AEF, Manston	
WK558	DH Chipmunk T10 (G-ARMG)	Privately owned, Wellesbourne Mountford	
WK559	DH Chipmunk T10 [M]	AAC BFWF, Middle Wallop	
WK562	DH Chipmunk T10 [91]	RAF No 10 AEF, Woodvale	
WK570	DH Chipmunk T10 (8211M) <ff>	No 424 Sqn ATC, Southampton	
WK572	DH Chipmunk T10 [92]	RAF No 10 AEF, Woodvale	
WK574	DH Chipmunk T10 (G-BVPC)	Privately owned, Husbands Bosworth	
WK576	DH Chipmunk T10 (8357M) <ff>	No 1206 Sqn ATC, Lichfield	
WK584	DH Chipmunk T10 (7556M) <ff>	No 216 Sqn ATC, Bawtry	
WK585	DH Chipmunk T10	RAF No 12 AEF, Turnhouse	
WK586	DH Chipmunk T10 [V]	AAC BFWF, Middle Wallop	
WK587	DH Chipmunk T10 (8212M) <ff>	*Scrapped by 1993*	
WK589	DH Chipmunk T10 [C]	RAF, stored Shawbury	
WK590	DH Chipmunk T10 [69]	RAF No 9 AEF, Finningley	
WK608	DH Chipmunk T10 [906]	RN Historic Flt, Yeovilton	
WK609	DH Chipmunk T10 [93]	RAF No 10 AEF, Woodvale	
WK611	DH Chipmunk T10 (G-ARWB)	Privately owned, White Waltham	
WK613	DH Chipmunk T10 [P]	Pennine Aviation Museum, Bacup	
WK620	DH Chipmunk T10 [T] (fuselage)	AAC, Middle Wallop, spares use	
WK621	DH Chipmunk T10 (G-BDBL)	*Sold to New Zealand, September 1994*	
WK622	DH Chipmunk T10 (G-BCZH)	Privately owned, Horsford	
WK624	DH Chipmunk T10 [M]	RAF, stored Shawbury	
WK626	DH Chipmunk T10 (8213M) <ff>	Wiltshire Historic Aviation Grp, Salisbury	
WK628	DH Chipmunk T10 (G-BBMW)	Privately owned, Shoreham	
WK630	DH Chipmunk T10 [11]	RAF No 2 AEF, Bournemouth	
WK633	DH Chipmunk T10 [B]	RAF, stored Shawbury	
WK634	DH Chipmunk T10 [902]	Privately owned	
WK635	DH Chipmunk T10	RN, stored Shawbury	
WK638	DH Chipmunk T10 [83]	RAF No 11 AEF, Leeming	
WK639	DH Chipmunk T10 [L]	RAF, stored Shawbury	
WK640	DH Chipmunk T10 [C]	RAF No 3 AEF, Colerne	
WK642	DH Chipmunk T10 [94]	RAF No 10 AEF, Woodvale	
WK643	DH Chipmunk T10 [G]	RAF CFS, Scampton	
WK654	Gloster Meteor F8 (8092M) [X]	RAF Neatishead, at main gate	
WK800	Gloster Meteor D16 [Z]	MoD(PE) T&EE, Llanbedr	
WK864	Gloster Meteor F8 (WL168/ 7750M) [C]	RAF Finningley on display	
WK935	Gloster Meteor Prone Pilot (7869M)	RAF Cosford Aerospace Museum	
WK991	Gloster Meteor F8 (7825M)	Imperial War Museum, Duxford	
WL131	Gloster Meteor F8 (7751M) <ff>	4th Guernsey Air Scouts,Guernsey Airport	
WL181	Gloster Meteor F8 [X]	North-East Aircraft Museum, Usworth	
WL332	Gloster Meteor. T7 [888]	Privately owned, Long Marston	
WL345	Gloster Meteor T7	Privately owned, Hollington, E Sussex	
WL349	Gloster Meteor T7 [Z]	Gloucestershire Airport, on display	
WL360	Gloster Meteor T7 (7920M) [G]	Gloucestershire Av'n Coll,Hucclecote	
WL375	Gloster Meteor T7	Dumfries & Galloway Av'n Mus, Tinwald Downs	

Notes	Serial	Type (other identity) [code]	Owner/operator, location or fate
	WL405	Gloster Meteor T7	Martin Baker Aircraft, Chalgrove, spares use
	WL419	Gloster Meteor T7	Martin Baker Aircraft, Chalgrove
	WL505	DH Vampire FB9 (7705M/G-FBIX)	Privately owned, Cranfield
	WL626	Vickers Varsity T1 (G-BHDD) [P]	East Midlands Airport Aero Park
	WL627	Vickers Varsity T1 (8488M) [D] <ff>	Privately owned, Preston, Humberside
	WL635	Vickers Varsity T1	RAF Machrihanish Police School
	WL679	Vickers Varsity T1 (9155M)	RAF Cosford Aerospace Museum
	WL732	BP Sea Balliol T21	RAF Cosford Aerospace Museum
	WL756	Avro Shackleton AEW2 (9101M)	RAF St Mawgan, Fire Section
	WL790	Avro Shackleton AEW2	*To USA as N790WL, Sep 1994*
	WL795	Avro Shackleton MR2C (8753M) [T]	RAF St Mawgan, on display
	WL798	Avro Shackleton MR2C (8114M) <ff>	*Scrapped at Elgin by 1993*
	WL925	Slingsby Cadet TX3 (WV925) <ff>	RAF No 633 VGS, Cosford
	WM145	AW Meteor NF11 <ff>	N Yorks Aircraft Recovery Centre, Chop Gate
	WM167	AW Meteor NF11 (G-LOSM)	Jet Heritage Ltd, Bournemouth
	WM223	AW Meteor TT20	SWWAPS, Lasham
	WM267	Gloster Meteor NF11 <ff>	Night Fighter Preservation Group, Elvington
	WM292	AW Meteor TT20 [841]	Wales Aircraft Museum, Cardiff
	WM311	AW Meteor TT20 (WM224/8177M)	Privately owned, North Weald
	WM366	AW Meteor NF13 (4X-FNA)	SWWAPS, Lasham
	WM367	AW Meteor NF13 <ff>	Privately owned, North Weald
	WM571	DH Sea Venom FAW21 [VL]	Southampton Hall of Aviation
	WM729	DH Vampire NF10 [A] <ff>	Mosquito Aircraft Museum, London Colney
	WM913	Hawker Sea Hawk FB5 (8162M) [456/J]	Newark Air Museum, Winthorpe
	WM961	Hawker Sea Hawk FB5 [J]	Caernarfon Air World
	WM969	Hawker Sea Hawk FB5 [10/Z]	Imperial War Museum, Duxford
	WM993	Hawker Sea Hawk FB5 [034]	Privately owned, Peasedown St John, Avon
	WM994	Hawker Sea Hawk FB5 (G-SEAH)	Jet Heritage Ltd, Bournemouth
	WN105	Hawker Sea Hawk FB3 (WF299/ 8164M)	Privately owned, Birlingham, Worcs
	WN108	Hawker Sea Hawk FB5 [033]	Ulster Aviation Society, Langford Lodge
	WN149	BP Balliol T2 <ff>	Boulton-Paul Society, Wolverhampton
	WN411	Fairey Gannet AS1 (fuselage)	Privately owned, Southampton
	WN493	WS51 Dragonfly HR5	FAA Museum, RNAS Yeovilton
	WN499	WS51 Dragonfly HR5 [Y]	Caernarfon Air World
	WN516	BP Balliol T2 <ff>	North-East Aircraft Museum, Usworth
	WN534	BP Balliol T2 <ff>	Boulton-Paul Society, Wolverhampton
	WN890	Hawker Hunter F2 <ff>	Robertsbridge Aviation Society
	WN904	Hawker Hunter F2 (7544M) [3]	RE 39 Regt, Waterbeach, on display
	WN907	Hawker Hunter F2 (7416M) <ff>	Blyth Valley Aviation Collection, Walpole
	WP180	Hawker Hunter F5 (WP190/ 7582M/8473M) [K]	Privately owned
	WP185	Hawker Hunter F5 (7583M)	Privately owned
	WP250	DH Vampire NF10 <ff>	Privately owned, Tamworth
	WP255	DH Vampire NF10 <ff>	South Yorkshire Aviation Museum, Firbeck
	WP270	EoN Eton TX1 (8598M)	Gtr Manchester Mus'm of Science & Industry
	WP271	EoN Eton TX1	Privately owned, stored, Keevil
	WP309	Percival Sea Prince T1 [570/CU]	RNAS Yeovilton Fire Section
	WP313	Percival Sea Prince T1 [568/CU]	FAA Museum, stored Wroughton
	WP314	Percival Sea Prince T1 (8634M) [573/CU]	Privately owned, Carlisle Airport
	WP321	Percival Sea Prince T1 (G-BRFC) [750/CU]	Aces High, North Weald
	WP503	WS51 Dragonfly HR3 [901]	Privately owned, Storwood, East Yorks
	WP515	EE Canberra B2 <ff>	Wales Aircraft Museum, Cardiff
	WP772	DH Chipmunk T10 [Q] (wreck)	Privately owned, St Athan
	WP776	DH Chipmunk T10 [817/CU]	RN, stored Shawbury
	WP784	DH Chipmunk T10 <ff>	Privately owned, Boston
	WP786	DH Chipmunk T10 [G]	RAF No 6 AEF, Benson
	WP788	DH Chipmunk T10 (G-BCHL)	Privately owned, Sleap
	WP790	DH Chipmunk T10 (G-BBNC) [T]	Mosquito Aircraft Museum, London Colney
	WP795	DH Chipmunk T10 [901]	Privately owned

Serial	Type (other identity) [code]	Owner/operator, location or fate	Notes
WP800	DH Chipmunk T10 (G-BCXN) [2]	Privately owned, Halton	
WP801	DH Chipmunk T10 [911]	Privately owned	
WP803	DH Chipmunk T10 [C]	RAF No 4 AEF, Exeter	
WP805	DH Chipmunk T10 [D]	RAF, stored Shawbury	
WP808	DH Chipmunk T10 (G-BDEU)	Privately owned, Binham	
WP809	DH Chipmunk T10 (G-BVTX) [778]	Privately owned, Lichfield	
WP833	DH Chipmunk T10 [A]	RAF No 4 AEF, Exeter	
WP835	DH Chipmunk T10 (G-BDCB)	Privately owned, Rochester	
WP837	DH Chipmunk T10 [L]	RAF No 5 AEF, Cambridge	
WP839	DH Chipmunk T10 [A]	RAF No 8 AEF, Shawbury	
WP840	DH Chipmunk T10 [9]	RAF No 2 AEF, Bournemouth	
WP844	DH Chipmunk T10 [85]	RAF No 11 AEF, Leeming	
WP845	DH Chipmunk T10 <ff>	Vintage Aircraft Team, Bruntingthorpe	
WP855	DH Chipmunk T10 [5]	RAF No 1 AEF, Manston	
WP856	DH Chipmunk T10 [904]	Privately owned	
WP857	DH Chipmunk T10 (G-BDRJ)[24]	Privately owned, Elstree	
WP859	DH Chipmunk T10 [E]	RAF No 8 AEF, Shawbury	
WP860	DH Chipmunk T10	RAF No 12 AEF, Turnhouse	
WP863	DH Chipmunk T10 (8360M/ G-ATJI) <ff>	No 2293 Sqn ATC, Marlborough	
WP864	DH Chipmunk T10 (8214M) <ff>	RAF No 7 AEF, Newton	
WP869	DH Chipmunk T10 (8215M) <ff>	RAF	
WP871	DH Chipmunk T10 [W]	AAC BFWF, Middle Wallop	
WP872	DH Chipmunk T10	RAF No 12 AEF, Turnhouse	
WP896	DH Chipmunk T10 [M]	RAF, stored Shawbury	
WP900	DH Chipmunk T10 [V]	RAF, stored Shawbury	
WP901	DH Chipmunk T10 [B]	RAF No 6 AEF, Benson	
WP903	DH Chipmunk T10 (G-BCGC)	RN Gliding Club, Culdrose	
WP904	DH Chipmunk T10 [909]	Privately owned	
WP906	DH Chipmunk T10 [816/CU]	RN, stored Shawbury	
WP907	DH Chipmunk T10 <ff> (7970M)	Privately owned, Reading	
WP912	DH Chipmunk T10 (8467M)	RAF Cosford Aerospace Museum	
WP914	DH Chipmunk T10 [E]	RAF No 6 AEF, Benson	
WP920	DH Chipmunk T10 [10]	RAF No 2 AEF, Bournemouth	
WP921	DH Chipmunk T10 <ff>	No 1924 Sqn ATC, Croydon	
WP925	DH Chipmunk T10 [C]	AAC BFWF, Middle Wallop	
WP927	DH Chipmunk T10 (8216M/ G-ATJK) <ff>	RAF No 10 AEF, Woodvale	
WP928	DH Chipmunk T10 [D]	AAC BFWF, Middle Wallop	
WP929	DH Chipmunk T10 [F]	RAF No 8 AEF, Shawbury	
WP930	DH Chipmunk T10 [J]	AAC BFWF, Middle Wallop	
WP962	DH Chipmunk T10 [C]	RAF No 5 AEF, Teversham	
WP964	DH Chipmunk T10 [Y]	AAC BFWF, Middle Wallop	
WP967	DH Chipmunk T10	RAF No 12 AEF, Turnhouse	
WP970	DH Chipmunk T10 [T]	RAF No 5 AEF, Cambridge	
WP971	DH Chipmunk T10 (G-ATHD)	Privately owned, Denham	
WP972	DH Chipmunk T10 (8667M) <ff>	CSDE, RAF Swanton Morley	
WP974	DH Chipmunk T10 [96]	RAF, stored Shawbury	
WP976	DH Chipmunk T10 (WP791/ G-APTS)	Privately owned, Booker	
WP977	DH Chipmunk T10 (G-BHRD) [N]	Privately owned, Kidlington	
WP978	DH Chipmunk T10 (7467M) <ff>	RAF No 2 AEF, Bournemouth	
WP979	DH Chipmunk T10 [J]	Scrapped at Swanton Morley by 1993	
WP981	DH Chipmunk T10 [D]	RAF No 5 AEF, Cambridge	
WP983	DH Chipmunk T10 [B]	AAC BFWF, Middle Wallop	
WP984	DH Chipmunk T10 [H]	RAF No 6 AEF, Benson	
WR410	DH Venom FB54 (G-BLKA) [N]	Vintage Aircraft Team, Bruntingthorpe	
WR539	DH Venom FB4 (8399M) [F]	Mosquito Aircraft Museum, London Colney	
WR960	Avro Shackleton AEW2 (8772M)	Gtr Manchester Mus'm of Science & Industry	
WR963	Avro Shackleton AEW2	Air Atlantique, Coventry	
WR971	Avro Shackleton MR3 (8119M) [Q]	Privately owned, Narborough, Norfolk	
WR974	Avro Shackleton MR3 (8117M) [K]	Privately owned, Charlwood, Surrey	
WR977	Avro Shackleton MR3 (8186M) [B]	Newark Air Museum, Winthorpe	
WR982	Avro Shackleton MR3 (8106M) [J]	Privately owned, Charlwood, Surrey	
WR985	Avro Shackleton MR3 (8103M) [H]	Privately owned, Long Marston	
WS103	Gloster Meteor T7 [709/VL]	FAA Museum, Crawley College	
WS692	Gloster Meteor NF12 (7605M) [C]	Newark Air Museum, Winthorpe	
WS726	Gloster Meteor NF14 (7960M) [G]	No 1855 Sqn ATC, Royton	
WS739	Gloster Meteor NF14 (7961M)	Newark Air Museum, Winthorpe	
WS760	Gloster Meteor NF14 (7964M)	Classic Jet Aircraft Coll, Loughborough	

Notes	Serial	Type (other identity) [code]	Owner/operator, location or fate
	WS774	Gloster Meteor NF14 (7959M)	Privately owned, Fearn, Highlands
	WS776	Gloster Meteor NF14 (7716M) [K]	RAF North Luffenham, at main gate
	WS788	Gloster Meteor NF14 (7967M) [Z]	Yorkshire Air Museum, Elvington
	WS792	Gloster Meteor NF14 (7965M) [K]	Privately owned, Brighouse Bay, D&G
	WS807	Gloster Meteor NF14 (7973M) [N]	Privately owned, Yatesbury
	WS832	Gloster Meteor NF14 [W]	Solway Aviation Society, Carlisle Airport
	WS838	Gloster Meteor NF14	Midland Air Museum, Coventry
	WS843	Gloster Meteor NF14 (7937M) [Y]	RAF Museum, Hendon
	WT121	Douglas Skyraider AEW1 (WT983) [415/CU]	FAA Museum, stored RNAS Yeovilton
	WT301	EE Canberra B6(mod)	*Scrapped at Chattenden, November 1993*
	WT308	EE Canberra B(I)6	RN, Predannack Fire School
	WT309	EE Canberra B(I)6	A&AEE Boscombe Down, Apprentice School
	WT327	EE Canberra B(I)8	MoD(PE) DRA, Bedford
	WT333	EE Canberra B(I)8	MoD(PE) Farnborough, wfu
	WT339	EE Canberra B(I)8 (8198M)	RAF Barkston Heath Fire Section
	WT480	EE Canberra T4 [AT]	RAF No 39(1 PRU) Sqn. Marham
	WT482	EE Canberra T4 <ff>	Privately owned,
	WT483	EE Canberra T4 [83]	Privately owned, Long Marston
	WT486	EE Canberra T4 (8102M) [C]	Belfast Airport Fire Section
	WT488	EE Canberra T4	BAe Dunsfold Fire Section
	WT507	EE Canberra PR7 (8131M/ 8548M) [44] <ff>	No 384 Sqn ATC, Mansfield
	WT509	EE Canberra PR7 [BR]	RAF No 39(1 PRU) Sqn, Marham
	WT510	EE Canberra T22 <ff>	Privately owned, Stock, Essex
	WT518	EE Canberra PR7 (8133M/ 8691M) <rf>	*Scrapped at Cardiff, 1992*
	WT519	EE Canberra PR7 [CH]	RAF Wyton, Fire Section
	WT520	EE Canberra PR7 (8094M/ 8184M)	Privately owned, Burntwood, Staffs
	WT525	EE Canberra T22 <ff>	Privately owned, South Woodham Ferrers
	WT532	EE Canberra PR7 (8728M/ 8890M) [Z]	Bournemouth Int'l Airport, Fire Section
	WT534	EE Canberra PR7 (8549M) [43] <ff>	No 492 Sqn ATC, Shirley, W. Midlands
	WT536	EE Canberra PR7 (8063M) <ff>	Privately owned, Bruntingthorpe
	WT537	EE Canberra PR7	BAe Samlesbury, on display
	WT555	Hawker Hunter F1 (7499M)	Privately owned, Greenford, London
	WT569	Hawker Hunter F1 (7491M)	No 2117 Sqn ATC, Kenfig Hill, Mid Glamorgan
	WT612	Hawker Hunter F1 (7496M)	RAF Henlow on display
	WT619	Hawker Hunter F1 (7525M)	Gtr Manchester Mus'm of Science & Industry
	WT648	Hawker Hunter F1 (7530M) <ff>	The Air Defence Collection, Salisbury
	WT651	Hawker Hunter F1 [C]	Newark Air Museum, Winthorpe
	WT660	Hawker Hunter F1 (7421M) [C]	Privately owned, New Byth, Grampian
	WT680	Hawker Hunter F1 (7533M) [Z]	No 1429 Sqn ATC, at T&EE Aberporth
	WT684	Hawker Hunter F1 (7422M)	Jet Aviation Preservation Grp, Long Marston
	WT694	Hawker Hunter F1 (7510M)	RAF Newton, at main gate
	WT711	Hawker Hunter GA11 [833/DD]	SAH, RNAS Culdrose
	WT720	Hawker Hunter F51 (RDAF E-408/8565M) [B]	RAF Sealand, on display
	WT722	Hawker Hunter T8C [878/VL]	RN stored, Yeovilton
	WT723	Hawker Hunter PR11 [866/VL,3]	SAH, RNAS Culdrose
	WT744	Hawker Hunter GA11 [868/VL]	Privately owned, Bodmin
	WT746	Hawker Hunter F4 (7770M) [A]	Army, Saighton, Chester
	WT799	Hawker Hunter T8C [879]	Privately owned
	WT804	Hawker Hunter GA11 [831/DD]	FETC, Moreton-in-Marsh
	WT806	Hawker Hunter GA11	Privately owned
	WT859	Supermarine 544 <ff>	Brooklands Aviation Museum, Weybridge
	WT867	Slingsby Cadet TX3	Privately owned, Eaglescott
	WT899	Slingsby Cadet TX3	Privately owned, Rush Green
	WT902	Slingsby Cadet TX3 (BGA 3147)	Privately owned, Lleweni Parc, Clwyd
	WT905	Slingsby Cadet TX3	Privately owned, Bridge of Don, Grampian
	WT910	Slingsby Cadet TX3 (BGA 3953)	Privately owned, Challock
	WT933	Bristol Sycamore 3 (G-ALSW/ 7709M)	Newark Air Museum, Winthorpe
	WV106	Douglas Skyraider AEW1 [427/C]	Flambards Village Theme Park, Helston
	WV198	S55 Whirlwind HAR21 (G-BJWY) [K]	South Yorkshire Aviation Museum, Firbeck

Serial	Type (other identity) [code]	Owner/operator, location or fate	Notes
WV256	Hawker Hunter GA11 [862/VL]	RN stored, Yeovilton	
WV267	Hawker Hunter GA11 [836/DD]	Sold to the USA, January 1994	
WV276	Hawker Hunter F4 (7847M) [D]	DRA Avionics & Sensors Dept, Farnborough	
WV309	Hawker Hunter F51 (RDAF E-409)	Painted as XF383	
WV318	Hawker Hunter T7B	TMTS, RAF Scampton	
WV322	Hawker Hunter T8C (9096M) [Y]	SIF, RAFC Cranwell	
WV332	Hawker Hunter F4 (7673M) <ff>	No 1254 Sqn ATC, Godalming	
WV372	Hawker Hunter T7 [877/VL,1]	SAH, RNAS Culdrose	
WV381	Hawker Hunter GA11 [732/VL]	UKAEA, Culham, Oxon	
WV383	Hawker Hunter T7	MoD(PE) DRA, Boscombe Down	
WV395	Hawker Hunter F4 (8001M)	BAe Dunsfold, Fire Section	
WV396	Hawker Hunter T8C (879/VL]	RN FRADU, Yeovilton	
WV483	Percival Provost T1 (7693M)[N-E]	Privately owned	
WV486	Percival Provost T1 (7694M)[N-D]	Privately owned, Grazeley, Berks	
WV493	Percival Provost T1 (G-BDYG/ 7696M)	Royal Scottish Mus'm of Flight, E Fortune	
WV495	Percival Provost T1 (7697M) [P-C]	Sold to the USA	
WV499	Percival Provost T1 (7698M) [P-G]	Privately owned, North Weald	
WV562	Percival Provost T1 (7606M) [P-C]	RAF Cosford Aerospace Museum, stored	
WV605	Percival Provost T1 [T-B]	Norfolk & Suffolk Aviation Museum, Flixton	
WV606	Percival Provost T1 (7622M)[P-B]	Newark Air Museum, Winthorpe	
WV666	Percival Provost T1 (7925M/ G-BTDH) [O-D]	Privately owned, Shoreham	
WV679	Percival Provost T1 (7615M) [O-J]	Privately owned, Wellesbourne Mountford	
WV686	Percival Provost T1 (7621M/ G-BLFT) [O-P]	Sold to Australia, 1993	
WV703	Percival Pembroke C1 (8108M/ G-IIIM)	Privately owned, Tattershall Thorpe	
WV705	Percival Pembroke C1 <ff>	Southampton Hall of Aviation, stored	
WV740	Percival Pembroke C1 (G-BNPH)	Privately owned, Cranfield	
WV746	Percival Pembroke C1 (8938M)	RAF Cosford Aerospace Museum	
WV753	Percival Pembroke C1 (8113M)	Cardiff Airport Fire Section	
WV781	Bristol Sycamore HR12 (G-ALTD/ 7839M)	Caernarfon Air World	
WV783	Bristol Sycamore HR12 (G-ALSP/ 7841M)	RNAY Fleetlands Museum	
WV787	EE Canberra B2/8 (8799M)	Newark Air Museum, Winthorpe	
WV795	Hawker Sea Hawk FGA6 (8151M)	Privately owned, Bournemouth	
WV797	Hawker Sea Hawk FGA6 (8155M) [491/J]	Midland Air Museum, Coventry	
WV798	Hawker Sea Hawk FGA6 [028/CU]	SWWAPS, Lasham	
WV826	Hawker Sea Hawk FGA6 [147/Z]	Wales Aircraft Museum, Cardiff	
WV843	Hawker Sea Hawk FGA4 <ff>	Wilts Historic Aviation Group, Salisbury	
WV856	Hawker Sea Hawk FGA6 [163]	FAA Museum, RNAS Yeovilton	
WV903	Hawker Sea Hawk FGA4 (8153M)	RN, stored Lee-on-Solent	
WV908	Hawker Sea Hawk FGA6 (8154M) [188/A]	RN Historic Flight, stored Yeovilton	
WV911	Hawker Sea Hawk FGA4 [115/C]	To Australia	
WW138	DH Sea Venom FAW22 [227/Z]	FAA Museum, RNAS Yeovilton	
WW145	DH Sea Venom FAW22 [680/LM]	Royal Scottish Mus'm of Flight, E Fortune	
WW217	DH Sea Venom FAW22 [736]	Newark Air Museum, Winthorpe	
WW388	Percival Provost T1 (7616M) [O-F]	South Yorkshire Aviation Museum, Firbeck	
WW421	Percival Provost T1 (7688M) [P-B]	Lincolnshire Aviation Museum, East Kirkby	
WW442	Percival Provost T1 (7618M) [N]	Privately owned, Kings Langley	
WW444	Percival Provost T1 [D]	Privately owned	
WW447	Percival Provost T1	Privately owned, Grazeley, Berks	
WW453	Percival Provost T1 (G-TMKI) [W-S]	Kennet Aircraft, Cranfield	
WW654	Hawker Hunter GA11 [834/DD]	Privately owned, Portsmouth	
WX660	Hover-Air HA-5 Hoverhawk III (XW660)	Privately owned, Cheltenham	
WX788	DH Venom NF3	Night Fighter Preservation Team, Elvington	
WX853	DH Venom NF3 (7443M)	Mosquito Aircraft Museum, London Colney	
WX905	DH Venom NF3 (7458M)	Newark Air Museum, Winthorpe	
WZ415	DH Vampire T11 [72]	No 2 Sqn ATC, Leavesden	
WZ425	DH Vampire T11	Privately owned, Birlingham	
WZ450	DH Vampire T11 <ff>	Lashenden Air Warfare Museum, Headcorn	

Notes	Serial	Type (other identity) [code]	Owner/operator, location or fate
	WZ458	DH Vampire T11 (7728M) [31] <ff>	Blyth Valley Aviation Collection, Walpole
	WZ464	DH Vampire T11 (N62430) [40]	Vintage Aircraft Team, Bruntingthorpe
	WZ476	DH Vampire T11 (XE985)	*Repainted as XE985*
	WZ507	DH Vampire T11 (G-VTII)	Vintage Aircraft Team, Bruntingthorpe
	WZ514	DH Vampire T11	Privately owned, Meols, Merseyside
	WZ515	DH Vampire T11 [60]	Solway Aviation Society, Carlisle
	WZ518	DH Vampire T11	North-East Aircraft Museum, Usworth
	WZ549	DH Vampire T11 (8118M) [F]	Ulster Heritage Centre, Langford Lodge
	WZ550	DH Vampire T11 (7902M) [NF]	Booker Aircraft Museum
	WZ553	DH Vampire T11 [40]	Privately owned, Cranfield
	WZ557	DH Vampire T11	N Yorks Aircraft Recovery Centre, Chop Gate
	WZ559	DH Vampire T11 (7736M) [45] <ff>	RAF Halton Fire Section
	WZ581	DH Vampire T11 <ff>	Privately owned, Hemel Hempstead
	WZ584	DH Vampire T11 [K]	Privately owned, Bridgend
	WZ589	DH Vampire T11 [19]	Lashenden Air Warfare Museum, Headcorn
	WZ590	DH Vampire T11 [19]	Imperial War Museum, Duxford
	WZ608	DH Vampire T11 [56] <ff>	Privately owned, Romford
	WZ620	DH Vampire T11 [68]	Avon Aviation Museum, Yatesbury
	WZ662	Auster AOP9 (G-BKVK)	Privately owned, Cranfield
	WZ679	Auster AOP9 (7863M)	*Painted as XP248*
	WZ706	Auster AOP9 (7851M/G-BURR)	Privately owned, Middle Wallop
	WZ711	Auster AOP9/Beagle E3 (G-AVHT)	Privately owned, Middle Wallop
	WZ721	Auster AOP9	Museum of Army Flying, Middle Wallop
	WZ724	Auster AOP9 (7432M)	AAC Middle Wallop, at main gate
	WZ736	Avro 707A (7868M)	Gtr Manchester Mus'm of Science & Industry
	WZ744	Avro 707C (7932M)	RAF Cosford Aerospace Museum
	WZ753	Slingsby Grasshopper TX1	Southampton Hall of Aviation
	WZ765	Slingsby Grasshopper TX1	RAFGSA, Bicester
	WZ767	Slingsby Grasshopper TX1	North-East Aircraft Museum, Usworth
	WZ769	Slingsby Grasshopper TX1	Privately owned, stored Rufforth
	WZ779	Slingsby Grasshopper TX1	Privately owned, Old Sarum
	WZ791	Slingsby Grasshopper TX1 (8944M)	RAF Museum, Hendon
	WZ792	Slingsby Grasshopper TX1	Privately owned, Falgunzeon, D&G
	WZ793	Slingsby Grasshopper TX1	Whitgift School, Croydon
	WZ796	Slingsby Grasshopper TX1	Privately owned, Nympsfield, stored
	WZ822	Slingsby Grasshopper TX1 (BGA 3875)	Robertsbridge Aviation Society, Mayfield
	WZ826	Vickers Valiant B(K)1 (XD826/7872M) <ff>	Privately owned, Rayleigh, Essex
	WZ829	Slingsby Grasshopper TX1	RAFGSA, stored Bicester
	WZ831	Slingsby Grasshopper TX1	Privately owned, Nympsfield
	WZ845	DH Chipmunk T10 [6]	RAF No 1 AEF, Manston
	WZ846	DH Chipmunk T10 (G-BCSC/8439M) <ff>	No 1404 Sqn ATC, Chatham
	WZ847	DH Chipmunk T10 [F]	RAF No 6 AEF, Benson
	WZ856	DH Chipmunk T10 [74]	RAF No 7 AEF, Newton
	WZ862	DH Chipmunk T10 [A]	RAF No 3 AEF, Colerne
	WZ866	DH Chipmunk T10 (8217M/G-ATEB) <ff>	No 2296 Sqn ATC, Dunoon, Strathclyde
	WZ868	DH Chipmunk T10 (G-BCIW) [H]	Privately owned, Fownhope, H&W
	WZ868	DH Chipmunk T10 (WG322/G-ARMF) [H]	Privately owned, Audley End
	WZ869	DH Chipmunk T10 (8019M) [R] <ff>	No 284 Sqn ATC, Cheadle
	WZ872	DH Chipmunk T10 [E]	RAF No 5 AEF, Cambridge
	WZ876	DH Chipmunk T10 (G-BBWN)	Privately owned, Netherthorpe
	WZ877	DH Chipmunk T10 [75]	RAF No 7 AEF, Newton
	WZ878	DH Chipmunk T10 [86]	RAF No 11 AEF, Leeming
	WZ879	DH Chipmunk T10	AAC BFWF, Middle Wallop
	WZ882	DH Chipmunk T10 [K]	AAC BFWF, Middle Wallop
	WZ884	DH Chipmunk T10 [P]	AAC BFWF, Middle Wallop
	XA109	DH Sea Vampire T22	Royal Scottish Mus'm of Flight, E Fortune
	XA127	DH Sea Vampire T22 <ff>	FAA Museum, stored RNAS Yeovilton
	XA129	DH Sea Vampire T22	FAA Museum, stored Wroughton
	XA225	Slingsby Grasshopper TX1	Churchers College, Petersfield, Hants
	XA230	Slingsby Grasshopper TX1 (BGA 4098)	Uppingham School, Leics
	XA231	Slingsby Grasshopper TX1 (8888M)	E Cheshire & S Manchester Wg ATC, Sealand

Serial	Type (other identity) [code]	Owner/operator, location or fate	Notes
XA243	Slingsby Grasshopper TX1 (8886M)	RAF, stored St Athan	
XA244	Slingsby Grasshopper TX1	RAF, stored Cosford	
XA282	Slingsby Cadet TX3	Caernarfon Air World	
XA286	Slingsby Cadet TX3	Privately owned, stored Rufforth	
XA289	Slingsby Cadet TX3	Privately owned, Eaglescott	
XA290	Slingsby Cadet TX3	Privately owned, stored Rufforth	
XA292	Slingsby Cadet TX3 (BGA3350)	Brooklands Museum, Weybridge	
XA293	Slingsby Cadet TX3	Privately owned, Breighton	
XA302	Slingsby Cadet TX3 (BGA3786)	Privately owned, Winthorpe	
XA454	Fairey Gannet COD4	RNAS Yeovilton Fire Section	
XA459	Fairey Gannet ECM6 [E]	Privately owned, Cirencester	
XA460	Fairey Gannet ECM6 [768/BY]	NE Wales Institute of HE, Connah's Quay	
XA466	Fairey Gannet COD4 [777/LM]	FAA Museum, stored Wroughton	
XA508	Fairey Gannet T2 [627/GN]	Midland Air Museum, Coventry	
XA553	Gloster Javelin FAW1 (7470M)	RAF Stanmore Park, on display	
XA564	Gloster Javelin FAW1 (7464M)	RAF Cosford Aerospace Museum	
XA571	Gloster Javelin FAW1 (7663M/ 7722M) <ff>	Privately owned, Catford	
XA634	Gloster Javelin FAW4 (7641M) [L]	RAF Leeming, on display	
XA699	Gloster Javelin FAW5 (7809M)	Midland Air Museum, Coventry	
XA801	Gloster Javelin FAW2 (7739M) <ff>	Privately owned, Stock, Essex	
XA847	EE P1B (8371M)	Privately owned, Southampton Docks	
XA862	WS55 Whirlwind HAR1 (G-AMJT) [9]	IHM, Weston-super-Mare	
XA864	WS55 Whirlwind HAR1	FAA Museum, stored	
XA868	WS55 Whirlwind HAR1	IHM, Weston-super-Mare	
XA870	WS55 Whirlwind HAR1	Flambards Village Theme Park, Helston	
XA880	DH Devon C2	Privately owned	
XA893	Avro Vulcan B1 (8591M) <ff>	RAF Cosford Aerospace Museum	
XA903	Avro Vulcan B1 <ff>	Privately owned, Sidcup	
XA909	Avro Vulcan B1 <ff>	Lincolnshire Av'n Heritage Centre, E Kirkby	
XB259	Blackburn Beverley C1 (G-AOAI)	Museum of Army Transport, Beverley	
XB261	Blackburn Beverley C1 <ff>	Imperial War Museum, Duxford	
XB446	Grumman Avenger ECM6B [992/C]	FAA Museum, stored Wroughton	
XB480	Hiller HT1 [537]	FAA Museum, stored Wroughton	
XB733	Canadair CL-13 Sabre 4 (G-ATBF)	Privately owned	
XB812	Canadair CL-13 Sabre F4 (9227M) [U]	RAF Museum, Hendon	
XD145	Saro SR53	RAF Cosford Aerospace Museum	
XD163	WS55 Whirlwind HAR10 (8645M) [X]	IHM, Weston-super-Mare	
XD165	WS55 Whirlwind HAR10 (8673M) [B]	AAC Netheravon, instructional use	
XD186	WS55 Whirlwind HAR10 (8730M)		
XD215	VS Scimitar F1 <ff>	Privately owned, Cheltenham	
XD219	VS Scimitar F1 (fuselage)	Scrapped at Yeovilton by March 1994	
XD234	VS Scimitar F1 [834]	DRA, derelict Farnborough	
XD235	VS Scimitar F1 <ff>	No 424 Sqn ATC, Southampton	
XD244	VS Scimitar F1 <ff>	Privately owned, Ottershaw	
XD317	VS Scimitar F1 [112/R]	FAA Museum, RNAS Yeovilton	
XD332	VS Scimitar F1 [194/C]	Flambards Village Theme Park, Helston	
XD375	DH Vampire T11 (7887M) [72]	Privately owned, Fakenham	
XD377	DH Vampire T11 (8203M) [A] <ff>	Yorkshire Air Museum, Elvington	
XD382	DH Vampire T11 (8033M)	Privately owned, Ripley, Derbys	
XD425	DH Vampire T11 [16]	Dumfries & Galloway Av'n Mus, stored	
XD434	DH Vampire T11 [25]	Fenland Aviation Museum, Wisbech	
XD435	DH Vampire T11 [26] <ff>	Privately owned, Lapworth, Warwicks	
XD445	DH Vampire T11 [51]	Bomber County Aviation Museum, Hemswell	
XD447	DH Vampire T11 [50]	Jet Aircraft Pres'n Grp., Long Marston	
XD452	DH Vampire T11 (7990M) <ff> [47]	Vampire Support Team, Sealand	
XD453	DH Vampire T11 (7890M) [64]	No 58 Sqn ATC, Elvington	
XD459	DH Vampire T11 [63] <ff>	Privately owned, Bruntingthorpe	
XD463	DH Vampire T11 (8023M)	No 1360 Sqn ATC, Stapleford, Notts	
XD506	DH Vampire T11 (7983M)	RAF Swinderby	
XD515	DH Vampire T11 (7998M/XM515)	Newark Air Museum, Winthorpe	
XD525	DH Vampire T11 (7882M) <ff>	Campbell College CCF, Belfast	
XD528	DH Vampire T11 (8159M)	South Yorkshire Air Museum, Firbeck	

XD534 – XE956

Notes	Serial	Type (other identity) [code]	Owner/operator, location or fate
	XD534	DH Vampire T11 [41]	Military Aircraft Pres'n Grp, Barton
	XD535	DH Vampire T11 <ff>	Macclesfield Historical Av'n Soc
	XD536	DH Vampire T11 (7734M) [H]	Alleyn's School CCF, Northolt
	XD542	DH Vampire T11 (7604M)[28]	RAF Edzell, Scotland, on display
	XD547	DH Vampire T11 [Z] (composite)	Dumfries & Galloway Av'n Mus, Tinwald Downs
	XD593	DH Vampire T11 [50]	Newark Air Museum, Winthorpe
	XD595	DH Vampire T11 <ff>	Privately owned, Glentham, Lincs
	XD596	DH Vampire T11 (7939M)	Southampton Hall of Aviation
	XD599	DH Vampire T11	Caernarfon Air World
	XD602	DH Vampire T11 (7737M) <ff>	Privately owned, Brands Hatch
	XD614	DH Vampire T11 (8124M) <ff>	Privately owned, Southampton
	XD616	DH Vampire T11 [56]	Mosquito Aircraft Museum, London Colney
	XD622	DH Vampire T11 (8160M)	No 2214 Sqn ATC, Usworth
	XD624	DH Vampire T11 [O]	Macclesfield Technical College
	XD626	DH Vampire T11 [Q]	Midland Air Museum, Coventry
	XD674	Hunting Jet Provost T1 (7570M)[T]	RAF Cosford Aerospace Museum
	XD816	Vickers Valiant B(K)1 <ff>	Brooklands Museum, Weybridge
	XD818	Vickers Valiant B(K)1 (7894M)	RAF Museum, Hendon
	XD857	Vickers Valiant B(K)1 <ff>	Privately owned, Rayleigh, Essex
	XD875	Vickers Valiant B(K)1 <ff>	Privately owned, Bruntingthorpe
	XE317	Bristol Sycamore HR14 (G-AMWO) [S-N]	Newark Air Museum, Winthorpe
	XE327	Hawker Sea Hawk FGA6 [644/LH]	Privately owned, Kings Langley, Herts
	XE339	Hawker Sea Hawk FGA6 (8156M) [149/E]	RNAS, stored Lee-on-Solent
	XE340	Hawker Sea Hawk FGA6 [131/Z]	Montrose Air Station Museum, Montrose
	XE368	Hawker Sea Hawk FGA6 [200/J]	Flambards Village Theme Park, Helston
	XE369	Hawker Sea Hawk FGA6 (8158M) [5]	*Scrapped at Yeovilton by March 1994*
	XE489	Hawker Sea Hawk FGA6 (G-JETH)	Privately owned, Charlwood, Surrey
	XE521	Fairey Rotodyne Y (parts)	IHM, Weston-super-Mare
	XE584	Hawker Hunter FGA9 <ff>	Macclesfield Historical Av'n Soc, Barton
	XE597	Hawker Hunter FGA9 (8874M) <ff>	RAF Halton
	XE601	Hawker Hunter FGA9	MoD(PE) A&AEE Boscombe Down
	XE624	Hawker Hunter FGA9 (8875M) [G]	RAF Brawdy, on display
	XE627	Hawker Hunter F6A [T]	Imperial War Museum, Duxford
	XE643	Hawker Hunter FGA9 (8586M) <ff>	RAF EP&TU, Aldergrove
	XE650	Hawker Hunter FGA9 (G-9-449) <ff>	Macclesfield Historical Av'n Soc
	XE653	Hawker Hunter F6A (8829M) [S]	Privately owned, Exeter
	XE656	Hawker Hunter F6 (8678M)	Privately owned, Ipswich
	XE665	Hawker Hunter T8C [876/VL]	RN stored, Yeovilton
	XE668	Hawker Hunter GA11 [832/DD]	RN Predannack Fire School
	XE670	Hawker Hunter F4 (7762M/8585M) <ff>	RAF EP&TU, St Athan
	XE677	Hawker Hunter F4 (G-HHUN)	Jet Heritage Ltd, Bournemouth
	XE682	Hawker Hunter GA11	*Burned at Culdrose*
	XE685	Hawker Hunter GA11 [861/VL]	Privately owned, Exeter
	XE689	Hawker Hunter GA11 [864/VL]	RN FRADU, Yeovilton
	XE707	Hawker Hunter GA11 [865/VL]	*Sold to USA, Dec 94*
	XE712	Hawker Hunter GA11 [708]	RN Predannack Fire School
	XE793	Slingsby Cadet TX3 (8666M)	RAF St Athan, instructional use
	XE799	Slingsby Cadet TX3 (8943M) [R]	RAF ACCGS Syerston, preserved
	XE802	Slingsby Cadet TX3	Privately owned, Cupar, Fife
	XE807	Slingsby Cadet TX3 (BGA3545)	Privately owned, Bath
	XE849	DH Vampire T11 (7928M) [V3]	
	XE852	DH Vampire T11 [H]	No 2247 Sqn ATC, Hawarden
	XE855	DH Vampire T11 <ff>	Midland Air Museum, Coventry
	XE856	DH Vampire T11	Privately owned, Catfoss
	XE864	DH Vampire T11 (composite with XD435)	Privately owned, Stretton, Cheshire
	XE872	DH Vampire T11 [62]	Midland Air Museum, Coventry
	XE874	DH Vampire T11 (8582M) [61]	Privately owned, New Byth, Grampian
	XE897	DH Vampire T11 (XD403)	Privately owned, Errol
	XE920	DH Vampire T11 (8196M) [D]	Allied Aeroplane Collection, RAF Sealand
	XE921	DH Vampire T11 [64] <ff>	South Yorkshire Air Museum, Firbeck
	XE935	DH Vampire T11 [30]	South Yorkshire Air Museum, Firbeck
	XE946	DH Vampire T11 (7473M) <ff>	RAF Museum Restoration Centre, Cardington
	XE956	DH Vampire T11	St Albans College of FE

Serial	Type (other identity) [code]	Owner/operator, location or fate	Notes
XE979	DH Vampire T11 [54]	Privately owned, Birlingham, Worcs	
XE982	DH Vampire T11 (7564M) [01]	Privately owned, Dunkeswell	
XE985	DH Vampire T11 (*WZ476*)	Mosquito Aircraft Museum, London Colney	
XE993	DH Vampire T11 (8161M)	Privately owned, Cosford	
XE995	DH Vampire T11 [53]	Privately owned, High Halden, Kent	
XE998	DH Vampire T11 [36]	Fenland Aviation Museum, stored Wisbech	
XF113	VS Swift F7 [19] <ff>	The Air Defence Collection, Salisbury	
XF114	VS Swift F7 (G-SWIF)	Jet Heritage Ltd, Bournemouth	
XF289	Hawker Hunter T8C [875/VL]	*Sold to USA, Dec 94*	
XF300	Hawker Hunter GA11 [860/VL]	RN FRADU, Yeovilton	
XF301	Hawker Hunter GA11 [834/VL]	Privately owned, Bournemouth	
XF310	Hawker Hunter T8C [869/VL,2]	SAH, RNAS Culdrose	
XF314	Hawker Hunter F51 (RDAF E-412) [N]	Tangmere Military Aviation Museum	
XF321	Hawker Hunter T7	RNAS Yeovilton, Fire Section	
XF357	Hawker Hunter T8C [871/VL]	RN FRADU, Yeovilton	
XF358	Hawker Hunter T8C [870/VL]	RN stored, Yeovilton	
XF368	Hawker Hunter GA11 [863/VL]	RN FRADU, Yeovilton	
XF375	Hawker Hunter F6A (8736M/ G-BUEZ) [05]	The Old Flying Machine Co, Duxford	
XF382	Hawker Hunter F6A [15]	Midland Air Museum, Coventry	
XF383	Hawker Hunter F51 (RDAF E-409)	Wales Aircraft Museum, Cardiff	
XF383	Hawker Hunter F6 (8706M) <ff>	Privately owned, Oxford	
XF509	Hawker Hunter F6 (8708M)	RAF Chivenor, at main gate	
XF515	Hawker Hunter F6A (8830M) [C]	TMTS, RAF Scampton	
XF516	Hawker Hunter F6A (8685M/ G-BVVC) [66,F]	Privately owned, Exeter	
XF519	Hawker Hunter FGA9 (8677M/ 8738M/9183M) (composite with XJ695) [J]	FSCTE, RAF Manston	
XF522	Hawker Hunter F6 <ff>	No 1365 Sqn ATC, Aylesbury	
XF526	Hawker Hunter F6 (8679M) [78/E]	RAF St Athan Fire Section	
XF527	Hawker Hunter F6 (8680M)	RAF Halton, on display	
XF545	Percival Provost T1 (7957M) [O-K]	Privately owned, Cranfield	
XF597	Percival Provost T1 (G-BKFW) [AH]	Privately owned, Aldermaston	
XF603	Percival Provost T1 [H]	Rolls-Royce Tech Coll, Filton	
XF690	Percival Provost T1 (8041M/ G-MOOS)	Kennet Aircraft, Cranfield	
XF708	Avro Shackleton MR3 [203/C]	Imperial War Museum, Duxford	
XF785	Bristol 173 (7648M/G-ALBN)	RAF Museum Restoration Centre, Cardington	
XF836	Percival Provost T1 (8043M/ G-AWRY) [JG]	Privately owned, Thatcham	
XF844	Percival Provost T1 [70]	DRA Farnborough Apprentice School	
XF877	Percival Provost T1 (G-AWVF)[JX]	Privately owned, Goodwood	
XF926	Bristol 188 (8368M)	RAF Cosford Aerospace Museum	
XF967	Hawker Hunter T8C (9186M) [T]	SIF, RAFC Cranwell	
XF994	Hawker Hunter T8C [873/VL]	RN FRADU, Yeovilton	
XF995	Hawker Hunter T8B (9237M) [K]	SIF, RAFC Cranwell	
XG154	Hawker Hunter FGA9 (8863M) [54]	RAF Museum, Hendon	
XG160	Hawker Hunter F6A (8831M) [U]	RJAF Historic Flight, Bournemouth	
XG164	Hawker Hunter F6 (8681M)	RAF Halton	
XG172	Hawker Hunter F6A (8832M) [A]	TMTS, RAF Scampton	
XG194	Hawker Hunter FGA9 (8839M) [55] <rf>	RAF North Luffenham Training Area	
XG195	Hawker Hunter FGA9 (comp with XG297)	Bomber County Aviation Museum, Hemswell	
XG196	Hawker Hunter F6A (8702M) [31]	RAF Bracknell, on display	
XG209	Hawker Hunter F6 (8709M) [69]	RAF Halton Fire Section	
XG210	Hawker Hunter F6	Privately owned, Beck Row, Suffolk	
XG225	Hawker Hunter F6A (8713M) [S]	RAF Cosford on display	
XG226	Hawker Hunter F6A (8800M)	Privately owned, Long Marston	
XG226	Hawker Hunter F6A (8800M) [28] <ff>	Privately owned, Faygate	
XG252	Hawker Hunter FGA9 (8840M) [U]	RAF Credenhill, on display	
XG254	Hawker Hunter FGA9 (8881M)	RAF Coltishall Fire Section	
XG274	Hawker Hunter F6 (8710M) [71]	Privately owned, Ipswich	
XG290	Hawker Hunter F6 (8711M) [74] (fuselage)	Jet Heritage Ltd, Bournemouth	
XG297	Hawker Hunter FGA9 <ff>	Pennine Aviation Museum, stored Bacup	

Notes	Serial	Type (other identity) [code]	Owner/operator, location or fate
	XG325	EE Lightning F1 <ff>	No 1312 Sqn ATC, Southend Airport
	XG329	EE Lightning F1 (8050M)	Norfolk & Suffolk Aviation Museum, Flixton
	XG331	EE Lightning F1 <ff>	Macclesfield Historical Av'n Soc, Marthall
	XG337	EE Lightning F1 (8056M) [M]	RAF Cosford Aerospace Museum
	XG452	Bristol Belvedere HC1 (7997M/ G-BRMB)	IHM, Weston-super-Mare
	XG454	Bristol Belvedere HC1 (8366M)	Gr Manchester Museum of Science & Industry
	XG462	Bristol Belvedere HC1 <ff>	IHM, Weston-super-Mare
	XG474	Bristol Belvedere HC1 (8367M) [O]	RAF Museum, Hendon
	XG496	DH Devon C2 (G-ANDX)	Solway Aviation Society, Carlisle
	XG502	Bristol Sycamore HR14	Museum of Army Flying, Middle Wallop
	XG506	Bristol Sycamore HR14 (7852M)	Bomber County Aviation Museum, Hemswell
	XG518	Bristol Sycamore HR14 (8009M) [S-E]	North-East Aircraft Museum, Usworth
	XG523	Bristol Sycamore HR14 <ff>	North-East Aircraft Museum, Usworth
	XG540	Bristol Sycamore HR14 (7899M/ 8345M) [Y-S]	Privately owned, Preston, Lancs
	XG544	Bristol Sycamore HR14	Privately owned, Lower Tremar
	XG547	Bristol Sycamore HR14 (G-HAPR) [S-T]	IHM, Weston-super-Mare
	XG573	WS55 Whirlwind HAR3	Scrapped
	XG574	WS55 Whirlwind HAR3	FAA Museum, stored Wroughton
	XG577	WS55 Whirlwind HAR3 (9050M)	RAF Leconfield Crash Rescue Training
	XG594	WS55 Whirlwind HAS7 [517/PO]	Royal Scottish Mus'm of Flight, E Fortune
	XG596	WS55 Whirlwind HAS7 [66]	IHM, Weston-super-Mare
	XG613	DH Sea Venom FAW21	Imperial War Museum, Duxford
	XG629	DH Sea Venom FAW22 <ff>	Privately owned,
	XG680	DH Sea Venom FAW22 [735/VL]	North-East Aircraft Museum, Usworth
	XG691	DH Sea Venom FAW22 [93/J]	Flambards Village Theme Park, Helston
	XG692	DH Sea Venom FAW22 [668/LM]	Midland Warplane Museum, Warwick
	XG730	DH Sea Venom FAW22 [499/A]	Mosquito Aircraft Museum, London Colney
	XG736	DH Sea Venom FAW22	Ulster Aviation Society, Newtownards
	XG737	DH Sea Venom FAW22 [220/Z]	Jet Aircraft Pres'n Grp., Long Marston
	XG743	DH Sea Vampire T22 [597/LM]	Wymondham College, Norfolk
	XG797	Fairey Gannet ECM6 [277]	Imperial War Museum, Duxford
	XG831	Fairey Gannet ECM6 [396]	Flambards Village Theme Park, Helston
	XG882	Fairey Gannet T5 (8754M) [771/LM]	Privately owned, Errol
	XG883	Fairey Gannet T5 [773/BY]	Wales Aircraft Museum, Cardiff
	XG888	Fairey Gannet T5 [LM]	To Australia
	XG900	Short SC1	FAA Museum, RNAS Yeovilton
	XG905	Short SC1	Ulster Folk & Transpt Mus, Holywood, Co Down
	XH131	EE Canberra PR9 [AF]	RAF No 39(1 PRU) Sqn, Marham
	XH132	Short SC9 Canberra (8915M) <ff>	Privately owned, St Austell
	XH133	EE Canberra PR9 <ff>	Privately owned, Stock, Essex
	XH134	EE Canberra PR9 [AA]	RAF No 39(1 PRU) Sqn, Marham
	XH135	EE Canberra PR9	RAF No 39(1 PRU) Sqn, Marham
	XH136	EE Canberra PR9 (8782M) <ff>	Privately owned, Bruntingthorpe
	XH165	EE Canberra PR9 <ff>	Blyth Valley Aviation Collection, Walpole
	XH168	EE Canberra PR9 [AB]	RAF No 39(1 PRU) Sqn, Marham
	XH169	EE Canberra PR9 [AC]	RAF No 39(1 PRU) Sqn, Marham
	XH170	EE Canberra PR9 (8739M)	RAF Wyton, on display
	XH171	EE Canberra PR9 (8746M) [U]	RAF Cosford Aerospace Museum
	XH174	EE Canberra PR9 <ff>	RAF, stored St Athan
	XH175	EE Canberra PR9 <ff>	Privately owned, Stock, Essex
	XH177	EE Canberra PR9 <ff>	Privately owned, Stock, Essex
	XH278	DH Vampire T11 (8595M/7866M)	Privately owned, Felton, Northumberland
	XH312	DH Vampire T11 [18]	Privately owned, Chester
	XH313	DH Vampire T11 [E]	St Albans College of FE
	XH328	DH Vampire T11	Jet Heritage Ltd, Bournemouth (dismantled)
	XH330	DH Vampire T11 [73]	Privately owned, Bridgnorth
	XH537	Avro Vulcan B2MRR (8749M) <ff>	Privately owned, Camberley
	XH558	Avro Vulcan B2	Privately owned, Bruntingthorpe
	XH560	Avro Vulcan K2 <ff>	Privately owned, Romford
	XH563	Avro Vulcan B2MRR <ff>	Privately owned, Banchory
	XH567	EE Canberra B6(mod)	MoD(PE) DRA, Boscombe Down
	XH568	EE Canberra B6(mod) (G-BVIC)	Privately owned, Bruntingthorpe
	XH584	EE Canberra T4 (G-27-374) <ff>	South Yorkshire Air Museum, Firbeck

Serial	Type (other identity) [code]	Owner/operator, location or fate	Notes
XH592	HP Victor K1A (8429M) <ff>	Privately owned, Bruntingthorpe	
XH648	HP Victor K1A	Imperial War Museum, Duxford	
XH669	HP Victor K2 (9092M)	RAF Waddington Fire Section	
XH670	HP Victor SR2 <ff>	Privately owned, Romford, Essex	
XH671	HP Victor K2	Scrapped at RAF Marham, February 1994	
XH672	HP Victor K2	RAF Cosford Aerospace Museum	
XH673	HP Victor K2 (8911M)	RAF Marham, on display	
XH675	HP Victor K2	Scrapped at Marham, January 1994	
XH767	Gloster Javelin FAW9 (7955M) [A]	City of Norwich Aviation Museum	
XH837	Gloster Javelin FAW7 (8032M) <ff>	Caernarfon Air World	
XH892	Gloster Javelin FAW9 (7982M) [J]	Norfolk & Suffolk Aviation Museum, Flixton	
XH897	Gloster Javelin FAW9	Imperial War Museum, Duxford	
XH903	Gloster Javelin FAW9 (7938M)	Gloucestershire Av'n Collection, Hucclecote	
XH980	Gloster Javelin FAW8 (7867M) [A]	Scrapped at West Raynham, Sept 1994	
XH992	Gloster Javelin FAW8 (7829M) [P]	Newark Air Museum, Winthorpe	
XJ314	RR Thrust Measuring Rig	FAA Museum, RNAS Yeovilton	
XJ380	Bristol Sycamore HR14 (8628M)	Privately owned, New Byth, Grampian	
XJ389	Fairey Jet Gyrodyne (XD759/ G-AJJP)	Museum of Berkshire Aviation, Woodley	
XJ393	WS55 Whirlwind HAR3	Privately owned, Codmore Hill, Sussex	
XJ396	WS55 Whirlwind HAR10	Burned at Farnborough	
XJ409	WS55 Whirlwind HAR10		
XJ435	WS55 Whirlwind HAR10 (8671M) [V]	AAC Netheravon, instructional use	
XJ445	WS55 Whirlwind HAR5	Scrapped	
XJ476	DH Sea Vixen FAW1 <ff>	No 424 Sqn ATC, Southampton Hall of Av'n	
XJ481	DH Sea Vixen FAW1 [VL]	RNAY Fleetlands Museum	
XJ482	DH Sea Vixen FAW1 [713/VL]	Norfolk & Suffolk Aviation Museum, Flixton	
XJ488	DH Sea Vixen FAW1 <ff>	Privately owned, New Milton, Hants	
XJ494	DH Sea Vixen FAW2	Privately owned, Kings Langley, Herts	
XJ560	DH Sea Vixen FAW2 (8142M) [242]	Newark Air Museum, Winthorpe	
XJ565	DH Sea Vixen FAW2 [127/E]	Mosquito Aircraft Museum, London Colney	
XJ571	DH Sea Vixen FAW2 (8140M) [242/R]	Brooklands Museum	
XJ575	DH Sea Vixen FAW2 <ff>	Wellesbourne Wartime Museum	
XJ579	DH Sea Vixen FAW2 <ff>	Midland Air Museum, Coventry	
XJ580	DH Sea Vixen FAW2 [131/E]	Christchurch Memorial Group	
XJ582	DH Sea Vixen FAW2 (8139M) [702]	Scrapped at Stock, November 1991	
XJ607	DH Sea Vixen FAW2 (8171M) [701/VL]	Privately owned, Dunsfold	
XJ634	Hawker Hunter F6A (8684M) [29]	Privately owned, Ipswich	
XJ639	Hawker Hunter F6A (8687M) [H]	SIF, RAFC Cranwell	
XJ676	Hawker Hunter F6A (8844M)	The Old Flying Machine Co, Duxford	
XJ690	Hawker Hunter FGA9 <ff>	Privately owned, Market Drayton	
XJ714	Hawker Hunter FR10	Jet Aviation Pres'n Grp, Long Marston	
XJ723	WS55 Whirlwind HAR10	Montrose Air Station Museum, Montrose	
XJ726	WS55 Whirlwind HAR10	Caernarfon Air World	
XJ727	WS55 Whirlwind HAR10 (8661M) [L]	AAC Dishforth, BDRT	
XJ729	WS55 Whirlwind HAR10 (8732M/ G-BVGE)	Privately owned, Cricklade, Wilts	
XJ758	WS55 Whirlwind HAR10 (8464M) <ff>	Privately owned, Oswestry	
XJ763	WS55 Whirlwind HAR10 (G-BKHA) [P]	Privately owned, Thornicombe, Dorset	
XJ772	DH Vampire T11 [H]	Mosquito Aircraft Museum, London Colney	
XJ823	Avro Vulcan B2A	Solway Aviation Society, Carlisle Airport	
XJ824	Avro Vulcan B2A	Imperial War Museum, Duxford	
XJ917	Bristol Sycamore HR14 [H-S]	Bristol Aero Collection, Banwell	
XJ918	Bristol Sycamore HR14 (8190M)	RAF Cosford Aerospace Museum	
XK149	Hawker Hunter F6A (8714M) [L]	Privately owned, Bruntingthorpe	
XK378	Auster AOP9 (TAD200)	Privately owned, Dale, Dyfed	
XK416	Auster AOP9 (7855M/G-AYUA)	Vintage Aircraft Team, Cranfield	
XK417	Auster AOP9 (G-AVXY)	Privately owned, Leicester East	
XK418	Auster AOP9 (7976M)	SWWAPS, Lasham	
XK421	Auster AOP9 (8365M) (frame)	British Classic Aircraft Rest'n, Hedge End	

Notes	Serial	Type (other identity) [code]	Owner/operator, location or fate
	XK482	Saro Skeeter AOP12 (7840M/ G-BJWC) [C]	Privately owned, Blackpool
	XK488	Blackburn Buccaneer S1	FAA Museum, RNAS Yeovilton
	XK526	Blackburn Buccaneer S2 (8648M)	RAF Honington, at main gate
	XK527	Blackburn Buccaneer S2D (8818M) <ff>	Privately owned, New Milton, Hants
	XK530	Blackburn Buccaneer S1	DRA, Bedford Fire Section
	XK532	Blackburn Buccaneer S1 (8867M) [632/LM]	The Fresson Trust, Inverness Airport
	XK533	Blackburn Buccaneer S1 <ff>	Royal Scottish Mus'm of Flight, E Fortune
	XK590	DH Vampire T11 [V]	Wellesbourne Wartime Museum
	XK623	DH Vampire T11 [56] (G-VAMP)	Caernarfon Air World
	XK624	DH Vampire T11 [32]	Norfolk & Suffolk Aviation Museum, Flixton
	XK625	DH Vampire T11 [12]	Brenzett Aeronautical Museum
	XK627	DH Vampire T11	Pennine Aviation Museum, Bacup
	XK632	DH Vampire T11 [67]	No 2 Sqn ATC, Leavesden
	XK637	DH Vampire T11 [56]	No 1855 Sqn ATC, Royton, Greater Manchester
	XK655	DH Comet C2(RC) <ff>	Privately owned, Maryport
	XK659	DH Comet C2(RC) <ff>	Privately owned, Elland, W. Yorks
	XK695	DH Comet C2(RC) (9164M) (fuselage)	RAF Newton, instructional use
	XK699	DH Comet C2 (7971M)	RAF Lyneham on display
	XK724	Folland Gnat F1 (7715M)	RAF Cosford Aerospace Museum
	XK740	Folland Gnat F1 (8396M)	Southampton Hall of Aviation
	XK741	Folland Gnat F1 (fuselage)	Midland Air Museum, Coventry
	XK776	ML Utility 1	Museum of Army Flying, Middle Wallop
	XK789	Slingsby Grasshopper TX1	Warwick School, Warwick
	XK819	Slingsby Grasshopper TX1	The Real Aeroplane Company, Breighton
	XK820	Slingsby Grasshopper TX1	Lancing School, West Sussex
	XK822	Slingsby Grasshopper TX1	Privately owned, West Malling
	XK824	Slingsby Grasshopper TX1	Sold to Germany
	XK895	DH Sea Devon C20 (G-SDEV) [19/CU]	Privately owned, North Weald
	XK896	DH Sea Devon C20 (G-RNAS)	Privately owned, stored Staverton
	XK907	WS55 Whirlwind HAS7 [U]	Midland Air Museum, Coventry
	XK911	WS55 Whirlwind HAS7 [519/PO]	Privately owned, Ipswich
	XK936	WS55 Whirlwind HAS7 [62]	Imperial War Museum, Duxford
	XK944	WS55 Whirlwind HAS7	No 617 Sqn ATC, Malpas School, Cheshire
	XK968	WS55 Whirlwind HAR10 (8445M) [E]	FSCTE, RAF Manston
	XK987	WS55 Whirlwind HAR10 (8393M)	MoD Swynnerton, Staffs
	XK988	WS55 Whirlwind HAR10 [D]	AAC Middle Wallop, Fire Section
	XL149	Blackburn Beverley C1 (7988M) <ff>	Newark Air Museum, Winthorpe
	XL160	HP Victor K2 (8910M) <ff>	Blyth Valley Aviation Collection, Walpole
	XL161	HP Victor K2 (9214M)	RAF Lyneham Fire Section
	XL162	HP Victor K2 (9114M)	FSCTE, RAF Manston
	XL163	HP Victor K2 (8916M)	Privately owned, Stock, Essex
	XL164	HP Victor K2 (9215M)	RAF Brize Norton Fire Section
	XL188	HP Victor K2 (9100M) (fuselage)	RAF Kinloss Fire Section
	XL190	HP Victor K2 (9216M)	RAF St Mawgan Fire Section
	XL192	HP Victor K2 (9024M)	RAF Marham Fire Section
	XL231	HP Victor K2	Yorkshire Air Museum, Elvington
	XL318	Avro Vulcan B2 (8733M)	RAF Museum, Hendon
	XL319	Avro Vulcan B2	North-East Aircraft Museum, Usworth
	XL360	Avro Vulcan B2A	Midland Air Museum, Coventry
	XL388	Avro Vulcan B2 <ff>	Blyth Valley Aviation Collection, Walpole
	XL391	Avro Vulcan B2	Privately owned, Blackpool
	XL426	Avro Vulcan B2 (G-VJET)	Privately owned, Southend
	XL427	Avro Vulcan B2 (8756M)	RAF Machrihanish Fire Section
	XL445	Avro Vulcan K2 (8811M) <ff>	Blyth Valley Aviation Collection, Walpole
	XL449	Fairey Gannet AEW3	Wales Aircraft Museum, Cardiff
	XL472	Fairey Gannet AEW3 [044/R]	Privately owned, Charlwood, Surrey
	XL497	Fairey Gannet AEW3 [041/R]	RN, Prestwick, on display
	XL500	Fairey Gannet AEW3 [LM]	RNAS Culdrose, for display
	XL502	Fairey Gannet AEW3 (8610M/ G-BMYP)	Privately owned, Sandtoft, S. Yorks
	XL503	Fairey Gannet AEW3 [070/E]	FAA Museum, RNAS Yeovilton
	XL563	Hawker Hunter T7 (9218M)	MoD(PE) Farnborough, for display
	XL564	Hawker Hunter T7 [4]	MoD(PE) ETPS, Boscombe Down

Serial	Type (other identity) [code]	Owner/operator, location or fate	Notes
XL565	Hawker Hunter T7 (parts of WT745)	Privately owned, Lincolnshire	
XL567	Hawker Hunter T7 (8723M) [84]	Privately owned, Exeter	
XL568	Hawker Hunter T7A (9224M) [C]	SIF, RAFC Cranwell	
XL569	Hawker Hunter T7 (8833M) [80]	East Midlands Airport Aero Park	
XL572	Hawker Hunter T7 (G-HNTR) [83]	Privately owned, Brough	
XL573	Hawker Hunter T7 (G-BVGH)	Lightning Flying Club, Exeter Airport	
XL577	Hawker Hunter T7 (8676M) [W]	SIF, RAFC Cranwell	
XL578	Hawker Hunter T7	Privately owned, Cranfield	
XL580	Hawker Hunter T8M [723]	FAA Museum, RNAS Yeovilton	
XL586	Hawker Hunter T7 <rf>	RNAY Fleetlands Apprentice School	
XL587	Hawker Hunter T7 (8807M) [Z]	TMTS, RAF Scampton	
XL591	Hawker Hunter T7	Privately owned, Lincolnshire	
XL592	Hawker Hunter T7 (8836M) [Y]	TMTS, RAF Scampton	
XL598	Hawker Hunter T8C [880/VL]	Privately owned	
XL600	Hawker Hunter T7 [Y/FL]	Privately owned, Southall	
XL601	Hawker Hunter T7 [874/VL,4]	SAH, RNAS Culdrose	
XL602	Hawker Hunter T8M	RN FRADU, Yeovilton	
XL603	Hawker Hunter T8M [724]	Privately owned	
XL612	Hawker Hunter T7 [2]	MoD(PE) ETPS, Boscombe Down	
XL613	Hawker Hunter T7 (G-BVMB)	Lightning Flying Club, Exeter	
XL614	Hawker Hunter T7	TMTS, RAF Scampton	
XL616	Hawker Hunter T7 (9223M) [D]	SIF, RAFC Cranwell	
XL618	Hawker Hunter T7 (8892M) [05]	RAF Cottesmore Fire Section	
XL623	Hawker Hunter T7 (8770M) [90]	RAF Newton	
XL629	EE Lightning T4	A&AEE, Boscombe Down, at main gate	
XL703	SAL Pioneer CC1 (8034M)	RAF Cosford Aerospace Museum, stored	
XL728	WS58 Wessex HAS1	RAF Brawdy, Fire Section	
XL735	Saro Skeeter AOP12	Privately owned	
XL738	Saro Skeeter AOP12 (7860M)	Museum of Army Flying, Middle Wallop	
XL762	Saro Skeeter AOP12 (8017M)	Royal Scottish Mus'm of Flight, E Fortune	
XL763	Saro Skeeter AOP12	Privately owned, Ottershaw	
XL764	Saro Skeeter AOP12 (7940M)	Newark Air Museum, Winthorpe	
XL765	Saro Skeeter AOP12	Privately owned, Pimlico	
XL770	Saro Skeeter AOP12 (8046M)	Southampton Hall of Aviation	
XL809	Saro Skeeter AOP12 (G-BLIX)	Privately owned, Wilden, Beds	
XL811	Saro Skeeter AOP12	IHM, Weston-super-Mare	
XL812	Saro Skeeter AOP12 (G-SARO)	Privately owned, Old Buckenham	
XL813	Saro Skeeter AOP12	Museum of Army Flying, Middle Wallop	
XL814	Saro Skeeter AOP12	AAC Historic Aircraft Flight, Middle Wallop	
XL824	Bristol Sycamore HR14 (8021M)	Gr Manchester Mus'm of Science & Industry	
XL829	Bristol Sycamore HR14	Bristol Industrial Museum	
XL836	WS55 Whirlwind HAS7 [65]	RN Predannack Fire School	
XL840	WS55 Whirlwind HAS7	Privately owned,	
XL847	WS55 Whirlwind HAS7 [83]	AAC Middle Wallop, Fire Section	
XL853	WS55 Whirlwind HAS7 [LS]	RNAY Fleetlands Museum	
XL875	WS55 Whirlwind HAR9	Air Service Training, Perth	
XL880	WS55 Whirlwind HAR9 [35]	RN Predannack Fire School	
XL898	WS55 Whirlwind HAR9 (8654M) [30/ED]	Scrapped, 1992	
XL929	Percival Pembroke C1 (G-BNPU)	Privately owned, Shoreham Airport	
XL954	Percival Pembroke C1 (9042M/ N4234C)	Privately owned, Tatenhill	
XL993	SAL Twin Pioneer CC1 (8388M)	RAF Cosford Aerospace Museum	
XM135	BAC Lightning F1 [135]	Imperial War Museum, Duxford	
XM144	BAC Lightning F1 (8417M) [J]	Scrapped at Burntwood, Staffs, January 1994	
XM169	BAC Lightning F1A (8422M) <ff>	N Yorks Aircraft Recovery Centre, Chop Gate	
XM172	BAC Lightning F1A (8427M) [B]	RAF Coltishall, gate guard	
XM173	BAC Lightning F1A (8414M) [A]	RAF Bentley Priory, at main gate	
XM191	BAC Lightning F1A (7854M/ 8590M) <ff>	RAF EP&TU, St Athan	
XM192	BAC Lightning F1A (8413M) [K]	Privately owned, Binbrook	
XM223	DH Devon C2 [J]	MoD(PE) T&EE, West Freugh	
XM279	EE Canberra B(I)8 <ff>	Privately owned, Flixton	
XM300	WS58 Wessex HAS1	Welsh Industrial & Maritime Mus'm, Cardiff	
XM327	WS58 Wessex HAS3 [401/KE]	College of Nautical Studies, Warsash	
XM328	WS58 Wessex HAS3	RNAS Culdrose, SAH	
XM329	WS58 Wessex HAS1	RN Predannack Fire School	

Notes	Serial	Type (other identity) [code]	Owner/operator, location or fate
	XM330	WS58 Wessex HAS1	IHM, Weston-super-Mare
	XM349	Hunting Jet Provost T3A (9046M) [T]	RAF No 1 SoTT, Cosford
	XM350	Hunting Jet Provost T3A (9036M) [89]	—
	XM351	Hunting Jet Provost T3 (8078M)	
	XM352	Hunting Jet Provost T3A [21]	*Sold to USA, July 1994*
	XM355	Hunting Jet Provost T3 (8229M) [D]	Arbury College, Cambridge
	XM357	Hunting Jet Provost T3A [45]	*Sold to USA, July 1994*
	XM358	Hunting Jet Provost T3A (8987M) [53]	Privately owned, RAF Cosford
	XM362	Hunting Jet Provost T3 (8230M)	RAF Halton
	XM363	Hunting Jet Provost T3 <ff>	RAF Cranwell
	XM365	Hunting Jet Provost T3A [37]	RAF, stored Shawbury
	XM367	Hunting Jet Provost T3 (8083M) [Z]	Privately owned
	XM369	Hunting Jet Provost T3 (8084M) [C]	Privately owned, New Byth, Grampian
	XM370	Hunting Jet Provost T3A (G-BVSP) [10]	Privately owned, Binbrook
	XM372	Hunting Jet Provost T3A (8917M) [55]	RAF Linton-on-Ouse Fire Section
	XM374	Hunting Jet Provost T3A [18]	RAF, stored Shawbury
	XM375	Hunting Jet Provost T3 (8231M) [B]	RAF Cottesmore Fire Section
	XM376	Hunting Jet Provost T3A [27]	RAF, stored Shawbury
	XM378	Hunting Jet Provost T3A [34]	RAF, stored Shawbury
	XM379	Hunting Jet Provost T3	Army Apprentice College, Arborfield
	XM381	Hunting Jet Provost T3 (8232M) [A]	RAF Marham Fire Section
	XM383	Hunting Jet Provost T3A [90]	Newark Air Museum, Winthorpe
	XM386	Hunting Jet Provost T3 (8076M) [08]	RAF St Athan
	XM387	Hunting Jet Provost T3A [I]	RAF, stored Shawbury
	XM401	Hunting Jet Provost T3A [17]	
	XM402	Hunting Jet Provost T3 (8055AM) [J]	Privately owned, Narborough, Norfolk
	XM403	Hunting Jet Provost T3A (9048M) [V]	RAF No 1 SoTT, Cosford
	XM404	Hunting Jet Provost T3 (8055BM)	FETC, Moreton-in-Marsh
	XM405	Hunting Jet Provost T3A (G-TORE) [42]	Kennet Aircraft, Cranfield
	XM408	Hunting Jet Provost T3 (8333M) [D]	Privately owned, Bruntingthorpe
	XM409	Hunting Jet Provost T3 (8082M) <rf>	RAF, stored St Athan
	XM410	Hunting Jet Provost T3 (8054AM) [B]	RAF North Luffenham Training Area
	XM412	Hunting Jet Provost T3A (9011M)	RAF CTTS, St Athan
	XM413	Hunting Jet Provost T3	Army Apprentice College, Arborfield
	XM414	Hunting Jet Provost T3A (8996M)	Flight Experience Workshop, Belfast
	XM417	Hunting Jet Provost T3 (8054BM)	RAF North Luffenham Training Area
	XM419	Hunting Jet Provost T3A (8990M) [102]	RAF CTTS, St Athan
	XM424	Hunting Jet Provost T3A	RAF, stored Shawbury
	XM425	Hunting Jet Provost T3A (8995M) [88]	RAF Halton
	XM426	Hunting Jet Provost T3 (XN511) [64] <ff>	Robertsbridge Aviation Museum, Mayfield
	XM455	Hunting Jet Provost T3A (8960M) [K]	RAF No 1 SoTT, Cosford
	XM459	Hunting Jet Provost T3A [F]	RAF, stored Shawbury
	XM463	Hunting Jet Provost T3A [38] (fuselage)	RAF Museum, Hendon
	XM464	Hunting Jet Provost T3A [23]	Privately owned, Colsterworth, Lincs
	XM465	Hunting Jet Provost T3A [55]	
	XM467	Hunting Jet Provost T3 (8085M)	
	XM468	Hunting Jet Provost T3 (8081M)	Privately owned, King's Lynn
	XM470	Hunting Jet Provost T3A [12]	RAF, stored Shawbury
	XM471	Hunting Jet Provost T3A (8968M) [L,93]	RAF No 1 SoTT, Cosford

Serial	Type (other identity) [code]	Owner/operator, location or fate	Notes
XM472	Hunting Jet Provost T3A (9051M) <ff>	*Scrapped*	
XM473	Hunting Jet Provost T3A (8974M/ G-TINY)	Privately owned, Norwich	
XM474	Hunting Jet Provost T3 (8121M)	No 1330 Sqn ATC, Warrington	
XM475	Hunting Jet Provost T3A (9112M) [44]	FSCTE, RAF Manston	
XM478	Hunting Jet Provost T3A (8983M) [33]	RAF, stored Shawbury	
XM479	Hunting Jet Provost T3A (G-BVEZ) [54]	Privately owned, Sandtoft	
XM480	Hunting Jet Provost T3 (8080M)	RAF Finningley, Fire Section	
XM529	Saro Skeeter AOP12 (7979M/ G-BDNS)	Privately owned, Handforth	
XM553	Saro Skeeter AOP12 (G-AWSV)	Privately owned, Middle Wallop	
XM555	Saro Skeeter AOP12 (8027M)	RAF Cosford Aerospace Museum, stored	
XM556	Saro Skeeter AOP12 (7870M/ G-HELI)	IHM, Weston-super-Mare	
XM561	Saro Skeeter AOP12 (7980M)	South Yorkshire Air Museum, Firbeck	
XM564	Saro Skeeter AOP12	Royal Armoured Corps Museum, Bovington	
XM569	Avro Vulcan B2	Wales Aircraft Museum, Cardiff	
XM575	Avro Vulcan B2A (G-BLMC)	East Midlands Airport Aero Park	
XM594	Avro Vulcan B2	Newark Air Museum, Winthorpe	
XM597	Avro Vulcan B2	Royal Scottish Mus'm of Flight, E Fortune	
XM598	Avro Vulcan B2 (8778M)	RAF Cosford Aerospace Museum	
XM602	Avro Vulcan B2 (8771M) <ff>	Avro Aircraft Restoration Society, Woodford	
XM603	Avro Vulcan B2	Avro Aircraft Restoration Society, Woodford	
XM607	Avro Vulcan B2 (8779M)	RAF Waddington, on display	
XM612	Avro Vulcan B2	City of Norwich Aviation Museum	
XM652	Avro Vulcan B2 <ff>	Privately owned, Burntwood, Staffs	
XM655	Avro Vulcan B2 (G-VULC)	Privately owned, Wellesbourne Mountford	
XM656	Avro Vulcan B2 (8757M) <ff>	Privately owned, Stock, Essex	
XM660	WS55 Whirlwind HAS7 [78]	North-East Aircraft Museum, Usworth	
XM665	WS55 Whirlwind HAS7	*Sold to South Africa*	
XM685	WS55 Whirlwind HAS7 (G-AYZJ) [513/PO]	Newark Air Museum, Winthorpe	
XM693	HS Gnat T1 (7891M)	BAe Hamble on display	
XM693	HS Gnat T1 (8618M/XP504/ G-TIMM)	Kennet Aircraft, Cranfield	
XM694	HS Gnat T1	Privately owned, Portsmouth	
XM697	HS Gnat T1 (G-NAAT)	Jet Heritage Ltd, Bournemouth	
XM706	HS Gnat T1 (8572M) [12]	*Scrapped at Swinderby, September 1993*	
XM708	HS Gnat T1 (8573M)	RAF Locking, on display	
XM709	HS Gnat T1 (8617M) [67]	Privately owned	
XM715	HP Victor K2	Privately owned, Bruntingthorpe	
XM717	HP Victor K2 <ff>	RAF Museum Restoration Centre, Cardington	
XM819	Lancashire EP9 Prospector (G-APXW)	Museum of Army Flying, Middle Wallop	
XM833	WS58 Wessex HAS3	SWWAPS, Lasham	
XM838	WS58 Wessex HAS3 [05]	RN Predannack Fire School	
XM843	WS58 Wessex HAS1 [527]	RN AES, Lee-on-Solent	
XM868	WS58 Wessex HAS1 [517]	RN Predannack Fire School	
XM870	WS58 Wessex HAS3 [PO]	RN AES, Lee-on-Solent	
XM874	WS58 Wessex HAS1 [521/CU]	RN Predannack Fire School	
XM923	WS58 Wessex HAS3	*Burnt at Fleetlands*	
XM927	WS58 Wessex HAS3 (8814M) [660/PO]	RAF Shawbury, Fire Section	
XN126	WS55 Whirlwind HAR10 (8655M) [S]	RAF Benson BDRT	
XN137	Hunting Jet Provost T3 <ff>	Privately owned, Ottershaw	
XN185	Slingsby Sedbergh TX1 (8942M)	*Repainted as BGA 4077*	
XN198	Slingsby Cadet TX3	Privately owned, Challock Lees	
XN238	Slingsby Cadet TX3 <ff>	Robertsbridge Aviation Society, Mayfield	
XN239	Slingsby Cadet TX3 (8889M) [G]	Imperial War Museum, Duxford	
XN243	Slingsby Cadet TX3 (BGA 3145)	RAFGSA, Bicester	
XN246	Slingsby Cadet TX3	Southampton Hall of Aviation	
XN258	WS55 Whirlwind HAR9 [589/CU]	North-East Aircraft Museum, Usworth	
XN259	WS55 Whirlwind HAS7	London City Airport, Fire Section	

Notes	Serial	Type (other identity) [code]	Owner/operator, location or fate
	XN263	WS55 Whirlwind HAS7	Privately owned, Chichester
	XN297	WS55 Whirlwind HAR9 (XN311) [12]	Privately owned, Hull
	XN298	WS55 Whirlwind HAR9 [810/LS]	International Fire Training Centre, Chorley
	XN299	WS55 Whirlwind HAS7 [ZZ]	Royal Marines' Museum, Portsmouth
	XN302	WS55 Whirlwind HAS7 (9037M)	RAF Finningley, Fire Section
	XN304	WS55 Whirlwind HAS7 [64]	Norfolk & Suffolk Aviation Museum, Flixton
	XN308	WS55 Whirlwind HAS7 [510]	*Scrapped at Yeovilton by March 1994*
	XN332	Saro P531 (G-APNV) [759]	FAA Museum, stored Wroughton
	XN334	Saro P531	FAA Museum, Crawley College of Technology
	XN341	Saro Skeeter AOP12 (8022M)	Privately owned, Luton Airport
	XN344	Saro Skeeter AOP12 (8018M)	Science Museum, South Kensington
	XN351	Saro Skeeter AOP12 (G-BKSC)	Privately owned, Shempston Fm, Lossiemouth
	XN359	WS55 Whirlwind HAR9 [34/ED]	RNAS Lee-on-Solent, Fire Section
	XN380	WS55 Whirlwind HAS7 [67]	Lashenden Air Warfare Museum, Headcorn
	XN385	WS55 Whirlwind HAS7	Privately owned, Bournemouth
	XN386	WS55 Whirlwind HAR9 [435/ED]	
	XN412	Auster AOP9	Cotswold Aircraft Rest'n Grp, Innsworth
	XN435	Auster AOP9 (G-BGBU)	Privately owned, Egham
	XN437	Auster AOP9 (G-AXWA)	Privately owned, Welling
	XN441	Auster AOP9 (G-BGKT)	Privately owned, Reymerston Hall
	XN458	Hunting Jet Provost T3 (8234M)	Wales Aircraft Museum, Cardiff
	XN459	Hunting Jet Provost T3A [N]	RAF, stored Shawbury
	XN461	Hunting Jet Provost T3A (G-BVBE)	Privately owned, Sandtoft
	XN462	Hunting Jet Provost T3A [17]	RAF, stored Shawbury
	XN466	Hunting Jet Provost T3A [29] <ff>	No 1005 Sqn ATC, Radcliffe, Gtr Manchester
	XN467	Hunting Jet Provost T4 (8559M) [B]	RAF Halton
	XN470	Hunting Jet Provost T3A [41]	RAF, stored Linton-on-Ouse
	XN472	Hunting Jet Provost T3A (8959M) [J,86]	RAF No 1 SoTT, Cosford
	XN473	Hunting Jet Provost T3A (8862M) [98] <ff>	
	XN492	Hunting Jet Provost T3 (8079M)	
	XN494	Hunting Jet Provost T3A (9012M) [43]	AAC Middle Wallop, Fire Section
	XN495	Hunting Jet Provost T3A (8786M) [102]	RAF Finningley, Fire Section
	XN497	Hunting Jet Provost T3A [52]	RAF St Athan
	XN498	Hunting Jet Provost T3A [16]	RAF, stored Shawbury
	XN500	Hunting Jet Provost T3A [48]	CSE Ltd, Oxford, ground instruction
	XN501	Hunting Jet Provost T3A (8958M) [G]	RAF No 1 SoTT, Cosford
	XN502	Hunting Jet Provost T3A [D]	RAF, stored Shawbury
	XN503	Hunting Jet Provost T3	Wiltshire Historic Av'n Group, Salisbury
	XN505	Hunting Jet Provost T3A [25]	RAF, stored Linton-on-Ouse
	XN508	Hunting Jet Provost T3A [47]	RAF St Athan
	XN509	Hunting Jet Provost T3A [50]	Privately owned, Colsterworth, Lincs
	XN510	Hunting Jet Provost T3A [40]	RAF, stored Linton-on-Ouse
	XN511	Hunting Jet Provost T3 [64] <ff>	*Painted as XM426*
	XN512	Hunting Jet Provost T3 (8435M)	Princess Alexandra Hospital, Wroughton
	XN549	Hunting Jet Provost T3 (8235M) [32,P]	RAF Shawbury Fire Section
	XN551	Hunting Jet Provost T3A (8984M)	RAF CTTS, St Athan
	XN552	Hunting Jet Provost T3A [32]	*Sold to USA, July 1994*
	XN553	Hunting Jet Provost T3A	*Sold to the USA as N57553, April 1994*
	XN554	Hunting Jet Provost T3 (8436M) [K]	RAF North Luffenham Training Area
	XN573	Hunting Jet Provost T3 [E] <ff>	Newark Air Museum, Winthrope
	XN577	Hunting Jet Provost T3A (8956M) [89,F]	RAF No 1 SoTT, Cosford
	XN579	Hunting Jet Provost T3A (9137M) [14]	RAF North Luffenham Training Area
	XN581	Hunting Jet Provost T3A [C]	*Scrapped at St Athan, 1992*
	XN582	Hunting Jet Provost T3A (8957M) [95,H]	Privately owned, Cambridge
	XN584	Hunting Jet Provost T3A (9014M) [E]	
	XN586	Hunting Jet Provost T3A (9039M) [91,S]	Brooklands Technical College

Serial	Type (other identity) [code]	Owner/operator, location or fate	Notes
XN589	Hunting Jet Provost T3A (9143M) [46]	RAF Linton-on-Ouse, on display	
XN592	Hunting Jet Provost T3 <ff>	No 1105 Sqn ATC, Winchester	
XN593	Hunting Jet Provost T3A (8988M) [97,Q]		
XN594	Hunting Jet Provost T3 (8077M) [W]	Privately owned	
XN595	Hunting Jet Provost T3A [43]	Privately owned, Peterborough	
XN597	Hunting Jet Provost T3 (7984M) <ff>	South Yorkshire Air Museum, Firbeck	
XN600	Hunting Jet Provost T3A <ff>	Yorkshire Air Museum, Elvington	
XN602	Hunting Jet Provost T3 (8088M)	FSCTE, RAF Manston	
XN606	Hunting Jet Provost T3A (9121M) [51]	Sold to USA 1993	
XN607	Hunting Jet Provost T3 <ff>	N Yorks Aircraft Recovery Centre, Chop Gate	
XN629	Hunting Jet Provost T3A (G-BVEG) [49]	Privately owned, North Weald	
XN632	Hunting Jet Provost T3 (8352M)	RAF Chivenor, crash rescue training	
XN634	Hunting Jet Provost T3A <ff>	BAe Warton Fire Section	
XN636	Hunting Jet Provost T3A (9045M) [15]	Privately owned	
XN637	Hunting Jet Provost T3 (G-BKOU) [3]	Vintage Aircraft Team, Bruntingthorpe	
XN640	Hunting Jet Provost T3A (9016M) [99,R]	Sold as N640XN, July 1994	
XN641	Hunting Jet Provost T3A (8865M) [47]	RAF Newton Fire Section	
XN643	Hunting Jet Provost T3A (8704M) <ff>	SIF, RAFC Cranwell	
XN647	DH Sea Vixen FAW2 [707/VL]	Flambards Village Theme Park, Helston	
XN649	DH Sea Vixen FAW2 [126]	MoD(PE), stored DRA Farnborough	
XN650	DH Sea Vixen FAW2 [VL]	Wales Aircraft Museum, Cardiff	
XN651	DH Sea Vixen FAW2 <ff>	Privately owned, Pucklechurch, Avon	
XN657	DH Sea Vixen D3 [TR-1]	T&EE Llanbedr Fire Section	
XN685	DH Sea Vixen FAW2 (8173M) [03/VL]	Midland Air Museum, Coventry	
XN688	DH Sea Vixen FAW2 (8141M) [511]	DRA Farnborough Fire Section	
XN691	DH Sea Vixen FAW2 (8143M) [247/H]	Aces High, North Weald	
XN692	DH Sea Vixen FAW2 [125/E]	Sold for scrapping, Nov 1994	
XN694	DH Sea Vixen FAW2	Scrapped at Llanbedr	
XN696	DH Sea Vixen FAW2 <ff>	Blyth Valley Aviation Collection, Walpole	
XN714	Hunting H126	RAF Cosford Aerospace Museum	
XN724	EE Lightning F2A (8513M) [F]	Privately owned, Newcastle-upon-Tyne	
XN728	EE Lightning F2A (8546M) [V]	Privately owned, Balderton, Notts	
XN734	EE Lightning F3A (8346M/ G-BNCA)	Privately owned, Cranfield	
XN769	EE Lightning F2 (8402M) [Z]	Scrapped at West Drayton, January 1994	
XN774	EE Lightning F2A (8551M) [F]	Coningsby, derelict	
XN776	EE Lightning F2A (8535M) [C]	Royal Scottish Mus'm of Flight, E Fortune	
XN817	AW Argosy C1	MoD(PE) T&EE, West Freugh Fire Section	
XN819	AW Argosy C1 (8205M) <ff>	Newark Air Museum, Winthorpe	
XN923	HS Buccaneer S1 [13]	Privately owned, Charlwood, Surrey	
XN928	HS Buccaneer S1 (8179M) [353]	Wales Aircraft Museum, Cardiff	
XN929	HS Buccaneer S1 (8051M) <ff>	SIF, RAF Cranwell	
XN930	HS Buccaneer S1 (8180M) [632/LM] <ff>	Privately owned, Stock, Essex	
XN934	HS Buccaneer S1 [631] (fuselage)	RN Predannack Fire School	
XN953	HS Buccaneer S1 [8182M]	RN Predannack Fire School	
XN957	HS Buccaneer S1 [630/LM]	FAA Museum, RNAS Yeovilton	
XN964	HS Buccaneer S1 [613/LM]	Newark Air Museum, Winthorpe	
XN967	HS Buccaneer S1 <ff>	Privately owned	
XN972	HS Buccaneer S1 (8183M/ XN962) <ff>	RAF EP&TU, St Athan	
XN974	HS Buccaneer S2A	Yorkshire Air Museum, Elvington	
XN979	HS Buccaneer S2 <ff>	ATC, RAF Stanbridge	
XN981	HS Buccaneer S2B	Scrapped at Lossiemouth, March 1994	
XN982	HS Buccaneer S2A	Scrapped at Brough, July 1992	
XN983	HS Buccaneer S2B	Scrapped at Shawbury, February 1994	
XP110	WS58 Wessex HAS3 [55/FL]	RNAY Fleetlands Apprentice School	

Notes	Serial	Type (other identity) [code]	Owner/operator, location or fate
	XP116	WS58 Wessex HAS3 [520]	*Scrapped at Lee-on-Solent*
	XP137	WS58 Wessex HAS3 [CU]	RN stored, Culdrose
	XP140	WS58 Wessex HAS3 (8806M) [653/PO]	RAF Chilmark, BDRT
	XP142	WS58 Wessex HAS3	FAA Museum, RNAS Yeovilton
	XP150	WS58 Wessex HAS3	FETC, Moreton-in-Marsh
	XP151	WS58 Wessex HAS1 [047/R]	RN Predannack Fire School
	XP157	WS58 Wessex HAS1 [AN]	RNAS Yeovilton, Fire Section
	XP158	WS58 Wessex HAS1 [522/CU]	RNAS Culdrose, Fire Section
	XP159	WS58 Wessex HAS1 (8877M) [047/R]	Privately owned, Brands Hatch
	XP160	WS58 Wessex HAS1 [521/CU]	RN Predannack Fire School
	XP165	WS Scout AH1	IHM, Weston-super-Mare
	XP166	WS Scout AH1 (G-APVL)	DRA Farnborough, Apprentice School
	XP190	WS Scout AH1	South Yorkshire Aviation Museum, Firbeck
	XP191	WS Scout AH1	AAC Middle Wallop, BDRT
	XP226	Fairey Gannet AEW3 [073/E]	Newark Air Museum, Winthorpe
	XP241	Auster AOP9	Rebel Air Museum, Andrewsfield
	XP242	Auster AOP9 (G-BUCI)	AAC Historic Aircraft Flight, MiddleWallop
	XP244	Auster AOP9 (7864M/*M7922*)	Army Apprentice College, Arborfield
	XP248	Auster AOP9 (7863M/WZ679)	Privately owned, Little Gransden
	XP254	Auster AOP11 (G-ASCC)	Privately owned, Longford, Salop
	XP279	Auster AOP9 (G-BWKK)	Privately owned, Popham
	XP280	Auster AOP9	Snibston Discovery Park, Coalville
	XP281	Auster AOP9	Imperial War Museum, Duxford
	XP282	Auster AOP9 (G-BGTC)	Privately owned, Widmerpoll
	XP283	Auster AOP9 (7859M)	Privately owned, Lichfield
	XP299	WS55 Whirlwind HAR10 (8726M)	RAF Cosford Aerospace Museum
	XP329	WS55 Whirlwind HAR10 (8791M) [V]	Privately owned, Tattershall Thorpe
	XP330	WS55 Whirlwind HAR10	CAA Fire School, Teesside Airport
	XP338	WS55 Whirlwind HAR10 (8647M) [N]	*Scrapped at Cosford, 1993*
	XP344	WS55 Whirlwind HAR10 (8764M) [X]	RAF North Luffenham
	XP345	WS55 Whirlwind HAR10 (8792M)	Privately owned, Storwood, East Yorks
	XP346	WS55 Whirlwind HAR10 (8793M)	Privately owned, Long Marston
	XP350	WS55 Whirlwind HAR10	Flambards Village Theme Park, Helston
	XP351	WS55 Whirlwind HAR10 (8672M) [Z]	RAF Shawbury, on display
	XP353	WS55 Whirlwind HAR10 (8720M)	Privately owned, Brands Hatch
	XP354	WS55 Whirlwind HAR10 (8721M)	Privately owned, Cricklade, Wilts
	XP355	WS55 Whirlwind HAR10 (8463M/G-BEBC)	City of Norwich Aviation Museum
	XP359	WS55 Whirlwind HAR10 (8447M)	RAF Stafford, Fire Section
	XP360	WS55 Whirlwind HAR10 [V]	Privately owned, Upper Hill, Hereford
	XP361	WS55 Whirlwind HAR10 (8731M)	RAF Coltishall, Fire Section
	XP393	WS55 Whirlwind HAR10 [U]	*Burned at Farnborough*
	XP395	WS55 Whirlwind HAR10 (8674M) [A]	Privately owned, Tattershall Thorpe
	XP398	WS55 Whirlwind HAR10 (8794M)	Privately owned, Charlwood, Surrey
	XP399	WS55 Whirlwind HAR10	Privately owned, Chelmsford, Essex
	XP404	WS55 Whirlwind HAR10 (8682M)	IHM, Weston-super-Mare
	XP405	WS55 Whirlwind HAR10 (8656M) [Y]	Junior Infantry Reg't, Shorncliffe, Kent
	XP411	AW Argosy C1 (8442M) [C]	RAF Cosford Aerospace Museum
	XP454	Slingsby Grasshopper TX1	Wellingborough School, Wellingborough
	XP458	Slingsby Grasshopper TX1	City of Norwich Aviation Museum
	XP463	Slingsby Grasshopper TX1	Privately owned, stored Rufforth
	XP488	Slingsby Grasshopper TX1	Fenland Aviation Museum, Wisbech
	XP490	Slingsby Grasshopper TX1	Ipswich School, Ipswich
	XP493	Slingsby Grasshopper TX1	Privately owned, stored Aston Down
	XP494	Slingsby Grasshopper TX1	Privately owned, Breighton
	XP502	HS Gnat T1 (8576M)	RAF CTTS, St Athan
	XP503	HS Gnat T1 (8568M) [73]	Privately owned, Bruntingthorpe
	XP505	HS Gnat T1	Science Museum, Wroughton
	XP516	HS Gnat T1 (8580M) [16]	DRA Structures Dept, Farnborough
	XP530	HS Gnat T1 (8606M) [60]	*Sold to USA as N530X, April 1994*
	XP532	HS Gnat T1 (8577M/8615M) [32]	*Sold to the USA*
	XP534	HS Gnat T1 (8620M/G-BVPP) [64]	Kennet Aircraft, Cranfield
	XP540	HS Gnat T1 (8608M) [62]	Privately owned, Bruntingthorpe
	XP542	HS Gnat T1 (8575M) [42]	

Serial	Type (other identity) [code]	Owner/operator, location or fate	Notes
XP547	Hunting Jet Provost T4 (8992M) [N,03]	RAF Benson	
XP556	Hunting Jet Provost T4 (9027M) [B]	RAF Halton	
XP557	Hunting Jet Provost T4 (8494M)	South Yorkshire Air Museum, Firbeck	
XP558	Hunting Jet Provost T4 (8627M)[20]	RAF St Athan Fire Section	
XP563	Hunting Jet Provost T4 (9028M) [C]	RAF Halton	
XP567	Hunting Jet Provost T4 (8510M) [23]	Privately owned, Ipswich	
XP568	Hunting Jet Provost T4	Jet Aviation Pres'n Grp, Long Marston	
XP573	Hunting Jet Provost T4 (8236M) [19]	Jersey Airport Fire Section	
XP585	Hunting Jet Provost T4 (8407M) [24]	NE Wales Institute, Wrexham	
XP627	Hunting Jet Provost T4	North-East Aircraft Museum, Usworth	
XP629	Hunting Jet Provost T4 (9026M) [P]	RAF North Luffenham Training Area	
XP638	Hunting Jet Provost T4 (9034M) [A]	RAF Waddington, BDRT	
XP640	Hunting Jet Provost T4 (8501M) [D]	Yorkshire Air Museum, Elvington	
XP672	Hunting Jet Provost T4 (8458M/ G-RAFI) [27]	Privately owned, Ramsey, Isle of Man	
XP677	Hunting Jet Provost T4 (8587M) <ff>	No 2530 Sqn ATC, Headley Court, Uckfield	
XP680	Hunting Jet Provost T4 (8460M)	RAF St Athan, Fire Section	
XP686	Hunting Jet Provost T4 (8401M/ 8502M) [G]	RAF North Luffenham Training Area	
XP688	Hunting Jet Provost T4 (9031M) [E]		
XP693	BAC Lightning F6 (G-FSIX)	Lightning Flying Club, Exeter Airport	
XP701	BAC Lightning F3 (8924M) <ff>	Robertsbridge Aviation Society, Mayfield	
XP703	BAC Lightning F3 <ff>	Lightning Preservation Grp, Bruntingthorpe	
XP706	BAC Lightning F3 (8925M)	Lincs Lightning Pres'n Soc, Strubby	
XP741	BAC Lightning F3 (8939M) [AR]	FSCTE, RAF Manston	
XP745	BAC Lightning F3 (8453M) [H]	Privately owned, Greenford, West London	
XP772	DHC Beaver AL1 (G-BUCJ)	The Aircraft Restoration Co, Duxford	
XP775	DHC Beaver AL1	Privately owned	
XP806	DHC Beaver AL1	Museum of Army Flying, Middle Wallop	
XP820	DHC Beaver AL1	AAC Historic Aircraft Flight, Middle Wallop	
XP821	DHC Beaver AL1 [MCO]	Museum of Army Flying, Middle Wallop	
XP822	DHC Beaver AL1	Privately owned	
XP831	Hawker P1127 (8406M)	Science Museum, South Kensington	
XP841	Handley-Page HP115	FAA Museum, RNAS Yeovilton	
XP846	WS Scout AH1 [B,H] (fuselage)		
XP847	WS Scout AH1	Museum of Army Flying, Middle Wallop	
XP848	WS Scout AH1	AAC SAE, Middle Wallop	
XP849	WS Scout AH1	MoD(PE) ETPS, Boscombe Down	
XP850	WS Scout AH1 (fuselage)	AAC, stored Dishforth	
XP853	WS Scout AH1	AAC SAE, Middle Wallop	
XP854	WS Scout AH1 (7898M/TAD043)	AAC SAE, Middle Wallop	
XP855	WS Scout AH1	Army Apprentice College, Arborfield	
XP856	WS Scout AH1	AAC Middle Wallop, BDRT	
XP857	WS Scout AH1	AAC Middle Wallop Fire Section	
XP883	WS Scout AH1	MoD(PE) ETPS, Boscombe Down	
XP884	WS Scout AH1	AAC SAE, Middle Wallop	
XP886	WS Scout AH1	Army Apprentice College, Arborfield	
XP888	WS Scout AH1	AAC SAE, Middle Wallop	
XP890	WS Scout AH1 [G] (fuselage)	AAC, stored RNAW Almondbank	
XP891	WS Scout AH1 [S]	AAC, stored RNAY Fleetlands	
XP893	WS Scout AH1	AAC, stored Middle Wallop	
XP899	WS Scout AH1 [D]	Army Apprentice College, Arborfield	
XP902	WS Scout AH1	AAC Netheravon	
XP905	WS Scout AH1	AAC SAE, Middle Wallop	
XP907	WS Scout AH1	AAC, stored RNAY Fleetlands	
XP908	WS Scout AH1 [Y]	AAC, stored Sek Kong	
XP910	WS Scout AH1	AAC SAE, Middle Wallop	
XP919	DH Sea Vixen FAW2 (8163M) [706/VL]	City of Norwich Aviation Museum	
XP924	DH Sea Vixen D3	MoD(PE), stored T&EE, Llanbedr	

Notes	Serial	Type (other identity) [code]	Owner/operator, location or fate
	XP925	DH Sea Vixen FAW2 [752] <ff>	DRA Farnborough, Fire Section
	XP956	DH Sea Vixen FAW2	Privately owned, Dunsfold
	XP980	Hawker P.1127	FAA Museum, RNAS Yeovilton
	XP984	Hawker P.1127	RN, stored Lee-on-Solent
	XR137	AW Argosy E1	Caernarfon Air World
	XR140	AW Argosy E1 (8579M) (fuselage)	*Burned at Halton*
	XR220	BAC TSR2 (7933M)	RAF Cosford Aerospace Museum
	XR222	BAC TSR2	Imperial War Museum, Duxford
	XR232	Sud Alouette AH2 (F-WEIP)	Museum of Army Flying, Middle Wallop
	XR240	Auster AOP9 (G-BDFH)	Privately owned, Cambridge
	XR241	Auster AOP9 (G-AXRR)	The Aircraft Restoration Co, Duxford
	XR244	Auster AOP9	AAC Historic Aircraft Flight, Middle Wallop
	XR246	Auster AOP9 (7862M/G-AZBU)	Privately owned, Reymerston Hall
	XR267	Auster AOP9 (G-BJXR)	Cotswold Aircraft Rest'n Grp, Innsworth
	XR271	Auster AOP9	Museum of Artillery, Woolwich
	XR363	SC5 Belfast C1 (G-OHCA)	*Scrapped at Southend, February 1994*
	XR371	SC5 Belfast C1	RAF Cosford Aerospace Museum
	XR379	Sud Alouette AH2	AAC Historic Aircraft Flight, Middle Wallop
	XR396	DH Comet C4 (8882M/G-BDIU) (fuselage)	*Remained as G-BDIU*
	XR436	Saro Scout AH1	AAC Middle Wallop, BDRT
	XR453	WS55 Whirlwind HAR10 (8873M) [A]	RAF Odiham, on gate
	XR458	WS55 Whirlwind HAR10 (8662M) [H]	Museum of Army Flying, Middle Wallop
	XR485	WS55 Whirlwind HAR10 [Q]	Norfolk & Suffolk Aviation Museum, Flixton
	XR486	WS55 Whirlwind HCC12 (8727M/G-RWWW)	Privately owned, Redhill
	XR497	WS58 Wessex HC2 [F]	RAF No 72 Sqn, Aldergrove
	XR498	WS58 Wessex HC2 [X]	RAF No 72 Sqn, Aldergrove
	XR499	WS58 Wessex HC2 [W]	RAF No 72 Sqn, Aldergrove
	XR501	WS58 Wessex HC2	RAF No 22 Sqn, St Mawgan
	XR502	WS58 Wessex HC2 [Z]	RAF No 60 Sqn, Benson
	XR503	WS58 Wessex HC2	MoD(PE), DRA Boscombe Down
	XR504	WS58 Wessex HC2	RAF No 84 Sqn, Akrotiri
	XR505	WS58 Wessex HC2 [WA]	RAF No 2 FTS, Shawbury
	XR506	WS58 Wessex HC2 [V]	RAF No 72 Sqn, Aldergrove
	XR507	WS58 Wessex HC2	RAF SARTU, Valley
	XR508	WS58 Wessex HC2 [D]	RAF No 28 Sqn, Sek Kong
	XR509	WS58 Wessex HC2 (8752M)	*Scrapped at Benson, December 1992*
	XR511	WS58 Wessex HC2 [L]	RAF No 60 Sqn, Benson
	XR515	WS58 Wessex HC2 [B]	RAF No 28 Sqn, Sek Kong
	XR516	WS58 Wessex HC2 [WB]	RAF No 2 FTS, Shawbury
	XR517	WS58 Wessex HC2 [N]	RAF No 60 Sqn, Benson
	XR518	WS58 Wessex HC2	RAF No 22 Sqn, C Flt/SARTU, Valley
	XR519	WS58 Wessex HC2 [WC] (wreck)	*Scrapped at Shawbury, March 1993*
	XR520	WS58 Wessex HC2	RAF SARTU, Valley
	XR521	WS58 Wessex HC2 [WD]	RAF No 2 FTS, Shawbury
	XR522	WS58 Wessex HC2 [A]	RAF No 28 Sqn, Sek Kong
	XR523	WS58 Wessex HC2 [M]	RAF No 60 Sqn, Benson
	XR525	WS58 Wessex HC2 [G]	RAF No 60 Sqn, Benson
	XR526	WS58 Wessex HC2 (8147M)	Westlands, Yeovil, instructional use
	XR527	WS58 Wessex HC2 [K]	RAF No 72 Sqn, Aldergrove
	XR528	WS58 Wessex HC2 [T]	RAF No 72 Sqn, Aldergrove
	XR529	WS58 Wessex HC2 [E]	RAF No 72 Sqn, Aldergrove
	XR534	HS Gnat T1 (8578M) [65]	RAF Valley on display
	XR535	HS Gnat T1 (8569M) [05]	RAF Halton
	XR537	HS Gnat T1 (8642M/G-NATY) [T]	Jet Heritage Ltd, Bournemouth
	XR538	HS Gnat T1 (8621M/G-RORI) [69]	Privately owned, Cranfield
	XR569	HS Gnat T1 (8560M) [08]	Privately owned, Bruntingthorpe
	XR571	HS Gnat T1 (8493M)	RAF *Red Arrows*, Scampton, on display
	XR574	HS Gnat T1 (8631M) [72]	RAF No 1 SoTT, Cosford
	XR588	WS58 Wessex HC2	RAF No 84 Sqn, Akrotiri
	XR595	WS Scout AH1 [M]	AAC, stored RNAY Fleetlands
	XR597	WS Scout AH1	AAC SAE, Middle Wallop
	XR600	WS Scout AH1 (fuselage)	AAC Netheravon, BDRT
	XR601	WS Scout AH1	Army Apprentice College, Arborfield
	XR627	WS Scout AH1 [X]	AAC SAE, Middle Wallop
	XR628	WS Scout AH1	AAC, stored RNAW Almondbank
	XR629	WS Scout AH1 (fuselage)	AAC, stored RNAW Almondbank
	XR630	WS Scout AH1 [U]	AAC Middle Wallop, BDRT
	XR632	WS Scout AH1	AAC, stored RNAY Fleetlands

Serial	Type (other identity) [code]	Owner/operator, location or fate	Notes
XR635	WS Scout AH1	AAC SAE, Middle Wallop	
XR639	WS Scout AH1 [X] (fuselage)	AAC, stored RNAW Almondbank	
XR650	Hunting Jet Provost T4 (8459M) [28]	MoD(PE) Boscombe Down, GI use	
XR651	Hunting Jet Provost T4 (8431M) [A]		
XR654	Hunting Jet Provost T4 [34]	Macclesfield Hist Av'n Society, Barton	
XR658	Hunting Jet Provost T4 (8192M)	N Wales Inst of HE, Connah's Quay	
XR662	Hunting Jet Provost T4 (8410M) [25]	RAF Finningley, Fire Section	
XR669	Hunting Jet Provost T4 (8062M) <ff>	*Scrapped at Halton*	
XR670	Hunting Jet Provost T4 (8498M)	RAF Odiham, Fire Section	
XR672	Hunting Jet Provost T4 (8495M) [50]	RAF Halton, Fire Section	
XR673	Hunting Jet Provost T4 (9032M) [L]	RAF Halton	
XR674	Hunting Jet Provost T4 (G-TOMG/9030M) [D]	Privately owned, North Weald	
XR679	Hunting Jet Provost T4 (8991M) [M,04]	RAF No 1 SoTT, Cosford	
XR681	Hunting Jet Provost T4 (8588M) <ff>	No 1218 Sqn ATC, Manston	
XR700	Hunting Jet Provost T4 (8589M) <ff>	RAF EP&TU, Aldergrove	
XR701	Hunting Jet Provost T4 (9025M) [K,21]	Privately owned, Ipswich	
XR704	Hunting Jet Provost T4 (8506M) [30]	Privately owned, Ipswich	
XR713	BAC Lightning F3 (8935M) [C]	RAF Leuchars, BDRT	
XR716	BAC Lightning F3 (8940M)	*Scrapped at Cottesmore, June 1994*	
XR718	BAC Lightning F6 (8932M) [DA]	Blyth Valley Aviation Collection, Walpole	
XR724	BAC Lightning F6 (G-BTSY)	Privately owned, Binbrook	
XR725	BAC Lightning F6	Privately owned, Binbrook	
XR726	BAC Lightning F6 <ff>	Privately owned, Harrogate	
XR728	BAC Lightning F6 [JS]	Lightning Preservation Grp, Bruntingthorpe	
XR747	BAC Lightning F6 <ff>	Privately owned, Plymouth	
XR749	BAC Lightning F3 (8934M)	Privately owned, Teeside Airport	
XR751	BAC Lightning F3	Privately owned, Lower Tremar, Cornwall	
XR753	BAC Lightning F6 (8969M) [BP]	RAF Leeming on display	
XR754	BAC Lightning F6 (8972M) <ff>	Blyth Valley Aviation Collection, Walpole	
XR755	BAC Lightning F6	Privately owned, Callington, Cornwall	
XR757	BAC Lightning F6 <ff>	Privately owned, New Waltham, Humberside	
XR759	BAC Lightning F6 <ff>	Privately owned, Haxey, Humberside	
XR770	BAC Lightning F6 [JS]	Privately owned, New Waltham, Humberside	
XR771	BAC Lightning F6 [BM]	Midland Air Museum, Coventry	
XR773	BAC Lightning F6 (G-OPIB)	Lightning Flying Club, Exeter Airport	
XR777	WS Scout AH1 (really XT625)	AAC, stored Middle Wallop	
XR806	BAC VC10 C1	RAF No 10 Sqn, Brize Norton	
XR807	BAC VC10 C1K	RAF No 10 Sqn, Brize Norton	
XR808	BAC VC10 C1	RAF No 10 Sqn, Brize Norton	
XR810	BAC VC10 C1K	RAF No 10 Sqn, Brize Norton	
XR944	Wallis WA116 (G-ATTB)	RAF Museum, Hendon	
XR953	HS Gnat T1 (8609M) [63]	RAF Halton	
XR954	HS Gnat T1 (8570M) [30]		
XR955	HS Gnat T1 [SAH-2]	Privately owned, Leavesden	
XR977	HS Gnat T1 (8640M) [3]	RAF Cosford Aerospace Museum	
XR980	HS Gnat T1 (8622M) [70]		
XR985	HS Gnat T1 (7886M)	Vintage Aircraft Team, Bruntingthorpe	
XR991	HS Gnat T1 (8624M/XS102/ G-MOUR)	Intrepid Aviation Co, North Weald	
XR998	HS Gnat T1 (8623M) [71]	RAF Halton	
XS101	HS Gnat T1 (8638M) (G-GNAT)	Privately owned, Cranfield	
XS122	WS58 Wessex HAS3 [655/PO]	RN AES, Lee-on-Solent	
XS128	WS58 Wessex HAS1 [37]	RNAS Yeovilton, Fire Section	
XS149	WS58 Wessex HAS3 [661/GL]	IHM, Weston-super-Mare	
XS153	WS58 Wessex HAS3 [662/PO]	*To AAC Sennelager, BDRT*	
XS165	Hiller UH12E (G-ASAZ) [37]	Privately owned	

47

Notes	Serial	Type (other identity) [code]	Owner/operator, location or fate
	XS176	Hunting Jet Provost T4 (8514M) [N]	University of Salford, Manchester
	XS177	Hunting Jet Provost T4 (9044M) [N]	RAF Valley Fire Section
	XS178	Hunting Jet Provost T4 (8994M) [P,05]	*Sold to Australia, April 1994*
	XS179	Hunting Jet Provost T4 (8237M) [20]	University of Salford, Manchester
	XS180	Hunting Jet Provost T4 (8238M) [21]	RAF St Athan (dismantled)
	XS181	Hunting Jet Provost T4 (9033M) [F]	RAF Halton
	XS183	Hunting Jet Provost T4 <ff>	Imperial War Museum, stored Duxford
	XS186	Hunting Jet Provost T4 (8408M) [M]	RAF North Luffenham Training Area
	XS209	Hunting Jet Provost T4 (8409M) [29]	RAF Halton
	XS215	Hunting Jet Provost T4 (8507M) [17]	RAF Halton, dismantled
	XS216	Hunting Jet Provost T4 <ff>	RAF Finningley Fire Section
	XS217	Hunting Jet Provost T4 (9029M) [O]	RAF Halton
	XS218	Hunting Jet Provost T4 (8508M) <ff>	Museum of Berkshire Aviation, Woodley
	XS219	Hunting Jet Provost T4 (8993M) [O,06]	*Sold as N219JP by July 1994*
	XS230	BAC Jet Provost T5P	Privately owned, North Weald
	XS231	BAC Jet Provost T5 (G-ATAJ)	Privately owned, Bruntingthorpe
	XS235	DH Comet 4C	MoD(PE) A&AEE, Boscombe Down
	XS241	WS58 Wessex HU5 (9102M)	*Scrapped at Benson, December 1992*
	XS416	BAC Lightning T5 <ff>	Privately owned, New Waltham, Humberside
	XS417	BAC Lightning T5	Newark Air Museum, Winthorpe
	XS420	BAC Lightning T5	Fenland Air Museum, Wisbech
	XS422	BAC Lightning T5	Privately owned, Southampton Docks
	XS451	BAC Lightning T5 (8503M/ G-LTNG)	Lightning Flying Club, Plymouth
	XS452	BAC Lightning T5 (G-BPFE) [BT]	Privately owned, Cranfield
	XS456	BAC Lightning T5	Privately owned, Wainfleet
	XS457	BAC Lightning T5 <ff>	Privately owned, New Waltham
	XS458	BAC Lightning T5 [DY]	*[Sold to Cyprus, Nov 1993]*, Cranfield
	XS459	BAC Lightning T5	Fenland Air Museum, Wisbech
	XS463	WS Wasp HAS1 (XT431)	IHM, Weston-super-Mare
	XS463	WS Wasp HAS1	RN Predannack Fire School
	XS479	WS58 Wessex HU5 (8819M) [XF]	JATE, RAF Brize Norton
	XS481	WS58 Wessex HU5	AAC 9 Regt Dishforth, BDRT
	XS482	WS58 Wessex HU5 [A-D]	DRA Farnborough Apprentice School
	XS483	WS58 Wessex HU5 [T/VL]	RN Lee-on-Solent, Fire Section
	XS484	WS58 Wessex HU5 [821/CU]	RAF Finningley, Fire Section
	XS485	WS58 Wessex HC5C [*Hearts*]	*Withdrawn from use, RAF Akrotori*
	XS486	WS58 Wessex HU5 [524/CU, F]	RN Recruiting Team, Lee-on-Solent
	XS488	WS58 Wessex HU5 (9056M) [XK]	RAF No 1 SoTT, Cosford
	XS489	WS58 Wessex HU5 [R]	RAF Odiham, instructional use
	XS491	WS58 Wessex HU5 [XM]	RAF No 16 MU Stafford, Fire Section
	XS492	WS58 Wessex HU5 [623]	RN, stored
	XS493	WS58 Wessex HU5	RN, stored Fleetlands
	XS496	WS58 Wessex HU5 [625/PO]	RN AES, Lee-on-Solent
	XS498	WS58 Wessex HC5C [*Joker*]	*Withdrawn from use, RAF Akrotori*
	XS506	WS58 Wessex HU5	*Scrapped at Shawbury, March 1993*
	XS507	WS58 Wessex HU5 [627/PO]	RN AES, Lee-on-Solent
	XS508	WS58 Wessex HU5	FAA Museum, RNAS Yeovilton
	XS509	WS58 Wessex HU5	MoD(PE) ETPS, Boscombe Down
	XS510	WS58 Wessex HU5 [626/PO]	RN AES, Lee-on-Solent
	XS511	WS58 Wessex HU5 [M]	RN AES, Lee-on-Solent
	XS513	WS58 Wessex HU5 [419/PO]	RN, Lee-on-Solent, BDRT
	XS514	WS58 Wessex HU5 [L]	RN AES, Lee-on-Solent
	XS515	WS58 Wessex HU5 [N]	RN AES, Lee-on-Solent
	XS516	WS58 Wessex HU5 [Q]	RN AES, Lee-on-Solent
	XS517	WS58 Wessex HC5C [*Diamonds*]	*Withdrawn from use, RAF Akrotiri*
	XS520	WS58 Wessex HU5 [F]	
	XS521	WS58 Wessex HU5	Army, Saighton, Cheshire
	XS522	WS58 Wessex HU5 [ZL]	RN AES, Lee-on-Solent
	XS523	WS58 Wessex HU5 [824/CU]	RN, Lee-on-Solent, BDRT

Serial	Type (other identity) [code]	Owner/operator, location or fate	Notes
XS527	WS Wasp HAS1	FAA Museum, RNAS Yeovilton	
XS529	WS Wasp HAS1 [461]	RN AES, Lee-on-Solent	
XS535	WS Wasp HAS1 [432]	RAOC, West Moors, Dorset	
XS538	WS Wasp HAS1 [451]	RN Predannack Fire School	
XS539	WS Wasp HAS1 [435]	RNAY Fleetlands Apprentice School	
XS541	WS Wasp HAS1 [602]	Sold to the USA, April 1994	
XS545	WS Wasp HAS1 [635]	RN AES, Lee-on-Solent	
XS562	WS Wasp HAS1 [605]	Sold to the USA, April 1994	
XS567	WS Wasp HAS1 [434/E]	Imperial War Museum, Duxford	
XS568	WS Wasp HAS1 [441]	RNAY Fleetlands Apprentice School	
XS569	WS Wasp HAS1	RNAY Fleetlands Apprentice School	
XS570	WS Wasp HAS1 [445/P]	Warship Preservation Trust, Birkenhead	
XS572	WS Wasp HAS1 (8845M) [414]	RAF No 16 MU Stafford, Fire Section	
XS576	DH Sea Vixen FAW2 [125/E]	Imperial War Museum, Duxford	
XS577	DH Sea Vixen D3	MoD(PE), stored T&EE Llanbedr	
XS587	DH Sea Vixen FAW(TT)2 (8828M/G-VIXN)	Privately owned, Charlwood, Surrey	
XS590	DH Sea Vixen FAW2 [131/E]	FAA Museum, RNAS Yeovilton	
XS596	HS Andover C1(PR)	MoD(PE), A&AEE Boscombe Down	
XS597	HS Andover C1	Sold as G-BVNJ, May 1994	
XS598	HS Andover C1 (fuselage)	FETC, Moreton-in-Marsh	
XS603	HS Andover E3	Hunting Air Services, East Midlands Airport	
XS605	HS Andover E3	Hunting Air Services, East Midlands Airport	
XS606	HS Andover C1	MoD(PE) ETPS, Boscombe Down	
XS607	HS Andover C1 (G-BEBY)	MoD(PE) Farnborough, wfu	
XS610	HS Andover E3	Hunting Air Services, East Midlands Airport	
XS637	HS Andover C1	Sold as G-BVNK, May 1994	
XS639	HS Andover E3A	RAF Cosford Aerospace Museum	
XS640	HS Andover E3	Hunting Air Services, East Midlands Airport	
XS641	HS Andover C1(PR) (9198M) [Z]	RAF No 1 SoTT, Cosford	
XS642	HS Andover C1 (8785M) [C]	Scrapped at Benson, July 1994	
XS643	HS Andover E3A	MoD(PE) A&AEE, Boscombe Down	
XS644	HS Andover E3A	Sold as VR-BOI, June 1994	
XS646	HS Andover C1(mod)	MoD(PE) DRA, Boscombe Down	
XS674	WS58 Wessex HC2 [R]	RAF No 60 Sqn, Benson	
XS675	WS58 Wessex HC2	RAF No 84 Sqn, Akrotiri	
XS676	WS58 Wessex HC2 [WJ]	RAF No 2 FTS, Shawbury	
XS677	WS58 Wessex HC2 [WK]	RAF No 2 FTS, Shawbury	
XS679	WS58 Wessex HC2 [WG]	RAF No 2 FTS, Shawbury	
XS695	HS Kestrel FGA1	RAF Museum Restoration Centre, Cardington	
XS709	HS Dominie T1 [M]	RAF No 6 FTS, Finningley	
XS710	HS Dominie T1 [O]	RAF No 6 FTS, Finningley	
XS711	HS Dominie T1 [L]	RAF No 6 FTS, Finningley	
XS712	HS Dominie T1 [A]	RAF No 6 FTS, Finningley	
XS713	HS Dominie T1 [C]	RAF No 6 FTS, Finningley	
XS714	HS Dominie T1 [P]	RAF No 6 FTS, Finningley	
XS726	HS Dominie T1 [T]	RAF No 6 FTS, Finningley	
XS727	HS Dominie T1	RAF St Athan	
XS728	HS Dominie T1 [E]	RAF No 6 FTS, Finningley	
XS729	HS Dominie T1 [G]	RAF No 6 FTS, Finningley	
XS730	HS Dominie T1 [H]	RAF No 6 FTS, Finningley	
XS731	HS Dominie T1 [J]	RAF No 6 FTS, Finningley	
XS732	HS Dominie T1 [B] (fuselage)	DRA, Fort Halstead, Kent	
XS733	HS Dominie T1 [Q]	RAF No 6 FTS, Finningley	
XS734	HS Dominie T1 [N]	RAF No 6 FTS, Finningley	
XS735	HS Dominie T1 [R]	RAF No 6 FTS, Finningley	
XS736	HS Dominie T1 [S]	RAF No 6 FTS, Finningley	
XS737	HS Dominie T1 [K]	RAF No 6 FTS, Finningley	
XS738	HS Dominie T1 [U]	RAF No 6 FTS, Finningley	
XS739	HS Dominie T1 [F]	RAF No 6 FTS, Finningley	
XS743	Beagle Basset CC1	MoD(PE) ETPS, Boscombe Down	
XS770	Beagle Basset CC1 (G-HRHI)	Privately owned, Cranfield	
XS789	HS Andover CC2	RAF No 32 Sqn, Northolt	
XS790	HS Andover CC2	MoD(PE) DRA, Boscombe Down	
XS791	HS Andover CC2	RAF, stored St Athan	
XS792	HS Andover CC2	Privately owned	
XS793	HS Andover CC2 (9178M) [Y]	RAF No 1 SoTT, Cosford	
XS794	HS Andover CC2	RAF No 32 Sqn, Northolt	

Notes	Serial	Type (other identity) [code]	Owner/operator, location or fate
	XS862	WS58 Wessex HAS3	NB&C Defence Centre, Winterbourne Gunner
	XS863	WS58 Wessex HAS1	Imperial War Museum, Duxford
	XS865	WS58 Wessex HAS1 [529/CU]	*Burnt at Lee-on-Solent, 1993*
	XS866	WS58 Wessex HAS1 [520/CU]	RN SAH, Culdrose
	XS868	WS58 Wessex HAS1	RNAY Fleetlands
	XS870	WS58 Wessex HAS1 [PO]	RN Portland, Fire Section
	XS871	WS58 Wessex HAS1 (8457M) [AI]	RAF Odiham, Fire Section
	XS872	WS58 Wessex HAS1 [572/CU]	RNAY Fleetlands Apprentice School
	XS873	WS58 Wessex HAS1	RN Predannack Fire School
	XS876	WS58 Wessex HAS1 [523]	RN SAH, Culdrose
	XS877	WS58 Wessex HAS1 [516/PO]	RN Predannack Fire School
	XS878	WS58 Wessex HAS1	*Burnt at Lee-on-Solent*
	XS881	WS58 Wessex HAS1 [046/CU]	RNAS Yeovilton, BDRT
	XS885	WS58 Wessex HAS1 [12/CU]	RN, SAH Culdrose
	XS886	WS58 Wessex HAS1 [527/CU]	Sea Scouts, Evesham, Worcs
	XS887	WS58 Wessex HAS1 [403/FI]	Flambards Village Theme Park, Helston
	XS888	WS58 Wessex HAS1 [521]	Guernsey Airport, Fire Section
	XS897	BAC Lightning F6	South Yorkshire Aviation Museum, Firbeck
	XS898	BAC Lightning F6 [BD]	*Scrapped at Cranfield, Nov 94*
	XS899	BAC Lightning F6 [BL]	*Scrapped at Cranfield, Nov 94*
	XS903	BAC Lightning F6 [BA]	Yorkshire Air Museum, Elvington
	XS904	BAC Lightning F6	Lightning Preservation Grp, Bruntingthorpe
	XS919	BAC Lightning F6	Privately owned, Lower Tremar, Cornwall
	XS922	BAC Lightning F6 (8973M) <ff>	Privately owned, Sidcup
	XS923	BAC Lightning F6 [BE]	*Scrapped at Cranfield, Nov 94*
	XS925	BAC Lightning F6 (8961M) [BA]	RAF Museum, Hendon
	XS928	BAC Lightning F6	BAe, Warton, stored
	XS932	BAC Lightning F6 <ff>	Privately owned, Bruntingthorpe
	XS933	BAC Lightning F6 <ff>	Privately owned, Terrington St Clement
	XS936	BAC Lightning F6	Privately owned, Liskeard, Cornwall
	XT108	Agusta-Bell Sioux AH1 [U]	Museum of Army Flying, Middle Wallop
	XT131	Agusta-Bell Sioux AH1 [B]	AAC Historic Aircraft Flight, Middle Wallop
	XT133	Agusta-Bell Sioux AH1 (7923M)	Royal Engineers' Museum, Chatham, stored
	XT140	Agusta-Bell Sioux AH1	Air Service Training, Perth
	XT148	Agusta-Bell Sioux AH1	Privately owned
	XT150	Agusta-Bell Sioux AH1 (7883M) [R]	AAC Netheravon, on display
	XT151	WS Sioux AH1 [W]	Museum of Army Flying, stored Middle Wallop
	XT175	WS Sioux AH1 (TAD175)	CSE Oxford for ground instruction
	XT176	WS Sioux AH1 [U]	FAA Museum, stored Wroughton
	XT190	WS Sioux AH1	AAC Wattisham, on display
	XT200	WS Sioux AH1 [F]	Newark Air Museum, Winthorpe
	XT236	WS Sioux AH1 (frame only)	North-East Aircraft Museum, Usworth
	XT242	WS Sioux AH1 (composite) [12]	The Aeroplane Coll'n, Hooton Park, Cheshire
	XT255	WS58 Wessex HAS3 (8751M)	RAF No 14 MU, Carlisle, BDRT
	XT257	WS58 Wessex HAS3 (8719M)	RAF Halton
	XT272	HS Buccaneer S2	DRA Farnborough Fire Section
	XT277	HS Buccaneer S2A (8853M) <ff>	Privately owned, Welshpool
	XT280	HS Buccaneer S2B	*Scrapped at Lossiemouth, March 1994*
	XT284	HS Buccaneer S2A (8855M)	RAF St Athan, BDRT
	XT288	HS Buccaneer S2B (9134M)	Royal Scottish Museum of Flight, E Fortune
	XT415	WS Wasp HAS1 [FIR3]	Airwork Ltd, Bournemouth
	XT420	WS Wasp HAS1 [606]	Privately owned, Sproughton
	XT422	WS Wasp HAS1 [324]	Privately owned, Burgess Hill
	XT427	WS Wasp HAS1 [606]	Flambards Village Theme Park, Helston
	XT434	WS Wasp HAS1 [455]	RNAY Fleetlands Apprentice School
	XT437	WS Wasp HAS1 [423]	RN AES, Lee-on-Solent
	XT439	WS Wasp HAS1 [605]	Cranfield Institute of Technology
	XT449	WS58 Wessex HU5 [C]	RN, Lee-on-Solent, Fire Section
	XT450	WS58 Wessex HU5 [V]	RN, Predannack Fire School
	XT451	WS58 Wessex HU5 [XN]	*Scrapped at Shawbury, March 1993*
	XT453	WS58 Wessex HU5 [VL]	RN AES, Lee-on-Solent
	XT455	WS58 Wessex HU5 [U]	RN AES, Lee-on-Solent
	XT456	WS58 Wessex HU5 (8941M) [XZ]	RAF Aldergrove, BDRT
	XT458	WS58 Wessex HU5 [622]	RN AES, Lee-on-Solent
	XT459	WS58 Wessex HU5 [D]	*Scrapped at Faygate by Oct 1993*
	XT460	WS58 Wessex HU5 [K]	RN AES, Lee-on-Solent

Serial	Type (other identity) [code]	Owner/operator, location or fate	Notes
XT463	WS58 Wessex HC5C [Clubs]	Withdrawn from use, RAF Akrotori	
XT466	WS58 Wessex HU5 (8921M) [XV]		
XT468	WS58 Wessex HU5 [628]	RN AES, Lee-on-Solent	
XT469	WS58 Wessex HU5 (8920M)	RAF No 16 MU, Stafford, ground instruction	
XT470	WS58 Wessex HU5 [A]	AAC, Netheravon, Fire Section	
XT471	WS58 Wessex HU5	AAC, 9 Regt Dishforth, BDRT	
XT472	WS58 Wessex HU5 [XC]	IHM, Weston-super-Mare	
XT475	WS58 Wessex HU5 (9108M) [624]	FSCTE, RAF Manston	
XT479	WS58 Wessex HC5C [Spades]	Withdrawn from use, RAF Akrotori	
XT480	WS58 Wessex HU5 [XQ]	RNAY Fleetlands Apprentice School	
XT481	WS58 Wessex HU5 [F]	RN Predannack Fire School	
XT482	WS58 Wessex HU5 [ZM/VL]	FAA Museum, RNAS Yeovilton	
XT484	WS58 Wessex HU5 [H]	RN AES, Lee-on-Solent	
XT485	WS58 Wessex HU5 [621/PO]	RN AES, Lee-on-Solent	
XT486	WS58 Wessex HU5 (8919M) [XR]	RAF JATE, preserved Brize Norton	
XT487	WS58 Wessex HU5 [815/LS]	Burned at Lee-on-Solent, 1993	
XT575	Vickers Viscount 837 <ff>	Privately owned, Stock, Essex	
XT595	McD Phantom FG1 (8851M) <ff>	RAF EP&TU, St Athan	
XT596	McD Phantom FG1	FAA Museum, RNAS Yeovilton	
XT597	McD Phantom FG1	MoD(PE), Boscombe Down, wfu	
XT601	WS58 Wessex HC2	RAF No 22 Sqn, C Flt/SARTU, Valley	
XT602	WS58 Wessex HC2	RAF No 22 Sqn, C Flt/SARTU, Valley	
XT603	WS58 Wessex HC2 [WF]	RAF No 2 FTS, Shawbury	
XT604	WS58 Wessex HC2	RAF SARTU, Valley	
XT605	WS58 Wessex HC2 [E]	RAF No 28 Sqn, Sek Kong	
XT606	WS58 Wessex HC2 [WL]	RAF No 2 FTS, Shawbury	
XT607	WS58 Wessex HC2 [P]	RAF No 72 Sqn, Aldergrove	
XT614	WS Scout AH1 [C]	Withdrawn from use at Sek Kong, 1993	
XT616	WS Scout AH1 (fuselage)	AAC, stored RNAW Almondbank	
XT617	WS Scout AH1	AAC, stored RNAW Almondbank	
XT620	WS Scout AH1	AAC Aldergrove, BDRT	
XT621	WS Scout AH1	R. Military College of Science, Shrivenham	
XT623	WS Scout AH1	Army Apprentice College, Arborfield	
XT624	WS Scout AH1 [D]	Privately owned, Lincolnshire	
XT626	WS Scout AH1 [Q]	AAC Historic Aircraft Flt, Middle Wallop	
XT628	WS Scout AH1 [E]	Withdrawn from use at Sek Kong, 1993	
XT630	WS Scout AH1 [X]	Privately owned, Lincolnshire	
XT631	WS Scout AH1 [D]	MoD(PE) A&AEE, Boscombe Down	
XT632	WS Scout AH1	AAC, stored RNAY Fleetlands	
XT633	WS Scout AH1	Army Apprentice College, Arborfield	
XT634	WS Scout AH1 [T]	AAC, stored RNAY Fleetlands	
XT636	WS Scout AH1 [F]	AAC, Brunei	
XT637	WS Scout AH1 (fuselage)	RNAS Yeovilton, Fire Section	
XT638	WS Scout AH1 [N]	AAC Middle Wallop, at gate	
XT639	WS Scout AH1 [Y] (fuselage)	AAC, stored RNAW Almondbank	
XT640	WS Scout AH1	RNAS Lee-on-Solent, BDRT	
XT642	WS Scout AH1 (fuselage)	AAC, stored RNAW Almondbank	
XT643	WS Scout AH1 [Z]		
XT644	WS Scout AH1 [Y]	AAC, stored RNAY Fleetlands	
XT645	WS Scout AH1 (fuselage)	AAC Thorney Island, BDRT	
XT646	WS Scout AH1 [Z]	AAC, stored RNAY Fleetlands	
XT649	WS Scout AH1	AAC, stored RNAY Fleetlands	
XT661	Vickers Viscount 838 <ff>	Privately owned, Bruntingthorpe	
XT667	WS58 Wessex HC2 [F]	Written off, Hong Kong, 17 Sept 1993	
XT668	WS58 Wessex HC2 [S]	RAF No 72 Sqn, Aldergrove	
XT669	WS58 Wessex HC2 (8894M) [T]	RAF Aldergrove, Fire Section	
XT670	WS58 Wessex HC2	RAF SARTU, Valley	
XT671	WS58 Wessex HC2 [D]	RAF No 60 Sqn, Benson	
XT672	WS58 Wessex FG2 [WE]	RAF No 2 FTS, Shawbury	
XT673	WS58 Wessex HC2 [G]	RAF No 28 Sqn, Sek Kong	
XT675	WS58 Wessex HC2 [C]	RAF No 28 Sqn, Sek Kong	
XT676	WS58 Wessex HC2 [I]	RAF No 72 Sqn, Aldergrove	
XT677	WS58 Wessex HC2 (8016M)	RAF Brize Norton Fire Section	
XT678	WS58 Wessex HC2 [H]	RAF No 28 Sqn, Sek Kong	
XT680	WS58 Wessex HC2	RAF No 84 Sqn, Akrotiri	
XT681	WS58 Wessex HC2 [U]	RAF No 72 Sqn, Aldergrove	
XT684	McD Phantom FG1 (8998M/ XT864) [BJ]	Repainted as XT864, 1994	
XT752	Fairey Gannet T5 (WN365/ G-APYO)	Privately owned	
XT755	WS58 Wessex HU5 (9053M) [V]	Privately owned, Bruntingthorpe	
XT756	WS58 Wessex HU5 [ZJ]	RN, Lee-on-Solent, Fire Section	

Notes	Serial	Type (other identity) [code]	Owner/operator, location or fate
	XT759	WS58 Wessex HU5 [XY]	RN Fleetlands, derelict
	XT760	WS58 Wessex HU5 [418]	RN ETS, Culdrose
	XT761	WS58 Wessex HU5	RN AES, Lee-on-Solent
	XT762	WS58 Wessex HU5	RNAS Culdrose, SAH
	XT765	WS58 Wessex HU5 [J]	RN AES, Lee-on-Solent
	XT766	WS58 Wessex HU5 (9054M) [822/CU]	Privately owned, Shawell, Leics
	XT768	WS58 Wessex HU5	*Sunk in Stoney Cove Lake, Leics, Feb 1992*
	XT769	WS58 Wessex HU5 [823]	FAA Museum, RNAS Yeovilton
	XT770	WS58 Wessex HU5 (9055M)	RAF Halton
	XT771	WS58 Wessex HU5 [620/PO]	RN AES, Lee-on-Solent
	XT772	WS58 Wessex HU5 (8805M)	RAF Valley, SARTU, ground instruction
	XT773	WS58 Wessex HU5 (9123M)	RAF St Athan, BDRT
	XT778	WS Wasp HAS1 [430]	RN AES, Lee-on-Solent
	XT780	WS Wasp HAS1 [636]	RNAY Fleetlands Apprentice School
	XT788	WS Wasp HAS1 [442] (G-BMIR)	Privately owned, Charlwood, Surrey
	XT793	WS Wasp HAS1 [456]	Privately owned, Bruntingthorpe
	XT803	WS Sioux AH1 [Y]	Privately owned
	XT827	WS Sioux AH1 [D] (spares)	AAC Historic Aircraft Flight, Middle Wallop
	XT852	McD Phantom FGR2	MoD(PE) T&EE, West Freugh Fire Section
	XT853	McD Phantom FGR2 (9071M)	RAF Scampton Fire Section
	XT858	McD Phantom FG1	MoD(PE), stored Aston Down
	XT864	McD Phantom FG1 (8998M/ XT684) [BJ]	RAF Leuchars on display
	XT867	McD Phantom FG1 (9064M) [BH]	RAF Leuchars BDRT
	XT874	McD Phantom FG1 (9068M) [BE]	*Scrapped at Bruntingthorpe, February 1994*
	XT891	McD Phantom FGR2 (9136M)	RAF Coningsby, on display
	XT895	McD Phantom FGR2 (9171M) [Q]	RAF Valley, Fire Section
	XT896	McD Phantom FGR2 [V]	RAF, stored Shawbury
	XT897	McD Phantom FGR2 [N]	RAF, stored Shawbury
	XT900	McD Phantom FGR2 (9099M) [CO]	RAF Honington, BDRT
	XT903	McD Phantom FGR2 [X]	RAF Leuchars, BDRT
	XT905	McD Phantom FGR2 [P]	RAF Coningsby, stored
	XT907	McD Phantom FGR2 (9151M) [W]	Defence School, Chattenden
	XT910	McD Phantom FGR2	RAF, stored Shawbury
	XT911	McD Phantom FGR2 <ff>	Wales Aircraft Museum, Cardiff
	XT914	McD Phantom FGR2 [Z]	RAF Leeming
	XV101	BAC VC10 C1K	RAF No 10 Sqn, Brize Norton
	XV102	BAC VC10 C1K	RAF No 10 Sqn, Brize Norton
	XV103	BAC VC10 C1K	RAF No 10 Sqn, Brize Norton
	XV104	BAC VC10 C1K	RAF No 10 Sqn, Brize Norton
	XV105	BAC VC10 C1K	RAF No 10 Sqn, Brize Norton
	XV106	BAC VC10 C1K	RAF No 10 Sqn, Brize Norton
	XV107	BAC VC10 C1	RAF No 10 Sqn, Brize Norton
	XV108	BAC VC10 C1	RAF No 10 Sqn, Brize Norton
	XV109	BAC VC10 C1K	RAF No 10 Sqn, Brize Norton
	XV118	WS Scout AH1 (9141M)	RAF Air Movements School, Brize Norton
	XV119	WS Scout AH1 [T]	AAC, Netheravon, BDRT
	XV121	WS Scout AH1	AAC, stored RNAY Fleetlands
	XV122	WS Scout AH1 [D]	AAC, stored RNAW Almondbank
	XV123	WS Scout AH1	AAC, stored RNAY Fleetlands
	XV124	WS Scout AH1 [W]	AAC SAE, Middle Wallop
	XV126	WS Scout AH1 [X]	AAC, stored RNAY Fleetlands
	XV127	WS Scout AH1	AAC, stored RNAY Fleetlands
	XV128	WS Scout AH1	AAC, stored RNAY Fleetlands
	XV129	WS Scout AH1 [V]	AAC, stored RNAY Fleetlands
	XV130	WS Scout AH1 [R]	AAC, stored RNAY Fleetlands
	XV131	WS Scout AH1 [Y]	AAC Middle Wallop, BDRT
	XV134	WS Scout AH1 [P]	AAC, stored RNAY Fleetlands
	XV135	WS Scout AH1	AAC
	XV136	WS Scout AH1 [X]	AAC Netheravon, on display
	XV137	WS Scout AH1	AAC, stored RNAY Fleetlands
	XV138	WS Scout AH1	AAC, stored RNAW Almondbank
	XV139	WS Scout AH1	Army Apprentice College, Arborfield
	XV140	WS Scout AH1 [K]	AAC, stored RNAY Fleetlands
	XV141	WS Scout AH1	Army Apprentice College, Arborfield
	XV147	HS Nimrod MR1(mod)	MoD(PE), BAe Warton
	XV148	HS Nimrod MR1(mod)	MoD(PE), BAe Woodford
	XV161	HS Buccaneer S2B (9117M)	*Scrapped at Lossiemouth, March 1994*
	XV163	HS Buccaneer S2A <ff>	Privately owned, Bruntingthorpe

Serial	Type (other identity) [code]	Owner/operator, location or fate	Notes
XV165	HS Buccaneer S2B	*Scrapped at Shawbury, February 1994*	
XV168	HS Buccaneer S2B	BAe Brough, on display	
XV176	Lockheed Hercules C3	RAF Lyneham Transport Wing	
XV177	Lockheed Hercules C3	RAF Lyneham Transport Wing	
XV178	Lockheed Hercules C1	RAF Lyneham Transport Wing	
XV179	Lockheed Hercules C1	RAF Lyneham Transport Wing	
XV181	Lockheed Hercules C1	RAF Lyneham Transport Wing	
XV182	Lockheed Hercules C1	RAF Lyneham Transport Wing	
XV183	Lockheed Hercules C3	RAF Lyneham Transport Wing	
XV184	Lockheed Hercules C3	RAF Lyneham Transport Wing	
XV185	Lockheed Hercules C1	RAF Lyneham Transport Wing	
XV186	Lockheed Hercules C1	RAF Lyneham Transport Wing	
XV187	Lockheed Hercules C1	RAF Lyneham Transport Wing	
XV188	Lockheed Hercules C3	RAF Lyneham Transport Wing	
XV189	Lockheed Hercules C3	RAF Lyneham Transport Wing	
XV190	Lockheed Hercules C3	RAF Lyneham Transport Wing	
XV191	Lockheed Hercules C1	RAF Lyneham Transport Wing	
XV192	Lockheed Hercules C1	RAF Lyneham Transport Wing	
XV195	Lockheed Hercules C1	RAF Lyneham Transport Wing	
XV196	Lockheed Hercules C1	RAF Lyneham Transport Wing	
XV197	Lockheed Hercules C3	RAF Lyneham Transport Wing	
XV199	Lockheed Hercules C3	RAF Lyneham Transport Wing	
XV200	Lockheed Hercules C1	RAF Lyneham Transport Wing	
XV201	Lockheed Hercules C1K	RAF Lyneham Transport Wing	
XV202	Lockheed Hercules C3	RAF Lyneham Transport Wing	
XV203	Lockheed Hercules C1K	RAF Lyneham Transport Wing	
XV204	Lockheed Hercules C1K	RAF No 1312 Flt, Mount Pleasant, FI	
XV205	Lockheed Hercules C1	RAF Lyneham Transport Wing	
XV206	Lockheed Hercules C1	RAF Lyneham Transport Wing	
XV207	Lockheed Hercules C3	RAF Lyneham Transport Wing	
XV208	Lockheed Hercules W2	MoD(PE) MRF, Boscombe Down	
XV209	Lockheed Hercules C3	RAF Lyneham Transport Wing	
XV210	Lockheed Hercules C1	RAF Lyneham Transport Wing	
XV211	Lockheed Hercules C1	RAF Lyneham Transport Wing	
XV212	Lockheed Hercules C3	RAF Lyneham Transport Wing	
XV213	Lockheed Hercules C1K	RAF Lyneham Transport Wing	
XV214	Lockheed Hercules C3	RAF Lyneham Transport Wing	
XV215	Lockheed Hercules C1	RAF Lyneham Transport Wing	
XV217	Lockheed Hercules C3	RAF Lyneham Transport Wing	
XV218	Lockheed Hercules C1	RAF Lyneham Transport Wing	
XV219	Lockheed Hercules C3	MoD(PE), A&AEE Boscombe Down	
XV220	Lockheed Hercules C3	RAF Lyneham Transport Wing	
XV221	Lockheed Hercules C3	RAF Lyneham Transport Wing	
XV222	Lockheed Hercules C3	RAF Lyneham Transport Wing	
XV223	Lockheed Hercules C3	RAF Lyneham Transport Wing	
XV226	HS Nimrod MR2	RAF No 120 Sqn, Kinloss	
XV227	HS Nimrod MR2	RAF No 120 Sqn, Kinloss	
XV228	HS Nimrod MR2	RAF No 201 Sqn, Kinloss	
XV229	HS Nimrod MR2	RAF No 206 Sqn, Kinloss	
XV230	HS Nimrod MR2	RAF No 201 Sqn, Kinloss	
XV231	HS Nimrod MR2	RAF No 206 Sqn, Kinloss	
XV232	HS Nimrod MR2	RAF No 201 Sqn, Kinloss	
XV233	HS Nimrod MR2	RAF No 206 Sqn, Kinloss	
XV234	HS Nimrod MR2	RAF, stored Kinloss	
XV235	HS Nimrod MR2	RAF No 120 Sqn, Kinloss	
XV236	HS Nimrod MR2	RAF No 42(R) Sqn, Kinloss	
XV238	HS Nimrod <R> (parts G-ALYW)	RAF EP&TU, St Athan	
XV240	HS Nimrod MR2	RAF No 120 Sqn, Kinloss	
XV241	HS Nimrod MR2	RAF No 201 Sqn, Kinloss	
XV242	HS Nimrod MR2	RAF, stored Kinloss	
XV243	HS Nimrod MR2	RAF No 120 Sqn, Kinloss	
XV244	HS Nimrod MR2	RAF No 201 Sqn, Kinloss	
XV245	HS Nimrod MR2	RAF No 120 Sqn, Kinloss	
XV246	HS Nimrod MR2	RAF No 206 Sqn, Kinloss	
XV247	HS Nimrod MR2	RAF, stored Kinloss	
XV248	HS Nimrod MR2	RAF No 206 Sqn, Kinloss	
XV249	HS Nimrod MR2	RAF, stored Kinloss	
XV250	HS Nimrod MR2	RAF No 120 Sqn, Kinloss	
XV251	HS Nimrod MR2	RAF No 206 Sqn, Kinloss	
XV252	HS Nimrod MR2	RAF No 206 Sqn, Kinloss	
XV253	HS Nimrod MR2 (9118M)	*Scrapped at Elgin, 1993*	
XV254	HS Nimrod MR2	RAF No 201 Sqn, Kinloss	

Notes	Serial	Type (other identity) [code]	Owner/operator, location or fate
	XV255	HS Nimrod MR2	RAF Kinloss MR Wing
	XV258	HS Nimrod MR2	RAF No 206 Sqn, Kinloss
	XV260	HS Nimrod MR2	RAF No 120 Sqn, Kinloss
	XV263	BAe Nimrod AEW3P (8967M)	RAF Air Engineer Sqn, Finningley
	XV268	DHC Beaver AL1 (G-BVER)	Privately owned
	XV269	DHC Beaver AL1 (8011M)	*Scrapped at Middle Wallop, 1990*
	XV277	HS Harrier GR3	RN ETS, Yeovilton
	XV279	HS Harrier GR1 (8566M) [44]	RAF Wittering WLT
	XV280	HS Harrier GR1 <ff>	RNAS Yeovilton, Fire Section
	XV281	HS Harrier GR3	BAe Warton, instructional use
	XV290	Lockheed Hercules C3	RAF Lyneham Transport Wing
	XV291	Lockheed Hercules C1	RAF Lyneham Transport Wing
	XV292	Lockheed Hercules C1	RAF Lyneham Transport Wing
	XV293	Lockheed Hercules C1	RAF Lyneham Transport Wing
	XV294	Lockheed Hercules C3	RAF Lyneham Transport Wing
	XV295	Lockheed Hercules C1	RAF Lyneham Transport Wing
	XV296	Lockheed Hercules C1K	RAF Lyneham Transport Wing
	XV297	Lockheed Hercules C1	RAF Lyneham Transport Wing
	XV298	Lockheed Hercules C1	RAF Lyneham Transport Wing
	XV299	Lockheed Hercules C3	RAF Lyneham Transport Wing
	XV300	Lockheed Hercules C1	RAF Lyneham Transport Wing
	XV301	Lockheed Hercules C3	RAF Lyneham Transport Wing
	XV302	Lockheed Hercules C3	RAF Lyneham Transport Wing
	XV303	Lockheed Hercules C3	RAF Lyneham Transport Wing
	XV304	Lockheed Hercules C3	RAF Lyneham Transport Wing
	XV305	Lockheed Hercules C3	RAF Lyneham Transport Wing
	XV306	Lockheed Hercules C1	RAF Lyneham Transport Wing
	XV307	Lockheed Hercules C3	RAF Lyneham Transport Wing
	XV328	BAC Lightning T5 [BZ]	*Scrapped at Cranfield, Nov 94*
	XV332	HS Buccaneer S2B	RAF Marham, Fire Section
	XV333	HS Buccaneer S2B [234/H]	FAA Museum, RNAS Yeovilton
	XV337	HS Buccaneer S2C (8852M)	RAF St Athan, BDRT
	XV338	HS Buccaneer S2A (8774M) <ff>	RAF EP&TU, St Athan
	XV344	HS Buccaneer S2C	MoD(PE), Farnborough, wfu
	XV350	HS Buccaneer S2B	East Midlands Aero Park
	XV352	HS Buccaneer S2B <ff>	RAF, stored St Athan
	XV353	HS Buccaneer S2B (9144M)	*Scrapped at Lossiemouth, February 1994*
	XV359	HS Buccaneer S2B	RN Predannack Fire School
	XV361	HS Buccaneer S2B	Ulster Aviation Society, Langford Lodge
	XV370	Sikorsky SH-3D	RN AES, Lee-on-Solent
	XV371	WS61 Sea King HAS1(DB)	MoD(PE) DRA, Boscombe Down
	XV372	WS61 Sea King HAS1	Privately owned, Trowbridge, Wilts
	XV393	McD Phantom FGR2 [Q]	RAF Marham, WLT
	XV399	McD Phantom FGR2 <ff>	Privately owned, Stock, Essex
	XV401	McD Phantom FGR2 [I]	MoD(PE) A&AEE, Boscombe Down, GI use
	XV402	McD Phantom FGR2 <ff>	Privately owned, Stock, Essex
	XV404	McD Phantom FGR2 [I]	*Scrapped at Stock, April 1994*
	XV406	McD Phantom FGR2 (9098M) [CK]	RAF Carlisle, on display
	XV408	McD Phantom FGR2 (9165M) [Z]	RAF Cranwell, on display
	XV411	McD Phantom FGR2 (9103M) [L]	FSCTE, RAF Manston
	XV415	McD Phantom FGR2 (9163M) [E]	RAF Boulmer, on display
	XV420	McD Phantom FGR2 [O]	AAC Wattisham, base museum
	XV422	McD Phantom FGR2 (9157M) [T]	Stornoway Airport, on display
	XV423	McD Phantom FGR2 [Y]	RAF Leeming, BDRT
	XV424	McD Phantom FGR2 (9152M) [I]	RAF Museum, Hendon
	XV426	McD Phantom FGR2 [P]	RAF Coningsby, BDRT
	XV433	McD Phantom FGR2 [E]	RAF, stored Shawbury
	XV435	McD Phantom FGR2 [R]	T&EE, Llanbedr, Fire Section
	XV460	McD Phantom FGR2 [R]	RAF Coningsby
	XV465	McD Phantom FGR2 [S]	RAF Leeming
	XV467	McD Phantom FGR2 (9158M) [F]	Benbecula Airport, on display
	XV468	McD Phantom FGR2 (9159M) [H]	RAF Woodvale, on display
	XV469	McD Phantom FGR2	RAF, stored Shawbury
	XV474	McD Phantom FGR2 [T]	The Old Flying Machine Company, Duxford
	XV482	McD Phantom FGR2 (9107M) [T]	RAF Leuchars, Fire Section
	XV487	McD Phantom FGR2 [G]	RAF, stored Shawbury
	XV489	McD Phantom FGR2 <ff>	Privately owned, Bruntingthorpe
	XV490	McD Phantom FGR2 <ff>	Privately owned, Bruntingthorpe
	XV497	McD Phantom FGR2 [W]	RAF Coningsby, BDRT
	XV499	McD Phantom FGR2	RAF Leeming, WLT
	XV500	McD Phantom FGR2 (9113M)	RAF St Athan, on display

Serial	Type (other identity) [code]	Owner/operator, location or fate	Notes
XV577	McD Phantom FG1 (9065M) [AM]	RAF Leuchars, BDRT	
XV581	McD Phantom FG1 (9070M) [AE]	RAF Buchan, on display	
XV582	McD Phantom FG1 (9066M) [M]	RAF Leuchars on display	
XV585	McD Phantom FG1 [AP]	RAF Leuchars	
XV586	McD Phantom FG1 (9067M) [AJ]	RAF Leuchars BDRT	
XV588	McD Phantom FG1 [007] <ff>	RN Predannack Fire School	
XV591	McD Phantom FG1 <ff>	RAF Cosford Aerospace Museum	
XV623	WS Wasp HAS1 [601]	*Scrapped at Portland*	
XV625	WS Wasp HAS1 [471]	RNEC Manadon, for instruction	
XV629	WS Wasp HAS1	AAC Middle Wallop, BDRT	
XV631	WS Wasp HAS1	*Scrapped at Farnborough, 1992*	
XV638	WS Wasp HAS1 (8826M) [430/A]	*Scrapped, 1991*	
XV639	WS Wasp HAS1 [612]	*Sold to the USA, April 1994*	
XV642	WS61 Sea King HAS2A	RN AES, Lee-on-Solent	
XV643	WS61 Sea King HAS6 [703/PW]	RN No 819 Sqn, Prestwick	
XV644	WS61 Sea King HAS6 [664]	RN Predannack Fire School	
XV647	WS61 Sea King HAR5 [820/CU]	RN No 771 Sqn, Culdrose	
XV648	WS61 Sea King HAS6 [582]	RN AMG, Culdrose	
XV649	WS61 Sea King AEW2A [184/R]	RN No 849 Sqn, Culdrose	
XV650	WS61 Sea King AEW2A [182/R]	RN No 849 Sqn, Culdrose	
XV651	WS61 Sea King HAS5 [591]	RNAY Fleetlands, stored	
XV653	WS61 Sea King HAS6 [500]	RN No 810 Sqn, Culdrose	
XV654	WS61 Sea King HAS6 [705/PW] (wreck)	RNAY Fleetlands, stored	
XV655	WS61 Sea King HAS5 [701/PW]	RN No 819 Sqn, Prestwick	
XV656	WS61 Sea King AEW2A [187/N]	RN AMG, Culdrose	
XV657	WS61 Sea King HAS5 [132]	RN ETS, Culdrose	
XV659	WS61 Sea King HAS6 [268/N]	RN No 814 Sqn, Culdrose	
XV660	WS61 Sea King HAS6 [698]	RN No 819 Sqn, Prestwick	
XV661	WS61 Sea King HAR5 [824/CU]	RN No 771 Sqn, Culdrose	
XV663	WS61 Sea King HAS6 [501/CU]	RN No 810 Sqn, Culdrose	
XV664	WS61 Sea King AEW2A [180]	RN No 849 Sqn, Culdrose	
XV665	WS61 Sea King HAS6 [505/CU]	RN No 810 Sqn, Culdrose	
XV666	WS61 Sea King HAR5 [823/CU]	RN No 771 Sqn, Culdrose	
XV669	WS61 Sea King HAS1 [10]	RN ETS, Culdrose	
XV670	WS61 Sea King HAS6 [592]	RNAY Fleetlands (conversion)	
XV671	WS61 Sea King AEW2A [186/R]	RN No 849 Sqn, Culdrose	
XV672	WS61 Sea King AEW2A [183/R]	RNAY Fleetlands	
XV673	WS61 Sea King HAS5 [588]	RNAY Fleetlands, stored	
XV674	WS61 Sea King HAS6	RN No 814 Sqn, Culdrose	
XV675	WS61 Sea King HAS6 [594]	RNAY Fleetlands	
XV676	WS61 Sea King HAS6 [515/CM]	RN No 810 Sqn, Culdrose	
XV677	WS61 Sea King HAS6 [269/N]	RN No 814 Sqn, Culdrose	
XV696	WS61 Sea King HAS6 [699]	RN No 814 Sqn, Culdrose	
XV697	WS61 Sea King AEW2A [185]	RN No 849 Sqn, Culdrose	
XV699	WS61 Sea King HAS6 [134]	RNAY Fleetlands (conversion)	
XV700	WS61 Sea King HAS6 [508]	RN No 810 Sqn, Culdrose	
XV701	WS61 Sea King HAS6 [010]	RN No 820 Sqn, Culdrose	
XV703	WS61 Sea King HAS6 [265/N]	RN No 814 Sqn, Culdrose	
XV704	WS61 Sea King AEW2A [183]	RN No 849 Sqn, Culdrose	
XV705	WS61 Sea King HAR5 [821/CU]	RN No 771 Sqn, Culdrose	
XV706	WS61 Sea King HAS6 [583/CU]	RN No 706 Sqn, Culdrose	
XV707	WS61 Sea King AEW2A [181]	RN No 849 Sqn, Culdrose	
XV708	WS61 Sea King HAS6 [510/CU]	RN No 810 Sqn, Culdrose	
XV709	WS61 Sea King HAS6 [585]	RNAY Fleetlands	
XV710	WS61 Sea King HAS6 [270/N]	RN AMG, Culdrose	
XV711	WS61 Sea King HAS6 [709/PW]	RN No 819 Sqn, Prestwick	
XV712	WS61 Sea King HAS6 [012]	RN No 820 Sqn, Culdrose	
XV713	WS61 Sea King HAS6 [018]	RN No 820 Sqn, Culdrose	
XV714	WS61 Sea King AEW2A [187/N]	RN No 849 Sqn, Culdrose	
XV720	WS58 Wessex HC2	RAF No 22 Sqn, C Flt/SARTU, Valley	
XV721	WS58 Wessex HC2 [H]	RAF No 72 Sqn, Aldergrove	
XV722	WS58 Wessex HC2 [WH]	RAF No 2 FTS, Shawbury	
XV723	WS58 Wessex HC2 [Q]	RAF No 72 Sqn, Aldergrove	
XV724	WS58 Wessex HC2	RAF No 22 Sqn, C Flt/SARTU, Valley	
XV725	WS58 Wessex HC2 [C]	RAF No 72 Sqn, Aldergrove	
XV726	WS58 Wessex HC2 [J]	RAF No 72 Sqn, Aldergrove	
XV728	WS58 Wessex HC2 [A]	RAF No 72 Sqn, Aldergrove	
XV729	WS58 Wessex HC2	RAF No 22 Sqn, C Flt/SARTU, Valley	
XV730	WS58 Wessex HC2	RAF No 84 Sqn, Akrotiri	
XV731	WS58 Wessex HC2 [Y]	RAF No 72 Sqn, Aldergrove	
XV732	WS58 Wessex HCC4	RAF, The Queen's Flight, Benson	
XV733	WS58 Wessex HCC4	RAF, The Queen's Flight, Benson	

Notes	Serial	Type (other identity) [code]	Owner/operator, location or fate
	XV738	HS Harrier GR3 (9074M) [B]	RAF Halton
	XV741	HS Harrier GR3 [1]	SAH, RNAS Culdrose
	XV744	HS Harrier GR3 (9167M) [3K]	R. Military College of Science, Shrivenham
	XV747	HS Harrier GR3 (8979M) (fuselage)	No 1803 Sqn ATC, Hucknall
	XV748	HS Harrier GR3 [3D]	Cranfield College of Aeronautics
	XV751	HS Harrier GR3	RN AES, Lee-on-Solent
	XV752	HS Harrier GR3 (9078M) [B]	RAF No 1 SoTT, Cosford
	XV753	HS Harrier GR3 (9075M) [3F]	SAH, RNAS Culdrose
	XV755	HS Harrier GR3 [M]	RNAS Yeovilton, Fire Section
	XV759	HS Harrier GR3 [O]	*To Pendine ranges by March 1994*
	XV760	HS Harrier GR3 [VL]	RNAS Yeovilton, ETS
	XV778	HS Harrier GR3 (9001M)	*Scrapped at RAF Valley, 1994*
	XV779	HS Harrier GR3 (8931M) [01,A]	RAF Wittering on display
	XV783	HS Harrier GR3 [N]	RN AES, Lee-on-Solent
	XV784	HS Harrier GR3 (8909M) <ff>	A&AEE, Boscombe Down
	XV786	HS Harrier GR3 <ff>	RN, Culdrose Fire Section
	XV786	HS Harrier GR3 [S] <rf>	RN, Predannack Fire School
	XV798	HS Harrier GR1 (mod)	Bristol Aero Collection, Banwell
	XV804	HS Harrier GR3	Defence NBC Centre, Winterbourne Gunner
	XV806	HS Harrier GR3 [E]	SAH, RNAS Culdrose
	XV808	HS Harrier GR3 (9076M) [3J]	SAH, RNAS Culdrose
	XV810	HS Harrier GR3 (9038M) [K]	RAF St Athan, BDRT
	XV814	DH Comet 4	MoD(PE) A&AEE, Boscombe Down, spares use
	XV863	HS Buccaneer S2B (9115M/ 9139M/9145M) [S]	RAF Lossiemouth, on display
	XV864	HS Buccaneer S2B	FSCTE, RAF Manston
	XV865	HS Buccaneer S2B (9226M)	RAF Coningsby, Fire Section
	XV867	HS Buccaneer S2B	RAF Lossiemouth
	XV869	HS Buccaneer S2B	*Scrapped at Shawbury, December 1993*
	XW175	HS Harrier T4A(mod)	MoD(PE), Cranfield Institute of Technology
	XW198	WS Puma HC1	RAF No 27(R) Sqn, Odiham
	XW199	WS Puma HC1	RAF No 27(R) Sqn, Odiham
	XW200	WS Puma HC1	RAF No 27(R) Sqn, Odiham
	XW201	WS Puma HC1	RAF No 27(R) Sqn, Odiham
	XW202	WS Puma HC1	RAF No 230 Sqn, Aldergrove
	XW204	WS Puma HC1	RAF No 33 Sqn, Odiham
	XW206	WS Puma HC1	RAF No 33 Sqn, Odiham
	XW207	VWS Puma HC1	RAF No 230 Sqn, Aldergrove
	XW208	WS Puma HC1 [C]	RAF No 33 Sqn, Aldergrove
	XW209	WS Puma HC1 [CF]	RAF No 230 Sqn, Aldergrove
	XW210	WS Puma HC1	RAF Odiham (on repair)
	XW211	WS Puma HC1 [CH]	MoD(PE) A&AEE, Boscombe Down
	XW212	WS Puma HC1	RAF No 230 Sqn, Aldergrove
	XW213	WS Puma HC1 [CJ]	RAF No 33 Sqn, Odiham
	XW214	WS Puma HC1	RAF No 33 Sqn, Odiham
	XW215	WS Puma HC1 [R]	Westland, Yeovil (on rebuild)
	XW216	WS Puma HC1	RAF No 230 Sqn, Aldergrove
	XW217	WS Puma HC1 [CS]	RAF No 230 Sqn, Aldergrove
	XW218	WS Puma HC1 [BW]	RAF No 18 Sqn, Laarbruch
	XW219	WS Puma HC1	RAF Odiham
	XW220	WS Puma HC1 [CZ]	RAF No 27(R) Sqn, Odiham
	XW221	WS Puma HC1 [CM]	RAF No 230 Sqn, Aldergrove
	XW222	WS Puma HC1 [BX]	RAF Odiham
	XW223	WS Puma HC1	RAF No 33 Sqn, Odiham
	XW224	WS Puma HC1	RAF No 18 Sqn, Laarbruch
	XW225	WS Puma HC1 [FE] (fuselage)	RAF Odiham
	XW226	WS Puma HC1 [BY]	RAF No 18 Sqn, Laarbruch
	XW227	WS Puma HC1 [BZ]	RAF No 18 Sqn, Laarbruch
	XW229	WS Puma HC1	RAF No 33 Sqn, Odiham
	XW231	WS Puma HC1	RAF No 27(R) Sqn, Odiham
	XW232	WS Puma HC1 [DJ]	RAF No 230 Sqn, Aldergrove
	XW234	WS Puma HC1	RAF No 230 Sqn, Aldergrove
	XW235	WS Puma HC1	RAF No 230 Sqn, Aldergrove
	XW236	WS Puma HC1	RAF No 33 Sqn, Odiham
	XW237	WS Puma HC1 [DL]	RAF No 230 Sqn, Aldergrove
	XW241	Sud SA330E Puma	DRA Avionics & Sensors Dept, Farnborough
	XW249	Cushioncraft CC7	Flambards Village Theme Park, Helston
	XW264	HS Harrier T2 <ff>	CARG store, RAF Innsworth

Serial	Type (other identity) [code]	Owner/operator, location or fate	Notes
XW265	HS Harrier T4A	RAF Wittering, instructional use	
XW266	HS Harrier T4N [719/VL]	RN No 899 Sqn, Yeovilton	
XW267	HS Harrier T4 [SA]	RAF SAOEU, Boscombe Down	
XW268	HS Harrier T4N [720]	RN AMG, Yeovilton	
XW269	HS Harrier T4	RAF Wittering	
XW270	HS Harrier T4 (fuselage)	Cranfield Institute of Technology	
XW271	HS Harrier T4 [X]	RAF Wittering, instructional use	
XW272	HS Harrier T4 (8783M) <ff>		
XW276	Aerospatiale SA341	North-East Aircraft Museum, Usworth	
XW280	WS Scout AH1 [Z]	*Withdrawn from use at Sek Kong, 1993*	
XW281	WS Scout AH1 [U]	AAC, stored RNAY Fleetlands	
XW282	WS Scout AH1 [W]	AAC, stored RNAY Fleetlands	
XW283	WS Scout AH1	AAC, stored RNAY Fleetlands	
XW284	WS Scout AH1 [A] (fuselage)	AAC, stored RNAW Almondbank	
XW287	BAC Jet Provost T5 [P]	*Sold to USA as N4107K, July 1994*	
XW289	BAC Jet Provost T5A [73]	RAF, stored Shawbury	
XW290	BAC Jet Provost T5A (9199M) [41]	RAF No 1 SoTT, Cosford	
XW291	BAC Jet Provost T5 [N]	RAF, stored Shawbury	
XW292	BAC Jet Provost T5A (9128M) [32]	RAF Halton	
XW293	BAC Jet Provost T5 [Z]	RAF, stored Shawbury	
XW294	BAC Jet Provost T5A (9129M) [45]	RAF Halton	
XW296	BAC Jet Provost T5 [Q]	*Sold to USA as N4107G, July 1994*	
XW299	BAC Jet Provost T5A (9146M) [60]	RAF No 1 SoTT, Cosford	
XW301	BAC Jet Provost T5A (9147M) [63]	RAF No 1 SoTT, Cosford	
XW302	BAC Jet Provost T5 [T]	RAF, stored Shawbury	
XW303	BAC Jet Provost T5A (9119M) [127]	RAF Halton	
XW304	BAC Jet Provost T5 (9172M) [MD]	RAF No 1 SoTT, Cosford	
XW305	BAC Jet Provost T5A [42]	RAF, stored Shawbury	
XW306	BAC Jet Provost T5 [O]	RAF, stored Shawbury	
XW307	BAC Jet Provost T5 [S]	*Sold to USA as N4107U, July 1994*	
XW309	BAC Jet Provost T5 (9179M) [V]	RAF No 1 SoTT, Cosford	
XW310	BAC Jet Provost T5A [37]	RAF, stored Shawbury	
XW311	BAC Jet Provost T5 (9180M) [W]	RAF No 1 SoTT, Cosford	
XW312	BAC Jet Provost T5A (9109M) [64]	RAF No 1 SoTT, Cosford	
XW315	BAC Jet Provost T5A	Privately owned, Long Marston	
XW317	BAC Jet Provost T5A [79]	RAF, stored Shawbury	
XW318	BAC Jet Provost T5A (9190M) [78]	RAF No 1 SoTT, Cosford	
XW319	BAC Jet Provost T5A [76]	RAF, stored Shawbury	
XW320	BAC Jet Provost T5A (9015M) [71]	RAF Halton	
XW321	BAC Jet Provost T5A (9154M) [62]	RAF No 1 SoTT, Cosford	
XW322	BAC Jet Provost T5B [D]	RAF, stored Shawbury	
XW323	BAC Jet Provost T5A (9166M) [86]	RAF Museum, Hendon	
XW324	BAC Jet Provost T5 [U]	RAF, stored Shawbury	
XW325	BAC Jet Provost T5B [E]	RAF, stored Shawbury	
XW326	BAC Jet Provost T5A [62]	RAF, stored Shawbury	
XW327	BAC Jet Provost T5A (9130M) [62]	RAF Halton	
XW328	BAC Jet Provost T5A (9177M) [MI]	RAF No 1 SoTT, Cosford	
XW330	BAC Jet Provost T5A (9195M) [82,MJ]	RAF No 1 SoTT, Cosford	
XW333	BAC Jet Provost T5A (G-BVTC) [79]	Privately owned, Binbrook	
XW335	BAC Jet Provost T5A (9061M) [74]	RAF Halton	
XW336	BAC Jet Provost T5A [67]	RAF, stored Shawbury	
XW351	BAC Jet Provost T5A (9062M) [31]	RAF Halton	
XW352	BAC Jet Provost T5 [R]	Privately owned, stored Tamworth	
XW353	BAC Jet Provost T5A (9090M) [3]	RAF Cranwell, on display	
XW354	BAC Jet Provost T5A [70]	*Sold to the USA as N300LT, Feb 1994*	
XW355	BAC Jet Provost T5A [20]	RAF, stored Shawbury	
XW358	BAC Jet Provost T5A (9181M) [59]	RAF No 1 SoTT, Cosford	
XW359	BAC Jet Provost T5B [65]	*Sold to USA as N400LT, Feb 1994*	
XW360	BAC Jet Provost T5A (9153M) [61,ML]	RAF No 1 SoTT, Cosford	
XW361	BAC Jet Provost T5A (9192M) [81,MM]	RAF No 1 SoTT, Cosford	
XW363	BAC Jet Provost T5A [36]	BAe, Training School, Warton	
XW364	BAC Jet Provost T5A (9188M) [35]	RAF No 1 SoTT, Cosford	
XW365	BAC Jet Provost T5A (9018M) [73]	RAF Halton	
XW366	BAC Jet Provost T5A (9097M) [75]	RAF Halton	
XW367	BAC Jet Provost T5A (9193M) [64]	RAF No 1 SoTT, Cosford	
XW368	BAC Jet Provost T5A [66]	*Sold to the USA as N600LT, Feb 1994*	

Notes	Serial	Type (other identity) [code]	Owner/operator, location or fate
	XW369	BAC Jet Provost T5A [69]	*Sold to the USA as N800LT, Feb 1994.*
	XW370	BAC Jet Provost T5A (9196M) [72]	RAF No 1 SoTT, Cosford
	XW372	BAC Jet Provost T5A [M]	RAF, stored Shawbury
	XW375	BAC Jet Provost T5A (9149M) [52]	RAF Halton
	XW404	BAC Jet Provost T5A (9049M)	RAF CTTS, St Athan
	XW405	BAC Jet Provost T5A (9187M) [J]	RAF No 1 SoTT, Cosford
	XW406	BAC Jet Provost T5A [23]	Privately owned, stored Tamworth
	XW409	BAC Jet Provost T5A (9047M)	RAF CTTS, St Athan
	XW410	BAC Jet Provost T5A (9125M) [80]	RAF No 1 SoTT, Cosford
	XW412	BAC Jet Provost T5A [74]	RAF, stored Shawbury
	XW413	BAC Jet Provost T5A (9126M) [69]	RAF Halton
	XW415	BAC Jet Provost T5A [80]	*Sold to the USA as N900LT, Feb 1994*
	XW416	BAC Jet Provost T5A (9191M) [84,MS]	RAF No 1 SoTT, Cosford
	XW418	BAC Jet Provost T5A (9173M) [60]	RAF No 1 SoTT, Cosford
	XW419	BAC Jet Provost T5A (9120M) [125]	RAF Halton
	XW420	BAC Jet Provost T5A (9194M) [83]	RAF No 1 SoTT, Cosford
	XW421	BAC Jet Provost T5A (9111M) [60]	RAF No 1 SoTT, Cosford
	XW422	BAC Jet Provost T5A [3]	RAF, stored Shawbury
	XW423	BAC Jet Provost T5A [14]	RAF, stored Shawbury
	XW425	BAC Jet Provost T5A (9200M) [H]	RAF No 1 SoTT, Cosford
	XW427	BAC Jet Provost T5A (9124M) [67]	RAF Halton
	XW428	BAC Jet Provost T5A [39]	DRA Farnborough Apprentice School
	XW429	BAC Jet Provost T5B [C]	RAF, stored Shawbury
	XW430	BAC Jet Provost T5A (9176M) [MW]	RAF No 1 SoTT, Cosford
	XW431	BAC Jet Provost T5B [A]	RAF, stored Shawbury
	XW432	BAC Jet Provost T5A (9127M) [76]	RAF No 1 SoTT, Cosford
	XW433	BAC Jet Provost T5A [63]	RAF, stored Shawbury
	XW434	BAC Jet Provost T5A (9091M) [78]	RAF No 1 SoTT, Cosford
	XW436	BAC Jet Provost T5A (9148M) [68]	RAF Halton
	XW437	BAC Jet Provost T5A [71]	RAF, stored Shawbury
	XW438	BAC Jet Provost T5B [B]	RAF, stored Shawbury
	XW527	HS Buccaneer S2B <ff>	RAF, stored St Athan
	XW528	HS Buccaneer S2B (8861M) [C]	RAF Coningsby Fire Section
	XW530	HS Buccaneer S2B	Privately owned, Elgin
	XW542	HS Buccaneer S2B	*Scrapped at Lossiemouth, February 1994*
	XW544	HS Buccaneer S2B (8857M) [Y]	Privately owned
	XW547	HS Buccaneer S2B (9095M/9169M) [R]	RAF Cosford Aerospace Museum
	XW549	HS Buccaneer S2B (8860M) (fuselage)	RAF Kinloss, BDRT
	XW550	HS Buccaneer S2B <ff>	Privately owned, West Horndon, Essex
	XW566	SEPECAT Jaguar T2	DRA Avionics & Sensors Dept, Farnborough
	XW612	WS Scout AH1 [A]	Privately owned, Lincolnshire
	XW613	WS Scout AH1 [W]	Privately owned, Lincolnshire
	XW614	WS Scout AH1	AAC Historic Flight, Middle Wallop
	XW616	WS Scout AH1	AAC No 70 MU, Middle Wallop
	XW626	DH Comet 4AEW	*Scrapped at Bedford, April 1994*
	XW630	HS Harrier GR3	RN AES, Lee-on-Solent
	XW635	Beagle D5/180 (G-AWSW)	Privately owned
	XW664	HS Nimrod R1	RAF No 51 Sqn, Wyton
	XW665	HS Nimrod R1	RAF No 51 Sqn, Wyton
	XW666	HS Nimrod R1	RAF No 51 Sqn, Wyton
	XW750	HS748 Series 107	MoD(PE), DRA Boscombe Down
	XW763	HS Harrier GR3 (9002M/9041M) (fuselage)	Imperial War Museum, stored Duxford
	XW764	HS Harrier GR3 (8981M)	RAF Leeming, Fire Section
	XW768	HS Harrier GR3 (9072M) [N]	RAF Halton
	XW784	Mitchell-Procter Kittiwake I (G-BBRN)	Privately owned, Haverfordwest
	XW788	HS125 CC1	*Sold as G-BVTP/N255TS, September 1994*
	XW789	HS125 CC1	*Sold as G-BVTR/N264TS, September 1994*
	XW790	HS125 CC1	*Sold as G-BVTS/N266TS, September 1994*
	XW791	HS125 CC1	*Sold as G-BVTT/N268TS, September 1994*
	XW795	WS Scout AH1 (fuselage)	AAC, stored Middle Wallop
	XW796	WS Scout AH1 [X]	AAC SAE, Middle Wallop
	XW797	WS Scout AH1 [G]	*Withdrawn from use at Sek Kong, 1993*
	XW798	WS Scout AH1	AAC, Middle Wallop
	XW799	WS Scout AH1	AAC, stored RNAY Fleetlands
	XW835	WS Lynx	AAC Dishforth, GI use

Serial	Type (other identity) [code]	Owner/operator, location or fate	Notes
XW836	WS Lynx	DRA, Lasham	
XW837	WS Lynx (fuselage)	IHM, Weston-super-Mare	
XW838	WS Lynx [TAD 009]	AAC SAE, Middle Wallop	
XW839	WS Lynx	RNAS Yeovilton, Fire Section	
XW843	WS Gazelle AH1	AAC SAE, Middle Wallop	
XW844	WS Gazelle AH1	AAC 1 Regiment, Gütersloh	
XW845	WS Gazelle HT2 [47/CU]	RN No 705 Sqn, Culdrose	
XW846	WS Gazelle AH1 [M]	AAC, RNAY Fleetlands	
XW847	WS Gazelle AH1	AAC No 665 Sqn, Aldergrove	
XW848	WS Gazelle AH1 [D]	AAC No 670 Sqn, Middle Wallop	
XW849	WS Gazelle AH1 [G]	RM 3 CBAS, Yeovilton	
XW851	WS Gazelle AH1 [H]	RM 3 CBAS, Yeovilton	
XW852	WS Gazelle HCC4	RAF No 32 Sqn, Northolt	
XW853	WS Gazelle HT2 [53/CU]	RN No 705 Sqn, Culdrose	
XW854	WS Gazelle HT2 [46/CU]	RN No 705 Sqn, Culdrose	
XW855	WS Gazelle HCC4	RAF No 32 Sqn, Northolt	
XW856	WS Gazelle HT2 [49/CU]	RN No 705 Sqn, Culdrose	
XW857	WS Gazelle HT2 [55/CU]	RN No 705 Sqn, Culdrose	
XW858	WS Gazelle HT3 [C]	RAF No 2 FTS, Shawbury	
XW860	WS Gazelle HT2	AAC SAE, Middle Wallop	
XW861	WS Gazelle HT2 [52/CU]	RN No 705 Sqn, Culdrose	
XW862	WS Gazelle HT3 [D]	RAF No 2 FTS, Shawbury	
XW863	WS Gazelle HT2 [42/CU]	AAC SAE, Middle Wallop	
XW864	WS Gazelle HT2 [54/CU]	RN No 705 Sqn, Culdrose	
XW865	WS Gazelle AH1 [C]	AAC No 670 Sqn, Middle Wallop	
XW866	WS Gazelle HT3 [E]	RAF No 2 FTS, Shawbury	
XW868	WS Gazelle HT2 [50/CU]	RN No 705 Sqn, Culdrose	
XW870	WS Gazelle HT3 [F]	RAF No 2 FTS, Shawbury	
XW871	WS Gazelle HT2 [44/CU]	RN No 705 Sqn, Culdrose	
XW884	WS Gazelle HT2 [41/CU]	RN No 705 Sqn, Culdrose	
XW885	WS Gazelle AH1 [B]	AAC, stored, RNAY Fleetlands	
XW887	WS Gazelle HT2 [FL]	RNAY Fleetlands Station Flight	
XW888	WS Gazelle AH1	AAC SAE, Middle Wallop	
XW889	WS Gazelle AH1	AAC SAE, Middle Wallop	
XW890	WS Gazelle HT2 [53] (fuselage)	RN, stored Fleetlands	
XW891	WS Gazelle HT2 [49] (fuselage)	RNAS Culdrose, Fire Section	
XW892	WS Gazelle AH1	AAC No 658 Sqn, Dishforth	
XW893	WS Gazelle AH1	AAC No 665 Sqn, Aldergrove	
XW894	WS Gazelle HT2 [37/CU]	RN No 705 Sqn, Culdrose	
XW895	WS Gazelle HT2 [51/CU]	RN FONA, Yeovilton	
XW897	WS Gazelle AH1 [Z]	AAC No 670 Sqn, Middle Wallop	
XW898	WS Gazelle HT3 [G]	RAF No 2 FTS, Shawbury	
XW899	WS Gazelle AH1 [K]	AAC, stored RNAY Fleetlands	
XW900	WS Gazelle AH1 (TAD-900)	AAC SAE, Middle Wallop	
XW902	WS Gazelle HT3 [H]	RAF No 18 Sqn, Laarbruch	
XW903	WS Gazelle AH1	AAC 1 Regiment, Gütersloh	
XW904	WS Gazelle AH1	AAC, stored RNAY Fleetlands	
XW906	WS Gazelle HT3 [J]	RAF No 2 FTS, Shawbury	
XW907	WS Gazelle HT2 [48/CU]	RN No 705 Sqn, Culdrose	
XW908	WS Gazelle AH1 [E]	AAC No 670 Sqn, Middle Wallop	
XW909	WS Gazelle AH1	AAC 1 Regiment, Gütersloh	
XW910	WS Gazelle HT3 [K]	RAF No 2 FTS, Shawbury	
XW911	WS Gazelle AH1 [I]	AAC No 670 Sqn, Middle Wallop	
XW912	WS Gazelle AH1	AAC, stored RNAY Fleetlands	
XW913	WS Gazelle AH1	AAC 3 Regiment, Wattisham	
XW916	HS Harrier GR3 [W]	RAF Wittering, Fire Section	
XW919	HS Harrier GR3 [W]	RN SAH, Culdrose	
XW923	HS Harrier GR3 (8724M) <ff>	RAF Wittering for rescue training	
XW924	HS Harrier GR3 (9073M) [G]	To Laarbruch for BDRT, 1994	
XW927	HS Harrier T4 [02]	RAF Laarbruch	
XW930	HS125-1B	MoD(PE), stored Farnborough	
XW934	HS Harrier T4 [Y]	RAF No 1 Sqn, Wittering	
XW986	HS Buccaneer S2B	MoD(PE), T&EE West Freugh, instructional use	
XW987	HS Buccaneer S2B	MoD(PE) A&AEE, Boscombe Down	
XW988	HS Buccaneer S2B	MoD(PE) A&AEE, Boscombe Down	
XX101	Cushioncraft CC7	IHM, Weston-super-Mare	
XX102	Cushioncraft CC7	Museum of Army Transport, Beverley	
XX105	BAC 1-11/201	MoD(PE) DRA, Boscombe Down	
XX108	SEPECAT Jaguar GR1	RAF St Athan	
XX109	SEPECAT Jaguar GR1 (8918M) [US]	RAF Coltishall, ground instruction	

Notes	Serial	Type (other identity) [code]	Owner/operator, location or fate
	XX110	SEPECAT Jaguar GR1 <R> (BAPC 169)	RAF Halton
	XX110	SEPECAT Jaguar GR1 (8955M) [EP]	RAF No 1 SoTT, Cosford
	XX112	SEPECAT Jaguar GR1A [EC]	RAF, stored Shawbury
	XX116	SEPECAT Jaguar GR1A	RAF No 16(R) Sqn, Lossiemouth
	XX117	SEPECAT Jaguar GR1A [06]	MoD(PE), DRA Boscombe Down
	XX119	SEPECAT Jaguar GR1A (8898M) [A]	RAF No 16(R) Sqn, Lossiemouth
	XX121	SEPECAT Jaguar GR1 [EQ]	RAF, stored Shawbury
	XX139	SEPECAT Jaguar T2A [T]	RAF No 16(R) Sqn, Lossiemouth
	XX140	SEPECAT Jaguar T2 (9008M) [D]	RAF No 1 SoTT, Cosford
	XX141	SEPECAT Jaguar T2A [Z]	RAF No 16(R) Sqn, Lossiemouth
	XX143	SEPECAT Jaguar T2A	RAF St Athan
	XX144	SEPECAT Jaguar T2A [U]	RAF No 16(R) Sqn, Lossiemouth
	XX145	SEPECAT Jaguar T2	MoD(PE) ETPS, Boscombe Down
	XX146	SEPECAT Jaguar T2A [X]	RAF No 16(R) Sqn, Lossiemouth
	XX150	SEPECAT Jaguar T2A [W]	RAF No 16(R) Sqn, Lossiemouth
	XX154	HS Hawk T1 [1]	MoD(PE), T&EE Llanbedr
	XX156	HS Hawk T1	MoD(PE), A&AEE Boscombe Down
	XX157	HS Hawk T1A [B]	RAF
	XX158	HS Hawk T1A	RAF
	XX159	HS Hawk T1A [PA]	RAF CFS/No 19(R) Sqn, Valley
	XX160	HS Hawk T1	MoD(PE), T&EE Llanbedr
	XX161	HS Hawk T1	RAF No 4 FTS/208(R) Sqn, Valley
	XX162	HS Hawk T1	MoD(PE) IAM, Boscombe Down
	XX163	HS Hawk T1 [PH] (wreck)	RAF Valley
	XX164	HS Hawk T1 [CN]	RAF No 100 Sqn, Finningley
	XX165	HS Hawk T1	RN FRADU, Yeovilton
	XX167	HS Hawk T1 [Q]	RAF No 4 FTS/74(R) Sqn, Valley
	XX168	HS Hawk T1	RAF No 6 FTS, Finningley
	XX169	HS Hawk T1	RAF No 6 FTS, Finningley
	XX170	HS Hawk T1	MoD(PE), T&EE Llanbedr
	XX171	HS Hawk T1 [DW]	RAF No 4 FTS/208(R) Sqn, Valley
	XX172	HS Hawk T1	RAF St Athan Station Flight
	XX173	HS Hawk T1	RAF No 6 FTS, Finningley
	XX174	HS Hawk T1	RAF No 4 FTS, Valley
	XX175	HS Hawk T1	RN FRADU, Yeovilton
	XX176	HS Hawk T1 [CO]	RAF No 100 Sqn, Finningley
	XX177	HS Hawk T1 [TD]	RAF No 4 FTS/74(R) Sqn, Valley
	XX178	HS Hawk T1 [M]	RAF CFS/No 19(R) Sqn, Valley
	XX179	HS Hawk T1 [E]	RAF No 4 FTS/74(R) Sqn, Valley
	XX181	HS Hawk T1	RAF No 4 FTS/208(R) Sqn, Valley
	XX183	HS Hawk T1	RN FRADU, Yeovilton
	XX184	HS Hawk T1	RAF St Athan Station Flight
	XX185	HS Hawk T1	RAF
	XX186	HS Hawk T1A [DD]	RAF No 4 FTS/208(R) Sqn, Valley
	XX187	HS Hawk T1A [PB]	RAF CFS/No 19(R) Sqn, Valley
	XX188	HS Hawk T1A [CG]	RAF No 100 Sqn, Finningley
	XX189	HS Hawk T1A [TB]	RAF No 4 FTS/74(R) Sqn, Valley
	XX190	HS Hawk T1A	RAF No 4 FTS, Valley
	XX191	HS Hawk T1A [DT]	RAF No 4 FTS/208(R) Sqn, Valley
	XX193	HS Hawk T1A [TT]	RAF No 4 FTS/74(R) Sqn, Valley
	XX194	HS Hawk T1A [TI]	RAF No 4 FTS/74(R) Sqn, Valley
	XX195	HS Hawk T1 [CA]	RAF No 100 Sqn, Finningley
	XX196	HS Hawk T1A [DB]	RAF No 4 FTS/208(R) Sqn, Valley
	XX198	HS Hawk T1A [DC]	RAF No 4 FTS/208(R) Sqn, Valley
	XX199	HS Hawk T1A [TG]	RAF No 4 FTS/74(R) Sqn, Valley
	XX200	HS Hawk T1A [CF]	RAF No 100 Sqn, Finningley
	XX201	HS Hawk T1A	RAF
	XX202	HS Hawk T1A	RAF No 4 FTS, Valley
	XX203	HS Hawk T1A [PC]	RAF CFS/No 19(R) Sqn, Valley
	XX204	HS Hawk T1A [H]	RAF No 4 FTS, Valley
	XX205	HS Hawk T1A	RAF
	XX217	HS Hawk T1A	RAF CFS/No 19(R) Sqn, Valley
	XX218	HS Hawk T1A [TQ]	RAF No 4 FTS/74(R) Sqn, Valley
	XX219	HS Hawk T1A	RAF
	XX220	HS Hawk T1A [PD]	RAF CFS/No 19(R) Sqn, Valley
	XX221	HS Hawk T1A [DG]	RAF No 4 FTS/208(R) Sqn, Valley
	XX222	HS Hawk T1A [TJ]	RAF No 4 FTS/74(R) Sqn, Valley
	XX223	HS Hawk T1 (fuselage)	Privately owned, Charlwood, Surrey
	XX224	HS Hawk T1 [PM]	RAF CFS/No 19(R) Sqn, Valley
	XX225	HS Hawk T1	RAF No 4 FTS/74 Sqn, Valley

Serial	Type (other identity) [code]	Owner/operator, location or fate	Notes
XX226	HS Hawk T1 [74]	RAF No 4 FTS/74(R) Sqn, Valley	
XX227	HS Hawk T1	RAF *Red Arrows*, Scampton	
XX228	HS Hawk T1 [CC]	RAF No 100 Sqn, Finningley	
XX230	HS Hawk T1A	RAF	
XX231	HS Hawk T1	RAF	
XX232	HS Hawk T1	RAF No 6 FTS, Finningley	
XX233	HS Hawk T1	RAF *Red Arrows*, Scampton	
XX234	HS Hawk T1	RN FRADU, Yeovilton	
XX235	HS Hawk T1	RAF No 4 FTS/74(R) Sqn, Valley	
XX236	HS Hawk T1 [PK]	RAF CFS/No 19(R) Sqn, Valley	
XX237	HS Hawk T1	RAF *Red Arrows*, Scampton	
XX238	HS Hawk T1	RAF No 6 FTS, Finningley	
XX239	HS Hawk T1 [PL]	RAF CFS/No 19(R) Sqn, Valley	
XX240	HS Hawk T1	RAF No 6 FTS, Finningley	
XX242	HS Hawk T1 [Y]	RN FRADU, Yeovilton	
XX244	HS Hawk T1	RAF No 4 FTS/74(R) Sqn, Valley	
XX245	HS Hawk T1	RN FRADU, Yeovilton	
XX246	HS Hawk T1A	RAF	
XX247	HS Hawk T1A [CM]	RAF No 100 Sqn, Finningley	
XX248	HS Hawk T1A [CJ]	RAF No 100 Sqn, Finningley	
XX249	HS Hawk T1 [DY]	RAF No 4 FTS/208(R) Sqn, Valley	
XX250	HS Hawk T1	RAF No 6 FTS, Finningley	
XX252	HS Hawk T1A	RAF *Red Arrows*, Scampton	
XX253	HS Hawk T1A	RAF *Red Arrows*, Scampton	
XX254	HS Hawk T1A	RAF	
XX255	HS Hawk T1A [TE]	RAF No 4 FTS/74(R) Sqn, Valley	
XX256	HS Hawk T1A	RAF	
XX257	HS Hawk T1	*Scrapped at Chivenor, Sept 1994*	
XX258	HS Hawk T1A [PE]	RAF CFS/No 19(R) Sqn, Valley	
XX260	HS Hawk T1A	RAF *Red Arrows*, Scampton	
XX261	HS Hawk T1A	RAF CFS/No 19(R) Sqn, Valley	
XX263	HS Hawk T1A	RAF	
XX263	HS Hawk T1 <R> (BAPC 152)	RAF EP&TU, St Athan	
XX264	HS Hawk T1A	RAF *Red Arrows*, Scampton	
XX265	HS Hawk T1A	RAF	
XX266	HS Hawk T1A	RAF *Red Arrows*, Scampton	
XX278	HS Hawk T1A	RAF CFS/No 19(R) Sqn, Valley	
XX280	HS Hawk T1A [DJ]	RAF No 4 FTS/208(R) Sqn, Valley	
XX281	HS Hawk T1A [O]	RAF St Athan (on repair)	
XX282	HS Hawk T1A	RAF No 4 FTS, Valley	
XX283	HS Hawk T1 [DY]	RAF No 4 FTS/208(R) Sqn, Valley	
XX284	HS Hawk T1A [CL]	RAF No 100 Sqn, Finningley	
XX285	HS Hawk T1A [CH]	RAF No 100 Sqn, Finningley	
XX286	HS Hawk T1A [DK]	RAF No 4 FTS/208(R) Sqn, Valley	
XX287	HS Hawk T1A	RAF	
XX288	HS Hawk T1 [DX]	RAF No 4 FTS/208(R) Sqn, Valley	
XX289	HS Hawk T1A [CI]	RAF No 100 Sqn, Finningley	
XX290	HS Hawk T1 [DV]	RAF No 4 FTS/208(R) Sqn, Valley	
XX292	HS Hawk T1 [R]	RAF CFS/No 19(R) Sqn, Valley	
XX294	HS Hawk T1	RAF *Red Arrows*, Scampton	
XX295	HS Hawk T1 [DW]	RAF No 4 FTS/208(R) Sqn, Valley	
XX296	HS Hawk T1 [DR]	MoD(PE) A&AEE, Boscombe Down	
XX297	HS Hawk T1A (8933M)	RAF Finningley Fire Section	
XX297	HS Hawk T1 <R> (BAPC 171)	RAF EP&TU, St Athan	
XX299	HS Hawk T1 [J]	RAF No 4 FTS/74(R) Sqn, Valley	
XX301	HS Hawk T1A	RAF	
XX302	HS Hawk T1A [TV]	RAF No 4 FTS/74(R) Sqn, Valley	
XX303	HS Hawk T1A [PF]	RAF CFS/No 19(R) Sqn, Valley	
XX304	HS Hawk T1A (fuselage)	RAF, stored Shawbury	
XX306	HS Hawk T1A	RAF *Red Arrows*, Scampton	
XX307	HS Hawk T1	RAF *Red Arrows*, Scampton	
XX308	HS Hawk T1	RAF *Red Arrows*, Scampton	
XX309	HS Hawk T1	RAF No 6 FTS, Finningley	
XX310	HS Hawk T1	RAF No 4 FTS/74(R) Sqn, Valley	
XX311	HS Hawk T1 [T]	RN FRADU, Yeovilton	
XX312	HS Hawk T1 [CF]	RAF No 4 FTSS/74(R) Sqn, Valley	
XX313	HS Hawk T1 [TX]	RAF No 4 FTS/74(R) Sqn, Valley	
XX314	HS Hawk T1	RAF No 4 FTS/74(R) Sqn, Valley	
XX315	HS Hawk T1A [DA]	RAF No 4 FTS/208(R) Sqn, Valley	
XX316	HS Hawk T1A [DF]	RAF No 4 FTS/208(R) Sqn, Valley	
XX317	HS Hawk T1A	RAF No 4 FTS/208(R) Sqn, Valley	
XX318	HS Hawk T1A [PG]	RAF CFS/No 19(R) Sqn, Valley	
XX319	HS Hawk T1A [TF]	RAF No 4 FTS/74(R) Sqn, Valley	

Notes	Serial	Type (other identity) [code]	Owner/operator, location or fate
	XX320	HS Hawk T1A	RAF
	XX321	HS Hawk T1A [DH]	RAF No 4 FTS/208(R) Sqn, Valley
	XX322	HS Hawk T1A [W]	RN FRADU, Yeovilton
	XX323	HS Hawk T1A [TD]	RAF No 4 FTS/74(R) Sqn, Valley
	XX324	HS Hawk T1A [DM]	RAF No 4 FTS/208(R) Sqn, Valley
	XX325	HS Hawk T1A [CE]	RAF No 100 Sqn, Finningley
	XX326	HS Hawk T1A	RAF
	XX327	HS Hawk T1	MoD(PE) IAM, Boscombe Down
	XX329	HS Hawk T1A [C]	RAF CFS/No 19(R) Sqn, Valley
	XX330	HS Hawk T1A [DE]	RAF No 4 FTS/208(R) Sqn, Valley
	XX331	HS Hawk T1A [CK]	RAF No 100 Sqn, Finningley
	XX332	HS Hawk T1A [F]	RAF No 4 FTS/74(R) Sqn, Valley
	XX335	HS Hawk T1A	RAF
	XX337	HS Hawk T1A [K]	RN FRADU, Yeovilton
	XX338	HS Hawk T1 [DZ]	RAF No 4 FTS/208(R) Sqn, Valley
	XX339	HS Hawk T1A [PJ]	RAF CFS/No 19(R) Sqn, Valley
	XX341	HS Hawk T1 ASTRA [1]	MoD(PE) ETPS, Boscombe Down
	XX342	HS Hawk T1 [2]	MoD(PE) ETPS, Boscombe Down
	XX343	HS Hawk T1 [3]	MoD(PE) ETPS, Boscombe Down
	XX344	HS Hawk T1 (8847M) (fuselage)	DRA Farnborough Fire Section
	XX345	HS Hawk T1A [DJ]	RAF No 4 FTS/208(R) Sqn, Valley
	XX346	HS Hawk T1A	RAF
	XX348	HS Hawk T1A [DN]	RAF No 4 FTS/208(R) Sqn, Valley
	XX349	HS Hawk T1	RAF No 4 FTS/74(R) Sqn, Valley
	XX350	HS Hawk T1A [TC]	RAF No 4 FTS/74(R) Sqn, Valley
	XX351	HS Hawk T1A	RAF No 4 FTS/208(R) Sqn, Valley
	XX352	HS Hawk T1A [CP]	RAF No 100 Sqn, Finningley
	XX370	WS Gazelle AH1	AAC No 665 Sqn, Aldergrove
	XX371	WS Gazelle AH1	AAC, RNAY Fleetlands
	XX372	WS Gazelle AH1 [1]	AAC, RNAY Fleetlands
	XX375	WS Gazelle AH1	AAC No 658 Sqn, Netheravon
	XX378	WS Gazelle AH1	AAC No 667 Sqn, Middle Wallop
	XX379	WS Gazelle AH1 [E]	AAC
	XX380	WS Gazelle AH1 [A]	RM 3 CBAS, Yeovilton
	XX381	WS Gazelle AH1	AAC, stored RNAY Fleetlands
	XX382	WS Gazelle HT3 [M]	RAF No 2 FTS, Shawbury
	XX383	WS Gazelle AH1 [E]	AAC No 658 Sqn, Netheravon
	XX384	WS Gazelle AH1	AAC No 663 Sqn, Wattisham
	XX385	WS Gazelle AH1 [X]	AAC No 670 Sqn, Middle Wallop
	XX386	WS Gazelle AH1	AAC, RNAY Fleetlands
	XX387	WS Gazelle AH1	AAC, stored RNAY Fleetlands
	XX388	WS Gazelle AH1	AAC 1 Regiment, Gütersloh
	XX389	WS Gazelle AH1	AAC 1 Regiment, Gütersloh
	XX391	WS Gazelle HT2 [56/CU]	RN No 705 Sqn, Culdrose
	XX392	WS Gazelle AH1 [A1]	AAC No 670 Sqn, Middle Wallop
	XX393	WS Gazelle AH1 [W]	AAC No 2(TA) Flt, Netheravon
	XX394	WS Gazelle AH1 [X]	AAC No 2(TA) Flt, Netheravon
	XX395	WS Gazelle AH1 [J]	AAC
	XX396	WS Gazelle HT3 (8718M) [N]	RAF EP&TU, Henlow
	XX398	WS Gazelle AH1	AAC No 661 Sqn, Gütersloh
	XX399	WS Gazelle AH1 [Y]	AAC, RNAY Fleetlands
	XX403	WS Gazelle AH1 [Y]	Westland, Weston-super-Mare (on rebuild)
	XX405	WS Gazelle AH1 [C1]	AAC No 670 Sqn, Middle Wallop
	XX406	WS Gazelle HT3 [P]	RAF No 7 Sqn, Odiham
	XX407	WS Gazelle AH1 [D1]	AAC No 670 Sqn, Middle Wallop
	XX408	WS Gazelle AH1 [Y]	AAC, stored RNAY Fleetlands
	XX409	WS Gazelle AH1	AAC 4 Regiment, Detmold
	XX410	WS Gazelle HT2 [58/CU]	RN AES, Lee-on-Solent
	XX411	WS Gazelle AH1 [X]	AAC Middle Wallop, BDRT
	XX411	WS Gazelle AH1 (tail only)	FAA Museum, RNAS Yeovilton
	XX412	WS Gazelle AH1 [B]	RM 3 CBAS, Yeovilton
	XX413	WS Gazelle AH1 [C]	RM 3 CBAS, Yeovilton
	XX414	WS Gazelle AH1	AAC 1 Regiment, Gütersloh
	XX416	WS Gazelle AH1	AAC No 29 Flt, BATUS, Suffield, Canada
	XX417	WS Gazelle AH1	AAC No 667 Sqn, Middle Wallop
	XX418	WS Gazelle AH1	AAC, RNAY Fleetlands
	XX419	WS Gazelle AH1 [W]	AAC 3 Regiment, Wattisham
	XX431	WS Gazelle HT2 [VL]	RN No 705 Sqn, Culdrose
	XX432	WS Gazelle AH1	AAC No 665 Sqn, Aldergrove
	XX433	WS Gazelle AH1	AAC No 665 Sqn, Aldergrove
	XX435	WS Gazelle AH1 [B]	AAC No 653 Sqn, Wattisham
	XX436	WS Gazelle HT2 [39/CU]	RN No 705 Sqn, Culdrose
	XX437	WS Gazelle AH1	AAC No 661 Sqn, Gütersloh

Serial	Type (other identity) [code]	Owner/operator, location or fate	Notes
XX438	WS Gazelle AH1 [N]	AAC No 661 Sqn, Gütersloh	
XX439	WS Gazelle AH1	AAC No 659 Sqn, Detmold	
XX440	WS Gazelle AH1	AAC No 665 Sqn, Aldergrove	
XX441	WS Gazelle HT2 [38/CU]	RN No 705 Sqn, Culdrose	
XX442	WS Gazelle AH1 [E]	AAC No 658 Sqn, Dishforth	
XX443	WS Gazelle AH1	AAC No 662 Sqn, Gütersloh	
XX444	WS Gazelle AH1 [E]	AAC, stored Fleetlands	
XX445	WS Gazelle AH1	AAC 9 Regiment, Dishforth	
XX446	WS Gazelle HT2 [57/CU]	RN No 705 Sqn, Culdrose	
XX447	WS Gazelle AH1	AAC No 658 Sqn, Dishforth	
XX448	WS Gazelle AH1	AAC No 654 Sqn, Detmold	
XX449	WS Gazelle AH1 [Y]	AAC No 657 Sqn, Dishforth	
XX450	WS Gazelle AH1 [D]	RM 3 CBAS, Yeovilton	
XX451	WS Gazelle HT2 [58/CU]	RN No 705 Sqn, Culdrose	
XX452	WS Gazelle AH1	AAC Middle Wallop Fire Section	
XX453	WS Gazelle AH1 [3]	AAC 4 Regiment, Detmold	
XX454	WS Gazelle AH1	AAC No 656 Sqn, Dishforth	
XX455	WS Gazelle AH1	AAC No 661 Sqn, Gütersloh	
XX456	WS Gazelle AH1	AAC No 2(TA) Flt, Netheravon	
XX457	WS Gazelle AH1 [Z]	AAC No 2(TA) Flt, Netheravon	
XX460	WS Gazelle AH1	AAC 4 Regiment, Detmold	
XX462	WS Gazelle AH1	AAC No 661 Sqn, Gütersloh	
XX466	HS Hunter T66B/T7 [830/DD]	RN Predannack Fire School	
XX467	HS Hunter T66B/T7	Air Service Training, Perth	
XX469	WS Lynx HAS2 (G-BNCL)	Lancashire Fire Brigade, Lancaster	
XX475	SA Jetstream T2 [572]	MoD(PE), TEE West Freugh	
XX476	SA Jetstream T2 [561/CU]	RN No 750 Sqn, Culdrose	
XX477	SA Jetstream T1 (8462M) <ff>	RAF Finningley for ground instruction	
XX478	SA Jetstream T2 [564/CU]	RN No 750 Sqn, Culdrose	
XX479	SA Jetstream T2 [563/CU]	RN No 750 Sqn, Culdrose	
XX480	SA Jetstream T2 [565/CU]	RN No 750 Sqn, Culdrose	
XX481	SA Jetstream T2 [560/CU]	RN No 750 Sqn, Culdrose	
XX482	SA Jetstream T1 [J]	RAF No 6 FTS/45(R) Sqn, Finningley	
XX483	SA Jetstream T2 [562/CU]	RN No 750 Sqn, Culdrose	
XX484	SA Jetstream T2 [566/CU]	RN No 750 Sqn, Culdrose	
XX485	SA Jetstream T2 [567/CU]	RN No 750 Sqn, Culdrose	
XX486	SA Jetstream T2 [569/CU]	RN No 750 Sqn, Culdrose	
XX487	SA Jetstream T2 [568/CU]	RN No 750 Sqn, Culdrose	
XX488	SA Jetstream T2 [571/CU]	RN No 750 Sqn, Culdrose	
XX490	SA Jetstream T2 [570/CU]	RN No 750 Sqn, Culdrose	
XX491	SA Jetstream T1 [K]	RAF No 6 FTS/45(R) Sqn, Finningley	
XX492	SA Jetstream T1 [A]	RAF No 6 FTS/45(R) Sqn, Finningley	
XX493	SA Jetstream T1 [L]	RAF No 6 FTS/45(R) Sqn, Finningley	
XX494	SA Jetstream T1 [B]	RAF No 6 FTS/45(R) Sqn, Finningley	
XX495	SA Jetstream T1 [C]	RAF No 6 FTS/45(R) Sqn, Finningley	
XX496	SA Jetstream T1 [D]	RAF No 6 FTS/45(R) Sqn, Finningley	
XX497	SA Jetstream T1 [E]	RAF No 6 FTS/45(R) Sqn, Finningley	
XX498	SA Jetstream T1 [F]	RAF No 6 FTS/45(R) Sqn, Finningley	
XX499	SA Jetstream T1 [G]	RAF No 6 FTS/45(R) Sqn, Finningley	
XX500	SA Jetstream T1 [H]	RAF No 6 FTS/45(R) Sqn, Finningley	
XX507	HS125 CC2	RAF No 32 Sqn, Northolt	
XX508	HS125 CC2	RAF No 32 Sqn, Northolt	
XX510	WS Lynx HAS2 [69/LS]	RN Lynx Training School, Lee-on-Solent	
XX513	SA Bulldog T1 [10]	RAF CFS, Scampton	
XX515	SA Bulldog T1 [A2]	RAF College Air Sqn, Cranwell	
XX516	SA Bulldog T1 [1]	RAF CFS, Scampton	
XX518	SA Bulldog T1 [Z]	RAF Cambridge UAS, Cambridge	
XX519	SA Bulldog T1 [A1]	RAF College Air Sqn, Cranwell	
XX520	SA Bulldog T1 [2]	RAF CFS, Scampton	
XX521	SA Bulldog T1 [01]	RAF East Lowlands UAS, Turnhouse	
XX522	SA Bulldog T1 [B2]	RAF College Air Sqn, Cranwell	
XX523	SA Bulldog T1 [X]	RAF Liverpool UAS, Woodvale	
XX524	SA Bulldog T1 [04]	RAF London UAS, Benson	
XX525	SA Bulldog T1 [03]	RAF East Lowlands UAS, Turnhouse	
XX526	SA Bulldog T1 [C]	RAF Oxford UAS, Benson	
XX527	SA Bulldog T1 [D]	RAF Aberdeen, Dundee & St Andrews UAS, Leuchars	
XX528	SA Bulldog T1 [D]	RAF Oxford UAS, Benson	
XX529	SA Bulldog T1 [W]	RAF No 6 FTS, Finningley	
XX531	SA Bulldog T1 [06]	RAF Wales UAS, St Athan	
XX532	SA Bulldog T1 [D]	RAF Yorkshire UAS, Finningley	
XX533	SA Bulldog T1 [U]	RAF Northumbria UAS, Leeming	
XX534	SA Bulldog T1 [B]	RAF Birmingham UAS, Cosford	

Notes	Serial	Type (other identity) [code]	Owner/operator, location or fate
	XX535	SA Bulldog T1 [11]	RAF East Midlands UAS, Newton
	XX536	SA Bulldog T1 [6]	RAF Manchester UAS, Woodvale
	XX537	SA Bulldog T1 [02]	RAF East Lowlands UAS, Turnhouse
	XX538	SA Bulldog T1 [V]	RAF No 6 FTS, Finningley
	XX539	SA Bulldog T1 [L]	RAF Liverpool UAS, Woodvale
	XX540	SA Bulldog T1 [C2]	RAF College Air Sqn, Cranwell
	XX541	SA Bulldog T1 [F]	RAF Bristol UAS, Colerne
	XX543	SA Bulldog T1 [F]	RAF Yorkshire UAS, Finningley
	XX544	SA Bulldog T1 [01]	RAF London UAS, Benson
	XX545	SA Bulldog T1 [02]	RAF East Lowlands UAS, Turnhouse, GI use
	XX546	SA Bulldog T1 [03]	RAF London UAS, Benson
	XX547	SA Bulldog T1 [05]	RAF London UAS, Benson
	XX548	SA Bulldog T1 [06]	RAF London UAS, Benson
	XX549	SA Bulldog T1	RAF Southampton UAS, Boscombe Down
	XX550	SA Bulldog T1 [Z]	RAF Northumbria UAS, Leeming
	XX551	SA Bulldog T1 [E]	RAF Oxford UAS, Benson
	XX552	SA Bulldog T1 [08]	RAF London UAS, Benson
	XX553	SA Bulldog T1 [07]	RAF London UAS, Benson
	XX554	SA Bulldog T1 [09]	RAF London UAS, Benson
	XX555	SA Bulldog T1 [10]	RAF CFS, Scampton
	XX556	SA Bulldog T1 [S]	RAF East Midlands UAS, Newton
	XX557	SA Bulldog T1	RAF Linton-on-Ouse, ground instruction
	XX558	SA Bulldog T1 [A]	RAF Birmingham UAS, Cosford
	XX559	SA Bulldog T1	RAF Glasgow & Strathclyde UAS, Glasgow
	XX560	SA Bulldog T1	RAF Glasgow & Strathclyde UAS, Glasgow
	XX561	SA Bulldog T1 [A]	RAF Aberdeen, Dundee & St Andrews UAS, Leuchars
	XX562	SA Bulldog T1 [E]	RAF No 13 AEF, Sydenham
	XX611	SA Bulldog T1	RAF Glasgow & Strathclyde UAS, Glasgow
	XX612	SA Bulldog T1 [05]	RAF Wales UAS, St Athan
	XX614	SA Bulldog T1 [6]	RAF CFS, Scampton
	XX615	SA Bulldog T1 [2]	RAF, stored Shawbury
	XX616	SA Bulldog T1 [3]	RAF Manchester UAS, Woodvale
	XX617	SA Bulldog T1 [4]	RAF Manchester UAS, Woodvale
	XX619	SA Bulldog T1 [B]	RAF Yorkshire UAS, Finningley
	XX620	SA Bulldog T1 [C]	RAF Yorkshire UAS, Finningley
	XX621	SA Bulldog T1 [X]	RAF No 6 FTS, Finningley
	XX622	SA Bulldog T1 [E]	RAF Yorkshire UAS, Finningley
	XX623	SA Bulldog T1 [M]	RAF East Midlands UAS, Newton
	XX624	SA Bulldog T1 [Y]	RAF No 6 FTS, Finningley
	XX625	SA Bulldog T1 [01]	RAF Wales UAS, St Athan
	XX626	SA Bulldog T1 [02]	RAF Wales UAS, St Athan
	XX627	SA Bulldog T1 [03]	RAF Wales UAS, St Athan
	XX628	SA Bulldog T1 [04]	RAF Wales UAS, St Athan
	XX629	SA Bulldog T1 [V]	RAF Northumbria UAS, Leeming
	XX630	SA Bulldog T1 [A]	RAF Liverpool UAS, Woodvale
	XX631	SA Bulldog T1 [W]	RAF Northumbria UAS, Leeming
	XX632	SA Bulldog T1 [D]	RAF Bristol UAS, Colerne
	XX633	SA Bulldog T1 [X]	RAF Northumbria UAS, Leeming
	XX634	SA Bulldog T1 [C]	RAF Cambridge UAS, Cambridge
	XX635	SA Bulldog T1 (8767M)	RAF CTTS, St Athan
	XX636	SA Bulldog T1 [Y]	RAF Northumbria UAS, Leeming
	XX637	SA Bulldog T1 (9197M) [U]	SERCO, RAF St Athan
	XX638	SA Bulldog T1 [H]	RAF Yorkshire UAS, Finningley
	XX639	SA Bulldog T1 [02]	RAF London UAS, Benson
	XX640	SA Bulldog T1 [B]	RAF Queen's UAS, Sydenham
	XX653	SA Bulldog T1 [E]	RAF Bristol UAS, Colerne
	XX654	SA Bulldog T1 [A]	RAF Bristol UAS, Colerne
	XX655	SA Bulldog T1 [B]	RAF Bristol UAS, Colerne
	XX656	SA Bulldog T1 [C]	RAF Bristol UAS, Colerne
	XX657	SA Bulldog T1 [U]	RAF Cambridge UAS, Cambridge
	XX658	SA Bulldog T1 [A]	RAF Cambridge UAS, Cambridge
	XX659	SA Bulldog T1 [S]	RAF Cambridge UAS, Cambridge
	XX660	SA Bulldog T1 [A]	*Scrapped at Prestwick, 1993*
	XX661	SA Bulldog T1 [B]	RAF Oxford UAS, Benson
	XX663	SA Bulldog T1 [B]	RAF Aberdeen, Dundee & St Andrews UAS, Leuchars
	XX664	SA Bulldog T1 [04]	RAF East Lowlands UAS, Turnhouse

Serial	Type (other identity) [code]	Owner/operator, location or fate	Notes
XX665	SA Bulldog T1 [E]	RAF Aberdeen, Dundee & St Andrews UAS, Leuchars	
XX666	SA Bulldog T1 [A]	RAF Queen's UAS, Sydenham	
XX667	SA Bulldog T1 [C1]	RAF College Air Sqn, Cranwell	
XX668	SA Bulldog T1 [1]	RAF Manchester UAS, Woodvale	
XX669	SA Bulldog T1 (8997M) [B]	Privately owned, Bruntingthorpe	
XX670	SA Bulldog T1 [C]	RAF Birmingham UAS, Cosford	
XX671	SA Bulldog T1 [D]	RAF Birmingham UAS, Cosford	
XX672	SA Bulldog T1 [E]	RAF, stored Shawbury	
XX685	SA Bulldog T1 [C]	RAF Aberdeen, Dundee & St Andrews UAS, Leuchars	
XX686	SA Bulldog T1	RAF Oxford UAS, Benson	
XX687	SA Bulldog T1 [A]	RAF East Midlands UAS, Newton	
XX688	SA Bulldog T1 [S]	RAF Liverpool UAS, Woodvale	
XX689	SA Bulldog T1 [3]	RAF CFS, Scampton	
XX690	SA Bulldog T1 [A]	RAF Yorkshire UAS, Finningley	
XX691	SA Bulldog T1 [G]	RAF Yorkshire UAS, Finningley	
XX692	SA Bulldog T1 [5]	RAF Yorkshire UAS, Finningley	
XX693	SA Bulldog T1 [4]	RAF CFS, Scampton	
XX694	SA Bulldog T1 [E]	RAF East Midlands UAS, Newton	
XX695	SA Bulldog T1 [A]	RAF Oxford UAS, Benson	
XX696	SA Bulldog T1 [8]	RAF CFS, Scampton	
XX697	SA Bulldog T1 [C]	RAF Queen's UAS, Sydenham	
XX698	SA Bulldog T1	RAF CFS/*Red Arrows*, Scampton	
XX699	SA Bulldog T1 [F]	RAF, stored Shawbury	
XX700	SA Bulldog T1 [B1]	RAF College Air Sqn, Cranwell	
XX701	SA Bulldog T1 [01]	RAF Southampton UAS, Boscombe Down	
XX702	SA Bulldog T1 [11]	RAF CFS, Scampton	
XX704	SA Bulldog T1 [U]	RAF East Midlands UAS, Newton	
XX705	SA Bulldog T1 [05]	RAF Southampton UAS, Boscombe Down	
XX706	SA Bulldog T1	RAF Southampton UAS, Boscombe Down	
XX707	SA Bulldog T1 [04]	RAF Southampton UAS, Boscombe Down	
XX708	SA Bulldog T1 [03]	RAF Southampton UAS, Boscombe Down	
XX709	SA Bulldog T1 [12]	RAF CFS, Scampton	
XX710	SA Bulldog T1 [5]	RAF Manchester UAS, Woodvale	
XX711	SA Bulldog T1 [D]	RAF Queen's UAS, Sydenham	
XX713	SA Bulldog T1 [Z]	RAF No 6 FTS, Finningley	
XX714	SA Bulldog T1 [7]	RAF CFS, Scampton	
XX719	SEPECAT Jaguar GR1A [EE]	BAe Warton (for Oman)	
XX720	SEPECAT Jaguar GR1A [EN]	RAF St Athan	
XX722	SEPECAT Jaguar GR1 [EF]	RAF, stored Shawbury	
XX723	SEPECAT Jaguar GR1A [GQ]	RAF No 54 Sqn, Coltishall	
XX724	SEPECAT Jaguar GR1A [GA]	RAF, stored Shawbury	
XX725	SEPECAT Jaguar GR1A [GU]	RAF No 54 Sqn, Coltishall	
XX725	SEPECAT Jaguar GR1 <R> (BAPC 150) [25]	RAF EP&TU, St Athan	
XX726	SEPECAT Jaguar GR1 (8947M) [EB]	RAF Halton	
XX727	SEPECAT Jaguar GR1 (8951M) [ER]	RAF No 1 SoTT, Cosford	
XX729	SEPECAT Jaguar GR1A [GC]	RAF St Athan	
XX730	SEPECAT Jaguar GR1 (8952M) [EC]	RAF No 1 SoTT, Cosford	
XX733	SEPECAT Jaguar GR1A [ER]	RAF No 6 Sqn, Coltishall	
XX736	SEPECAT Jaguar GR1 (9110M)	RAF Coltishall, BDRT	
XX737	SEPECAT Jaguar GR1A [EG]	RAF St Athan	
XX738	SEPECAT Jaguar GR1A [GJ]	RAF St Athan	
XX739	SEPECAT Jaguar GR1 (8902M)	RAF Halton	
XX741	SEPECAT Jaguar GR1A [04]	RAF, stored Shawbury	
XX743	SEPECAT Jaguar GR1 (8949M) [EG]	RAF Halton	
XX744	SEPECAT Jaguar GR1 [DJ]	RAF, stored Shawbury	
XX745	SEPECAT Jaguar GR1A [EG]	RAF No 6 Sqn, Coltishall	
XX746	SEPECAT Jaguar GR1A (8895M) [09]		
XX747	SEPECAT Jaguar GR1 (8903M)	ATF, RAFC Cranwell	
XX748	SEPECAT Jaguar GR1A [GK]	RAF No 54 Sqn, Coltishall	
XX751	SEPECAT Jaguar GR1 (8937M) [10]	RAF No 1 SoTT, Cosford	
XX752	SEPECAT Jaguar GR1A [EQ]	RAF No 6 Sqn, Coltishall	
XX753	SEPECAT Jaguar GR1 (9087M) <ff>	RAF EP&TU, St Athan	

Notes	Serial	Type (other identity) [code]	Owner/operator, location or fate
	XX756	SEPECAT Jaguar GR1 (8899M) [AM]	RAF No 1 SoTT, Cosford
	XX757	SEPECAT Jaguar GR1 (8948M) [CU]	RAF Halton
	XX761	SEPECAT Jaguar GR1 (8600M) <ff>	BAe Warton, instructional use
	XX763	SEPECAT Jaguar GR1 (9009M)	RAF CTTS, St Athan
	XX764	SEPECAT Jaguar GR1 (9010M)	RAF CTTS, St Athan
	XX765	SEPECAT Jaguar ACT	Loughborough University
	XX766	SEPECAT Jaguar GR1A [EA]	RAF No 6 Sqn, Coltishall
	XX767	SEPECAT Jaguar GR1A [GE]	RAF No 54 Sqn, Coltishall
	XX818	SEPECAT Jaguar GR1 (8945M) [DE]	RAF No 1 SoTT, Cosford
	XX819	SEPECAT Jaguar GR1 (8923M) [CE]	RAF No 1 SoTT, Cosford
	XX821	SEPECAT Jaguar GR1 (8896M) [P]	SIF, RAFC Cranwell
	XX824	SEPECAT Jaguar GR1 (9019M) [AD]	RAF Halton
	XX825	SEPECAT Jaguar GR1 (9020M) [BN]	RAF Halton
	XX826	SEPECAT Jaguar GR1 (9021M) [34]	RAF No 1 SoTT, Cosford
	XX829	SEPECAT Jaguar T2A [Y]	RAF No 16(R) Sqn, Lossiemouth
	XX830	SEPECAT Jaguar T2	MoD(PE) ETPS, Boscombe Down
	XX832	SEPECAT Jaguar T2A [S]	RAF, stored Shawbury
	XX833	SEPECAT Jaguar T2A [N]	RAF SAOEU, Boscombe Down
	XX835	SEPECAT Jaguar T2	MoD(PE) DRA, Boscombe Down
	XX836	SEPECAT Jaguar T2A	RAF, stored Shawbury
	XX837	SEPECAT Jaguar T2 (8978M) [Z]	RAF No 1 SoTT, Cosford
	XX838	SEPECAT Jaguar T2A [X]	RAF, stored Shawbury
	XX839	SEPECAT Jaguar T2A [GW]	RAF No 54 Sqn, Coltishall
	XX840	SEPECAT Jaguar T2A [X]	RAF, stored Shawbury
	XX841	SEPECAT Jaguar T2A [ES]	RAF No 6 Sqn, Coltishall
	XX842	SEPECAT Jaguar T2A [EW]	RAF, stored Shawbury
	XX844	SEPECAT Jaguar T2 (9023M) [F]	RAF No 1 SoTT, Cosford
	XX845	SEPECAT Jaguar T2A [A]	RAF No 41 Sqn, Coltishall
	XX846	SEPECAT Jaguar T2A [Y]	RAF No 41 Sqn, Coltishall
	XX847	SEPECAT Jaguar T2A	RAF No 41 Sqn, Coltishall
	XX885	HS Buccaneer S2B (9225M)	RAF Lossiemouth, BDRT
	XX886	HS Buccaneer S2B	RAF Honington, WLT use
	XX888	HS Buccaneer S2B <ff>	Privately owned, Dundonald
	XX889	HS Buccaneer S2B	RAF, stored St Athan
	XX892	HS Buccaneer S2B	*Scrapped at Lossiemouth, March 1994*
	XX893	HS Buccaneer S2B	*Scrapped at Lossiemouth, March 1994*
	XX894	HS Buccaneer S2B [020/R]	Privately owned, Bruntingthorpe
	XX895	HS Buccaneer S2B	RAF, stored St Athan
	XX897	HS Buccaneer S2B	Privately owned, Bournemouth
	XX899	HS Buccaneer S2B <ff>	*Scrapped at RAF St Athan, Oct 1994*
	XX900	HS Buccaneer S2B	Privately owned, Bruntingthorpe
	XX901	HS Buccaneer S2B	Privately owned, Hucclecote
	XX907	WS Lynx AH1	DRA Structures Dept, Farnborough
	XX910	WS Lynx HAS2	DRA Structures Dept, Farnborough
	XX914	BAC VC10 srs 1103 (8777M) <rf>	RAF AMS, Brize Norton
	XX919	BAC 1-11/402	MoD(PE) DRA, Boscombe Down
	XX946	Panavia Tornado (P02) (8883M)	RAF Museum, Hendon
	XX947	Panavia Tornado (P03) (8797M)	RAF Marham, Fire Section
	XX948	Panavia Tornado (P06) (8879M) [P]	RAF No 1 SoTT, Cosford
	XX955	SEPECAT Jaguar GR1A [GK]	RAF, stored Shawbury
	XX956	SEPECAT Jaguar GR1 (8950M) [BE]	RAF Halton
	XX958	SEPECAT Jaguar GR1 (9022M) [BK]	RAF No 1 SoTT, Cosford
	XX959	SEPECAT Jaguar GR1 (8953M) [CJ]	RAF No 1 SoTT, Cosford
	XX962	SEPECAT Jaguar GR1A [EK]	RAF No 6 Sqn, Coltishall
	XX965	SEPECAT Jaguar GR1A [C]	RAF No 16(R) Sqn, Lossiemouth
	XX966	SEPECAT Jaguar GR1A (8904M)	RAF Halton
	XX967	SEPECAT Jaguar GR1 (9006M) [AC]	RAF No 1 SoTT, Cosford
	XX968	SEPECAT Jaguar GR1 (9007M) [AJ]	RAF No 1 SoTT, Cosford

Serial	Type (other identity) [code]	Owner/operator, location or fate	Notes
XX969	SEPECAT Jaguar GR1A (8897M) [01]	RAF No 1 SoTT, Cosford	
XX970	SEPECAT Jaguar GR1A [EH]	RAF No 6 Sqn, Coltishall	
XX974	SEPECAT Jaguar GR1A [GH]	RAF No 54 Sqn, Coltishall	
XX975	SEPECAT Jaguar GR1 (8905M) [07]	RAF No 1 SoTT, Cosford	
XX976	SEPECAT Jaguar GR1 (8906M) [BD]	RAF Halton	
XX977	SEPECAT Jaguar GR1 (9132M) [DL,05]	RAF St Athan, BDRT	
XX979	SEPECAT Jaguar GR1A	MoD(PE), A&AEE Boscombe Down	
XZ101	SEPECAT Jaguar GR1A [D]	RAF No 16(R) Sqn, Lossiemouth	
XZ103	SEPECAT Jaguar GR1A [P]	RAF No 41 Sqn, Coltishall	
XZ104	SEPECAT Jaguar GR1A [FM]	RAF No 41 Sqn, Coltishall	
XZ106	SEPECAT Jaguar GR1A [FR]	RAF No 41 Sqn, Coltishall	
XZ107	SEPECAT Jaguar GR1A [H]	RAF No 41 Sqn, Coltishall	
XZ108	SEPECAT Jaguar GR1A [E]	RAF No 16(R) Sqn, Lossiemouth	
XZ109	SEPECAT Jaguar GR1A [EN]	RAF No 6 Sqn, Coltishall	
XZ111	SEPECAT Jaguar GR1A [EL]	RAF, stored Shawbury	
XZ112	SEPECAT Jaguar GR1A [GA]	RAF No 54 Sqn, Coltishall	
XZ113	SEPECAT Jaguar GR1A [FD]	RAF No 41 Sqn, Coltishall	
XZ114	SEPECAT Jaguar GR1A [FB]	RAF No 41 Sqn, Coltishall	
XZ115	SEPECAT Jaguar GR1A [FC]	RAF, stored Shawbury	
XZ117	SEPECAT Jaguar GR1A [GG]	RAF, stored Shawbury	
XZ118	SEPECAT Jaguar GR1A [FF]	RAF No 41 Sqn, Coltishall	
XZ119	SEPECAT Jaguar GR1A	RAF No 41 Sqn, Coltishall	
XZ129	HS Harrier GR3 [ETS]	RN ETS, Yeovilton	
XZ130	HS Harrier GR3 (9079M) [A]	RAF No 1 SoTT, Cosford	
XZ131	HS Harrier GR3 (9174M) <ff>	RAF EP&TU, St Athan	
XZ132	HS Harrier GR3 (9168M) [C]	ATF, RAFC Cranwell	
XZ133	HS Harrier GR3 [10]	Imperial War Museum, Duxford	
XZ135	HS Harrier GR3 (8848M) <ff>	RAF EP&TU, St Athan	
XZ138	HS Harrier GR3 (9040M) <ff>	RAFC Cranwell, Trenchard Hall	
XZ145	HS Harrier T4 [T]	RAF HOCU/No 20(R) Sqn, Wittering	
XZ146	HS Harrier T4 [S]	RAF HOCU/No 20(R) Sqn, Wittering	
XZ170	WS Lynx AH7(mod)	MoD(PE)/Westland, Yeovil	
XZ171	WS Lynx AH7 [L]	AAC No 657 Sqn, Dishforth	
XZ172	WS Lynx AH7	AAC No 655 Sqn, Aldergrove	
XZ173	WS Lynx AH7	AAC 3 Regiment, Wattisham	
XZ174	WS Lynx AH7	AAC No 655 Sqn, Aldergrove	
XZ175	WS Lynx AH7 [Z]	AAC No 671 Sqn, Middle Wallop	
XZ176	WS Lynx AH7 [O]	AAC No 663 Sqn, Wattisham	
XZ177	WS Lynx AH7	AAC, stored RNAY Fleetlands	
XZ178	WS Lynx AH7	AAC No 656 Sqn, Dishforth	
XZ179	WS Lynx AH7	AAC No 669 Sqn, Detmold	
XZ180	WS Lynx AH7 [R]	RM 3 CBAS, Yeovilton	
XZ181	WS Lynx AH1	AAC, stored RNAY Fleetlands	
XZ182	WS Lynx AH7 [M]	RM 3 CBAS, Yeovilton	
XZ183	WS Lynx AH7	AAC No 671 Sqn, Middle Wallop	
XZ184	WS Lynx AH7 [W]	AAC, RNAY Fleetlands	
XZ185	WS Lynx AH7	AAC 3 Regiment, Wattisham	
XZ186	WS Lynx AH7 (wreckage)	AAC, RNAY Fleetlands	
XZ187	WS Lynx AH7	AAC No 667 Sqn, Middle Wallop	
XZ188	WS Lynx AH7	AAC 3 Regiment, Wattisham	
XZ190	WS Lynx AH7	AAC 3 Regiment, Wattisham	
XZ191	WS Lynx AH7 [X]	AAC, RNAY Fleetlands (conversion)	
XZ192	WS Lynx AH7	AAC No 655 Sqn, Aldergrove	
XZ193	WS Lynx AH7 [I]	AAC No 671 Sqn, Middle Wallop	
XZ194	WS Lynx AH7	AAC No 663 Sqn, Wattisham	
XZ195	WS Lynx AH7 [T]	AAC SAE, Middle Wallop	
XZ196	WS Lynx AH7 [A]	AAC, RNAY Fleetlands (conversion)	
XZ197	WS Lynx AH7	AAC 4 Regiment, Detmold	
XZ198	WS Lynx AH7	AAC No 655 Sqn, Aldergrove	
XZ199	WS Lynx AH7	AAC No 664 Sqn, Dishforth	
XZ203	WS Lynx AH7	AAC, stored RNAY Fleetlands	
XZ205	WS Lynx AH7	AAC No 655 Sqn, Aldergrove	
XZ206	WS Lynx AH7 [B]	AAC, RNAY Fleetlands (conversion)	
XZ207	WS Lynx AH7	AAC 4 Regiment, Detmold	
XZ208	WS Lynx AH7 [M]	AAC No 657 Sqn, Dishforth	
XZ209	WS Lynx AH1 [T]	AAC, stored RNAY Fleetlands	
XZ210	WS Lynx AH7	AAC No 662 Sqn, Wattisham	
XZ211	WS Lynx AH7 [X]	AAC No 671 Sqn, Middle Wallop	

Notes	Serial	Type (other identity) [code]	Owner/operator, location or fate
	XZ212	WS Lynx AH7 [P]	AAC, RNAY Fleetlands (conversion)
	XZ213	WS Lynx AH1 [TAD 213]	RNAY Fleetlands Apprentice School
	XZ214	WS Lynx AH7	AAC No 664 Sqn, Dishforth
	XZ215	WS Lynx AH7	AAC No 655 Sqn, Aldergrove
	XZ216	WS Lynx AH7 [6]	AAC No 656 Sqn, Dishforth
	XZ217	WS Lynx AH7	AAC No 661 Sqn, Gütersloh
	XZ218	WS Lynx AH7	AAC, stored RNAY Fleetlands
	XZ219	WS Lynx AH7	AAC 1 Regiment, Gütersloh
	XZ220	WS Lynx AH7	AAC No 669 Sqn, Detmold
	XZ221	WS Lynx AH7	AAC No 651 Sqn, Gütersloh
	XZ222	WS Lynx AH7 [P]	AAC No 657 Sqn, Dishforth
	XZ227	WS Lynx HAS3	Sold to Pakistan, August 1994
	XZ228	WS Lynx HAS3S [334/SN]	RN No 815 Sqn, Portland
	XZ229	WS Lynx HAS3S [338/CT]	RN No 815 Sqn, Portland
	XZ230	WS Lynx HAS3S [336/CV]	RN No 815 Sqn, Portland
	XZ231	WS Lynx HAS3 [303/BT]	RN No 815 Sqn, Portland
	XZ232	WS Lynx HAS3S [305]	RN No 815 Sqn, Portland
	XZ233	WS Lynx HAS3 [435/ED]	RN No 815 Sqn, Portland
	XZ234	WS Lynx HAS3S [361/NF]	RN No 815 Sqn, Portland
	XZ235	WS Lynx HAS3S [635]	RN No 702 Sqn, Portland
	XZ236	WS Lynx HAS8	MoD(PE) A&AEE, Boscombe Down
	XZ237	WS Lynx HAS3S [PO]	RN AMG, Portland
	XZ238	WS Lynx HAS8	MoD(PE)/Westland, Yeovil (conversion)
	XZ239	WS Lynx HAS3 [307]	RN No 815 Sqn, Portland
	XZ240	WS Lynx HAS3	Sold to Pakistan, August 1994
	XZ241	WS Lynx HAS3S [346/BW]	RN No 815 Sqn, Portland
	XZ243	WS Lynx HAS3 [635] (wreck)	RN Portland, GI use
	XZ245	WS Lynx HAS3S [352/SD]	RN No 815 Sqn, Portland
	XZ246	WS Lynx HAS3 [434/ED]	RNAY Fleetlands
	XZ248	WS Lynx HAS3S [345/NC]	RN No 815 Sqn, Portland
	XZ250	WS Lynx HAS3S [645]	RN No 702 Sqn, Portland
	XZ252	WS Lynx HAS3 [644]	RN No 702 Sqn, Portland
	XZ254	WS Lynx HAS3S [360/MC]	RN No 815 Sqn, Portland
	XZ255	WS Lynx HAS3S [335/CF]	RN No 815 Sqn, Portland
	XZ256	WS Lynx HAS8	MoD(PE)/Westland, Yeovil (conversion)
	XZ257	WS Lynx HAS3S [304]	RN No 815 Sqn, Portland
	XZ284	HS Nimrod MR2	RAF No 206 Sqn, Kinloss
	XZ287	BAe Nimrod AEW3 (9140M) (fuselage)	RAF TSW Stafford
	XZ290	WS Gazelle AH1 [F]	AAC No 670 Sqn, Middle Wallop
	XZ291	WS Gazelle AH1	AAC, RNAY Fleetlands
	XZ292	WS Gazelle AH1 [4]	AAC No 656 Sqn, Dishforth
	XZ294	WS Gazelle AH1	AAC 4 Regiment, Detmold
	XZ295	WS Gazelle AH1	AAC No 6(TA) Flt, Shawbury
	XZ296	WS Gazelle AH1	AAC No 664 Sqn, Dishforth
	XZ298	WS Gazelle AH1 [X]	AAC No 657 Sqn, Dishforth
	XZ299	WS Gazelle AH1 [G1]	AAC, stored RNAY Fleetlands
	XZ300	WS Gazelle AH1 [L]	AAC No 670 Sqn, Middle Wallop
	XZ301	WS Gazelle AH1	AAC No 29 Flt, BATUS, Suffield, Canada
	XZ302	WS Gazelle AH1	AAC, stored RNAY Fleetlands
	XZ303	WS Gazelle AH1 [S]	AAC No 663 Sqn, Wattisham
	XZ304	WS Gazelle AH1	AAC, stored RNAY Fleetlands
	XZ305	WS Gazelle AH1	AAC 3 Regiment, Wattisham
	XZ307	WS Gazelle AH1	AAC No 665 Sqn, Aldergrove
	XZ308	WS Gazelle AH1 [V]	AAC No 657 Sqn, Dishforth
	XZ309	WS Gazelle AH1	AAC No 6(TA) Flt, Shawbury
	XZ310	WS Gazelle AH1 [U]	AAC No 670 Sqn, Middle Wallop
	XZ311	WS Gazelle AH1	AAC No 6(TA) Flt, Shawbury
	XZ312	WS Gazelle AH1	AAC, stored RNAY Fleetlands
	XZ313	WS Gazelle AH1 [K]	AAC No 670 Sqn, Middle Wallop
	XZ314	WS Gazelle AH1 [A]	AAC No 666(TA) Sqn, Netheravon
	XZ315	WS Gazelle AH1	AAC, RNAY Fleetlands
	XZ316	WS Gazelle AH1 [B]	AAC No 657 Sqn, Dishforth
	XZ317	WS Gazelle AH1 [R]	AAC No 670 Sqn, Middle Wallop
	XZ318	WS Gazelle AH1	AAC No 664 Sqn, Dishforth
	XZ320	WS Gazelle AH1	RM, stored Fleetlands
	XZ321	WS Gazelle AH1	AAC No 665 Sqn, Aldergrove
	XZ322	WS Gazelle AH1 [N]	AAC No 670 Sqn, Middle Wallop
	XZ323	WS Gazelle AH1	AAC, RNAY Fleetlands
	XZ324	WS Gazelle AH1	AAC No 3(TA) Flt, Turnhouse
	XZ325	WS Gazelle AH1 [T]	AAC No 670 Sqn, Middle Wallop
	XZ326	WS Gazelle AH1	RM, stored Fleetlands
	XZ327	WS Gazelle AH1 [B1]	AAC, RNAY Fleetlands

Serial	Type (other identity) [code]	Owner/operator, location or fate	Notes
XZ328	WS Gazelle AH1	AAC 4 Regiment, Detmold	
XZ329	WS Gazelle AH1 [J]	AAC No 670 Sqn, Middle Wallop	
XZ330	WS Gazelle AH1 [Y]	AAC No 670 Sqn, Middle Wallop	
XZ331	WS Gazelle AH1 [X]	AAC No 657 Sqn, Dishforth	
XZ332	WS Gazelle AH1 [O]	AAC No 670 Sqn, Middle Wallop	
XZ333	WS Gazelle AH1 [A]	AAC No 670 Sqn, Middle Wallop	
XZ334	WS Gazelle AH1 [S]	AAC No 670 Sqn, Middle Wallop	
XZ335	WS Gazelle AH1	AAC No 669 Sqn, Detmold	
XZ337	WS Gazelle AH1 [5]	AAC No 656 Sqn, Dishforth	
XZ338	WS Gazelle AH1	AAC No 661 Sqn, Gütersloh	
XZ339	WS Gazelle AH1	AAC No 667 Sqn, Middle Wallop	
XZ340	WS Gazelle AH1	AAC No 29 Flt, BATUS, Suffield, Canada	
XZ341	WS Gazelle AH1	AAC No 3(TA) Flt, Turnhouse	
XZ342	WS Gazelle AH1	AAC, RNAY Fleetlands	
XZ343	WS Gazelle AH1	AAC 1 Regiment, Gütersloh	
XZ344	WS Gazelle AH1 [F1]	AAC No 670 Sqn, Middle Wallop	
XZ345	WS Gazelle AH1	AAC 4 Regiment, Detmold	
XZ346	WS Gazelle AH1	AAC No 665 Sqn, Aldergrove	
XZ347	WS Gazelle AH1	AAC No 664 Sqn, Dishforth	
XZ348	WS Gazelle AH1 (wreckage)	AAC, stored RNAY Fleetlands	
XZ349	WS Gazelle AH1	AAC, stored RNAY Fleetlands	
XZ355	SEPECAT Jaguar GR1A [J]	RAF No 41 Sqn, Coltishall	
XZ356	SEPECAT Jaguar GR1A [EP]	RAF No 6 Sqn, Coltishall	
XZ357	SEPECAT Jaguar GR1A [FK]	RAF No 41 Sqn, Coltishall	
XZ358	SEPECAT Jaguar GR1A [L]	RAF No 41 Sqn, Coltishall	
XZ360	SEPECAT Jaguar GR1A [FN]	RAF No 41 Sqn, Coltishall	
XZ361	SEPECAT Jaguar GR1A [T]	RAF No 41 Sqn, Coltishall	
XZ362	SEPECAT Jaguar GR1A [GC]	RAF No 54 Sqn, Coltishall	
XZ363	SEPECAT Jaguar GR1A [O]	RAF No 41 Sqn, Coltishall	
XZ363	SEPECAT Jaguar GR1A <R> (BAPC 151) [A]	RAF EP&TU, St Athan	
XZ364	SEPECAT Jaguar GR1A [GJ]	RAF No 54 Sqn, Coltishall	
XZ366	SEPECAT Jaguar GR1A [S]	RAF No 41 Sqn, Coltishall	
XZ367	SEPECAT Jaguar GR1A [GP]	RAF No 54 Sqn, Coltishall	
XZ368	SEPECAT Jaguar GR1 [8900M] [AG]	RAF No 1 SoTT, Cosford	
XZ369	SEPECAT Jaguar GR1A [EF]	RAF No 6 Sqn, Coltishall	
XZ370	SEPECAT Jaguar GR1 (9004M) [JB]	RAF No 1 SoTT, Cosford	
XZ371	SEPECAT Jaguar GR1 (8907M) [AP]	RAF No 1 SoTT, Cosford	
XZ372	SEPECAT Jaguar GR1A [ED]	RAF No 6 Sqn, Coltishall	
XZ373	SEPECAT Jaguar GR1A [GF]	RAF No 54 Sqn, Coltishall	
XZ374	SEPECAT Jaguar GR1 (9005M) [JC]	RAF No 1 SoTT, Cosford	
XZ375	SEPECAT Jaguar GR1A [GR]	RAF No 54 Sqn, Coltishall	
XZ377	SEPECAT Jaguar GR1A [EB]	RAF No 6 Sqn, Coltishall	
XZ378	SEPECAT Jaguar GR1A [EP]	RAF, stored Shawbury	
XZ381	SEPECAT Jaguar GR1A [EC]	RAF No 6 Sqn, Coltishall	
XZ382	SEPECAT Jaguar GR1 (8908M) [AE]	RAF Coltishall BDRF	
XZ383	SEPECAT Jaguar GR1 (8901M) [AF]	RAF No 1 SoTT, Cosford	
XZ384	SEPECAT Jaguar GR1 (8954M) [BC]	RAF No 1 SoTT, Cosford	
XZ385	SEPECAT Jaguar GR1A [F]	RAF No 16(R) Sqn, Lossiemouth	
XZ389	SEPECAT Jaguar GR1 (8946M) [BL]	RAF Halton	
XZ390	SEPECAT Jaguar GR1A (9003M) [35]	RAF No 1 SoTT, Cosford	
XZ391	SEPECAT Jaguar GR1A [GM]	RAF No 54 Sqn, Coltishall	
XZ392	SEPECAT Jaguar GR1A [GQ]	RAF, stored Shawbury	
XZ394	SEPECAT Jaguar GR1A [GN]	RAF No 54 Sqn, Coltishall	
XZ396	SEPECAT Jaguar GR1A [EM]	RAF No 6 Sqn, Coltishall	
XZ398	SEPECAT Jaguar GR1A [A]	RAF No 41 Sqn, Coltishall	
XZ399	SEPECAT Jaguar GR1A [EJ]	RAF No 6 Sqn, Coltishall	
XZ400	SEPECAT Jaguar GR1A [EG]	RAF, stored Shawbury	
XZ431	HS Buccaneer S2B	RAF Marham, Fire Section	
XZ439	BAe Sea Harrier F/A2 [2]	MoD(PE)/BAe Dunsfold	
XZ440	BAe Sea Harrier FRS1 [126/N]	RN, BAe Brough, on rebuild	
XZ445	BAe Harrier T4A	RN No 899 Sqn, Yeovilton	
XZ455	BAe Sea Harrier F/A2 [001]	RN No 801 Sqn, Yeovilton	
XZ457	BAe Sea Harrier F/A2 [714]	RN No 899 Sqn, Yeovilton	

XZ459 – XZ669

Notes	Serial	Type (other identity) [code]	Owner/operator, location or fate
	XZ459	BAe Sea Harrier F/A2	MoD(PE)/BAe Dunsfold (under conversion)
	XZ492	BAe Sea Harrier FRS1	RN, St Athan
	XZ493	BAe Sea Harrier FRS1 [126]	RN No 800 Sqn, Yeovilton
	XZ494	BAe Sea Harrier FRS1 [122]	RN No 800 Sqn, Yeovilton
	XZ495	BAe Sea Harrier FRS2 [713/OEU]	*Written off, 5 Jan 1994, Bristol Channel*
	XZ497	BAe Sea Harrier F/A2 [R]	MoD(PE) A&AEE Boscombe Down
	XZ498	BAe Sea Harrier FRS1	*Written off, 16 April 1994, Gorazde*
	XZ499	BAe Sea Harrier FRS1 [123]	RN No 800 Sqn, Yeovilton
	XZ557	Slingsby Venture T2 [7]	*To G-BVKU, February 1994*
	XZ570	WS61 Sea King HAS5 (mod)	MoD(PE)/Westland, Yeovil
	XZ571	WS61 Sea King HAS6 [014]	RN No 820 Sqn, Culdrose
	XZ574	WS61 Sea King HAS6 [704/PW]	RN No 819 Sqn, Prestwick
	XZ575	WS61 Sea King HAS5 [599]	RN No 706 Sqn, Culdrose
	XZ576	WS61 Sea King HAS6	MoD(PE), A&AEE Boscombe Down
	XZ577	WS61 Sea King HAS5 [138]	*Written off, 31 May 1991, Bay of Bengal*
	XZ578	WS61 Sea King HAS6 [581]	RN No 706 Sqn, Culdrose
	XZ579	WS61 Sea King HAS6 [706/PW]	RN No 819 Sqn, Prestwick
	XZ580	WS61 Sea King HAS6 [267]	RN No 814 Sqn, Culdrose
	XZ581	WS61 Sea King HAS6 [BD]	RN AMG, Culdrose
	XZ585	WS61 Sea King HAR3	RAF No 22 Sqn, A Flt, Chivenor
	XZ586	WS61 Sea King HAR3 [S]	RAF No 22 Sqn, B Flt, Wattisham
	XZ587	WS61 Sea King HAR3	RAF SKTU, St Mawgan
	XZ588	WS61 Sea King HAR3	RAF SKTU, St Mawgan
	XZ589	WS61 Sea King HAR3	RAF No 202 Sqn, D Flt, Lossiemouth
	XZ590	WS61 Sea King HAR3	RAF No 22 Sqn, B Flt, Wattisham
	XZ591	WS61 Sea King HAR3 [S]	RAF No 202 Sqn, St Mawgan
	XZ592	WS61 Sea King HAR3 [S]	RAF No 78 Sqn, Mount Pleasant, FI
	XZ593	WS61 Sea King HAR3	RAF SAREW, St Mawgan
	XZ594	WS61 Sea King HAR3	RAF No 202 Sqn, B Flt, Brawdy
	XZ595	WS61 Sea King HAR3	RAF No 22 Sqn, A Flt, Chivenor
	XZ596	WS61 Sea King HAR3	RAF SAREW, St Mawgan
	XZ597	WS61 Sea King HAR3 [S]	RAF SKTU, St Mawgan
	XZ598	WS61 Sea King HAR3	RAF No 202 Sqn, E Flt, Leconfield
	XZ599	WS61 Sea King HAR3 [S]	RAF SAREW, St Mawgan
	XZ605	WS Lynx AH7 [Y]	RM 3 CBAS, Yeovilton
	XZ606	WS Lynx AH7	AAC No 667 Sqn, Middle Wallop
	XZ607	WS Lynx AH7	AAC 3 Regiment, Wattisham
	XZ608	WS Lynx AH7 [1]	AAC No 656 Sqn, Dishforth
	XZ609	WS Lynx AH7	AAC No 669 Sqn, Detmold
	XZ610	WS Lynx AH7	AAC No 669 Sqn, Detmold
	XZ611	WS Lynx AH7 [Y]	AAC No 671 Sqn, Middle Wallop
	XZ612	WS Lynx AH7 [N]	RM 3 CBAS, Yeovilton
	XZ613	WS Lynx AH7 [F]	AAC SAE, Middle Wallop
	XZ614	WS Lynx AH7 [X]	RM 3 CBAS, Yeovilton
	XZ615	WS Lynx AH7	AAC No 655 Sqn, Aldergrove
	XZ616	WS Lynx AH7 [2]	AAC No 656 Sqn, Dishforth
	XZ617	WS Lynx AH7	AAC, RNAY Fleetlands
	XZ631	Panavia Tornado GR4	MoD(PE)/BAe, Warton
	XZ641	WS Lynx AH7 [G]	AAC No 671 Sqn, Middle Wallop
	XZ642	WS Lynx AH7	AAC 1 Regiment, Gütersloh
	XZ643	WS Lynx AH7 [N]	AAC No 661 Sqn, Gütersloh
	XZ644	WS Lynx AH7 (wreck)	AAC, Detmold
	XZ645	WS Lynx AH7 [M]	AAC No 663 Sqn, Wattisham
	XZ646	WS Lynx AH7	AAC 1 Regiment, Gütersloh
	XZ647	WS Lynx AH7	AAC No 655 Sqn, Aldergrove
	XZ648	WS Lynx AH7	AAC No 662 Sqn, Wattisham
	XZ649	WS Lynx AH7	AAC No 655 Sqn, Aldergrove
	XZ650	WS Lynx AH7	AAC 1 Regiment, Gütersloh
	XZ651	WS Lynx AH7 [3]	AAC No 656 Sqn, Dishforth
	XZ652	WS Lynx AH7 [T]	AAC No 671 Sqn, Middle Wallop
	XZ653	WS Lynx AH7	AAC No 664 Sqn, Dishforth
	XZ654	WS Lynx AH7	AAC, stored RNAY Fleetlands
	XZ655	WS Lynx AH7	AAC No 664 Sqn, Dishforth
	XZ661	WS Lynx AH7	AAC, stored RNAY Fleetlands
	XZ662	WS Lynx AH7	AAC No 655 Sqn, Aldergrove
	XZ663	WS Lynx AH7	AAC No 655 Sqn, Aldergrove
	XZ664	WS Lynx AH7	AAC No 661 Sqn, Gütersloh
	XZ665	WS Lynx AH7	AAC 1 Regiment, Gütersloh
	XZ666	WS Lynx AH7	AAC No 661 Sqn, Gütersloh
	XZ667	WS Lynx AH7	AAC No 665 Sqn, Aldergrove
	XZ668	WS Lynx AH7	AAC 3 Regiment, Wattisham
	XZ669	WS Lynx AH7	AAC No 661 Sqn, Gütersloh

Serial	Type (other identity) [code]	Owner/operator, location or fate	Notes
XZ670	WS Lynx AH7 [O]	AAC No 657 Sqn, Topcliffe	
XZ671	WS Lynx AH9 <ff>	AAC, stored RNAY Fleetlands	
XZ672	WS Lynx AH7	AAC No 655 Sqn, Aldergrove	
XZ673	WS Lynx AH7	AAC No 655 Sqn, Aldergrove	
XZ674	WS Lynx AH1 [Y]	AAC No 663 Sqn, Wattisham	
XZ675	WS Lynx AH7 [E]	AAC No 671 Sqn, Middle Wallop	
XZ676	WS Lynx AH7 [N]	AAC No 671 Sqn, Middle Wallop	
XZ677	WS Lynx AH7	AAC 3 Regiment, Wattisham	
XZ678	WS Lynx AH7	AAC No 662 Sqn, Wattisham	
XZ679	WS Lynx AH7 [5]	AAC No 656 Sqn, Dishforth	
XZ680	WS Lynx AH7	AAC No 652 Sqn, Gütersloh	
XZ681	WS Lynx AH1	AAC Middle Wallop, BDRT	
XZ689	WS Lynx HAS3S [403/BX]	RN No 815 Sqn, Portland	
XZ690	WS Lynx HAS3S [462]	RN No 815 Sqn, Portland	
XZ691	WS Lynx HAS8 [300]	Westland, Yeovil (conversion)	
XZ692	WS Lynx HAS3S [301]	RN No 815 Sqn, Portland	
XZ693	WS Lynx HAS3S [632]	RN No 702 Sqn, Portland	
XZ694	WS Lynx HAS3S [307]	RN No 815 Sqn, Portland	
XZ695	WS Lynx HAS3S [411/EB]	RN No 815 Sqn, Portland	
XZ696	WS Lynx HAS3S [479]	RN No 815 Sqn, Portland	
XZ697	WS Lynx HAS3CTS [341]	RNAY Fleetlands	
XZ698	WS Lynx HAS3	RNAY Fleetlands	
XZ699	WS Lynx HAS3 [301]	RN No 815 Sqn, Portland	
XZ719	WS Lynx HAS3S [638]	RN No 702 Sqn, Portland	
XZ720	WS Lynx HAS3S [332/LP]	RN No 815 Sqn, Portland	
XZ721	WS Lynx HAS3S [344/GW]	RN No 815 Sqn, Portland	
XZ722	WS Lynx HAS3S [304]	RN No 815 Sqn, Portland	
XZ723	WS Lynx HAS3S [374/VB]	RN No 815 Sqn, Portland	
XZ724	WS Lynx HAS3S [376/XB]	RN No 815 Sqn, Portland	
XZ725	WS Lynx HAS3S [342/BT]	RN No 815 Sqn, Portland	
XZ726	WS Lynx HAS3S [672]	RN No 815 Sqn OEU, Portland	
XZ727	WS Lynx HAS3S	RNAY Fleetlands (conversion)	
XZ728	WS Lynx HAS3S [641]	RN No 702 Sqn, Portland	
XZ729	WS Lynx HAS3S [642]	RN No 702 Sqn, Portland	
XZ730	WS Lynx HAS3CTS [634]	RN No 702 Sqn, Portland	
XZ731	WS Lynx HAS3S [457/LA]	RN No 815 Sqn, Portland	
XZ732	WS Lynx HAS8	RN No 815 Sqn, Portland	
XZ733	WS Lynx HAS3S [308]	RN No 815 Sqn, Portland	
XZ735	WS Lynx HAS3S	RNAY Fleetlands (conversion)	
XZ736	WS Lynx HAS3S [374/VB]	RN No 815 Sqn, Portland	
XZ918	WS61 Sea King HAS5 [589]	RN No 706 Sqn, Culdrose	
XZ920	WS61 Sea King HAR5 [822]	RN AMG, Culdrose	
XZ921	WS61 Sea King HAS6 [593/CU]	RNAY Fleetlands	
XZ922	WS61 Sea King HAS6 [514/BD]	RN No 810 Sqn, Boscombe Down	
XZ930	WS Gazelle HT3 [Q]	RAF No 2 FTS, Shawbury	
XZ931	WS Gazelle HT3 [R]	RAF No 2 FTS, Shawbury	
XZ932	WS Gazelle HT3 [S]	RAF No 2 FTS, Shawbury	
XZ933	WS Gazelle HT3 [T]	RAF No 2 FTS, Shawbury	
XZ934	WS Gazelle HT3 [U]	RAF No 2 FTS, Shawbury	
XZ935	WS Gazelle HCC4	RAF No 32 Sqn, Northolt	
XZ936	WS Gazelle HT2	MoD(PE) ETPS, Boscombe Down	
XZ937	WS Gazelle HT2 [Y]	RAF No 2 FTS, Shawbury	
XZ938	WS Gazelle HT2 [45/CU]	RN No 705 Sqn, Culdrose	
XZ939	WS Gazelle HT2 [Z]	MoD(PE) ETPS, Boscombe Down	
XZ940	WS Gazelle HT2 [O]	RAF No 2 FTS, Shawbury	
XZ941	WS Gazelle HT2 [B]	RAF No 2 FTS, Shawbury	
XZ942	WS Gazelle HT2 [42/CU]	RN No 705 Sqn, Culdrose	
XZ964	BAe Harrier GR3 [D]	Royal Engineers Museum, Chatham	
XZ965	BAe Harrier GR3 (9184M) [L]	RAF Stafford, GI use	
XZ966	BAe Harrier GR3 (9221M) [G]	RAF Cottesmore, Fire Section	
XZ967	BAe Harrier GR3 (9077M) [F]	RAF Halton	
XZ968	BAe Harrier GR3 (9222M) [3G]	RAF Marham, Fire Section	
XZ969	BAe Harrier GR3 [D]	RNEC Manadon	
XZ970	BAe Harrier GR3	RAF, stored St Athan	
XZ971	BAe Harrier GR3 (9219M) [G]	RAF Benson, at main gate	
XZ987	BAe Harrier GR3 (9185M) [C]	RAF Stafford, at main gate	
XZ990	BAe Harrier GR3 (wreck)	RAF Wittering, derelict	
XZ991	BAe Harrier GR3 (9162M) [3A]	RAF St Athan, BDRT	
XZ993	BAe Harrier GR3 [M]	RAF St Athan, Fire Section	
XZ994	BAe Harrier GR3 (9170M) [U]	RAF Air Movements School, Brize Norton	
XZ995	BAe Harrier GR3 (9220M) [3G]	RAF St Mawgan, Fire Section	
XZ996	BAe Harrier GR3 [2]	SAH, RNAS Culdrose	
XZ997	BAe Harrier GR3 (9122M) [V]	RAF Museum, Hendon	

Notes	Serial	Type (other identity) [code]	Owner/operator, location or fate
	XZ998	BAe Harrier GR3 (9161M) [D]	CSDE Swanton Morley, GI use
	ZA101	BAe Hawk 100 (G-HAWK)	BAe, Warton
	ZA105	WS61 Sea King HAR3 [S]	RAF No 78 Sqn, Mount Pleasant, FI
	ZA110	BAe Jetstream T2 [573/CU]	RN No 750 Sqn, Culdrose
	ZA111	BAe Jetstream T2 [574/CU]	RN No 750 Sqn, Culdrose
	ZA126	WS61 Sea King HAS6 [509]	RN No 810 Sqn, Culdrose
	ZA127	WS61 Sea King HAS6 [592]	RN No 706 Sqn, Culdrose
	ZA128	WS61 Sea King HAS6 [598]	RNAY Fleetlands
	ZA129	WS61 Sea King HAS6 [502/CU]	RN No 810 Sqn, Culdrose
	ZA130	WS61 Sea King HAS6 [587]	RN No 706 Sqn, Culdrose
	ZA131	WS61 Sea King HAS6 [011]	RN No 820 Sqn, Culdrose
	ZA133	WS61 Sea King HAS6 [013]	RN No 820 Sqn, Culdrose
	ZA134	WS61 Sea King HAS6 [598]	RN No 706 Sqn, Culdrose
	ZA135	WS61 Sea King HAS5 [015]	RN, stored Fleetlands
	ZA136	WS61 Sea King HAS5 [015]	RN No 820 Sqn, Culdrose
	ZA137	WS61 Sea King HAS5 [597]	RN No 706 Sqn, Culdrose
	ZA140	BAe VC10 K2 [A]	RAF St Athan
	ZA141	BAe VC10 K2 [B]	RAF No 101 Sqn, Brize Norton
	ZA142	BAe VC10 K2 [C]	RAF, stored St Athan
	ZA143	BAe VC10 K2 [D]	RAF No 101 Sqn, Brize Norton
	ZA144	BAe VC10 K2 [E]	RAF stored, Brize Norton
	ZA147	BAe VC10 K3 [F]	RAF No 101 Sqn, Brize Norton
	ZA148	BAe VC10 K3 [G]	RAF No 101 Sqn, Brize Norton
	ZA149	BAe VC10 K3	RAF No 101 Sqn, Brize Norton
	ZA150	BAe VC10 K3 [J]	RAF No 101 Sqn, Brize Norton
	ZA166	WS61 Sea King HAS6 [590]	RNAY Fleetlands
	ZA167	WS61 Sea King HAS6 [131]	RNAY Fleetlands
	ZA168	WS61 Sea King HAS6 [512]	RN No 810 Sqn, Culdrose
	ZA169	WS61 Sea King HAS6 [266/N]	RN No 814 Sqn, Culdrose
	ZA170	WS61 Sea King HAS6 [584]	RN No 706 Sqn, Culdrose
	ZA175	BAe Sea Harrier FRS1	RN AMG, Yeovilton
	ZA176	BAe Sea Harrier F/A2 [000]	RN No 801 Sqn, Yeovilton
	ZA195	BAe Sea Harrier F/A2	MoD(PE), A&AEE Boscombe Down
	ZA250	BAe Harrier T52 (G-VTOL)	Brooklands Aviation Museum, Weybridge
	ZA254	Panavia Tornado F2	MoD(PE), BAe Warton
	ZA267	Panavia Tornado F2	MoD(PE), BAe Warton
	ZA283	Panavia Tornado F2	MoD(PE), BAe Warton
	ZA291	WS61 Sea King HC4 [ZX]	RN No 707 Sqn, Yeovilton
	ZA292	WS61 Sea King HC4 [ZW]	MoD(PE)/Westland, Yeovil
	ZA293	WS61 Sea King HC4 [ZT]	RN No 707 Sqn, Yeovilton
	ZA295	WS61 Sea King HC4 [ZU]	RN AMG, Yeovilton
	ZA296	WS61 Sea King HC4 [VO]	RN No 846 Sqn, Yeovilton
	ZA297	WS61 Sea King HC4 [25]	RN No 772 Sqn, Portland
	ZA298	WS61 Sea King HC4 [G]	RN No 845 Sqn, Yeovilton
	ZA299	WS61 Sea King HC4 [ZZ]	RN No 707 Sqn, Yeovilton
	ZA310	WS61 Sea King HC4 [ZV]	RN No 707 Sqn, Yeovilton
	ZA312	WS61 Sea King HC4 [ZS]	RN No 707 Sqn, Yeovilton
	ZA313	WS61 Sea King HC4 [E]	RN No 845 Sqn, Yeovilton
	ZA314	WS61 Sea King HC4 [F]	RN AMG, Yeovilton
	ZA319	Panavia Tornado GR1 [B-11]	RAF TTTE, Cottesmore
	ZA320	Panavia Tornado GR1 [B-01]	RAF TTTE, Cottesmore
	ZA321	Panavia Tornado GR1 [B-58]	RAF TTTE, Cottesmore
	ZA322	Panavia Tornado GR1 [B-50]	RAF TTTE, Cottesmore
	ZA323	Panavia Tornado GR1 [B-14]	RAF TTTE, Cottesmore
	ZA324	Panavia Tornado GR1 [B-02]	RAF TTTE, Cottesmore
	ZA325	Panavia Tornado GR1 [B-03]	RAF TTTE, Cottesmore
	ZA326	Panavia Tornado GR1	MoD(PE) DRA, Boscombe Down
	ZA327	Panavia Tornado GR1 [B-51]	RAF TTTE, Cottesmore
	ZA328	Panavia Tornado GR1	MoD(PE) A&AEE, Boscombe Down
	ZA330	Panavia Tornado GR1 [B-08]	RAF TTTE, Cottesmore
	ZA352	Panavia Tornado GR1 [B-04]	RAF TTTE, Cottesmore
	ZA353	Panavia Tornado GR1 [B-53]	RAF TTTE, Cottesmore
	ZA354	Panavia Tornado GR1	MoD(PE) A&AEE, Boscombe Down
	ZA355	Panavia Tornado GR1 [B-54]	RAF TTTE, Cottesmore
	ZA356	Panavia Tornado GR1 [B-07]	RAF TTTE, Cottesmore
	ZA357	Panavia Tornado GR1 [B-05]	RAF TTTE, Cottesmore
	ZA358	Panavia Tornado GR1 [B-06]	RAF TTTE, Cottesmore
	ZA359	Panavia Tornado GR1 [B-55]	RAF TTTE, Cottesmore
	ZA360	Panavia Tornado GR1 [B-56]	RAF TTTE, Cottesmore
	ZA361	Panavia Tornado GR1 [B-57]	RAF TTTE, Cottesmore
	ZA362	Panavia Tornado GR1 [B-09]	RAF TTTE, Cottesmore
	ZA365	Panavia Tornado GR1 [JT]	RAF No 12 Sqn, Lossiemouth

Serial	Type (other identity) [code]	Owner/operator, location or fate	Notes
ZA367	Panavia Tornado GR1 [Z]	RAF No 2 Sqn, Marham	
ZA368	Panavia Tornado GR1 [AJ-P]	*Written off, 19 July 1994, Moray Firth*	
ZA369	Panavia Tornado GR1A [II]	RAF No 2 Sqn, Marham	
ZA370	Panavia Tornado GR1A [A]	RAF No 2 Sqn, Marham	
ZA371	Panavia Tornado GR1A [C]	RAF No 2 Sqn, Marham	
ZA372	Panavia Tornado GR1A [E]	RAF No 2 Sqn, Marham	
ZA373	Panavia Tornado GR1A [H]	RAF No 2 Sqn, Marham	
ZA374	Panavia Tornado GR1 [CN]	RAF No 17 Sqn, Bruggen	
ZA375	Panavia Tornado GR1B [AJ-W]	RAF No 617 Sqn, Lossiemouth	
ZA393	Panavia Tornado GR1 [BE]	RAF No 14 Sqn, Bruggen	
ZA395	Panavia Tornado GR1A [N]	RAF No 2 Sqn, Marham	
ZA397	Panavia Tornado GR1A [O]	*Written off, Radisson, Canada, 1 Aug*	
1994			
ZA398	Panavia Tornado GR1A [S]	RAF No 2 Sqn, Marham	
ZA399	Panavia Tornado GR1B [AJ-C]	RAF No 617 Sqn, Lossiemouth	
ZA400	Panavia Tornado GR1A [T]	RAF No 2 Sqn, Marham	
ZA401	Panavia Tornado GR1A [R]	RAF No 2 Sqn, Marham	
ZA402	Panavia Tornado GR1	MoD(PE), A&AEE Boscombe Down	
ZA404	Panavia Tornado GR1A [W]	RAF No 2 Sqn, Marham	
ZA405	Panavia Tornado GR1A [Y]	RAF No 2 Sqn, Marham	
ZA406	Panavia Tornado GR1 [CI]	RAF No 17 Sqn, Bruggen	
ZA407	Panavia Tornado GR1B [AJ-G]	RAF No 617 Sqn, Lossiemouth	
ZA409	Panavia Tornado GR1B [FQ]	RAF No 12 Sqn, Lossiemouth	
ZA410	Panavia Tornado GR1B [FZ]	RAF No 12 Sqn, Lossiemouth	
ZA411	Panavia Tornado GR1B [AJ-S]	RAF No 617 Sqn, Lossiemouth	
ZA412	Panavia Tornado GR1B [FX]	RAF, stored St Athan	
ZA446	Panavia Tornado GR1B [AJ-H]	RAF SAOEU, Boscombe Down	
ZA446	Panavia Tornado GR1 <R>	RAF EP&TU, St Athan	
	(BAPC 155) [F]		
ZA447	Panavia Tornado GR1B [FA]	RAF No 12 Sqn, Lossiemouth	
ZA449	Panavia Tornado GR1	MoD(PE), A&AEE Boscombe Down	
ZA450	Panavia Tornado GR1B [FB]	RAF No 12 Sqn, Lossiemouth	
ZA452	Panavia Tornado GR1B [FC]	RAF No 12 Sqn, Lossiemouth	
ZA453	Panavia Tornado GR1B [FD]	RAF No 12 Sqn, Lossiemouth	
ZA455	Panavia Tornado GR1B [FE]	RAF No 12 Sqn, Lossiemouth	
ZA456	Panavia Tornado GR1 [AJ-Q]	RAF No 617 Sqn, Lossiemouth	
ZA457	Panavia Tornado GR1 [AJ-J]	RAF No 617 Sqn, Lossiemouth	
ZA458	Panavia Tornado GR1 [CE]	RAF No 17 Sqn, Bruggen	
ZA459	Panavia Tornado GR1B [AJ-B]	RAF No 617 Sqn, Lossiemouth	
ZA460	Panavia Tornado GR1 [AJ-A]	RAF No 617 Sqn, Lossiemouth	
ZA461	Panavia Tornado GR1 [AJ-M]	RAF No 617 Sqn, Lossiemouth	
ZA462	Panavia Tornado GR1 [CG]	RAF No 17 Sqn, Bruggen	
ZA463	Panavia Tornado GR1 [CR]	RAF No 17 Sqn, Bruggen	
ZA465	Panavia Tornado GR1B [AJ-F]	RAF No 617 Sqn, Lossiemouth	
ZA466	Panavia Tornado GR1 <ff>	RAF St Athan, BDRT	
ZA469	Panavia Tornado GR1 [AJ-O]	RAF No 617 Sqn, Lossiemouth	
ZA470	Panavia Tornado GR1 [BQ]	RAF No 14 Sqn, Bruggen	
ZA471	Panavia Tornado GR1B [AJ-K]	RAF No 617 Sqn, Lossiemouth	
ZA472	Panavia Tornado GR1 [CT]	RAF No 17 Sqn, Bruggen	
ZA473	Panavia Tornado GR1B [FG]	RAF No 12 Sqn, Lossiemouth	
ZA474	Panavia Tornado GR1B [FF]	RAF No 12 Sqn, Lossiemouth	
ZA475	Panavia Tornado GR1B [FH]	RAF No 12 Sqn, Lossiemouth	
ZA490	Panavia Tornado GR1B [FJ]	RAF No 12 Sqn, Lossiemouth	
ZA491	Panavia Tornado GR1B [FK]	RAF No 12 Sqn, Lossiemouth	
ZA492	Panavia Tornado GR1B [FL]	RAF No 12 Sqn, Lossiemouth	
ZA541	Panavia Tornado GR1	RAF No 15(R) Sqn, Lossiemouth	
ZA542	Panavia Tornado GR1 [JA]	RAF, stored St Athan	
ZA543	Panavia Tornado GR1	RAF, stored St Athan	
ZA544	Panavia Tornado GR1 [TP]	RAF No 15(R) Sqn, Lossiemouth	
ZA546	Panavia Tornado GR1 [AJ-C]	RAF Cottesmore, instructional use	
ZA547	Panavia Tornado GR1 [JC]	RAF, stored St Athan	
ZA548	Panavia Tornado GR1 [TQ]	RAF No 15(R) Sqn, Lossiemouth	
ZA549	Panavia Tornado GR1 [TR]	RAF No 15(R) Sqn, Lossiemouth	
ZA550	Panavia Tornado GR1 [JD]	RAF, stored St Athan	
ZA551	Panavia Tornado GR1 [X]	RAF No 2 Sqn, Marham	
ZA552	Panavia Tornado GR1 [TS]	RAF No 15(R) Sqn, Lossiemouth	
ZA553	Panavia Tornado GR1 [JE]	RAF, stored St Athan	
ZA554	Panavia Tornado GR1 [DM]	RAF, stored St Athan	
ZA556	Panavia Tornado GR1 [TA]	RAF No 15(R) Sqn, Lossiemouth	
ZA557	Panavia Tornado GR1	RAF, stored St Athan	
ZA559	Panavia Tornado GR1 [F]	RAF No 15(R) Sqn, Lossiemouth	
ZA560	Panavia Tornado GR1 [B-59]	RAF TTTE, Cottesmore	
ZA562	Panavia Tornado GR1 [TT]	RAF No 15(R) Sqn, Lossiemouth	

Notes	Serial	Type (other identity) [code]	Owner/operator, location or fate
	ZA563	Panavia Tornado GR1 [TC]	RAF No 15(R) Sqn, Lossiemouth
	ZA564	Panavia Tornado GR1 [JK]	RAF, stored St Athan
	ZA585	Panavia Tornado GR1	RAF, stored St Athan
	ZA587	Panavia Tornado GR1 [TD]	RAF No 15(R) Sqn, Lossiemouth
	ZA588	Panavia Tornado GR1 [B-52]	RAF, stored St Athan
	ZA589	Panavia Tornado GR1 [TE]	RAF No 15(R) Sqn, Lossiemouth
	ZA590	Panavia Tornado GR1	RAF, stored St Athan
	ZA591	Panavia Tornado GR1	RAF, stored St Athan
	ZA592	Panavia Tornado GR1 [B]	RAF, stored St Athan
	ZA594	Panavia Tornado GR1 [TU]	RAF No 15(R) Sqn, Lossiemouth
	ZA595	Panavia Tornado GR1 [TV]	RAF No 15(R) Sqn, Lossiemouth
	ZA596	Panavia Tornado GR1	RAF, stored St Athan
	ZA597	Panavia Tornado GR1	RAF, stored St Athan
	ZA598	Panavia Tornado GR1 [S]	RAF, stored St Athan
	ZA599	Panavia Tornado GR1 [B-16]	RAF TTTE, Cottesmore
	ZA600	Panavia Tornado GR1 [TH]	RAF No 15(R) Sqn, Lossiemouth
	ZA601	Panavia Tornado GR1 [TI]	RAF No 15(R) Sqn, Lossiemouth
	ZA602	Panavia Tornado GR1 [B-17]	RAF TTTE, Cottesmore
	ZA604	Panavia Tornado GR1 [TY]	RAF No 15(R) Sqn, Lossiemouth
	ZA606	Panavia Tornado GR1	RAF, stored St Athan
	ZA607	Panavia Tornado GR1 [TJ]	RAF No 15(R) Sqn, Lossiemouth
	ZA608	Panavia Tornado GR1 [TK]	RAF No 15(R) Sqn, Lossiemouth
	ZA609	Panavia Tornado GR1 [J]	RAF, stored St Athan
	ZA611	Panavia Tornado GR1	RAF, stored St Athan
	ZA612	Panavia Tornado GR1 [TZ]	RAF No 15(R) Sqn, Lossiemouth
	ZA613	Panavia Tornado GR1	RAF, stored St Athan
	ZA614	Panavia Tornado GR1 [TB]	RAF No 15(R) Sqn, Lossiemouth
	ZA654	Slingsby Venture T2 [4]	*Sold as G-BVLX, March 1994*
	ZA665	Slingsby Venture T2	*Sold as G-BVKK, February 1994*
	ZA670	B-V Chinook HC2 [BG]	Boeing, Philadelphia (conversion)
	ZA671	B-V Chinook HC2 [BB]	RAF No 18 Sqn, Laarbruch
	ZA673	B-V Chinook HC2 [BF]	Boeing, Philadelphia (conversion)
	ZA674	B-V Chinook HC2 [A]	RAF No 7 Sqn, Odiham
	ZA675	B-V Chinook HC2 [EB]	RAF No 7 Sqn, Odiham
	ZA676	B-V Chinook HC1 [FG] (wreck)	RAF, stored Fleetlands
	ZA677	B-V Chinook HC2 [U]	RAF No 7 Sqn, Odiham
	ZA678	B-V Chinook HC1 (9229M) [EZ] (wreck)	RAF Odiham, BDRT
	ZA679	B-V Chinook HC2 [C]	RAF No 7 Sqn, Odiham
	ZA680	B-V Chinook HC2 [EM]	Boeing, Philadelphia (conversion)
	ZA681	B-V Chinook HC2 [S]	RAF No 7 Sqn/27(R) Sqn, Odiham
	ZA682	B-V Chinook HC2 [N]	RAF No 7 Sqn, Odiham
	ZA683	B-V Chinook HC2 [EW]	Boeing, Philadelphia (conversion)
	ZA684	B-V Chinook HC2 [L]	RAF No 7 Sqn, Odiham
	ZA704	B-V Chinook HC2 [J]	RAF No 7 Sqn, Odiham
	ZA705	B-V Chinook HC2 [EO]	Boeing, Philadelphia (conversion)
	ZA707	B-V Chinook HC2 [EV]	Boeing, Philadelphia (conversion)
	ZA708	B-V Chinook HC2 [BK]	Boeing, Philadelphia (conversion)
	ZA709	B-V Chinook HC2	Boeing, Philadelphia (conversion)
	ZA710	B-V Chinook HC2 [Y]	RAF No 78 Sqn, Mount Pleasant, FI
	ZA711	B-V Chinook HC2 [ET]	Boeing, Philadelphia (conversion)
	ZA712	B-V Chinook HC2	RAF No 7 Sqn/27(R) Sqn, Odiham
	ZA713	B-V Chinook HC2 [EM]	RAF No 7 Sqn, Odiham
	ZA714	B-V Chinook HC2 [BA]	RAF No 18 Sqn, Laarbruch
	ZA717	B-V Chinook HC1 (wreck)	RAF St Athan, BDRT
	ZA718	B-V Chinook HC2 [BN]	MoD(PE), A&AEE Boscombe Down
	ZA720	B-V Chinook HC2 [EP]	Boeing, Philadelphia (conversion)
	ZA726	WS Gazelle AH1	AAC, stored Fleetlands
	ZA728	WS Gazelle AH1 [E]	RM 3 CBAS, Yeovilton
	ZA729	WS Gazelle AH1	AAC No 656 Sqn, Dishforth
	ZA730	WS Gazelle AH1	AAC, RNAY Fleetlands
	ZA731	WS Gazelle AH1 [A]	AAC No 29 Flt, BATUS, Suffield, Canada
	ZA733	WS Gazelle AH1	AAC No 665 Sqn, Aldergrove
	ZA734	WS Gazelle AH1	AAC, stored Fleetlands
	ZA735	WS Gazelle AH1	AAC No 25 Flt, Belize
	ZA736	WS Gazelle AH1 [S]	AAC No 29 Flt, BATUS, Suffield, Canada
	ZA737	WS Gazelle AH1 [V]	AAC No 670 Sqn, Middle Wallop
	ZA765	WS Gazelle AH1	AAC No 25 Flt, Belize
	ZA766	WS Gazelle AH1 [W]	AAC
	ZA767	WS Gazelle AH1	AAC No 25 Flt, Belize
	ZA768	WS Gazelle AH1 [F] (wreck)	AAC, stored Fleetlands
	ZA769	WS Gazelle AH1 [K]	AAC No 670 Sqn, Middle Wallop
	ZA771	WS Gazelle AH1	AAC No 664 Sqn, Dishforth

Serial	Type (other identity) [code]	Owner/operator, location or fate	Notes
ZA772	WS Gazelle AH1	AAC, stored Fleetlands	
ZA773	WS Gazelle AH1	AAC No 665 Sqn, Aldergrove	
ZA774	WS Gazelle AH1	AAC No 665 Sqn, Aldergrove	
ZA775	WS Gazelle AH1 [E1]	AAC, stored Fleetlands	
ZA776	WS Gazelle AH1 [F]	RM 3 CBAS, Yeovilton	
ZA777	WS Gazelle AH1 [B]	AAC No 670 Sqn, Middle Wallop	
ZA802	WS Gazelle HT3 [W]	RAF No 2 FTS, Shawbury	
ZA803	WS Gazelle HT3 [X]	RAF No 2 FTS, Shawbury	
ZA804	WS Gazelle HT3 [I]	RAF No 2 FTS, Shawbury	
ZA934	WS Puma HC1 [BX]	RAF No 18 Sqn, Laarbruch	
ZA935	WS Puma HC1 [DM]	RAF No 230 Sqn, Aldergrove	
ZA936	WS Puma HC1	RAF No 33 Sqn, Odiham	
ZA937	WS Puma HC1 [CV]	RAF No 230 Sqn, Aldergrove	
ZA938	WS Puma HC1	RAF No 33 Sqn, Odiham	
ZA939	WS Puma HC1 [DN]	RAF No 230 Sqn, Aldergrove	
ZA940	WS Puma HC1 [CY]	RAF No 230 Sqn, Aldergrove	
ZA947	Douglas Dakota C3 [YS-DM]	RAF BBMF, Coningsby	
ZB506	WS61 Sea King Mk 4X	MoD(PE), DRA Boscombe Down	
ZB507	WS61 Sea King Mk 4X	MoD(PE), ETPS Boscombe Down	
ZB600	BAe Harrier T4 [Z]	RAF HOCU/No 20(R) Sqn, Wittering	
ZB601	BAe Harrier T4 [721]	RAF St Athan Fire Section	
ZB602	BAe Harrier T4 [R]	RAF HOCU/No 20(R) Sqn, Wittering	
ZB603	BAe Harrier T4 [718]	RN No 899 Sqn, Yeovilton	
ZB604	BAe Harrier T4N [722]	RN No 899 Sqn, Yeovilton	
ZB605	BAe Harrier T8	MoD(PE), A&AEE Boscombe Down	
ZB615	SEPECAT Jaguar T2A	MoD(PE), A&AEE Boscombe Down	
ZB625	WS Gazelle HT3 [N]	RAF No 2 FTS, Shawbury	
ZB626	WS Gazelle HT3 [L]	RAF No 2 FTS, Shawbury	
ZB627	WS Gazelle HT3 [A]	RAF No 7 Sqn, Odiham	
ZB629	WS Gazelle HCC4	RAF No 32 Sqn, Northolt	
ZB646	WS Gazelle HT2 [59/CU]	RN No 705 Sqn, Culdrose	
ZB647	WS Gazelle HT2 [40/CU]	RN No 705 Sqn, Culdrose	
ZB648	WS Gazelle HT2 [40/CU] (wreck)	RN Predannack Fire School	
ZB649	WS Gazelle HT2 [43/CU]	RN No 705 Sqn, Culdrose	
ZB665	WS Gazelle AH1	AAC No 16 Flt, Dhekelia, Cyprus	
ZB666	WS Gazelle AH1 [G]	AAC No 670 Sqn, Middle Wallop	
ZB667	WS Gazelle AH1	AAC, UNFICYP, Nicosia	
ZB668	WS Gazelle AH1 [UN]	AAC, stored Fleetlands	
ZB669	WS Gazelle AH1	AAC, Fleetlands	
ZB670	WS Gazelle AH1	AAC No 665 Sqn, Aldergrove	
ZB671	WS Gazelle AH1	AAC No 29 Flt, BATUS, Suffield, Canada	
ZB672	WS Gazelle AH1 [V]	AAC No 662 Sqn, Wattisham	
ZB673	WS Gazelle AH1 [P]	AAC No 670 Sqn, Middle Wallop	
ZB674	WS Gazelle AH1	AAC No 665 Sqn, Aldergrove	
ZB676	WS Gazelle AH1 [E1]	AAC, stored Fleetlands	
ZB677	WS Gazelle AH1	AAC No 29 Flt, BATUS, Suffield, Canada	
ZB678	WS Gazelle AH1	AAC No 16 Flt, Dhekelia, Cyprus	
ZB679	WS Gazelle AH1	AAC No 16 Flt, Dhekelia, Cyprus	
ZB682	WS Gazelle AH1	AAC No 665 Sqn, Aldergrove	
ZB683	WS Gazelle AH1	AAC, RNAY Fleetlands	
ZB684	WS Gazelle AH1	AAC No 665 Sqn, Aldergrove	
ZB685	WS Gazelle AH1	AAC No 665 Sqn, Aldergrove	
ZB686	WS Gazelle AH1	AAC, RNAY Fleetlands	
ZB688	WS Gazelle AH1 [H]	AAC No 670 Sqn, Middle Wallop	
ZB689	WS Gazelle AH1 [W]	AAC No 670 Sqn, Middle Wallop	
ZB690	WS Gazelle AH1	AAC No 16 Flt, Dhekelia, Cyprus	
ZB691	WS Gazelle AH1 [C]	AAC No 664 Sqn, Dishforth	
ZB692	WS Gazelle AH1	AAC No 664 Sqn, Dishforth	
ZB693	WS Gazelle AH1	AAC AETW, Middle Wallop	
ZD230	BAC Super VC10 K4	MoD(PE), BAe Filton	
ZD232	BAC Super VC10 (8699M)	RAF Brize Norton Fire Section	
ZD234	BAC Super VC10 (8700M)	RAF Brize Norton, tanker simulator	
ZD235	BAC Super VC10 K4	MoD(PE), BAe Filton	
ZD239	BAC Super VC10	FSCTE, RAF Manston	
ZD240	BAC Super VC10 K4 [M]	RAF No 101 Sqn, Brize Norton	
ZD241	BAC Super VC10 K4	MoD(PE), BAe Filton	
ZD242	BAC Super VC10 K4 [P]	RAF No 101 Sqn, Brize Norton	
ZD243	BAC Super VC10	BAe, Filton (spares use)	
ZD249	WS Lynx HAS3S	RNAY Fleetlands (conversion)	
ZD250	WS Lynx HAS3S [417/NM]	RN No 815 Sqn, Portland	
ZD251	WS Lynx HAS3S [415/MM]	RN No 815 Sqn, Portland	
ZD252	WS Lynx HAS3S [302]	RN No 815 Sqn, Portland	

ZD253 – ZD406

Notes	Serial	Type (other identity) [code]	Owner/operator, location or fate
	ZD253	WS Lynx HAS3S	RNAY Fleetlands
	ZD254	WS Lynx HAS3S [631]	RNAY Fleetlands (conversion)
	ZD255	WS Lynx HAS3S [412/CW]	RN No 815 Sqn, Portland
	ZD256	WS Lynx HAS3S [328/BV]	RN No 815 Sqn, Portland
	ZD257	WS Lynx HAS3S [363]	RN No 815 Sqn, Portland
	ZD258	WS Lynx HAS3S	RN No 702 Sqn, Portland
	ZD259	WS Lynx HAS3S [363/MA]	RN No 815 Sqn, Portland
	ZD260	WS Lynx HAS3S [352]	RN No 815 Sqn, Portland
	ZD261	WS Lynx HAS8 [636]	MoD(PE), Westland Yeovil
	ZD262	WS Lynx HAS3S [641]	RN No 702 Sqn, Portland
	ZD263	WS Lynx HAS3S	RN No 815 Sqn, Portland
	ZD264	WS Lynx HAS3S [420/EX]	RN No 815 Sqn, Portland
	ZD265	WS Lynx HAS3S [306]	RN No 815 Sqn, Portland
	ZD266	WS Lynx HAS8	MoD(PE), Westland Yeovil (conversion)
	ZD267	WS Lynx HAS8	MoD(PE), Westland Yeovil
	ZD268	WS Lynx HAS3S [344/GW]	RN No 815 Sqn, Portland
	ZD272	WS Lynx AH7 [H]	AAC No 671 Sqn, Middle Wallop
	ZD273	WS Lynx AH7	AAC, stored RNAY Fleetlands
	ZD274	WS Lynx AH7 [N]	AAC No 657 Sqn, Dishforth
	ZD275	WS Lynx AH7	*Written off, Crossmaglen, 19 March 1994*
	ZD276	WS Lynx AH7 [6]	AAC No 656 Sqn, Dishforth
	ZD277	WS Lynx AH7	AAC No 669 Sqn, Detmold
	ZD278	WS Lynx AH7 [A]	AAC No 671 Sqn, Middle Wallop
	ZD279	WS Lynx AH7 [C]	AAC No 671 Sqn, Middle Wallop
	ZD280	WS Lynx AH7	AAC, stored RNAY Fleetlands
	ZD281	WS Lynx AH7	AAC No 667 Sqn, Middle Wallop
	ZD282	WS Lynx AH7 [L]	RM 3 CBAS, Yeovilton
	ZD283	WS Lynx AH1 [P]	AAC No 671 Sqn, Middle Wallop
	ZD284	WS Lynx AH7 [H]	AAC 1 Regiment, Gütersloh
	ZD285	WS Lynx AH7	MoD(PE), DRA Boscombe Down
	ZD318	BAe Harrier GR7	MoD(PE), A&AEE Boscombe Down
	ZD319	BAe Harrier GR7	MoD(PE), A&AEE Boscombe Down
	ZD320	BAe Harrier GR5A	MoD(PE), A&AEE Boscombe Down
	ZD321	BAe Harrier GR5	MoD(PE), A&AEE Boscombe Down
	ZD322	BAe Harrier GR7	MoD(PE)/BAe Dunsfold (under conversion)
	ZD323	BAe Harrier GR7	RAF HSF, Wittering
	ZD324	BAe Harrier GR7	MoD(PE)/BAe Dunsfold
	ZD326	BAe Harrier GR7 [F]	RAF HOCU/No 20(R) Sqn, Wittering
	ZD327	BAe Harrier GR7	RAF, stored Shawbury
	ZD328	BAe Harrier GR7 [CB]	RAF No 4 Sqn, Laarbruch
	ZD329	BAe Harrier GR7	MoD(PE)/BAe Dunsfold (under conversion)
	ZD330	BAe Harrier GR7 [J]	RAF, stored Shawbury
	ZD345	BAe Harrier GR7 [J]	RAF HOCU/No 20(R) Sqn, Wittering
	ZD346	BAe Harrier GR7	MoD(PE)/BAe Dunsfold (under conversion)
	ZD347	BAe Harrier GR7	MoD(PE)/BAe Dunsfold (under conversion)
	ZD348	BAe Harrier GR7	RAF, stored Shawbury
	ZD349	BAe Harrier GR7 [C]	*Written off near Evesham, 14 Jan 1994*
	ZD350	BAe Harrier GR5 (9189M) [A]	RAF St Athan, BDRT
	ZD351	BAe Harrier GR7	MoD(PE)/BAe Dunsfold (under conversion)
	ZD352	BAe Harrier GR7 [01]	RAF, stored Shawbury
	ZD353	BAe Harrier GR7	MoD(PE)/BAe Brough (under conversion)
	ZD354	BAe Harrier GR7	MoD(PE)/BAe Dunsfold (under conversion)
	ZD375	BAe Harrier GR5 [5D]	RAF HOCU/No 20(R) Sqn, Wittering
	ZD376	BAe Harrier GR7	MoD(PE)/BAe Dunsfold (under conversion)
	ZD377	BAe Harrier GR7	MoD(PE)/BAe Dunsfold (under conversion)
	ZD378	BAe Harrier GR7 [A]	RAF HOCU/No 20(R) Sqn, Wittering
	ZD379	BAe Harrier GR7 [H]	RAF, stored Shawbury
	ZD380	BAe Harrier GR7 [06]	RAF No 1 Sqn, Wittering
	ZD400	BAe Harrier GR7 [02]	RAF, stored Shawbury
	ZD401	BAe Harrier GR7	RAF, stored Shawbury
	ZD402	BAe Harrier GR7 [E]	RAF HOCU/No 20(R) Sqn, Wittering
	ZD403	BAe Harrier GR7 (fuselage)	RAF HSF, Wittering
	ZD404	BAe Harrier GR7 [H]	RAF HOCU/No 20(R) Sqn, Wittering
	ZD405	BAe Harrier GR7 [WC]	RAF No 4 Sqn, Incirlik
	ZD406	BAe Harrier GR7 [WB]	RAF No 3 Sqn, Laarbruch

Serial	Type (other identity) [code]	Owner/operator, location or fate	Notes
ZD407	BAe Harrier GR7 [WM]	RAF No 4 Sqn, Laarbruch	
ZD408	BAe Harrier GR7 [WK]	RAF No 4 Sqn, Incirlik	
ZD409	BAe Harrier GR7 [B]	RAF HOCU/No 20(R) Sqn, Wittering	
ZD410	BAe Harrier GR7 [C]	RAF HOCU/No 20(R) Sqn, Wittering	
ZD411	BAe Harrier GR7 [L]	RAF HOCU/No 20(R) Sqn, Wittering	
ZD412	BAe Harrier GR5 (wreck)	BAe Brough (rebuild)	
ZD431	BAe Harrier GR7 [02]	RAF No 1 Sqn, Wittering	
ZD432	BAe Harrier GR7 [WF]	*Written off, 23 Nov 1993, Northern Iraq*	
ZD433	BAe Harrier GR7 [D]	RAF HOCU/No 20(R) Sqn, Wittering	
ZD434	BAe Harrier GR7 [WE]	RAF No 4 Sqn, Incirlik	
ZD435	BAe Harrier GR7 [04]	RAF No 1 Sqn, Wittering	
ZD436	BAe Harrier GR7	MoD(PE)/BAe Dunsfold	
		(under conversion)	
ZD437	BAe Harrier GR7 [05]	RAF No 1 Sqn, Wittering	
ZD438	BAe Harrier GR7 [03]	RAF No 1 Sqn, Wittering	
ZD461	BAe Harrier GR7 [WH]	RAF No 1 Sqn, Wittering	
ZD462	BAe Harrier GR7 [07]	RAF No 1 Sqn, Wittering	
ZD463	BAe Harrier GR7 [09]	RAF No 1 Sqn, Wittering	
ZD464	BAe Harrier GR7 [10]	RAF No 1 Sqn, Wittering	
ZD465	BAe Harrier GR7 (fuselage)	RAF HSF, Wittering	
ZD466	BAe Harrier GR7	RAF HSF, Wittering	
ZD467	BAe Harrier GR7 [AV]	RAF No 3 Sqn, Laarbruch	
ZD468	BAe Harrier GR7 [12]	RAF No 1 Sqn, Wittering	
ZD469	BAe Harrier GR7	RAF AMF, Laarbruch	
ZD470	BAe Harrier GR7 [01]	RAF No 1 Sqn, Wittering	
ZD472	Harrier GR5 <R> (BAPC 191) [01]	RAF EP&TU, St Athan	
ZD476	WS61 Sea King HC4 [ZU]	RN No 707 Sqn, Yeovilton	
ZD477	WS61 Sea King HC4 [A]	RN No 845 Sqn, Yeovilton	
ZD478	WS61 Sea King HC4 [VM]	RN No 846 Sqn, Yeovilton	
ZD479	WS61 Sea King HC4 [ZV]	RN No 707 Sqn, Yeovilton	
ZD480	WS61 Sea King HC4 [C]	RNAY Fleetlands	
ZD559	WS Lynx AH5X	MoD(PE), DRA Boscombe Down	
ZD560	WS Lynx Mk 7	MoD(PE), ETPS, Boscombe Down	
ZD565	WS Lynx HAS3S [630]	RN No 702 Sqn, Portland	
ZD566	WS Lynx HAS3S [637]	RN No 702 Sqn, Portland	
ZD567	WS Lynx HAS3S [365/AY]	*Written off, West Indies, 26 March 1994*	
ZD574	B-V Chinook HC2 [EH]	Boeing, Philadelphia (conversion)	
ZD575	B-V Chinook HC2 [BL]	Boeing, Philadelphia (conversion)	
ZD576	B-V Chinook HC2 [G]	*Written off, Mull of Kintyre, 2 June 1994*	
ZD578	BAe Sea Harrier FRS1 [124]	RN, St Athan	
ZD579	BAe Sea Harrier F/A2	RN AMG, Yeovilton	
ZD580	BAe Sea Harrier F/A2 [122]	RN, St Athan	
ZD581	BAe Sea Harrier FRS1 [124]	RN No 800 Sqn, Yeovilton	
ZD582	BAe Sea Harrier F/A2 [710]	RN No 899 Sqn OEU, Boscombe Down	
ZD607	BAe Sea Harrier FRS1 [001]	RN, St Athan	
ZD608	BAe Sea Harrier F/A2	RN No 899 Sqn, Yeovilton	
ZD610	BAe Sea Harrier FRS1 [004]	RN, St Athan	
ZD611	BAe Sea Harrier F/A2	RN No 899 Sqn, Yeovilton	
ZD612	BAe Sea Harrier F/A2 [724]	RN No 899 Sqn, Yeovilton	
ZD613	BAe Sea Harrier F/A2	RN No 801 Sqn, Yeovilton	
ZD614	BAe Sea Harrier FRS1 [126]	RN, St Athan	
ZD615	BAe Sea Harrier F/A2 [723/OEU]	RN No 899 Sqn OEU, Yeovilton	
ZD620	BAe 125 CC3	RAF No 32 Sqn, Northolt	
ZD621	BAe 125 CC3	RAF No 32 Sqn, Northolt	
ZD625	WS61 Sea King HC4 [VJ]	RN No 846 Sqn, Yeovilton	
ZD626	WS61 Sea King HC4 [ZY]	RN No 707 Sqn, Yeovilton	
ZD627	WS61 Sea King HC4 [VL]	RN No 846 Sqn, Yeovilton	
ZD630	WS61 Sea King HAS6 [271]	RN No 814 Sqn, Culdrose	
ZD631	WS61 Sea King HAS6 [66]	RN, ETS Yeovilton	
	(fuselage)		
ZD633	WS61 Sea King HAS6 [507]	RN No 810 Sqn, Culdrose	
ZD634	WS61 Sea King HAS6 [506]	RN No 810 Sqn, Culdrose	
ZD636	WS61 Sea King HAR5 [702]	RN AMG, Culdrose	
ZD637	WS61 Sea King HAS6 [700/PW]	RN No 819 Sqn, Prestwick	
ZD657	Schleicher Valiant TX1	RAF ACCGS, Syerston	
ZD658	Schleicher Valiant TX1	RAF, stored Syerston	
ZD659	Schleicher Valiant TX1	RAF ACCGS, Syerston	
ZD660	Schleicher Valiant TX1	RAF, stored Syerston	
ZD667	BAe Harrier GR3 [3]	SAH, RNAS Culdrose	
ZD668	BAe Harrier GR3 [3E]	RAF, stored Wittering	
ZD669	BAe Harrier GR3	*Preserved in Belize, 1993*	
ZD670	BAe Harrier GR3 [3A]	RAF, stored Wittering	
ZD703	BAe 125 CC3	RAF No 32 Sqn, Northolt	

Notes	Serial	Type (other identity) [code]	Owner/operator, location or fate
	ZD704	BAe 125 CC3	RAF No 32 Sqn, Northolt
	ZD707	Panavia Tornado GR1 [BK]	RAF No 14 Sqn, Bruggen
	ZD708	Panavia Tornado GR4	MoD(PE), BAe Warton
	ZD709	Panavia Tornado GR1 [BR]	RAF No 14 Sqn, Bruggen
	ZD711	Panavia Tornado GR1 [DY]	RAF No 31 Sqn, Bruggen
	ZD712	Panavia Tornado GR1 [BY]	RAF No 14 Sqn, Bruggen
	ZD713	Panavia Tornado GR1 [BX]	RAF No 14 Sqn, Bruggen
	ZD714	Panavia Tornado GR1 [AP]	RAF No 9 Sqn, Bruggen
	ZD715	Panavia Tornado GR1 [DB]	RAF No 31 Sqn, Bruggen
	ZD716	Panavia Tornado GR1 [O]	RAF SAOEU, Boscombe Down
	ZD719	Panavia Tornado GR1 [AD]	RAF No 9 Sqn, Bruggen
	ZD720	Panavia Tornado GR1 [AG]	RAF No 9 Sqn, Bruggen
	ZD739	Panavia Tornado GR1 [AC]	RAF No 9 Sqn, Bruggen
	ZD740	Panavia Tornado GR1 [DA]	RAF No 31 Sqn, Bruggen
	ZD741	Panavia Tornado GR1 [DZ]	RAF No 31 Sqn, Bruggen
	ZD742	Panavia Tornado GR1 [CZ]	RAF No 17 Sqn, Bruggen
	ZD743	Panavia Tornado GR1 [CX]	RAF No 17 Sqn, Bruggen
	ZD744	Panavia Tornado GR1 [BD]	RAF No 14 Sqn, Bruggen
	ZD745	Panavia Tornado GR1 [BM]	RAF No 14 Sqn, Bruggen
	ZD746	Panavia Tornado GR1 [AB]	RAF No 9 Sqn, Bruggen
	ZD747	Panavia Tornado GR1 [AL]	RAF No 9 Sqn, Bruggen
	ZD748	Panavia Tornado GR1 [AK]	RAF No 9 Sqn, Bruggen
	ZD749	Panavia Tornado GR1 [U]	RAF SAOEU, Boscombe Down
	ZD788	Panavia Tornado GR1 [CB]	RAF No 17 Sqn, Bruggen
	ZD789	Panavia Tornado GR1 [AM]	RAF No 9 Sqn, Bruggen
	ZD790	Panavia Tornado GR1 [DL]	RAF No 31 Sqn, Bruggen
	ZD792	Panavia Tornado GR1 [CF]	RAF No 17 Sqn, Bruggen
	ZD793	Panavia Tornado GR1 [CA]	RAF No 17 Sqn, Bruggen
	ZD809	Panavia Tornado GR1 [BA]	RAF No 14 Sqn, Bruggen
	ZD810	Panavia Tornado GR1 [AA]	RAF No 9 Sqn, Bruggen
	ZD811	Panavia Tornado GR1 [DF]	RAF No 31 Sqn, Bruggen
	ZD812	Panavia Tornado GR1 [BW]	RAF No 14 Sqn, Bruggen
	ZD842	Panavia Tornado GR1 [CY]	RAF No 17 Sqn, Bruggen
	ZD843	Panavia Tornado GR1 [DH]	RAF No 31 Sqn, Bruggen
	ZD844	Panavia Tornado GR1 [DE]	RAF No 31 Sqn, Bruggen
	ZD845	Panavia Tornado GR1 [AF]	RAF No 9 Sqn, Bruggen
	ZD846	Panavia Tornado GR1 [BL]	RAF No 14 Sqn, Bruggen
	ZD847	Panavia Tornado GR1 [CH]	RAF No 17 Sqn, Bruggen
	ZD848	Panavia Tornado GR1 [DM]	RAF No 31 Sqn, Bruggen
	ZD849	Panavia Tornado GR1 [BT]	RAF No 14 Sqn, Bruggen
	ZD850	Panavia Tornado GR1 [CL]	RAF No 17 Sqn, Bruggen
	ZD851	Panavia Tornado GR1 [AJ]	RAF No 9 Sqn, Bruggen
	ZD890	Panavia Tornado GR1 [AE]	RAF No 9 Sqn, Bruggen
	ZD892	Panavia Tornado GR1 [BJ]	RAF No 14 Sqn, Bruggen
	ZD895	Panavia Tornado GR1 [BF]	RAF No 14 Sqn, Bruggen
	ZD899	Panavia Tornado F2	MoD(PE), BAe Warton
	ZD900	Panavia Tornado F2	MoD(PE), A&AEE Boscombe Down
	ZD901	Panavia Tornado F2 (fuselage)	MoD(PE)/BAe Warton
	ZD902	Panavia Tornado F2TIARA	MoD(PE), DRA Boscombe Down
	ZD903	Panavia Tornado F2 [AB]	RAF, stored St Athan
	ZD904	Panavia Tornado F2 [AE]	RAF, stored St Athan
	ZD905	Panavia Tornado F2	RAF, stored St Athan
	ZD906	Panavia Tornado F2 [AN]	RAF, stored St Athan
	ZD932	Panavia Tornado F2 [AM]	RAF, stored St Athan
	ZD933	Panavia Tornado F2	RAF, stored St Athan
	ZD934	Panavia Tornado F2 [AD]	RAF, stored St Athan
	ZD936	Panavia Tornado F2	RAF, stored St Athan
	ZD937	Panavia Tornado F2 [A]	RAF St Athan, BDRT
	ZD938	Panavia Tornado F2	RAF, stored St Athan
	ZD939	Panavia Tornado F2 [AS]	BAe Warton, instructional use
	ZD940	Panavia Tornado F2	RAF, stored St Athan
	ZD941	Panavia Tornado F2 [AU]	RAF, stored St Athan
	ZD948	Lockheed Tristar KC1	RAF No 216 Sqn, Brize Norton
	ZD949	Lockheed Tristar K1	RAF No 216 Sqn, Brize Norton
	ZD950	Lockheed Tristar KC1	RAF No 216 Sqn, Brize Norton
	ZD951	Lockheed Tristar K1	RAF No 216 Sqn, Brize Norton
	ZD952	Lockheed Tristar KC1	RAF No 216 Sqn, Brize Norton
	ZD953	Lockheed Tristar KC1	RAF No 216 Sqn, Brize Norton
	ZD974	Schempp-Hirth Kestrel TX1	RAF ACCGS, Syerston
	ZD975	Schempp-Hirth Kestrel TX1	RAF, stored Syerston
	ZD980	B-V Chinook HC2	Boeing, Philadelphia (conversion)
	ZD981	B-V Chinook HC2 [BD]	RAF No 7 Sqn, Odiham
	ZD982	B-V Chinook HC2 [BI]	RAF No 7 Sqn, Odiham

Serial	Type (other identity) [code]	Owner/operator, location or fate	Notes
ZD983	B-V Chinook HC2 [EF]	Boeing, Philadelphia (conversion)	
ZD984	B-V Chinook HC2 [EE]	RAF No 7 Sqn, Odiham	
ZD990	BAe Harrier T4A [Q]	RAF HOCU/No 20(R) Sqn, Wittering	
ZD991	BAe Harrier T4A [V]	RAF HOCU/No 20(R) Sqn, Wittering	
ZD992	BAe Harrier T4	SAH, RNAS Culdrose	
ZD993	BAe Harrier T4 [U]	RN AMG, Yeovilton	
ZD996	Panavia Tornado GR1A [I]	RAF No 2 Sqn, Marham	
ZE116	Panavia Tornado GR1A [K]	RAF No 2 Sqn, Marham	
ZE154	Panavia Tornado F3 (fuselage)	MoD(PE)/BAe Warton	
ZE155	Panavia Tornado F3	MoD(PE)/BAe Warton	
ZE156	Panavia Tornado F3 [HE]	RAF No 11 Sqn, Leuchars	
ZE157	Panavia Tornado F3 [AI]	RAF F3 OCU/No 56(R) Sqn, Coningsby	
ZE158	Panavia Tornado F3 [DC]	RAF, ASF Leeming (on rebuild)	
ZE159	Panavia Tornado F3 [EG]	RAF	
ZE160	Panavia Tornado F3 [DV]	RAF No 11 Sqn, Leeming	
ZE161	Panavia Tornado F3 [FG]	RAF No 25 Sqn, Leeming	
ZE162	Panavia Tornado F3 [FK]	RAF No 25 Sqn, Leeming	
ZE163	Panavia Tornado F3 [AA]	RAF F3 OCU/No 56(R) Sqn, Coningsby	
ZE164	Panavia Tornado F3 [DA]	RAF No 11 Sqn, Leeming	
ZE165	Panavia Tornado F3 [FO]	RAF No 25 Sqn, Leeming	
ZE166	Panavia Tornado F3 [AF]	RAF F3 OCU/No 56(R) Sqn, Coningsby	
ZE167	Panavia Tornado F3 [HX]	RAF No 111 Sqn, Leuchars	
ZE168	Panavia Tornado F3 [EB]	RAF, St Athan	
ZE199	Panavia Tornado F3 [FL]	RAF No 25 Sqn, Leeming	
ZE200	Panavia Tornado F3 [DB]	RAF No 11 Sqn, Leeming	
ZE201	Panavia Tornado F3 [DO]	RAF No 11 Sqn, Leeming	
ZE202	Panavia Tornado F3 [AG]	RAF F3 OCU/No 56(R) Sqn, Coningsby	
ZE203	Panavia Tornado F3 [FI]	RAF No 25 Sqn, Leeming	
ZE204	Panavia Tornado F3 [DD]	RAF No 11 Sqn, Leeming	
ZE205	Panavia Tornado F3 [DT]	RAF No 11 Sqn, Leeming	
ZE206	Panavia Tornado F3 [FH]	RAF No 25 Sqn, Leeming	
ZE207	Panavia Tornado F3 [GC]	RAF No 43 Sqn, Leuchars	
ZE208	Panavia Tornado F3 [AN]	RAF F3 OCU/No 56(R) Sqn, Coningsby	
ZE209	Panavia Tornado F3 [AV]	RAF F3 OCU/No 56(R) Sqn, Coningsby	
ZE210	Panavia Tornado F3 [FB]	RAF No 25 Sqn, Leeming	
ZE250	Panavia Tornado F3 [HZ]	RAF, ASF Leuchars (on repair)	
ZE251	Panavia Tornado F3 [DE]	RAF, stored St Athan	
ZE252	Panavia Tornado F3 [HH]	RAF No 111 Sqn, Leuchars	
ZE253	Panavia Tornado F3 [AC]	RAF F3 OCU/No 56(R) Sqn, Coningsby	
ZE254	Panavia Tornado F3 [CA]	RAF, stored St Athan	
ZE255	Panavia Tornado F3	RAF, stored St Athan	
ZE256	Panavia Tornado F3 [AJ]	RAF F3 OCU/No 56(R) Sqn, Coningsby	
ZE257	Panavia Tornado F3 [FZ]	RAF No 25 Sqn, Leeming	
ZE258	Panavia Tornado F3 (fuselage)	RAF, stored St Athan	
ZE287	Panavia Tornado F3 [AH]	RAF F3 OCU/No 56(R) Sqn, Coningsby	
ZE288	Panavia Tornado F3 [GG]	RAF, stored St Athan	
ZE289	Panavia Tornado F3 [HF]	RAF No 111 Sqn, Leuchars	
ZE290	Panavia Tornado F3 [AD]	RAF F3 OCU/No 56(R) Sqn, Coningsby	
ZE291	Panavia Tornado F3 [GQ]	RAF No 43 Sqn, Leuchars	
ZE292	Panavia Tornado F3	RAF, stored St Athan	
ZE293	Panavia Tornado F3 [HT]	RAF No 111 Sqn, Leuchars	
ZE294	Panavia Tornado F3 [AQ]	RAF, stored St Athan	
ZE295	Panavia Tornado F3 [AW]	RAF, stored Coningsby	
ZE296	Panavia Tornado F3 [GR]	RAF No 43 Sqn, Leuchars	
ZE338	Panavia Tornado F3 [HG]	RAF No 111 Sqn, Leuchars	
ZE339	Panavia Tornado F3 [FQ]	RAF No 25 Sqn, Leeming	
ZE340	Panavia Tornado F3 [AE]	RAF F3 OCU/No 56(R) Sqn, Coningsby	
ZE341	Panavia Tornado F3 [HD]	RAF No 111 Sqn, Leuchars	
ZE342	Panavia Tornado F3 [HW]	RAF No 111 Sqn, Leuchars	
ZE343	Panavia Tornado F3 [AI]	RAF, stored St Athan	
ZE351	McD Phantom F-4J(UK) (9058M) [I]	RAF Finningley Fire Section	
ZE353	McD Phantom F-4J(UK) (9083M) [E]	FSCTE, RAF Manston	
ZE354	McD Phantom F-4J(UK) (9084M) [R]	RAF Coningsby Fire Section	
ZE356	McD Phantom F-4J(UK) (9060M) [Q]	RAF Waddington Fire Section	
ZE359	McD Phantom F-4J(UK) [J]	Imperial War Museum, Duxford	
ZE360	McD Phantom F-4J(UK) (9059M) [O]	FSCTE, RAF Manston	

Notes	Serial	Type (other identity) [code]	Owner/operator, location or fate
	ZE361	McD Phantom F-4J(UK) (9057M) [P]	RAF Honington Fire Section
	ZE364	McD Phantom F-4J(UK) (9085M) [Z]	RAF Coltishall Fire Section
	ZE368	WS61 Sea King HAR3	RAF SKTU, St Mawgan
	ZE369	WS61 Sea King HAR3	RAF No 202 Sqn, St Mawgan
	ZE370	WS61 Sea King HAR3	RAF No 202 Sqn, St Mawgan
	ZE375	WS Lynx AH9 [2]	AAC No 659 Sqn, Detmold
	ZE376	WS Lynx AH9 [4]	AAC No 653 Sqn, Wattisham
	ZE378	WS Lynx AH7	AAC, RNAY Fleetlands
	ZE379	WS Lynx AH7	AAC No 667 Sqn, Middle Wallop
	ZE380	WS Lynx AH9 [1]	AAC No 659 Sqn, Detmold
	ZE381	WS Lynx AH7	AAC No 655 Sqn, Aldergrove
	ZE382	WS Lynx AH9 [3]	AAC No 659 Sqn, Detmold
	ZE395	BAe 125 CC3	RAF No 32 Sqn, Northolt
	ZE396	BAe 125 CC3	RAF No 32 Sqn, Northolt
	ZE410	Agusta A109A	AAC No 8 Flight, Netheravon
	ZE411	Agusta A109A	AAC No 8 Flight, Netheravon
	ZE412	Agusta A109A	AAC No 8 Flight, Netheravon
	ZE413	Agusta A109A	AAC No 8 Flight, Netheravon
	ZE418	WS61 Sea King HAS5 [826]	RN No 771 Sqn, Culdrose
	ZE420	WS61 Sea King HAS5 [592]	RN No 706 Sqn, Culdrose
	ZE422	WS61 Sea King HAS6 [588]	RN No 706 Sqn, Culdrose
	ZE425	WS61 Sea King HC4 [26]	RN No 772 Sqn, Portland
	ZE426	WS61 Sea King HC4 [ZW]	RN No 707 Sqn, Yeovilton
	ZE427	WS61 Sea King HC4 [B]	RN No 845 Sqn, Yeovilton
	ZE428	WS61 Sea King HC4 [VH]	RNAY Fleetlands
	ZE432	BAC 1-11/479	MoD(PE), ETPS Boscombe Down
	ZE433	BAC 1-11/479	MoD(PE) GEC/Ferranti, Edinburgh
	ZE438	BAe Jetstream T3 [576]	RN, stored Shawbury
	ZE439	BAe Jetstream T3 [577]	RN FONA/Heron Flight, Yeovilton
	ZE440	BAe Jetstream T3 [578]	RN FONA/Heron Flight, Yeovilton
	ZE441	BAe Jetstream T3 [579]	RN FONA/Heron Flight, Yeovilton
	ZE477	WS Lynx 3	IHM, Weston-super-Mare
	ZE495	Grob Viking T1 (BGA3000)	RAF No 622 VGS, Upavon
	ZE496	Grob Viking T1 (BGA3001)	RAF No 613 VGS, Halton
	ZE497	Grob Viking T1 (BGA3002)	RAFGSA, Syerston
	ZE498	Grob Viking T1 (BGA3003)	RAF No 614 VGS, Wethersfield
	ZE499	Grob Viking T1 (BGA3004)	RAF ACCGS, Syerston
	ZE501	Grob Viking T1 (BGA3006)	RAF ACCGS, Syerston
	ZE502	Grob Viking T1 (BGA3007)	RAF ACCGS, Syerston
	ZE503	Grob Viking T1 (BGA3008)	RAF No 625 VGS, Hullavington
	ZE504	Grob Viking T1 (BGA3009)	RAF No 645 VGS, Catterick
	ZE520	Grob Viking T1 (BGA3010)	RAF No 622 VGS, Upavon
	ZE521	Grob Viking T1 (BGA3011)	RAF No 626 VGS, Catterick
	ZE522	Grob Viking T1 (BGA3012)	RAF No 618 VGS, Challock
	ZE524	Grob Viking T1 (BGA3014)	RAF No 626 VGS, Predannack
	ZE525	Grob Viking T1 (BGA3015)	ATC, Congleton, Cheshire
	ZE526	Grob Viking T1 (BGA3016)	RAF No 634 VGS, St Athan
	ZE527	Grob Viking T1 (BGA3017)	RAF CGMF, Syerston
	ZE528	Grob Viking T1 (BGA3018)	RAF No 645 VGS, Catterick
	ZE529	Grob Viking T1 (BGA3019)	RAF No 636 VGS, Swansea
	ZE530	Grob Viking T1 (BGA3020)	RAF No 611 VGS, Swanton Morley
	ZE531	Grob Viking T1 (BGA3021)	RAF No 662 VGS, Arbroath
	ZE532	Grob Viking T1 (BGA3022)	RAF No 618 VGS, Challock
	ZE533	Grob Viking T1 (BGA3023)	RAF No 622 VGS, Upavon
	ZE534	Grob Viking T1 (BGA3024)	RAF No 614 VGS, Wethersfield
	ZE550	Grob Viking T1 (BGA3025)	RAF No 622 VGS, Upavon
	ZE551	Grob Viking T1 (BGA3026)	RAF No 614 VGS, Wethersfield
	ZE552	Grob Viking T1 (BGA3027)	RAF ACCGS, Syerston
	ZE553	Grob Viking T1 (BGA3028)	RAF No 611 VGS, Swanton Morley
	ZE554	Grob Viking T1 (BGA3029)	RAF ACCGS, Syerston
	ZE555	Grob Viking T1 (BGA3030)	RAF No 645 VGS, Catterick
	ZE556	Grob Viking T1 (BGA3031)	RAF CGMF, Syerston
	ZE557	Grob Viking T1 (BGA3032)	RAF No 622 VGS, Upavon
	ZE558	Grob Viking T1 (BGA3033)	RAF No 615 VGS, Kenley
	ZE559	Grob Viking T1 (BGA3034)	RAF CGMF, Syerston
	ZE560	Grob Viking T1 (BGA3035)	RAF No 625 VGS, Hullavington
	ZE561	Grob Viking T1 (BGA3036)	RAF No 621 VGS, Hullavington
	ZE562	Grob Viking T1 (BGA3037)	RAF No 631 VGS, Samlesbury
	ZE563	Grob Viking T1 (BGA3038)	RAF No 631 VGS, Samlesbury
	ZE564	Grob Viking T1 (BGA3039)	RAF No 636 VGS, Swansea
	ZE584	Grob Viking T1 (BGA3040)	RAF CGMF, Syerston

Serial	Type (other identity) [code]	Owner/operator, location or fate	Notes
ZE585	Grob Viking T1 (BGA3041)	RAF No 614 VGS, Wethersfield	
ZE586	Grob Viking T1 (BGA3042)	RAF No 618 VGS, Challock	
ZE587	Grob Viking T1 (BGA3043)	RAF No 611 VGS, Swanton Morley	
ZE589	Grob Viking T1 (BGA3045)	RAF CGMF, Syerston	
ZE590	Grob Viking T1 (BGA3046)	RAF No 645 VGS, Catterick	
ZE591	Grob Viking T1 (BGA3047)	RAF CGMF, Syerston	
ZE592	Grob Viking T1 (BGA3048)	RAF No 661 VGS, Kirknewton	
ZE593	Grob Viking T1 (BGA3049)	RAF No 631 VGS, Samlesbury	
ZE594	Grob Viking T1 (BGA3050)	RAF No 615 VGS, Kenley	
ZE595	Grob Viking T1 (BGA3051)	RAF No 662 VGS, Arbroath	
ZE600	Grob Viking T1 (BGA3052)	RAF ACCGS, Syerston	
ZE601	Grob Viking T1 (BGA3053)	RAF No 615 VGS, Kenley	
ZE602	Grob Viking T1 (BGA3054)	RAF CGMF, Syerston	
ZE603	Grob Viking T1 (BGA3055)	RAF No 617 VGS, Manston	
ZE604	Grob Viking T1 (BGA3056)	RAF No 617 VGS, Manston	
ZE605	Grob Viking T1 (BGA3057)	RAF CGMF, Syerston	
ZE606	Grob Viking T1 (BGA3058)	RAF No 617 VGS, Manston	
ZE607	Grob Viking T1 (BGA3059)	RAF No 625 VGS, Hullavington	
ZE608	Grob Viking T1 (BGA3060)	RAF ACCGS, Syerston	
ZE609	Grob Viking T1 (BGA3061)	RAF No 636 VGS, Swansea	
ZE610	Grob Viking T1 (BGA3062)	RAF CGMF, Syerston	
ZE611	Grob Viking T1 (BGA3063)	RAF No 621 VGS, Hullavington	
ZE612	Grob Viking T1 (BGA3064)	RAF CGMF, Syerston (wreck)	
ZE613	Grob Viking T1 (BGA3065)	RAF ACCGS, Syerston	
ZE614	Grob Viking T1 (BGA3066)	RAF No 661 VGS, Kirknewton	
ZE625	Grob Viking T1 (BGA3067)	RAF No 634 VGS, St Athan	
ZE626	Grob Viking T1 (BGA3068)	RAF No 636 VGS, Swansea	
ZE627	Grob Viking T1 (BGA3069)	RAF ACCGS, Syerston	
ZE628	Grob Viking T1 (BGA3070)	RAF No 615 VGS, Kenley	
ZE629	Grob Viking T1 (BGA3071)	RAF ACCGS, Syerston	
ZE630	Grob Viking T1 (BGA3072)	RAF ACCGS, Syerston	
ZE631	Grob Viking T1 (BGA3073)	RAF CGMF, Syerston	
ZE632	Grob Viking T1 (BGA3074)	RAF No 618 VGS, Challock	
ZE633	Grob Viking T1 (BGA3075)	RAF No 614 VGS, Wethersfield	
ZE634	Grob Viking T1 (BGA3076)	RAF CGMF, Syerston (wreck)	
ZE635	Grob Viking T1 (BGA3077)	RAF CGMF, Syerston	
ZE636	Grob Viking T1 (BGA3078)	RAF ACCGS, Syerston	
ZE637	Grob Viking T1 (BGA3079)	RAF No 622 VGS, Upavon	
ZE650	Grob Viking T1 (BGA3080)	RAF No 636 VGS, Swansea	
ZE651	Grob Viking T1 (BGA3081)	RAF No 625 VGS, Hullavington	
ZE652	Grob Viking T1 (BGA3082)	RAF ACCGS, Syerston	
ZE653	Grob Viking T1 (BGA3083)	RAF No 631 VGS, Samlesbury	
ZE654	Grob Viking T1 (BGA3084)	RAF No 631 VGS, Samlesbury	
ZE655	Grob Viking T1 (BGA3085)	RAF No 631 VGS, Samlesbury	
ZE656	Grob Viking T1 (BGA3086)	RAF No 617 VGS, Manston	
ZE657	Grob Viking T1 (BGA3087)	RAF No 626 VGS, Predannack	
ZE658	Grob Viking T1 (BGA3088)	RAF ACCGS, Syerston	
ZE659	Grob Viking T1 (BGA3089)	RAF No 611 VGS, Swanton Morley	
ZE677	Grob Viking T1 (BGA3090)	RAF No 631 VGS, Samlesbury	
ZE678	Grob Viking T1 (BGA3091)	RAF No 621 VGS, Hullavington	
ZE679	Grob Viking T1 (BGA3092)	RAF CGMF, Syerston	
ZE680	Grob Viking T1 (BGA3093)	RAF No 661 VGS, Kirknewton	
ZE681	Grob Viking T1 (BGA3094)	RAF No 615 VGS, Kenley	
ZE682	Grob Viking T1 (BGA3095)	RAF No 611 VGS, Swanton Morley	
ZE683	Grob Viking T1 (BGA3096)	RAF No 645 VGS, Catterick	
ZE684	Grob Viking T1 (BGA3097)	RAF No 618 VGS, Challock	
ZE685	Grob Viking T1 (BGA3098)	RAF No 661 VGS, Kirknewton	
ZE686	Grob Viking T1 (BGA3099)	MoD(PE), Slingsby Kirkbymoorside	
ZE690	BAe Sea Harrier F/A2 [003]	RN No 801 Sqn, Yeovilton	
ZE691	BAe Sea Harrier FRS1	RN, St Athan	
ZE692	BAe Sea Harrier FRS1 [001]	RN, St Athan	
ZE693	BAe Sea Harrier FRS1 [003]	RN No 801 Sqn, Yeovilton	
ZE694	BAe Sea Harrier FRS1 [125]	RN, St Athan	
ZE695	BAe Sea Harrier F/A2 [711]	RN No 899 Sqn, Yeovilton	
ZE696	BAe Sea Harrier F/A2 [712$\frac{1}{2}$]	RN No 899 Sqn, Yeovilton	
ZE697	BAe Sea Harrier F/A2 [715]	RN No 899 Sqn, Yeovilton	
ZE698	BAe Sea Harrier FRS1 [005]	RN No 801 Sqn, Yeovilton	
ZE700	BAe 146 CC2	RAF, The Queen's Flight, Benson	
ZE701	BAe 146 CC2	RAF, The Queen's Flight, Benson	
ZE702	BAe 146 CC2	RAF, The Queen's Flight, Benson	
ZE704	Lockheed Tristar C2	RAF No 216 Sqn, Brize Norton	
ZE705	Lockheed Tristar C2	RAF No 216 Sqn, Brize Norton	
ZE706	Lockheed Tristar C2A	RAF No 216 Sqn, Brize Norton	

Notes	Serial	Type (other identity) [code]	Owner/operator, location or fate
	ZE728	Panavia Tornado F3 [AL]	RAF, stored St Athan
	ZE729	Panavia Tornado F3 (fuselage)	RAF, stored St Athan
	ZE730	Panavia Tornado F3 [GL]	RAF No 43 Sqn, Leuchars
	ZE731	Panavia Tornado F3 [GK]	RAF No 43 Sqn, Leuchars
	ZE732	Panavia Tornado F3 [GI]	RAF No 43 Sqn, Leuchars
	ZE733	Panavia Tornado F3 [GE]	RAF No 43 Sqn, Leuchars
	ZE734	Panavia Tornado F3 [GB]	RAF No 43 Sqn, Leuchars
	ZE735	Panavia Tornado F3 [AL]	RAF ASF, Coningsby
	ZE736	Panavia Tornado F3 [HA]	RAF, stored St Athan
	ZE737	Panavia Tornado F3 [FF]	RAF No 25 Sqn, Leeming
	ZE755	Panavia Tornado F3 [GJ]	RAF No 43 Sqn, Leuchars
	ZE756	Panavia Tornado F3	RAF F3 OEU, Coningsby
	ZE757	Panavia Tornado F3 [GF]	RAF No 43 Sqn, Leuchars
	ZE758	Panavia Tornado F3 [HV]	RAF No 111 Sqn, Leuchars
	ZE759	Panavia Tornado F3 (fuselage)	RAF, stored St Athan
	ZE760	Panavia Tornado F3 [GP]	RAF No 43 Sqn, Leuchars
	ZE761	Panavia Tornado F3 [AP]	RAF F3 OCU/No 56(R) Sqn, Coningsby
	ZE762	Panavia Tornado F3 [GM]	RAF No 43 Sqn, Leuchars
	ZE763	Panavia Tornado F3 [DG]	RAF No 11 Sqn, Leeming
	ZE764	Panavia Tornado F3 [DH]	RAF No 11 Sqn, Leeming
	ZE785	Panavia Tornado F3 [AT]	RAF F3 OCU/No 56(R) Sqn, Coningsby
	ZE786	Panavia Tornado F3 (fuselage)	RAF, stored St Athan
	ZE787	Panavia Tornado F3 [HM]	RAF No 111 Sqn, Leuchars
	ZE788	Panavia Tornado F3 [DF]	RAF No 11 Sqn, Leeming
	ZE789	Panavia Tornado F3 [AU]	RAF F3 OCU/No 56(R) Sqn, Coningsby
	ZE790	Panavia Tornado F3 [AW]	RAF F3 OCU/No 56(R) Sqn, Coningsby
	ZE791	Panavia Tornado F3 [FP]	RAF No 25 Sqn, Leeming
	ZE792	Panavia Tornado F3 [HL]	RAF No 111 Sqn, Leuchars
	ZE793	Panavia Tornado F3	RAF, stored St Athan
	ZE794	Panavia Tornado F3 [HQ]	RAF No 111 Sqn, Leuchars
	ZE808	Panavia Tornado F3 [FA]	RAF No 25 Sqn, Leeming
	ZE809	Panavia Tornado F3 [HP]	*Written off, North Sea, 7 June 1994*
	ZE810	Panavia Tornado F3 [HP]	RAF No 111 Sqn, Leuchars
	ZE811	Panavia Tornado F3 [HB]	RAF No 111 Sqn, Leuchars
	ZE812	Panavia Tornado F3	RAF F3 OCU/No 56(R) Sqn, Coningsby
	ZE830	Panavia Tornado F3 [GD]	RAF No 43 Sqn, Leuchars
	ZE831	Panavia Tornado F3 [GG]	RAF No 43 Sqn, Leuchars
	ZE832	Panavia Tornado F3 [A7]	RAF F3 OCU/No 56(R) Sqn, Coningsby
	ZE834	Panavia Tornado F3	RAF, on repair Leeming
	ZE835	Panavia Tornado F3 [HK]	RAF No 111 Sqn, Leuchars
	ZE836	Panavia Tornado F3 [AS]	RAF F3 OCU/No 56(R) Sqn, Coningsby
	ZE837	Panavia Tornado F3 [HY]	RAF No 111 Squadron, Leuchars
	ZE838	Panavia Tornado F3 [GH]	RAF No 43 Sqn, Leuchars
	ZE839	Panavia Tornado F3 [AR]	RAF F3 OCU/No 56(R) Sqn, Coningsby
	ZE862	Panavia Tornado F3	RAF F3 OEU, Coningsby
	ZE887	Panavia Tornado F3 [DJ]	RAF No 11 Sqn, Leeming
	ZE888	Panavia Tornado F3 [FV]	RAF No 25 Sqn, Leeming
	ZE889	Panavia Tornado F3 [SB]	RAF F3 OEU, Coningsby
	ZE907	Panavia Tornado F3 [FM]	RAF No 25 Sqn, Leeming
	ZE908	Panavia Tornado F3 [FC]	RAF No 25 Sqn, Leeming
	ZE911	Panavia Tornado F3[BE]	RAF No 29 Sqn, Coningsby
	ZE934	Panavia Tornado F3 [DX]	RAF No 11 Sqn, Leeming
	ZE936	Panavia Tornado F3 [DL]	RAF No 11 Sqn, Leeming
	ZE941	Panavia Tornado F3 [FE]	RAF No 25 Sqn, Leeming
	ZE942	Panavia Tornado F3 [DK]	RAF No 11 Sqn, Leeming
	ZE961	Panavia Tornado F3 [FD]	RAF No 25 Sqn, Leeming
	ZE962	Panavia Tornado F3 [FJ]	RAF No 25 Sqn, Leeming
	ZE963	Panavia Tornado F3 [FT]	RAF No 25 Sqn, Leeming
	ZE964	Panavia Tornado F3 [DY]	RAF No 11 Sqn, Leeming
	ZE965	Panavia Tornado F3 [DW]	RAF No 11 Sqn, Leeming
	ZE966	Panavia Tornado F3 [DZ]	RAF No 11 Sqn, Leeming
	ZE967	Panavia Tornado F3 [FU]	RAF No 25 Sqn, Leeming
	ZE968	Panavia Tornado F3	RAF F3 OEU, Coningsby
	ZE969	Panavia Tornado F3 [DI]	RAF No 11 Sqn, Leeming
	ZE982	Panavia Tornado F3 [DM]	RAF No 11 Sqn, Leeming
	ZE983	Panavia Tornado F3 [HP]	RAF No 111 Sqn, Leuchars
	ZF115	WS61 Sea King HC4	MoD(PE), ETPS, Boscombe Down
	ZF116	WS61 Sea King HC4 [25]	RN No 772 Sqn, Portland
	ZF117	WS61 Sea King HC4 [VK]	RN No 846 Sqn, Yeovilton
	ZF118	WS61 Sea King HC4 [VP]	RN No 846 Sqn, Yeovilton
	ZF119	WS61 Sea King HC4 [VH]	RN No 846 Sqn, Yeovilton
	ZF120	WS61 Sea King HC4 [20/PO]	RN No 772 Sqn, Portland

Serial	Type (other identity) [code]	Owner/operator, location or fate	Notes
ZF121	WS61 Sea King HC4 [21]	RN AMG, Yeovilton	
ZF122	WS61 Sea King HC4 [22/PO]	RN No 772 Sqn, Portland	
ZF123	WS61 Sea King HC4 [23]	RN No 772 Sqn, Portland	
ZF124	WS61 Sea King HC4 [24]	RN No 772 Sqn, Portland	
ZF130	BAe 125-600B	MoD(PE), BAe Dunsfold	
ZF135	Shorts Tucano T1	RAF No 3 FTS, Cranwell	
ZF136	Shorts Tucano T1	RAF No 1 FTS, Linton-on-Ouse	
ZF137	Shorts Tucano T1	RAF No 1 FTS, Linton-on-Ouse	
ZF138	Shorts Tucano T1	RAF CFS, Scampton	
ZF139	Shorts Tucano T1	RAF No 3 FTS, Cranwell	
ZF140	Shorts Tucano T1	RAF No 3 FTS, Cranwell	
ZF141	Shorts Tucano T1	RAF No 3 FTS, Cranwell	
ZF142	Shorts Tucano T1	RAF, stored Shawbury	
ZF143	Shorts Tucano T1	RAF No 3 FTS, Cranwell	
ZF144	Shorts Tucano T1	RAF, stored Shawbury	
ZF145	Shorts Tucano T1	RAF, stored Shawbury	
ZF160	Shorts Tucano T1	RAF No 3 FTS, Cranwell	
ZF161	Shorts Tucano T1	RAF No 6 FTS, Finningley	
ZF162	Shorts Tucano T1	RAF No 6 FTS, Finningley	
ZF163	Shorts Tucano T1	RAF No 1 FTS, Linton-on-Ouse	
ZF164	Shorts Tucano T1	RAF No 1 FTS, Linton-on-Ouse	
ZF165	Shorts Tucano T1	RAF No 3 FTS, Cranwell	
ZF166	Shorts Tucano T1	RAF CFS, Scampton	
ZF167	Shorts Tucano T1	RAF No 3 FTS, Cranwell	
ZF168	Shorts Tucano T1	RAF, stored Shawbury	
ZF169	Shorts Tucano T1	RAF CFS, Scampton	
ZF170	Shorts Tucano T1	RAF, stored Shawbury	
ZF171	Shorts Tucano T1	RAF No 3 FTS, Cranwell	
ZF172	Shorts Tucano T1	RAF CFS, Scampton	
ZF200	Shorts Tucano T1	RAF No 3 FTS, Cranwell	
ZF201	Shorts Tucano T1	RAF No 3 FTS, Cranwell	
ZF202	Shorts Tucano T1	RAF, stored Shawbury	
ZF203	Shorts Tucano T1	RAF CFS, Scampton	
ZF204	Shorts Tucano T1	RAF CFS, Scampton	
ZF205	Shorts Tucano T1	RAF CFS, Scampton	
ZF206	Shorts Tucano T1	RAF CFS, Scampton	
ZF207	Shorts Tucano T1	RAF, stored Shawbury	
ZF208	Shorts Tucano T1	RAF, stored Shawbury	
ZF209	Shorts Tucano T1	RAF CFS, Scampton	
ZF210	Shorts Tucano T1	RAF No 3 FTS, Cranwell	
ZF211	Shorts Tucano T1	RAF No 1 FTS, Linton-on-Ouse	
ZF212	Shorts Tucano T1	RAF No 3 FTS, Cranwell	
ZF238	Shorts Tucano T1	RAF No 1 FTS, Linton-on-Ouse	
ZF239	Shorts Tucano T1	RAF, stored Shawbury	
ZF240	Shorts Tucano T1	RAF, stored Shawbury	
ZF241	Shorts Tucano T1	RAF No 3 FTS, Cranwell	
ZF242	Shorts Tucano T1	RAF No 6 FTS, Finningley	
ZF243	Shorts Tucano T1	RAF No 1 FTS, Linton-on-Ouse	
ZF244	Shorts Tucano T1	RAF, stored Shawbury	
ZF245	Shorts Tucano T1	RAF CFS, Scampton	
ZF263	Shorts Tucano T1	RAF No 3 FTS, Cranwell	
ZF264	Shorts Tucano T1	RAF No 3 FTS, Cranwell	
ZF265	Shorts Tucano T1	RAF CFS, Scampton	
ZF266	Shorts Tucano T1	RAF CFS, Scampton	
ZF267	Shorts Tucano T1	RAF No 3 FTS, Cranwell	
ZF268	Shorts Tucano T1	RAF CFS, Scampton	
ZF269	Shorts Tucano T1	RAF CFS, Scampton	
ZF270	Shorts Tucano T1	RAF No 3 FTS, Cranwell	
ZF284	Shorts Tucano T1	RAF No 3 FTS, Cranwell	
ZF285	Shorts Tucano T1	RAF No 3 FTS, Cranwell	
ZF286	Shorts Tucano T1	RAF CFS, Scampton	
ZF287	Shorts Tucano T1	RAF, stored Shawbury	
ZF288	Shorts Tucano T1	RAF CFS, Scampton	
ZF289	Shorts Tucano T1	RAF, stored Shawbury	
ZF290	Shorts Tucano T1	RAF No 1 FTS, Linton-on-Ouse	
ZF291	Shorts Tucano T1	RAF, stored Shawbury	
ZF292	Shorts Tucano T1	RAF, stored Shawbury	
ZF293	Shorts Tucano T1	RAF, stored Shawbury	
ZF294	Shorts Tucano T1	RAF, stored Shawbury	
ZF295	Shorts Tucano T1	RAF, stored Shawbury	
ZF315	Shorts Tucano T1	RAF No 1 FTS, Linton-on-Ouse	
ZF317	Shorts Tucano T1	RAF, stored Shawbury	
ZF318	Shorts Tucano T1	RAF CFS, Scampton	

Notes	Serial	Type (other identity) [code]	Owner/operator, location or fate
	ZF319	Shorts Tucano T1	RAF, stored Shawbury
	ZF320	Shorts Tucano T1	RAF No 1 FTS, Linton-on-Ouse
	ZF338	Shorts Tucano T1	RAF, stored Shawbury
	ZF339	Shorts Tucano T1	RAF, stored Shawbury
	ZF340	Shorts Tucano T1	RAF No 3 FTS, Cranwell
	ZF341	Shorts Tucano T1	RAF, stored Shawbury
	ZF342	Shorts Tucano T1	RAF, stored Shawbury
	ZF343	Shorts Tucano T1	RAF CFS, Scampton
	ZF344	Shorts Tucano T1	RAF No 3 FTS, Cranwell
	ZF345	Shorts Tucano T1	RAF CFS, Scampton
	ZF346	Shorts Tucano T1	RAF No 1 FTS, Linton-on-Ouse
	ZF347	Shorts Tucano T1	RAF, stored Shawbury
	ZF348	Shorts Tucano T1	RAF No 3 FTS, Cranwell
	ZF349	Shorts Tucano T1	RAF No 3 FTS, Cranwell
	ZF350	Shorts Tucano T1	RAF, stored Shawbury
	ZF372	Shorts Tucano T1	RAF CFS, Scampton
	ZF373	Shorts Tucano T1	RAF No 3 FTS, Cranwell
	ZF374	Shorts Tucano T1	RAF No 3 FTS, Cranwell
	ZF375	Shorts Tucano T1	RAF No 3 FTS, Cranwell
	ZF376	Shorts Tucano T1	RAF No 1 FTS, Linton-on-Ouse
	ZF377	Shorts Tucano T1	RAF No 3 FTS, Cranwell
	ZF378	Shorts Tucano T1	RAF CFS, Scampton
	ZF379	Shorts Tucano T1	RAF No 1 FTS, Linton-on-Ouse
	ZF380	Shorts Tucano T1	RAF CFS, Scampton
	ZF405	Shorts Tucano T1	RAF No 6 FTS, Finningley
	ZF406	Shorts Tucano T1	RAF CFS, Scampton
	ZF407	Shorts Tucano T1	RAF, stored Shawbury
	ZF408	Shorts Tucano T1	RAF No 1 FTS, Linton-on-Ouse
	ZF409	Shorts Tucano T1	RAF No 3 FTS, Cranwell
	ZF410	Shorts Tucano T1	RAF No 1 FTS, Linton-on-Ouse
	ZF411	Shorts Tucano T1	RAF No 1 FTS, Linton-on-Ouse
	ZF412	Shorts Tucano T1	RAF No 1 FTS, Linton-on-Ouse
	ZF413	Shorts Tucano T1	RAF No 6 FTS, Finningley
	ZF414	Shorts Tucano T1	RAF No 3 FTS, Cranwell
	ZF415	Shorts Tucano T1	RAF No 3 FTS, Cranwell
	ZF416	Shorts Tucano T1	RAF No 1 FTS, Linton-on-Ouse
	ZF417	Shorts Tucano T1	RAF, stored Shawbury
	ZF418	Shorts Tucano T1	RAF No 6 FTS, Finningley
	ZF445	Shorts Tucano T1	RAF No 6 FTS, Finningley
	ZF446	Shorts Tucano T1	RAF No 6 FTS, Finningley
	ZF447	Shorts Tucano T1	RAF No 3 FTS, Cranwell
	ZF448	Shorts Tucano T1	RAF No 6 FTS, Finningley
	ZF449	Shorts Tucano T1	RAF No 1 FTS, Linton-on-Ouse
	ZF450	Shorts Tucano T1	RAF No 1 FTS, Linton-on-Ouse
	ZF483	Shorts Tucano T1	RAF No 1 FTS, Linton-on-Ouse
	ZF484	Shorts Tucano T1	RAF No 1 FTS, Linton-on-Ouse
	ZF485	Shorts Tucano T1	RAF, stored Shawbury
	ZF486	Shorts Tucano T1	RAF No 1 FTS, Linton-on-Ouse
	ZF487	Shorts Tucano T1	RAF No 1 FTS, Linton-on-Ouse
	ZF488	Shorts Tucano T1	RAF No 1 FTS, Linton-on-Ouse
	ZF489	Shorts Tucano T1	RAF No 3 FTS, Cranwell
	ZF490	Shorts Tucano T1	RAF No 1 FTS, Linton-on-Ouse
	ZF491	Shorts Tucano T1	RAF, stored Shawbury
	ZF492	Shorts Tucano T1	RAF No 1 FTS, Linton-on-Ouse
	ZF510	Shorts Tucano T1	MoD(PE) ETPS, Boscombe Down
	ZF511	Shorts Tucano T1	MoD(PE) ETPS, Boscombe Down
	ZF512	Shorts Tucano T1	RAF No 3 FTS, Cranwell
	ZF513	Shorts Tucano T1	RAF No 1 FTS, Linton-on-Ouse
	ZF514	Shorts Tucano T1	RAF No 1 FTS, Linton-on-Ouse
	ZF515	Shorts Tucano T1	RAF, stored Shawbury
	ZF516	Shorts Tucano T1	RAF No 3 FTS, Cranwell
	ZF520	Piper PA-31 Navajo Chieftain 350	MoD(PE), A&AEE Boscombe Down
	ZF521	Piper PA-31 Navajo Chieftain 350	MoD(PE), T&EE Llanbedr
	ZF522	Piper PA-31 Navajo Chieftain 350	MoD(PE), A&AEE Boscombe Down
	ZF534	BAe EAP	MoD(PE), stored BAe Warton
	ZF537	WS Lynx AH9	AAC, stored RNAY Fleetlands
	ZF538	WS Lynx AH9	AAC No 653 Sqn, Wattisham
	ZF539	WS Lynx AH9 [5]	AAC, RNAY Fleetlands
	ZF540	WS Lynx AH9 [6]	AAC No 659 Sqn, Detmold
	ZF557	WS Lynx HAS8 [670]	MoD(PE)/Westland, Yeovil (conversion)
	ZF558	WS Lynx HAS3CTS [672]	RN No 815 Sqn OEU, Portland
	ZF560	WS Lynx HAS8 [323]	MoD(PE)/Westland, Yeovil (conversion)
	ZF562	WS Lynx HAS8	MoD(PE)/Westland, Yeovil (conversion)

Serial	Type (other identity) [code]	Owner/operator, location or fate	Notes
ZF563	WS Lynx HAS3CTS [671]	RN No 815 Sqn OEU, Portland	
ZF573	PBN 2T Islander CC2A (G-SRAY)	RAF Northolt Station Flight	
ZF577	BAC Lightning F53	Privately owned, stored Warrington	
ZF578	BAC Lightning F53	Wales Aircraft Museum, Cardiff Airport	
ZF579	BAC Lightning F53	Privately owned, stored Warrington	
ZF580	BAC Lightning F53	BAe Samlesbury, at main gate	
ZF581	BAC Lightning F53	Privately owned, stored Warrington	
ZF582	BAC Lightning F53	Privately owned, stored Warrington	
ZF583	BAC Lightning F53	Solway Aviation Society, Carlisle	
ZF584	BAC Lightning F53	Ferranti Ltd, South Gyle, Edinburgh	
ZF585	BAC Lightning F53	Privately owned, stored Warrington	
ZF586	BAC Lightning F53	Privately owned, stored Warrington	
ZF587	BAC Lightning F53	Privately owned, stored Warrington	
ZF588	BAC Lightning F53	East Midlands Airport Aero Park	
ZF589	BAC Lightning F53	Privately owned, stored Warrington	
ZF590	BAC Lightning F53	Privately owned, stored Warrington	
ZF591	BAC Lightning F53	Privately owned, stored Warrington	
ZF592	BAC Lightning F53	Privately owned, stored Warrington	
ZF594	BAC Lightning F53	North-East Aircraft Museum, Usworth	
ZF595	BAC Lightning T55	Privately owned, stored Warrington	
ZF596	BAC Lightning T55	Privately owned, stored Warrington	
ZF597	BAC Lightning T55	Privately owned, stored Warrington	
ZF598	BAC Lightning T55	Midland Air Museum, Coventry	
ZF622	Piper PA-31 Navajo Chieftain 350	MoD(PE), A&AEE Boscombe Down	
ZF641	WS/Agusta EH-101 [PP1]	MoD(PE)/Westland, Yeovil	
ZF644	WS/Agusta EH-101 [PP4]	MoD(PE)/Westland, Yeovil	
ZF649	WS/Agusta EH-101 Merlin [PP5]	MoD(PE)/Westland, Yeovil	
ZG101	WS/Agusta EH-101 (mock-up) [GB]	Westland/Agusta, Yeovil	
ZG468	WS70 Blackhawk	Westland Helicopters, Yeovil	
ZG471	BAe Harrier GR7 [WN]	RAF No 4 Sqn, Incirlik	
ZG472	BAe Harrier GR7	RAF SAOEU, Boscombe Down	
ZG474	BAe Harrier GR7 [WL]	RAF No 3 Sqn, Laarbruch	
ZG475	BAe Harrier GR7	RAF SAOEU, Boscombe Down	
ZG476	BAe Harrier GR7 [WT]	RAF No 4 Sqn, Incirlik	
ZG477	BAe Harrier GR7 [WI]	RAF No 4 Sqn, Incirlik	
ZG478	BAe Harrier GR7 [WY]	RAF No 4 Sqn, Incirlik	
ZG479	BAe Harrier GR7 [CM]	RAF No 4 Sqn, Laarbruch	
ZG480	BAe Harrier GR7 [WZ]	RAF No 4 Sqn, Incirlik	
ZG500	BAe Harrier GR7 [WV]	RAF No 3 Sqn, Laarbruch	
ZG501	BAe Harrier GR7 [E]	RAF SAOEU, Boscombe Down	
ZG502	BAe Harrier GR7 [WF]	RAF No 1 Sqn, Wittering	
ZG503	BAe Harrier GR7	RAF, St Athan	
ZG504	BAe Harrier GR7 [CM]	RAF No 4 Sqn, Laarbruch	
ZG505	BAe Harrier GR7 [WJ]	RAF No 4 Sqn, Laarbruch	
ZG506	BAe Harrier GR7 [AF]	RAF No 3 Sqn, Laarbruch	
ZG507	BAe Harrier GR7 [CA]	RAF No 4 Sqn, Laarbruch	
ZG508	BAe Harrier GR7 [AB]	RAF No 3 Sqn, Laarbruch	
ZG509	BAe Harrier GR7 [CH]	RAF No 4 Sqn, Laarbruch	
ZG510	BAe Harrier GR7 [AE]	RAF No 3 Sqn, Laarbruch	
ZG511	BAe Harrier GR7 [AL]	RAF No 3 Sqn, Laarbruch	
ZG512	BAe Harrier GR7	RAF No 4 Sqn, Laarbruch	
ZG530	BAe Harrier GR7 [CL]	RAF No 4 Sqn, Laarbruch	
ZG531	BAe Harrier GR7	RAF, St Athan	
ZG532	BAe Harrier GR7	RAF, St Athan	
ZG533	BAe Harrier GR7 [CF]	RAF No 4 Sqn, Laarbruch	
ZG705	Panavia Tornado GR1A [A]	RAF No 13 Sqn, Marham	
ZG706	Panavia Tornado GR1A [E]	RAF SAOEU, Boscombe Down	
ZG707	Panavia Tornado GR1A [B]	RAF No 13 Sqn, Marham	
ZG708	Panavia Tornado GR1A [C]	*Written off, Glen Ogle, 1 Sept 1994*	
ZG709	Panavia Tornado GR1A [I]	RAF No 13 Sqn, Marham	
ZG710	Panavia Tornado GR1A [D]	RAF No 13 Sqn, Marham	
ZG711	Panavia Tornado GR1A [E]	RAF No 13 Sqn, Marham	
ZG712	Panavia Tornado GR1A [F]	RAF No 13 Sqn, Marham	
ZG713	Panavia Tornado GR1A [G]	RAF No 13 Sqn, Marham	
ZG714	Panavia Tornado GR1A [H]	RAF No 13 Sqn, Marham	
ZG725	Panavia Tornado GR1A [J]	*Written off, off Sardinia, 19 Sept 1994*	
ZG726	Panavia Tornado GR1A [K[	RAF No 13 Sqn, Marham	
ZG727	Panavia Tornado GR1A [L]	RAF No 13 Sqn, Marham	
ZG728	Panavia Tornado F3 [CI]	RAF No 5 Sqn, Coningsby	
ZG729	Panavia Tornado GR1A [M]	RAF No 13 Sqn, Marham	
ZG730	Panavia Tornado F3 [CC]	RAF No 5 Sqn, Coningsby	

Notes	Serial	Type (other identity) [code]	Owner/operator, location or fate
	ZG731	Panavia Tornado F3 [CG]	RAF No 5 Sqn, Coningsby
	ZG732	Panavia Tornado F3 [BC]	RAF No 29 Sqn, Coningsby
	ZG733	Panavia Tornado F3 [BK]	RAF No 29 Sqn, Coningsby
	ZG734	Panavia Tornado F3 [BA]	RAF No 29 Sqn, Coningsby
	ZG735	Panavia Tornado F3 [CO]	RAF No 5 Sqn, Coningsby
	ZG750	Panavia Tornado GR1 [Y]	RAF No 13 Sqn, Marham
	ZG751	Panavia Tornado F3 [CW]	RAF ASF, Coningsby
	ZG752	Panavia Tornado GR1 [Z]	RAF No 13 Sqn, Marham
	ZG753	Panavia Tornado F3	RAF No 1435 Flt, Mount Pleasant, FI
	ZG754	Panavia Tornado GR1	RAF, stored St Athan
	ZG755	Panavia Tornado F3	RAF No 1435 Flt, Mount Pleasant, FI
	ZG756	Panavia Tornado GR1 [AX]	RAF No 9 Sqn, Bruggen
	ZG757	Panavia Tornado F3 [CA]	RAF No 5 Sqn, Coningsby
	ZG768	Panavia Tornado F3 [AX]	RAF F3 OCU/No 56(R) Sqn, Coningsby
	ZG769	Panavia Tornado GR1 [AY]	RAF No 9 Sqn, Bruggen
	ZG770	Panavia Tornado F3 [BD]	RAF No 29Sqn, Coningsby
	ZG771	Panavia Tornado GR1 [DW]	RAF No 31 Sqn, Bruggen
	ZG772	Panavia Tornado F3	RAF No 1435 Flt, Mount Pleasant, FI
	ZG773	Panavia Tornado GR4	MoD(PE), BAe Warton (conversion)
	ZG774	Panavia Tornado F3 [AY]	RAF F3 OCU/No 56(R) Sqn, Coningsby
	ZG775	Panavia Tornado GR1 [CC]	RAF No 17 Sqn, Bruggen
	ZG776	Panavia Tornado F3	RAF No 1435 Flt, Mount Pleasant, FI
	ZG777	Panavia Tornado GR1 [DP]	RAF No 31 Sqn, Bruggen
	ZG778	Panavia Tornado F3	RAF No 25 Sqn, Leeming
	ZG779	Panavia Tornado GR1 [DK]	RAF No 31 Sqn, Bruggen
	ZG780	Panavia Tornado F3 [BH]	RAF No 29 Sqn, Coningsby
	ZG791	Panavia Tornado GR1 [DC]	RAF No 31 Sqn, Bruggen
	ZG792	Panavia Tornado GR1 [DD]	RAF No 31 Sqn, Bruggen
	ZG793	Panavia Tornado F3 [CY]	RAF No 5 Sqn, Coningsby
	ZG794	Panavia Tornado GR1 [DJ]	RAF No 31 Sqn, Bruggen
	ZG795	Panavia Tornado F3 [CB]	RAF No 5 Sqn, Coningsby
	ZG796	Panavia Tornado F3 [CE]	RAF No 5 Sqn, Coningsby
	ZG797	Panavia Tornado F3 [BF]	RAF No 29 Sqn, Coningsby
	ZG798	Panavia Tornado F3 [CD]	RAF No 5 Sqn, Coningsby
	ZG799	Panavia Tornado F3 [BB]	RAF No 29 Sqn, Coningsby
	ZG816	WS61 Sea King HAS6 [708/PW]	RN No 819 Sqn, Prestwick
	ZG817	WS61 Sea King HAS6 [504]	RN No 810 Sqn, Culdrose
	ZG818	WS61 Sea King HAS6 [271/N]	RN AMG, Culdrose
	ZG819	WS61 Sea King HAS6 [270/N]	RN No 814 Sqn, Culdrose
	ZG820	WS61 Sea King HC4 [A]	RN No 845 Sqn, Yeovilton
	ZG821	WS61 Sea King HC4 [D]	RN No 845 Sqn, Yeovilton
	ZG822	WS61 Sea King HC4 [VN]	RN No 846 Sqn, Yeovilton
	ZG844	PBN 2T Islander AL1	AAC No 1 Flt, Aldergrove
	ZG845	PBN 2T Islander AL1	AAC Islander Training Flt, Middle Wallop
	ZG846	PBN 2T Islander AL1	AAC No 1 Flt, Aldergrove
	ZG847	PBN 2T Islander AL1	AAC No 1 Flt, Aldergrove
	ZG848	PBN 2T Islander AL1	AAC No 1 Flt, Aldergrove
	ZG856	BAe Harrier GR7 [CJ]	RAF No 3 Sqn, Laarbruch
	ZG857	BAe Harrier GR7 [AH]	RAF No 3 Sqn, Laarbruch
	ZG858	BAe Harrier GR7 [CB]	RAF No 4 Sqn, Laarbruch
	ZG859	BAe Harrier GR7	RAF No 4 Sqn, Laarbruch
	ZG860	BAe Harrier GR7 [T]	RAF SAOEU, Boscombe Down
	ZG861	BAe Harrier GR7 [AA]	RAF No 3 Sqn, Laarbruch
	ZG862	BAe Harrier GR7 [CO]	RAF No 4 Sqn, Laarbruch
	ZG875	WS61 Sea King HAS6 [702/PW]	RN No 819 Sqn, Prestwick
	ZG879	Powerchute Raider Mk 1	MoD(PE)/Powerchute, Hereford
	ZG884	WS Lynx AH9	MoD(PE)/Westland, Yeovil
	ZG885	WS Lynx AH9 [2]	AAC No 659 Sqn, Detmold
	ZG886	WS Lynx AH9 [3]	AAC No 653 Sqn, Wattisham
	ZG887	WS Lynx AH9 [4]	AAC No 653 Sqn, Wattisham
	ZG888	WS Lynx AH9 [5]	AAC No 653 Sqn, Wattisham
	ZG889	WS Lynx AH9 [6]	AAC No 653 Sqn, Wattisham
	ZG914	WS Lynx AH9 [G]	AAC No 653 Sqn, Wattisham
	ZG915	WS Lynx AH9 [7]	AAC No 653 Sqn, Wattisham
	ZG916	WS Lynx AH9 [8]	AAC No 659 Sqn, Detmold
	ZG917	WS Lynx AH9 [9]	AAC No 659 Sqn, Detmold
	ZG918	WS Lynx AH9 [10]	AAC No 659 Sqn, Detmold
	ZG919	WS Lynx AH9 [7]	AAC No 653 Sqn, Wattisham
	ZG920	WS Lynx AH9 [8]	AAC No 653 Sqn, Wattisham
	ZG921	WS Lynx AH9 [11]	AAC No 659 Sqn, Detmold
	ZG922	WS Lynx AH9 [9]	AAC No 653 Sqn, Wattisham
	ZG923	WS Lynx AH9 [10]	AAC No 653 Sqn, Wattisham
	ZG969	Pilatus PC-9	BAe Warton

Serial	Type (other identity) [code]	Owner/operator, location or fate	Notes
ZG989	PBN 2T Islander Astor (G-DLRA)	MoD(PE), stored Wyton	
ZG993	PBN 2T Islander AL1	AAC Islander Flight, Middle Wallop	
ZG994	PBN 2T Islander AL1	AAC No 1 Flight, Aldergrove	
ZH101	Boeing E-3D Sentry AEW1	RAF No 8 Sqn, Waddington	
ZH102	Boeing E-3D Sentry AEW1	RAF No 8 Sqn, Waddington	
ZH103	Boeing E-3D Sentry AEW1	RAF No 8 Sqn, Waddington	
ZH104	Boeing E-3D Sentry AEW1	RAF No 8 Sqn, Waddington	
ZH105	Boeing E-3D Sentry AEW1	RAF No 8 Sqn, Waddington	
ZH106	Boeing E-3D Sentry AEW1	RAF No 8 Sqn, Waddington	
ZH107	Boeing E-3D Sentry AEW1	RAF No 8 Sqn, Waddington	
ZH115	Grob Vigilant T1	RAF ACCGS, Syerston	
ZH116	Grob Vigilant T1	RAF No 632 VGS, Ternhill	
ZH117	Grob Vigilant T1	RAF CGMF, Syerston	
ZH118	Grob Vigilant T1	RAF ACCGS, Syerston	
ZH119	Grob Vigilant T1	RAF No 635 VGS, Samlesbury	
ZH120	Grob Vigilant T1	RAF No 642 VGS, Linton-on-Ouse	
ZH121	Grob Vigilant T1	RAF ACCGS, Syerston	
ZH122	Grob Vigilant T1	RAF No 616 VGS, Henlow	
ZH123	Grob Vigilant T1	RAF No 624 VGS, Chivenor	
ZH124	Grob Vigilant T1	RAF No 637 VGS, Little Rissington	
ZH125	Grob Vigilant T1	RAF No 633 VGS, Cosford	
ZH126	Grob Vigilant T1	RAF No 616 VGS, Henlow	
ZH127	Grob Vigilant T1	RAF CGMF, Syerston	
ZH128	Grob Vigilant T1	RAF ACCGS, Syerston	
ZH129	Grob Vigilant T1	RAF No 616 VGS, Henlow	
ZH144	Grob Vigilant T1	RAF No 616 VGS, Henlow	
ZH145	Grob Vigilant T1	RAF No 632 VGS, Ternhill	
ZH146	Grob Vigilant T1	RAF No 637 VGS, Little Rissington	
ZH147	Grob Vigilant T1	RAF No 637 VGS, Little Rissington	
ZH148	Grob Vigilant T1	RAF No 637 VGS, Little Rissington	
ZH184	Grob Vigilant T1	RAF ACCGS, Syerston	
ZH185	Grob Vigilant T1	RAF No 632 VGS, Ternhill	
ZH186	Grob Vigilant T1	RAF No 633 VGS, Cosford	
ZH187	Grob Vigilant T1	RAF ACCGS, Syerston	
ZH188	Grob Vigilant T1	RAF ACCGS, Syerston	
ZH189	Grob Vigilant T1	RAF ACCGS, Syerston	
ZH190	Grob Vigilant T1	RAF ACCGS, Syerston	
ZH191	Grob Vigilant T1	RAF No 635 VGS, Samlesbury	
ZH192	Grob Vigilant T1	RAF No 663 VGS, Kinloss	
ZH193	Grob Vigilant T1	RAF No 663 VGS, Kinloss	
ZH194	Grob Vigilant T1	RAF No 612 VGS, Halton	
ZH195	Grob Vigilant T1	RAF ACCGS, Syerston	
ZH196	Grob Vigilant T1	RAF No 633 VGS, Cosford	
ZH197	Grob Vigilant T1	RAF No 642 VGS, Linton-on-Ouse	
ZH200	BAe Hawk 200	MoD(PE), stored BAe Warton	
ZH205	Grob Vigilant T1	RAF No 624 VGS, Chivenor	
ZH206	Grob Vigilant T1	RAF No 642 VGS, Linton-on-Ouse	
ZH207	Grob Vigilant T1	RAF ACCGS, Syerston	
ZH208	Grob Vigilant T1	RAF No 642 VGS, Linton-on-Ouse	
ZH209	Grob Vigilant T1	RAF No 613 VGS, Halton	
ZH210	Grob Vigilant T1 (wreck)	RAF CGMF Syerston	
ZH211	Grob Vigilant T1	RAF No 663 VGS, Kinloss	
ZH247	Grob Vigilant T1	RAF No 635 VGS, Samlesbury	
ZH248	Grob Vigilant T1	RAF No 642 VGS, Linton-on-Ouse	
ZH249	Grob Vigilant T1	RAF No 616 VGS, Henlow	
ZH257	B-V CH-47C Chinook	To the USA, September 1993	
ZH263	Grob Vigilant T1	RAF No 635 VGS, Samlesbury	
ZH264	Grob Vigilant T1	RAF No 642 VGS, Linton-on-Ouse	
ZH265	Grob Vigilant T1	RAF No 633 VGS, Cosford	
ZH266	Grob Vigilant T1	RAF No 633 VGS, Cosford	
ZH267	Grob Vigilant T1	RAF No 635 VGS, Samlesbury	
ZH268	Grob Vigilant T1	RAF No 613 VGS, Halton	
ZH269	Grob Vigilant T1	RAF No 624 VGS, Chivenor	
ZH270	Grob Vigilant T1	RAF No 632 VGS, Ternhill	
ZH271	Grob Vigilant T1	RAF ACCGS, Syerston	
ZH506	Shorts Tucano T52 (KAF 101)	Shorts, Belfast	
ZH507	Shorts Tucano T52 (KAF 102)	Shorts, Belfast	
ZH508	Shorts Tucano T52 (KAF 103)	Shorts, Belfast	
ZH509	Shorts Tucano T52 (KAF 104)	Shorts, Belfast	
ZH510	Shorts Tucano T52 (KAF 105)	Shorts, Belfast	
ZH511	Shorts Tucano T52 (KAF 106)	Shorts, Belfast	
ZH512	Shorts Tucano T52 (KAF 107)	Shorts, stored Shawbury	

Notes	Serial	Type (other identity) [code]	Owner/operator, location or fate
	ZH513	Shorts Tucano T52 (KAF 108)	Shorts, stored Shawbury
	ZH526	Shorts Tucano T52 (KAF 109)	Shorts, stored Shawbury
	ZH527	Shorts Tucano T52 (KAF 110)	Shorts, stored Shawbury
	ZH528	Shorts Tucano T52 (KAF 111)	Shorts, stored Shawbury
	ZH529	Shorts Tucano T52 (KAF 112)	Shorts, stored Shawbury
	ZH530	Shorts Tucano T52 (KAF 113)	Shorts, Belfast
	ZH531	Shorts Tucano T52 (KAF 114)	Shorts, stored Shawbury
	ZH532	Shorts Tucano T52 (KAF 115)	Shorts, stored Shawbury
	ZH533	Shorts Tucano T52 (KAF 116)	Shorts, stored Shawbury
	ZH536	PBN 2T Islander CC2 (G-BSAH)	RAF Northolt Station Flight
	ZH540	WS61 Sea King HAR3A	Westland, for RAF
	ZH541	WS61 Sea King HAR3A	Westland, for RAF
	ZH542	WS61 Sea King HAR3A	Westland, for RAF
	ZH543	WS61 Sea King HAR3A	Westland, for RAF
	ZH552	Panavia Tornado F3	RAF F3 OEU, Coningsby
	ZH553	Panavia Tornado F3 [BY]	RAF No 29 Sqn, Coningsby
	ZH554	Panavia Tornado F3 [BZ]	RAF No 29 Sqn, Coningsby
	ZH555	Panavia Tornado F3 [CV]	RAF No 5 Sqn, Coningsby
	ZH556	Panavia Tornado F3 [AK]	RAF F3 OCU/No 56(R) Sqn, Coningsby
	ZH557	Panavia Tornado F3 [CT]	RAF No 5 Sqn, Coningsby
	ZH558	Panavia Tornado F3 [GF]	*Written off, 8 July 1994, off Cyprus*
	ZH559	Panavia Tornado F3 [AO]	RAF F3 OCU/No 56(R) Sqn, Coningsby
	ZH563	DH115 Vampire T55 (U-1216/ G-BVLM)	*To RJAF Historic Flight as 209*
	ZH582	WS Lynx Mk 95	For Portuguese Navy as 9203
	ZH583	WS Lynx Mk 95	*To Portuguese Navy as 9204, 13 Nov 1993*
	ZH584	WS Lynx Mk 95	*To Portuguese Navy as 9205, 13 Nov 1993*
	ZH586	Eurofighter 2000 (DA1/98+29)	BAe Warton
	ZH588	Eurofighter 2000 (DA2)	MoD(PE), BAe Warton
	ZH590	Eurofighter 2000(T) (DA4)	MoD(PE), BAe Warton
	ZH629	BAe Hawk 102	For Abu Dhabi AF as 1059
	ZH634	BAe Hawk 102	For Abu Dhabi AF as 1060
	ZH635	BAe Hawk 102	For Abu Dhabi AF as 1061
	ZH636	BAe Hawk 102	For Abu Dhabi AF as 1062
	ZH637	BAe Hawk 102	For Abu Dhabi AF as 1063
	ZH638	BAe Hawk 102	For Abu Dhabi AF as 1064
	ZH639	BAe Hawk 102	For Abu Dhabi AF as 1065
	ZH640	BAe Hawk 102	For Abu Dhabi AF as 1066
	ZH641	BAe Hawk 102	For Abu Dhabi AF as 1067
	ZH642	BAe Hawk 102	For Abu Dhabi AF as 1068
	ZH647	WS/Agusta EH-101 (G-EHIL)	MoD(PE) Westland, Yeovil
	ZH653	BAe Harrier T10	MoD(PE), A&AEE Boscombe Down
	ZH654	BAe Harrier T10	MoD(PE) BAe, Warton
	ZH655	BAe Harrier T10	MoD(PE) BAe, Warton
	ZH656	BAe Harrier T10	BAe, for RAF
	ZH657	BAe Harrier T10	BAe, for RAF
	ZH658	BAe Harrier T10	BAe, for RAF
	ZH659	BAe Harrier T10	BAe, for RAF
	ZH660	BAe Harrier T10	BAe, for RAF
	ZH661	BAe Harrier T10	BAe, for RAF
	ZH662	BAe Harrier T10	BAe, for RAF
	ZH663	BAe Harrier T10	BAe, for RAF
	ZH664	BAe Harrier T10	BAe, for RAF
	ZH665	BAe Harrier T10	BAe, for RAF
	ZH670	BAe Hawk 103 (Omani AF 102)	BAe Brough (on rebuild)
	ZH700	BAe Hawk 51A	For Finnish AF as HW-353
	ZH701	BAe Hawk 51A	*To Finnish AF as HW-354, 23 March 1994*
	ZH702	BAe Hawk 51A	For Finnish AF as HW-355
	ZH703	BAe Hawk 51A	For Finnish AF as HW-356
	ZH704	BAe Hawk 51A	For Finnish AF as HW-357
	ZH710	BAe Hawk 203	For RAF of Oman as 121
	ZH711	BAe Hawk 203	For RAF of Oman as 122
	ZH712	BAe Hawk 203	For RAF of Oman as 123
	ZH713	BAe Hawk 203	*To RAF of Oman as 124, 26 May 1994*
	ZH714	BAe Hawk 203	For RAF of Oman as 125
	ZH719	BAe Hawk 203	For RAF of Oman as 126
	ZH720	BAe Hawk 203	For RAF of Oman as 127
	ZH721	BAe Hawk 203	For RAF of Oman as 128
	ZH722	BAe Hawk 203	For RAF of Oman as 129
	ZH729	BAe Hawk 203	For RAF of Oman as 130
	ZH730	BAe Hawk 203	For RAF of Oman as 131

Serial	Type (other identity) [code]	Owner/operator, location or fate	Notes
ZH731	BAe Hawk 203	For RAF of Oman as 132	
ZH735	BAe Hawk 108	*To R Malaysian AF as M40-01, 14 March 1994*	
ZH738	BAe Hawk 108	*To R Malaysian AF as M40-02, February 1994*	
ZH745	BAe Hawk 108	*To R Malaysian AF as M40-03, 14 March 1994*	
ZH746	BAe Hawk 108	*To R Malaysian AF as M40-04, 11 April 1994*	
ZH747	BAe Hawk 108	*To R Malaysian AF as M40-05, 11 April 1994*	
ZH748	BAe Hawk 108	*To R Malaysian AF as M40-06, 11 April 1994*	
ZH752	BAe Hawk 108	For R Malaysian AF as M40-07	
ZH753	BAe Hawk 108	*To R Malaysian AF as M40-08, 26 May 1994*	
ZH754	BAe Hawk 108	*To R Malaysian AF as M40-09, 26 May 1994*	
ZH757	BAe Hawk 108	*To R Malaysian AF as M40-10*	
ZH762	Westinghouse Skyship 500 (G-SKSC)	MoD(PE), A&AEE Boscombe Down	
ZH763	BAC 1-11/539GL (G-BGKE)	MoD(PE), DRA Boscombe Down	
ZH778	BAe Hawk 208	*To R Malaysian AF as M40-21, 25 July 1994*	
ZH779	BAe Hawk 208	*To R Malaysian AF as M40-22, 19 August 1994*	
ZH780	BAe Hawk 208 (*ZH779*)	*To R Malaysian AF as M40-23, 19 August 1994*	
ZH781	BAe Hawk 208	*To R Malaysian AF as M40-24*	
ZH782	BAe Hawk 208	*To R Malaysian AF as M40-25*	
ZH783	BAe Hawk 208	*To R Malaysian AF as M40-26*	
ZH784	BAe Hawk 208	*To R Malaysian AF as M40-27*	
ZH785	BAe Hawk 208	For R Malaysian AF as M40-28	
ZH786	BAe Hawk 208	For R Malaysian AF as M40-29	
ZH787	BAe Hawk 208	For R Malaysian AF as M40-30	
ZH788	BAe Hawk 208	For R Malaysian AF as M40-31	
ZH789	BAe Hawk 208	For R Malaysian AF as M40-32	
ZH790	BAe Hawk 208	For R Malaysian AF as M40-33	
ZH814	Bell 212 (G-BGMH)	AAC No 7 Flt, Brunei	
ZH815	Bell 212 (G-BGCZ)	AAC No 7 Flt, Brunei	
ZH816	Bell 212 (G-BGMG)	AAC No 7 Flt, Brunei	
ZJ100	BAe Hawk 102D	BAe Warton	
ZJ201	BAe Hawk 200RDA	BAe Warton	

VS Spitfire LF/Xe ML417 (G-BJSG) display by The Fighter Collection at Duxford. *PRM*

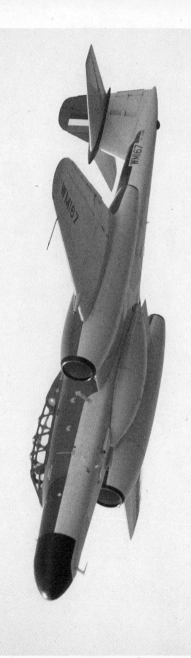

Meteor NF11 WM167 is displayed by Jet Heritage. *PRM*

Jet Heritage's red Hunter F4 XE677/G-HHUN and the Royal Jordanian Air Force Historic Flight's T7 G-BOOM. *PRM*

XX519, a Bulldog T1 carries the Cranwell light blue band round its rear fuselage. *PRM*

93

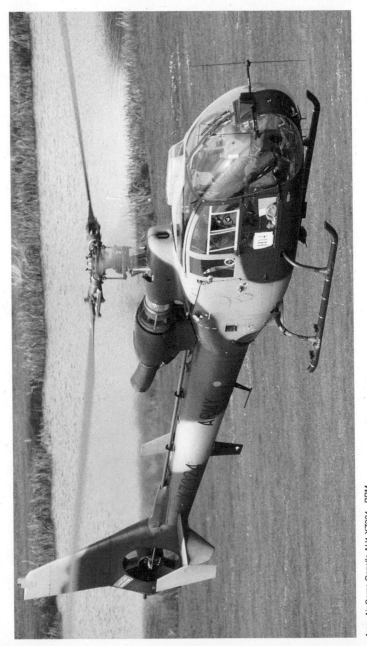

Army Air Corps Gazelle AH1 XZ324. *PRM*

No 101 Squadron VC10 K3 ZA147 based at RAF Brize Norton. *PRM*

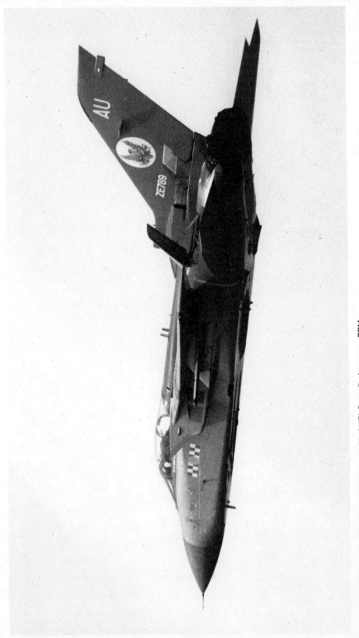

Tornado F3 ZE789 in specially colourful markings for No 56(R) Sqns display crew. *PRM*

RAF Maintenance Command/ Support Command 'M' number cross-reference

1764M/K4972	7525M/WT619	7817M/TX214	7984M/XN597
2015M/K5600	7530M/WT648	7825M/WK991	7986M/WG777
2292M/K8203	7532M/WT651	7829M/XH992	7988M/XL149
2361M/K6035	7533M/WT680	7839M/WV781	7990M/XD452
3118M/H5199/BK892	7544M/WN904	7840M/XK482	7997M/XG452
3858M/X7688	7548M/PS915	7841M/WV783	7998M/*XM515*/(XD515)
4354M/BL614	7554M/FS890	7851M/WZ706	8001M/WV395
5377M/EP120	7555M/AR614	7852M/XG506	8005M/WG768
5378M/AR614	7556M/WK584	7854M/XM191	8009M/XG518
5405M/LF738	7564M/XE982	7855M/XK416	8010M/XG547
5466M/*BN230*/(LF751)	7570M/XD674	7859M/XP283	8012M/VS562
5690M/MK356	7582M/*WP180*/(WP190)	7860M/XL738	8016M/XT677
5718M/BM597	7583M/WP185	7862M/XR246	8017M/XL762
5758M/DG202	7602M/WE600	7863M/*XP248*	8018M/XN344
5854M/WH903	7605M/WS692	7864M/XP244	8019M/WZ869
6457M/ML427	7606M/WV562	7865M/TX226	8021M/XL824
6490M/LA255	7607M/TJ138	7866M/XH278	8022M/XN341
6850M/TE184	7615M/WV679	7867M/XH980	8023M/XD463
6946M/RW388	7616M/WW388	7868M/WZ736	8027M/XM555
6948M/DE673	7618M/WW442	7869M/WK935	8032M/XH837
6960M/MT847	7622M/WV606	7870M/XM556	8033M/XD382
7008M/EE549	7625M/WD356	7872M/*WZ826*/(XD826)	8034M/XL703
7014M/N6720	7631M/VX185	7881M/WD413	8041M/XF690
7015M/NL985	7641M/XA634	7882M/XD525	8043M/XF836
7035M/*K2567*/(DE306)	7645M/WD293	7883M/XT150	8046M/XL770
7060M/VF301	7646M/VX461	7886M/XR985	8049M/WE168
7090M/EE531	7648M/XF785	7887M/XD375	8050M/XG329
7118M/LA198	7663M/XA571	7890M/XD453	8051M/XN929
7119M/LA226	7673M/WV332	7891M/XM693	8052M/WH166
7150M/PK683	7688M/WW421	7894M/XD818	8054AM/XM410
7154M/WB188	7693M/WV483	7895M/WF784	8054BM/XM417
7174M/VX272	7696M/WV493	7898M/XP854	8055AM/XM402
7175M/VV106	7698M/WV499	7899M/XG540	8055BM/XM404
7200M/VT812	7703M/WG725	7900M/WA576	8056M/XG337
7241M/*X4474*/(TE311)	7704M/TW536	7902M/WZ550	8057M/XR243
7243M/TE462	7705M/WL505	7906M/WH132	8063M/WT536
7244M/*X4277*/(TB382)	7706M/WB584	7917M/WA591	8070M/EP120
7246M/TD248	7709M/WT933	7920M/WL360	8072M/PK624
7256M/TB752	7711M/PS915	7923M/XT133	8073M/TB252
7257M/TB252	7712M/WK281	7925M/WV666	8076M/XM386
7279M/TB752	7715M/XK724	7928M/XE849	8077M/XN594
7281M/TB252	7716M/WS776	7930M/WH301	8078M/XM351
7288M/PK724	7718M/WA577	7931M/RD253	8079M/XN492
7293M/RW393	7719M/WK277	7932M/WZ744	8080M/XM480
7323M/VV217	7722M/XA571	7933M/XR220	8081M/XM468
7325M/R5868	7728M/WZ458	7937M/WS843	8082M/XM409
7326M/VN485	7729M/WB758	7938M/XH903	8085M/XM467
7362M/475081/(VP546)	7734M/XD536	7939M/XD596	8086M/TB752
7416M/WN907	7736M/WZ559	7940M/XL764	8088M/XN602
7421M/WT660	7737M/XD602	7955M/XH767	8092M/WK654
7422M/WT684	7739M/XA801	7957M/XF545	8094M/WT520
7428M/WK198	7741M/VZ477	7959M/WS774	8101M/WH984
7432M/WZ724	7750M/*WK864*/(WL168)	7960M/WS726	8102M/WT486
7438M/WP905	7751M/WL131	7961M/WS739	8103M/WR985
7443M/WX853	7755M/WG760	7964M/WS760	8106M/WR982
7451M/TE476	7758M/PM651	7965M/WS792	8108M/WV703
7458M/WX905	7759M/PK664	7967M/WS788	8113M/WV753
7464M/XA564	7761M/XH318	7970M/WP907	8117M/WR974
7467M/WP978	7762M/XE670	7971M/XK699	8118M/WZ549
7470M/XA553	7770M/WT746	7973M/WS807	8119M/WR971
7473M/XE946	7793M/XG523	7976M/XK418	8121M/XM474
7491M/WT569	7796M/WJ676	7979M/XM529	8124M/XD614
7496M/WT612	7806M/TA639	7980M/XM561	8128M/WH775
7499M/WT555	7809M/XA699	7982M/XH892	8131M/WT507
7510M/WT694	7816M/WG763	7983M/XD506	8140M/XJ571

8141M/XN688	8367M/XG474	8483M/420430	8640M/XR977
8142M/XJ560	8368M/XF926	8484M/5439	8642M/XR537
8143M/XN691	8369M/WE139	8485M/997	8645M/XD163
8147M/XR526	8370M/N1671	8486M/BAPC 99	8648M/XK526
8151M/WV795	8371M/XA847	8487M/J-1172	8653M/XS120
8153M/WV903	8372M/K8042	8488M/WL627	8655M/XN126
8154M/WV908	8373M/P2617	8491M/WJ880	8656M/XP405
8155M/WV797	8375M/NX611	8492M/WJ872	8657M/VZ634
8156M/XE339	8376M/RF398	8493M/XR571	8661M/XJ727
8158M/XE369	8377M/R9125	8494M/XP557	8662M/XR458
8159M/XD528	8378M/*T9707*	8495M/XR672	8664M/WJ603
8160M/XD622	8379M/DG590	8498M/XR670	8666M/XE793
8161M/XE993	8380M/Z7197	8501M/XP640	8667M/WP972
8162M/WM913	8382M/VR930	8502M/XP686	8668M/WJ821
8163M/XP919	8383M/K9942	8503M/XS451	8671M/XJ435
8164M/*WN105*/(WF299)	8384M/X4590	8506M/XR704	8672M/XP351
8165M/WH791	8385M/N5912	8507M/XS215	8673M/XD165
8169M/WH364	8386M/NV778	8508M/XS218	8674M/XP395
8171M/XJ607	8387M/T6296	8509M/XT141	8676M/XL577
8173M/XN685	8388M/XL993	8510M/XP567	8677M/*XF519*/(XJ6
8176M/WH791	8389M/VX573	8513M/XN724	8678M/XE656
8177M/*WM311*/(WM224)	8392M/SL674	8514M/XS176	8679M/XF526
8179M/XN928	8393M/XK987	8535M/XN776	8680M/XF527
8180M/XN930	8394M/WG422	8538M/XN781	8681M/XG164
8182M/XN953	8395M/WF408	8546M/XN728	8682M/XP404
8183M/*XN972*/(XN962)	8396M/XK740	8548M/WT507	8684M/XJ634
8184M/WT520	8399M/WR539	8549M/WT534	8685M/XF516
8185M/WH946	8401M/XP686	8551M/XN774	8687M/XJ639
8186M/WR977	8402M/XN769	8554M/TG511	8689M/WK144
8187M/WH791	8406M/XP831	8559M/XN467	8693M/WH863
8189M/WD646	8407M/XP585	8560M/XR569	8696M/WH773
8190M/XJ918	8408M/XS186	8565M/*WT720*/(E-408)	8699M/ZD232
8192M/XR658	8409M/XS209	8566M/XV279	8700M/ZD234
8196M/XE920	8410M/XR662	8568M/XP503	8702M/XG196
8198M/WT339	8413M/XM192	8569M/XR535	8703M/VW453
8203M/XD377	8414M/XM173	8570M/XR954	8704M/XN643
8205M/XN819	8417M/XM144	8573M/XM708	8706M/XF383
8206M/WG419	8422M/XM169	8575M/XP542	8708M/XF509
8207M/WD318	8427M/XM172	8576M/XP502	8709M/XG209
8208M/WG303	8429M/XH592	8578M/XR534	8710M/XG274
8209M/WG418	8431M/XR651	8581M/WJ775	8711M/XG290
8210M/WG471	8435M/XN512	8582M/XE874	8713M/XG225
8211M/WK570	8436M/XN554	8583M/BAPC 94	8714M/XK149
8213M/WK626	8437M/WG362	8585M/XE670	8718M/XX396
8214M/WP864	8439M/WZ846	8586M/XE643	8719M/XT257
8215M/WP869	8440M/WD935	8587M/XP677	8720M/XP353
8216M/WP927	8442M/XP411	8588M/XR681	8721M/XP354
8217M/WZ866	8445M/XK968	8589M/XR700	8723M/XL567
8229M/XM355	8447M/XP359	8590M/XM191	8724M/XW923
8230M/XM362	8453M/XP745	8591M/XA813	8726M/XP299
8231M/XM375	8457M/XS871	8595M/XH278	8727M/XR486
8232M/XM381	8458M/XP672	8596M/LH208	8728M/WT532
8234M/XN458	8459M/XR650	8598M/WP270	8729M/WJ815
8235M/XN549	8460M/XP680	8600M/XX761	8730M/XD186
8236M/XP573	8462M/XX477	8602M/*PF179*/(XR541)	8731M/XP361
8237M/XS179	8463M/XP355	8606M/XP530	8732M/XJ729
8238M/XS180	8464M/XJ758	8608M/XP540	8733M/XL318
8333M/XM408	8465M/W1048	8609M/XR953	8736M/XF375
8344M/WH960	8466M/L-866	8610M/XL502	8739M/XH170
8345M/XG540	8467M/WP912	8611M/WF128	8740M/WE173
8346M/XN734	8468M/MM5701/(BT474)	8617M/XM709	8741M/XW329
8350M/WH840	8470M/584219	8618M/*XM693*/(XP504)	8743M/WD790
8352M/XN632	8471M/701152	8620M/XP534	8746M/XH171
8355M/*KG374*/(KN645)	8472M/120227/(VN679)	8621M/XR538	8749M/XH537
8357M/WK576	8473M/WP180/(WP190)	8622M/XR980	8751M/XT255
8359M/WF825	8474M/494083	8623M/XR998	8753M/WL795
8360M/WP863	8475M/360043/(PJ876)	8624M/*XR991*/(XS102)	8755M/*WH699*/(W.
8361M/WB670	8476M/24	8627M/XP558	8756M/XL427
8362M/WG477	8477M/4101/(DG200)	8628M/XJ380	8757M/XM656
8363M/WG463	8478M/10639	8630M/WG362	8762M/WH740
8364M/WG464	8479M/730301	8631M/XR574	8763M/WH665
8365M/XK421	8481M/191614	8634M/WP314	8764M/XP344
8366M/XG454	8482M/112372/(VK893)	8638M/XS101	8767M/XX635

8768M/A-522	8884M/VX275	8984M/XN551	9071M/XT853
8769M/A-528	8886M/XA243	8985M/WK127	9072M/XW768
8770M/XL623	8888M/XA231	8986M/XV261	9073M/XW924
8771M/XM602	8889M/XN239	8987M/XM358	9074M/XV738
8772M/WR960	8890M/WT532	8988M/XN593	9075M/XV753
8774M/XV338	8892M/XL618	8990M/XM419	9076M/XV808
8777M/XX914	8894M/XT669	8991M/XR679	9077M/XZ967
8778M/XM598	8895M/XX746	8992M/XP547	9078M/XV752
8779M/XM607	8896M/XX821	8995M/XM425	9079M/XZ130
8780M/WK102	8897M/XX969	8996M/XM414	9083M/ZE353
8781M/WE982	8898M/XX119	8997M/XX669	9084M/ZE354
8782M/XH136	8899M/XX756	8998M/XT864	9085M/ZE364
8783M/XW272	8900M/XZ368	9001M/XV778	9087M/XX753
8785M/XS642	8901M/XZ383	9002M/XW763	9090M/XW353
8786M/XN495	8902M/XX739	9003M/XZ390	9091M/XW434
8791M/XP329	8903M/XX747	9004M/XZ370	9092M/XH669
8792M/XP345	8904M/XX966	9005M/XZ374	9093M/WK124
8793M/XP346	8905M/XX975	9006M/XX967	9095M/XW547
8794M/XP398	8906M/XX976	9007M/XX968	9096M/WV322
8796M/XK943	8907M/XZ371	9008M/XX140	9097M/XW366
8797M/XX947	8908M/XZ382	9009M/XX763	9098M/XV406
8799M/WV787	8909M/XV784	9010M/XX764	9099M/XT900
8800M/XG226	8910M/XL160	9011M/XM412	9100M/XL188
8805M/XT772	8911M/XH673	9012M/XN494	9101M/WL756
8806M/XP140	8915M/XH132	9014M/XN584	9103M/XV411
8807M/XL587	8916M/XL163	9015M/XW320	9107M/XV482
8810M/XJ825	8917M/XM372	9017M/ZE449	9108M/XT475
8813M/VT260	8918M/XX109	9018M/XW365	9109M/XW312
8814M/XM927	8919M/XT486	9019M/XX824	9110M/XX736
8818M/XK527	8920M/XT469	9020M/XX825	9111M/XW421
8819M/XS479	8921M/XT466	9021M/XX826	9112M/XM475
8820M/VP952	8923M/XX819	9022M/XX958	9113M/XV500
8822M/VP957	8924M/XP701	9023M/XX844	9114M/XL162
8824M/VP971	8925M/XP706	9025M/XR701	9115M/XV863
8828M/XS587	8931M/XV779	9026M/XP629	9119M/XW303
8829M/XE653	8932M/XR718	9027M/XP556	9120M/XW419
8830M/XF515	8933M/XX297	9028M/XP563	9122M/XZ997
8831M/XG160	8934M/XR749	9029M/XS217	9123M/XT773
8832M/XG172	8935M/XR713	9030M/XR674	9124M/XW427
8833M/XL569	8937M/XX751	9031M/XP688	9125M/XW410
8834M/XL572	8938M/WV746	9032M/XR673	9126M/XW413
8836M/XL592	8939M/XP741	9033M/XS181	9127M/XW432
8838M/*34037*/(429356)	8941M/XT456	9034M/XP638	9128M/XW292
8839M/XG194	8942M/XN185	9036M/XM350	9129M/XW294
8840M/XG252	8943M/XE799	9037M/XN302	9130M/XW327
8844M/XJ676	8944M/WZ791	9038M/XV810	9131M/*DD931*
8845M/XS572	8945M/XX818	9039M/XN586	9132M/XX977
8847M/XX344	8946M/XZ389	9040M/XZ138	9133M/*413573*
8848M/XZ121	8947M/XX726	9041M/XW763	9134M/XT288
8851M/XT595	8948M/XX757	9042M/XL954	9136M/XT891
8852M/XV337	8949M/XX743	9044M/XS177	9137M/XN579
8853M/XT277	8950M/XX956	9045M/XN636	9139M/XV863
8855M/XT284	8951M/XX727	9046M/XM349	9140M/XZ287
8857M/XW544	8952M/XX730	9047M/XW409	9141M/XV118
8860M/XW549	8953M/XX959	9048M/XM403	9143M/XN589
8861M/XW528	8954M/XZ384	9049M/XW404	9145M/XV863
8862M/XN473	8955M/XX110	9050M/XG577	9146M/XW299
8863M/XG154	8956M/XN577	9052M/WJ717	9147M/XW301
8865M/XN641	8957M/XN582	9053M/XT755	9148M/XW436
8867M/XK532	8958M/XN501	9054M/XT766	9149M/XW375
8868M/WH775	8959M/XN472	9055M/XT770	9150M/*FX760*
8869M/WH957	8960M/XM455	9056M/XS488	9151M/XT907
8870M/WH964	8961M/XS925	9057M/ZE361	9152M/XV424
8871M/WJ565	8967M/XV263	9058M/ZE351	9153M/XW360
8873M/XR453	8968M/XM471	9059M/ZE360	9154M/XW321
8874M/XE597	8969M/XR753	9060M/ZE356	9155M/WL679
8875M/XE624	8972M/XR754	9061M/XW335	9157M/XV422
8876M/*VM791*/(XA312)	8973M/XS922	9062M/XW351	9158M/XV467
8877M/XP159	8974M/XM473	9064M/XT867	9159M/XV468
8879M/XX948	8978M/XX837	9065M/XV577	9161M/XZ998
8880M/XF435	8979M/XV747	9066M/XV582	9162M/XZ991
8881M/XG254	8981M/XW764	9067M/XV586	9163M/XV415
8883M/XX946	8983M/XM478	9070M/XV581	9164M/XK695

RAF Maintenance cross-reference

9165M/XV408	9183M/*XF519*	9201M	9220M/XZ995
9166M/XW323	9184M/XZ965	9202M/*433*	9221M/XZ966
9167M/XV744	9185M/XZ987	9203M/*3066*	9222M/XZ968
9168M/XZ132	9186M/XF967	9205M/*E449*	9223M/XL616
9169M/XW547	9187M/XW405	9206M/F6314	9224M/XL568
9170M/XZ994	9188M/XW364	9207M/8417/18	9225M/XX885
9171M/XT895	9189M/ZD350	9208M/F938	9226M/XV865
9172M/XW304	9190M/XW318	9209M/164	9227M/XB812
9173M/XW418	9191M/XW416	9210M/MF628	9228M
9174M/XZ131	9192M/XW361	9211M/733682	9229M/ZA678
9175M/P1344	9193M/XW367	9212M/13064	9230M
9176M/XW430	9194M/XW420	9213M/N5182	9231M
9177M/XW328	9195M/XW330	9214M/XL161	9232M
9178M/XS793	9196M/XW370	9215M/XL164	9233M
9179M/XW309	9197M	9216M/XL190	9234M
9180M/XW311	9198M/XS641	9217M	9235M
9181M/XW358	9199M/XW290	9218M/XL563	9236M
9182M	9200M/XW425	9219M/XZ971	9237M/XF995

Ships' Numeric Code — Deck Letters Analysis

	0	1	2	3	4	5	6	7	8	9
32	AZ	GIB	AV	AB			AW	AL	BA	BA
33	BZ	BZ	LP	BM	SN	CF	CV	CV	CT	CT
34		AG	BT	BT	GW	NC	BW	BW		
35	CL	CL	SD	SD		SM				
36	MC	NF	NF	MA	MA	AY	AY			
37			NL		VB	VB	XB			
40			BX	BX	IR	LN	LN	YK		
41	GC	EB	CW	CW		MM		NM		
42	EX		SU							
43					ED	ED		GT		
44					MR					
45								LA		
46			WM							
47			AM		RM					

RN Code – Squadron – Base – Aircraft Cross-Check

Code Numbers	Deck/Base Letters	Unit	Location	Aircraft Type(s)
000 — 005	R	801 Sqn	Yeovilton	Sea Harrier F/A2
010 — 020	R	820 Sqn	Culdrose	Sea King HAS6
122 — 129	N	800 Sqn	Yeovilton	Sea Harrier FRS1
180 — 187	R	849 Sqn	Culdrose	Sea King AEW2A
264 — 274	N	814 Sqn	Culdrose	Sea King HAS6
300 — 308	PO	815 Sqn	Portland	Lynx HAS3
320 — 479	*	815 Sqn	Portland	Lynx HAS3
500 — 510	CU	810 Sqn	Culdrose	Sea King HAS6
538 — 559	CU	705 Sqn	Culdrose	Gazelle HT2
560 — 575	CU	750 Sqn	Culdrose	Jetstream T2
576 — 579	—	FONA	Yeovilton	Jetstream T3
580 — 599	—	706 Sqn	Culdrose	Sea King HAS6
620 — 628	PO	772 Sqn	Portland	Sea King HC4
630 — 638	PO	702 Sqn	Portland	Lynx HAS3
640 — 648	PO	702 Sqn	Portland	Lynx HAS3
670 — 672	PO	815 Sqn OEU	Portland	Lynx HAS3 CTS
699 — 709	PW	819 Sqn	Prestwick	Sea King HAS6
710 — 717	VL	899 Sqn	Yeovilton	Sea Harrier FRS1/F/A2
718 — 722	VL	899 Sqn	Yeovilton	Harrier T4/T4N
820 — 826	CU	771 Sqn	Culdrose	Sea King HAR5

*See foregoing separate ships' Deck Letter Analysis
Note that only the 'last two' digits of the Code are worn by some aircraft types, especially helicopters.

RN Landing Platform and Shore Station Code-letters

Code	Deck Letters	Vessel Name & Pennant No	Vessel Type & Unit
323	AB	HMS *Ambuscade* (F172)	Type 21 (815 Sqn)
341	AG	HMS *Avenger* (F185)	Type 21 (815 Sqn)
327	AL	HMS *Alacrity* (F174)	Type 21 (815 Sqn)
472	AM	HMS *Andromeda* (F57)	Leander (815 Sqn)
—	AS	RFA *Argus* (A135)	Aviation Training ship
322	AV	HMS *Active* (F171)	Type 21 (815 Sqn)
326	AW	HMS *Arrow* (F173)	Type 21 (815 Sqn)
365/6	AY	HMS *Argyll* (F232)	Type 23 (815 Sqn)
320	AZ	HMS *Amazon* (F169)	Type 21 (815 Sqn)
328/9	BA	HMS *Brave* (F94)	Type 22 (815 Sqn)
—	BD	RFA *Sir Bedivere* (L3004)	Landing ship
—	BE	RFA *Blue Rover* (A270)	Fleet tanker
333	BM	HMS *Birmingham* (D86)	Type 42 (815 Sqn)
342/3	BT	HMS *Brilliant* (F90)	Type 22 (815 Sqn)
—	BV	RFA *Black Rover* (A273)	Fleet tanker
346/7	BW	HMS *Broadsword* (F88)	Type 22 (815 Sqn)
402/3	BX	HMS *Battleaxe* (F89)	Type 22 (815 Sqn)
330/1	BZ	HMS *Brazen* (F91)	Type 22 (815 Sqn)
335	CF	HMS *Cardiff* (D108)	Type 42 (815 Sqn)
350/1	CL	HMS *Cumberland* (F85)	Type 22 (815 Sqn)
515	CM	HMS *Chatham* (F87)	Type 22 (810 Sqn)
338/9	CT	HMS *Campbeltown* (F86)	Type 22 (815 Sqn)
—	CU	RNAS Culdrose (HMS *Seahawk*)	
336/7	CV	HMS *Coventry* (F98)	Type 22 (815 Sqn)
412/3	CW	HMS *Cornwall* (F99)	Type 22 (815 Sqn)
—	DC	HMS *Dumbarton Castle* (P268)	Fishery protection
—	DG	RFA *Diligence* (A132)	Maintenance
411	EB	HMS *Edinburgh* (D97)	Type 42 (815 Sqn)
434/5	ED	HMS *Endurance* (A176)	Ice Patrol (815 Sqn)
420	EX	HMS *Exeter* (D89)	Type 42 (815 Sqn)
—	FA	RFA *Fort Austin* (A386)	Support ship
—	FG	RFA *Fort Grange* (A385)	Support ship
—	FL	RNAY Fleetlands	
—	FS	HMS *Fearless* (L10)	Assault
410	GC	HMS *Gloucester* (D96)	Type 42 (815 Sqn)
321	GIB	Gibraltar Airport	(815 Sqn)
—	GD	RFA *Sir Galahad* (L3005)	Landing ship
—	GN	RFA *Green Rover* (A268)	Fleet tanker
—	GR	RFA *Sir Geraint* (L3027)	Landing ship
437	GT	HMS *Grafton* (F241)	Type 23
—	GV	RFA *Gold Rover* (A271)	Fleet tanker
344	GW	HMS *Glasgow* (D88)	Type 42 (815 Sqn)
—	GY	RFA *Grey Rover* (A269)	Fleet tanker
—	HC	HMS *Hecla* (A133)	Survey ship
—	HR	HMS *Herald*	Survey ship
—	ID	HMS *Intrepid* (L11)	Assault
404	IR	HMS *Iron Duke* (F234)	Type 23 (815 Sqn)
—	L	HMS *Illustrious* (R06)	Carrier
457	LA	HMS *Lancaster* (F229)	Type 23 (815 Sqn)
—	LC	HMS *Leeds Castle* (P258)	Fishery protection
405/6	LN	HMS *London* (F95)	Type 22 (815 Sqn)
332	LP	HMS *Liverpool* (D92)	Type 42 (815 Sqn)
—	LS	RNAS Lee-on-Solent (HMS *Daedalus*)	
363/4	MA	HMS *Marlborough* (F233)	Type 23 (815 Sqn)
360	MC	HMS *Manchester* (D95)	Type 42 (815 Sqn)
415	MM	HMS *Monmouth* (F235)	Type 23
444	MR	HMS *Montrose* (F236)	Type 23
—	N	HMS *Invincible* (R05)	Carrier
345	NC	HMS *Newcastle* (D87)	Type 42 (815 Sqn)
361/2	NF	HMS *Norfolk* (F230)	Type 23 (815 Sqn)
372	NL	HMS *Northumberland* (F238)	Type 23
417	NM	HMS *Nottingham* (D91)	Type 42 (815 Sqn)
—	OD	RFA *Olmeda* (A124)	Fleet tanker
—	ON	RFA *Olna* (A123)	Fleet tanker
—	OW	RFA *Olwen* (A122)	Fleet tanker

RN Landing Platforms

Code	Deck Letters	Vessel Name & Pennant No	Vessel Type & Unit
—	PO	RNAS Portland (HMS *Osprey*)	
—	PV	RFA *Sir Percival* (L3036)	Landing ship
—	PW	Prestwick Airport (HMS *Gannet*)	
—	R	HMS *Ark Royal* (R09)	Carrier
—	RG	RFA *Regent* (A486)	Support ship
474	RM	HMS *Richmond* (F239)	Type 23
—	RS	RFA *Resource* (A480)	Support ship
352/3	SD	HMS *Sheffield* (F96)	Type 23 (815 Sqn)
355	SM	HMS *Somerset* (F240)	Type 23
334	SN	HMS *Southampton* (D90)	Type 42 (815 Sqn)
422	SU	HMS *Sutherland* (F242)	Type 23
—	TM	RFA *Sir Tristram* (L3505)	Landing ship
374/5	VB	HMS *Beaver* (F93)	Type 22 (815 Sqn)
—	VL	RNAS Yeovilton (HMS *Heron*)	
462	WM	HMS *Westminster* (F237)	Type 23
376	XB	HMS *Boxer* (F92)	Type 22 (815 Sqn)
407	YK	HMS *York* (D98)	Type 42 (815 Sqn)
—	—	RFA *Fort Victoria* (A387)	Auxiliary Oiler
—	—	RFA *Fort George* (A388)	Auxiliary Oiler

ZD634 one of 810 Naval Air Squadrons Sea King HAS6's based at RNAS Culdrose. *PRM*

John Griffin flying his Russian marked Yakovlev Yak-50 822303/LY-ANJ. *PRM*

The Slovak Air Force donated this MiG-21 7708 to the RAF Benevolent Fund in 1994. It is now based at Boscombe Down. *Andrew March*

British-based Historic Aircraft in Overseas Markings

Some *historic, classic and warbird* aircraft carry the markings of overseas air arms and can be seen in the UK, mainly preserved in museums and collections or taking part in air shows.

Notes	Serial	Type (other identity)	Owner/operator, location
	Argentina		
	0729	Beech T-34C Turbo Mentor	FAA Museum, stored Wroughton
	0767	Aermacchi MB339AA	Rolls-Royce, Filton
	A-515	FMA IA58 Pucara (ZD485)	RAF Cosford Aerospace Museum
	A-517	FMA IA58 Pucara (G-BLRP)	Privately owned, Channel Islands
	A-522	FMA IA58 Pucara (8768M)	North-East Aircraft Museum, Usworth
	A-528	FMA IA58 Pucara (8769M)	Norfolk & Suffolk Aviation Museum, Flixton
	A-533	FMA IA58 Pucara (ZD486)	Museum of Army Flying, Middle Wallop
	A-549	FMA IA58 Pucara (ZD487)	Imperial War Museum, Duxford
	AE-406	Bell UH-1H Iroquois	Museum of Army Flying, Middle Wallop
	AE-409	Bell UH-1H Iroquois [656]	Museum of Army Flying, Middle Wallop
	AE-422	Bell UH-1H Iroquois	FAA Museum, RNAS Yeovilton
	PA-12	SA330L Puma HC1 (9017M)	RAF Odiham, BDRT
	Australia		
	A2-4	Supermarine Seagull V (VH-ALB)	RAF Museum, Hendon
	A8-324	Bristol Beaufighter X	The Fighter Collection, Duxford
	A16-199	Lockheed Hudson IIIA (G-BEOX) [SF-R]	RAF Museum, Hendon
	A17-48	DH Tiger Moth (G-BPHR)	Privately owned, Swindon
	A68-192	CAC-18 Mustang 23 (G-HAEC)	The Old Flying Machine Company, Duxford
	A92-480	GAF Jindivik 4A	T&EE Llanbedr, on display
	A92-664	GAF Jindivik 4A	Maes Artro Craft Village, Llanbedr
	Belgium		
	FT-36	Lockheed T-33A	Dumfries & Galloway Av'n Mus, Tinwald Downs
	HD-75	Hanriot HD1 (G-AFDX)	RAF Museum, Hendon
	MT-11	Fouga CM-170R Magister (G-BRFU)	Privately owned, North Weald
	SG-3	VS Spitfire FR.XIV (SG-31/G-BSKP)	Privately owned, Duxford
	V-58	Stampe SV4B (G-DANN)	Privately owned, Redhill
	Brazil		
	1317	Embraer T-27 Tucano	Shorts, Belfast (engine test bed)
	Canada		
	232	Hawker Sea Fury FB11 (TG114/ G-BVOE)	Privately owned, North Weald
	622	Piasecki HUP-3 Retriever (116622/N6699D)	IHM, Weston-super-Mare
	920	VS Stranraer (CF-BXO) [Q-N]	RAF Museum, Hendon
	9059	Bristol Bolingbroke IVT	Privately owned, Portsmouth
	9754	Consolidated PBY-5A Catalina (VR-BPS) [P]	Plane Sailing Ltd, Duxford
	9893	Bristol Bolingbroke IVT	Imperial War Museum store, Duxford
	9940	Bristol Bolingbroke IVT	Royal Scottish Mus'm of Flight, E Fortune
	16693	Auster J/1N Alpha (G-BLPG) [693]	Privately owned, Headcorn
	18013	DHC Chipmunk 22 (G-TRIC) [013]	Privately owned, North Weald
	18393	Avro Canada CF-100 (G-BCYK)	Imperial War Museum, Duxford
	18671	DHC Chipmunk 22 (G-BNZC) [671]	Privately owned, Wombleton
	20310	CCF Harvard IV (G-BSBG)	Privately owned, Shoreham
	20385	CCF T-6J Harvard IV (G-BGPB)	British Aerial Museum, Duxford
	21417	Canadair CT-133 Silver Star	Yorkshire Air Museum, Elvington
	23140	NA Sabre [AX] (fuselage)	Midland Air Museum, Coventry
	Croatia		
	5	Nord 1203 (G-BEDB)	Privately owned, Chirk
	Czech Republic		
	3309	Mikoyan MiG-15	Royal Scottish Museum of Flight, East Fortune

Serial	Type (other identity)	Owner/operator, location	Notes
3794	Letov S-102 (MiG-15) (623794)	Imperial War Museum, Duxford	
9147	Mil Mi-4	IHM, Weston-super-Mare	

Denmark

AR-107	SAAB S-35XD Draken	Newark Air Museum, Winthrope	
E-402	Hawker Hunter F51	Privately owned, Bournemouth	
E-419	Hawker Hunter F51	North-East Aircraft Museum, Usworth	
E-420	Hawker Hunter F51 (G-9-442)	Privately owned, Marlow	
E-421	Hawker Hunter F51	Brooklands Museum, Weybridge	
E-423	Hawker Hunter F51 (G-9-444)	SWWAPS, Lasham	
E-424	Hawker Hunter F51 (G-9-445)	South Yorkshire Air Museum, Firbeck	
E-425	Hawker Hunter F51	Midland Air Museum, Coventry	
E-427	Hawker Hunter F51 (G-9-447)	Privately owned, Bruntingthorpe	
E-430	Hawker Hunter F51	Privately owned, Charlwood, Surrey	
ET-272	Hawker Hunter T7	South Yorkshire Air Museum, Firbeck	
ET-273	Hawker Hunter T7 <ff>	Jet Heritage Ltd, Bournemouth	
L-866	Consolidated Catalina (8466M)	RAF Cosford Aerospace Museum	
R-756	Lockheed F-104G Starfighter	Midland Air Museum, Coventry	
S-881	Sikorsky S-55C	IHM, Weston-super-Mare	
S-882	Sikorsky S-55C	IHM, Weston-super-Mare	
S-885	Sikorsky S-55C	Privately owned,	
S-886	Sikorsky S-55C	IHM, Weston-super-Mare	
S-887	Sikorsky S-55C	IHM, Weston-super-Mare	

Egypt

0446	Mikoyan MiG-21UM <ff>	The Air Defence Collection, Salisbury	
2684	Mikoyan MiG-19	DRA Farnborough Fire Section	
7907	Sukhoi Su-7 <ff>	Robertsbridge Aviation Society, Headcorn	

France

37	Nord 3400 (G-ZARA) [MAB]	Privately owned, Boston	
57	Dassault Mystère IVA [8-MT]	Imperial War Museum, Duxford	
59	Dassault Mystère IVA [2-SF]	Wales Aircraft Museum, Cardiff	
68	Nord 3400 [MHA]	Privately owned, Coventry	
70	Dassault Mystère IVA [8-NV]	Midland Air Museum, Coventry	
79	Dassault Mystère IVA [8-NB]	Norfolk & Suffolk Aviation Museum, Flixton	
83	Dassault Mystère IVA [8-MS]	Newark Air Museum, Winthorpe	
84	Dassault Mystère IVA [8-NF]	Robertsbridge Aviation Society, Headcorn	
85	Dassault Mystère IVA	Privately owned, Bruntingthorpe	
101	Dassault Mystère IVA [8-MN]	Bomber County Aviation Museum, Hemswell	
FR108	SO1221 Djinn [CDL]	IHM, Weston-super-Mare	
120	SNCAN Stampe SV4C (G-AZGC)	Privately owned, Reading	
121	Dassault Mystère IVA [8-MY]	City of Norwich Aviation Museum	
143	MS733 Alcyon (G-MSAL)	Privately owned, Booker	
FR145	SO1221 Djinn [CDL]	Privately owned, Luton Airport	
146	Dassualt Mystère IVA [8-MC]	North-East Aircraft Museum, Usworth	
157	Morane MS230 (G-AVEB) [01/M573]	Privately owned, Booker	
192	MH1521M Broussard (G-BKPT) [44-GI]	Privately owned, Rednal	
318	Dassault Mystère IVA [8-NY]	Dumfries & Galloway Av'n Mus, Tinwald Downs	
319	Dassault Mystère IVA [8-ND]	Rebel Air Museum, Andrewsfield	
14286	Lockheed T-33A [WK]	Imperial War Museum, Duxford	
16718	Lockheed T-33A [314-UJ]	City of Norwich Aviation Museum	
42204	NA F-100D Super Sabre [11-MQ]	RAF Alconbury	
63938	NA F-100F Super Sabre [11-MU]	Lashenden Air Warfare Museum, Headcorn	
18-1528	PA-18 Cub 95 (F-MBCH)	Privately owned, stored Southampton	
MS824	Morane-Saulnier Type N <R> (G-AWBU)	Privately owned, Booker	
S3398	Spad X.III <R> (G-BFYO) [2]	FAA Museum, RNAS Yeovilton	
S4523	Spad S.VII (N4727V) [1]	Imperial War Museum, Duxford	

Germany

C850/17	Albatros D.V <R>	Macclesfield Hist Av'n Society, Marthall	
D5397/17	Albatros D.VA <R> (G-BFXL)	FAA Museum, RNAS Yeovilton	
1Z+NK	Amiot AAC1 (Port.AF 6316)	IWM, Duxford	
LG+01	Bucker Bu.133C Jungmeister (G-AYSJ)	The Fighter Collection, Duxford	
LG+03	Bucker Bu.133C Jungmeister (G-AEZX)	Privately owned, Milden	

Historic Aircraft

Notes	Serial	Type (other identity)	Owner/operator, location
	BU+CC	CASA 1.131E Jungmann (G-BUEM)	Privately owned, Billingshurst
	BU+CK	CASA 1.131E Jungmann (G-BUCK)	Privately owned, White Waltham
	S5+B06	CASA 1.131E Jungmann 2000 (G-BSFB)	Privately owned, Stretton
	6J+PR	CASA 2.111D (G-AWHB)	Aces High Ltd, North Weald
	14	Fiat G.46-3B (G-BBII)	Privately owned, stored Rendcomb
	-	Fieseler Fi103 (V-1) (BAPC36)	Kent Battle of Britain Mus'm, Hawking
	-	Fieseler Fi103 (V-1) (BAPC91)	Lashenden Air Warfare Museum, Headcorn
	-	Fieseler Fi103 (V-1) (BAPC 92)	RAF Museum, Hendon
	-	Fieseler Fi103 (V-1) (BAPC 93)	Imperial War Museum, Duxford
	-	Fieseler Fi103 (V-1) (8583M/ BAPC 94)	RAF Cosford Aerospace Museum
	-	Fieseler Fi103 (V-1) (BAPC 158)	Defence School, Chattenden
	477663	Fieseler Fi103 (V-1) (BAPC198)	Imperial War Museum, Lambeth
	442795	Fieseler Fi103 (V-1) (BAPC 199)	Science Museum, South Kensington
	475081	Fieseler Fi156C-7 Storch (7362M) [GM+AK]	RAF Cosford Aerospace Museum
	28368	Flettner Fl282/B-V20 Kolibri (frame only)	Midland Air Museum, Coventry
	100143	Focke-Achgelis Fa330A	Imperial War Museum, Duxford
	100502	Focke-Achgelis Fa330A	The Real Aeroplane Company, Breighton
	100509	Focke-Achgelis Fa330A	Science Museum, stored South Kensington
	100545	Focke-Achgelis Fa330A	Fleet Air Arm Museum stored, Wroughton
	100549	Focke-Achgelis Fa330A	Lashenden Air Warfare Museum, Headcorn
	112100	Focke Wulf Fw189A-1 [V7+1H]	Privately owned, Lancing
	2+1	Focke Wulf Fw190 <R> (G-SYFW) [7334]	Privately owned, Guernsey, CI
	4	Focke Wulf Fw190 <R> (G-BSLX)	Privately owned, Shoreham
	8	Focke Wulf Fw190 <R> (G-WULF)	Privately owned, Dunkeswell
	5415	Focke Wulf Fw190A-4	The Old Flying Machine Company, Duxford
	733682	Focke Wulf Fw190A-8/R7 (9211M)	Imperial War Museum, Lambeth
	584219	Focke Wulf Fw190F-8/U1 (8470M) [38]	RAF Museum, Hendon
	4253/18	Fokker D.VII <R> (G-BFPL)	Privately owned, North Weald
	626/18	Fokker D.VII <R> (N6268)	Blue Max Movie Aircraft Museum, Booker
	8417/18	Fokker D.VII (9207M)	RAF Museum Restoration Centre, Cardington
	102/17	Fokker Dr.1 Dreidekker <R> (BAPC 88)	FAA Museum, RNAS Yeovilton
	152/17	Fokker Dr.1 Dreidekker <R> (G-ATJM)	The Old Flying Machine Company, Duxford
	152/17	Fokker Dr.1 Dreidekker <R> (G-BTYV)	Privately owned, North Weald
	425/17	Fokker Dr.1 Dreidekker <R> (BAPC 133)	Newark Air Museum, Winthorpe
	425/17	Fokker Dr.1 Dreidekker <R> (G-BEFR)	Privately owned, Dunkeswell
	450/17	Fokker Dr.1 Dreidekker <R> (G-BVGZ)	Museum of Army Flying, Middle Wallop
	210/16	Fokker EIII (BAPC 56)	Science Museum, South Kensington
	422/15	Fokker EIII <R> (G-AVJO)	Privately owned, Booker
	701152	Heinkel He111H-23 (8471M) [NT+SL]	RAF Museum, Hendon
	120227	Heinkel He162A-2 Salamander (8472M) [2]	RAF Museum, Hendon
	120235	Heinkel He162A-2 Salamander	Imperial War Museum, Lambeth
	14	Hispano HA 1112 (G-BOML)	The Old Flying Machine Company, Duxford
	494083	Junkers Ju87G-2 (8474M) [RI+JK]	RAF Museum, Hendon
	360043	Junkers Ju88R-1 (8475M) [D5+EV]	RAF Museum, Hendon
	22+35	Lockheed F104G Starfighter	SWWAPS, Lasham
	22+57	Lockheed F104G Starfighter	Starfighter Pres'n Grp, New Waltham
	7198/18	LVG C.VI (G-AANJ)	Shuttleworth Collection, Old Warden
	14	Messerschmitt Bf109 <R> (BAPC 67)	Kent Battle of Britain Museum, Hawkinge
	1480	Messerschmitt Bf109 <R> (BAPC 66) [6]	Kent Battle of Britain Museum, Hawkinge

Serial	Type (other identity)	Owner/operator, location	Notes
6357	Messerschmitt Bf109 <R> (BAPC 74) [6]	Kent Battle of Britain Museum, Hawkinge	
1190	Messerschmitt Bf109E-3	Privately owned, Bournemouth	
1342	Messerschmitt Bf109E	Privately owned, Colchester	
3579	Messerschmitt Bf109E-1	Privately owned, Colchester	
4101	Messerschmitt Bf109E-3 (8477M) [12]	RAF Museum, Hendon	
8147	Messerschmitt Bf109F-4	Privately owned, Colchester	
10639	Messerschmitt Bf109G-2/Trop (8478M/G-USTV) [6]	Imperial War Museum, Duxford	
3235	Messerschmitt Bf110C-4 [LN+ER]	Privately owned, Lancing	
4502	Messerschmitt Bf110E-2 [M8+ZE]	Privately owned, Lancing	
5052	MesserschmittBf110F-2	Privately owned, Lancing	
730301	Messerschmitt Bf110G-4 (8479M) [D5+RL]	RAF Museum, Hendon	
191316	Messerschmitt Me163B Komet	Science Museum, South Kensington	
191614	Messerschmitt Me163B Komet (8481M)	RAF Cosford Aerospace Museum	
191659	Messerschmitt Me163B Komet (8480M) [15]	Royal Scottish Mus'm of Flight, E Fortune	
191660	Messerschmitt Me163B Komet [3]	Imperial War Museum, Duxford	
112372	Messerschmitt Me262A-2a (8482M) [9K-XK]	RAF Cosford Aerospace Museum	
420430	Messerschmitt Me410A-1/U2 (8483M) [3U+CC]	RAF Cosford Aerospace Museum	
20+48	Mikoyan MiG-23BN [702]	A&AEE, Boscombe Down	
7A+WN	Morane-Saulnier MS500 (G-AZMH)	Privately owned, Chalmington, Dorset	
FI+S	Morane-Saulnier MS505 (G-BIRW)	Royal Scottish Mus'm of Flight, E Fortune	
TA+RC	Morane-Saulnier MS505 (G-BPHZ)	The Aircraft Restoration Co., Duxford	
NJ+C11	Nord 1002 (G-ATBG)	Privately owned, Duxford	
14	Pilatus P-2 (G-BJAX)	Privately owned, Duxford	
CC+43	Pilatus P-2 (G-CJCI)	Privately owned, Norwich	
97+04	Putzer Elster B (G-APVF)	Privately owned, Tadlow	
+114	SNCAN 1101 Noralpha (G-BSMD)	Privately owned, Abbotsley	
D-692	Staaken Z-1 Flitzer (G-BVAW)	Privately owned, Aberdare	
98+10	Sukhoi Su-22M-4	A&AEE, Boscombe Down	

Greece

52-6541	Republic F-84F Thunderflash	North-East Aircraft Museum, Usworth	
51-6151	Canadair F-86D Sabre (51-6171)	North-East Aircraft Museum, Usworth	

Hungary

501	Mikoyan MiG-21PF	Privately owned, St Athan	
503	Mikoyan MiG-21SMT (G-BRAM)	Aces High, North Weald	

India

Q497	EE Canberra T4(fuselage)	BAe Warton Fire Service	

Iraq

243	Hawker Fury FB10 (G-BTTA)	The Old Flying Machine Co, Duxford	
333	DH Vampire T55	Military Aircraft Pres'n Grp, Barton	
26186	Bell 214ST (tail only)	Museum of Army Flying, Middle Wallop	

Israel

41	NA P-51D Mustang	Privately owned, Teesside Airport	

Italy

MM5701	Fiat CR42 (8468M) [13-95]	RAF Museum, Hendon	
MM12822	Fieseler Fi156C-3 Storch (G-FIST) [20]	Privately owned, Duxford	
MM53211	Fiat G.46-4 (BAPC 79) [ZI-4]	The Aircraft Restoration Co., Duxford	
MM53432	NA T-6D Texan [RM-11]	Privately owned, South Wales	
MM53692	CCF T-6G Texan	RAeS Medway Branch, Rochester	
MM54099	NA T-6G Texan (G-BRBC) [RR-56]	Privately owned, Chigwell	
MM542372	PA.18-95 Super Cub	Privately owned, Kesgrave	
W7	Avia FL.3 (G-AGFT)	Privately owned, Leicester	

Japan

24	Kawasaki Ki100-1B (8476M/ BAPC 83)	RAF Cosford Aerospace Museum	
5439	Mitsubishi Ki46-III (8484M/ BAPC 84)	RAF Cosford Aerospace Museum	

Historic Aircraft

Notes	Serial	Type (other identity)	Owner/operator, location
	15-1585	Yokosuka MXY 7 Ohka II (BAPC 58)	FAA Museum, RNAS Yeovilton
	997	Yokosuka MXY 7 Ohka II (8485M/ BAPC 98)	Gtr Manchester Mus'm of Science & Industry
	I-13	Yokosuka MXY 7 Ohka II (8486M/ BAPC 99)	RAF Cosford Aerospace Museum
	-	Yokosuka MXY 7 Ohka II (BAPC 159)	Defence School, Chattenden

Jordan

	209	DH Vampire T55 (G-BVLM/ZH563)	RJAF Historic Flight, Bournemouth
	800	Hawker Hunter T7 (G-BOOM) [F]	RJAF Historic Flight, Bournemouth

Netherlands

	204	Lockheed SP-2H Neptune [V]	RAF Cosford Aerospace Museum
	361	Hawker Fury FB10 (N36SF)	Privately owned, Bournemouth
	B-168	NA AT-16 Harvard IIB	British Aerial Museum, Duxford (spares use)
	E-15	Fokker S-11 Instructor (G-BIYU)	Privately owned, White Waltham
	E-31	Fokker S-11 Instructor (G-BEPV)	Privately owned, Elstree
	N-202	Hawker Hunter F6 [10] <ff>	Pinewood Studios, Elstree
	N-250	Hawker Hunter F6 <ff>	Science Museum, Wroughton
	N-268	Hawker Hunter F6 (Qatar QA-10)	Yorkshire Air Museum, Elvington
	N-315	Hawker Hunter T7	Gloucestershire Aviation Collection
	R-163	Piper L-21B Super Cub (G-BIRH)	Privately owned, Lee-on-Solent
	R-167	Piper L-21B Super Cub (54-2457/ G-LION)	Privately owned, Bishops Stortford

New Zealand

	NZ233	Vickers Varsity T1 (WJ944)	Wales Aircraft Museum, Cardiff
	NZ5648	Goodyear FG-1D Corsair (NX55JP) [1]	Old Flying Machine Co, Duxford

Norway

	56321	Saab S91B Safir (G-BKPY) [U-AB]	Newark Air Museum, Winthorpe

Poland

	05	WSK SM-2 (Mi-2) (1005)	IHM, Weston-super-Mare
	07	WSK SM-1 (Mi-1) (2007)	IHM, Weston-super-Mare
	1120	MiG-15bis	RAF Museum Restoration Centre, Cardington
	3309	WSK SBLim-2A (MiG-15UTI)	Royal Scottish Museum of Flight, East Fortune
	6247	WSK SBLim-2A (MiG-15UTI) (622047/G-OMIG)	The Old Flying Machine Company, Duxford
	09008	WSK SBLim-2A (MiG-15UTI)	Privately owned, Shoreham

Portugal

	1662	NA Harvard III (G-ELMH/EZ341)	Privately owned, Sudbury
	1741	CCF Harvard IV (G-HRVD)	Privately owned, Wellesbourne

Qatar

	QA12	Hawker Hunter FGA 78	Lovaux Ltd., Bournemouth (dismantled)
	QP30	WS Lynx Mk 28	RNAS Lee-on-Solent
	QP31	WS Lynx Mk 28	RNAY Fleetlands
	QP32	WS Lynx Mk 28	RNAW Almondbank

Russia (& former Soviet Union)

	03	Mil Mi-24D (3532461715415)	Privately owned, Hawarden
	04	Mikoyan MiG-23ML (024003607)	Privately owned, Hawarden
	05	Yakovlev Yak-50 (832507/YL/YAK)	Privately owned, Strathallan
	06	Let L-29 Delfin (591636)	Privately owned, Cumbernauld
	06	Mil Mi-24D (3532464505029)	Privately owned, Hawarden
	07	Yakovlev Yak-18M (G-BMJY)	Privately owned, North Weald
	09	Let L-29 Delfin (591378)	Privately owned, Cumbernauld
	15	Yakovlev Yak-52 (844605/ RA-01361)	Privately owned, Wellesbourne Mountford
	18	Let L-29 Delfin (591771)	Privately owned, Hawarden
	19	Yakovlev Yak-52 (811202)	Privately owned, Strathallan
	20	Lavochkin La-11	The Fighter Collection, Duxford
	20	Yakovlev Yak-52 (790404)	Privately owned, Strathallan
	23	Mikoyan MiG-27D (83712515040)	Privately owned, Hawarden
	27	SPP Yak C-11 (G-OYAK)	Privately owned, North Weald

Serial	Type (other identity)	Owner/operator, location	Notes
35	Sukhoi Su-17M-3 (25102)	Privately owned, Hawarden	
36	Let/Yak C-11 (F-AZHQ)	The Fighter Collection, Duxford	
37	Let L-29 Delfin (491119)	Privately owned, Cumbernauld	
40	Let L-29 Delfin (491165)	Privately owned, Cumbernauld	
50	Mikoyan MiG-23MF (023003508)	Privately owned, Hawarden	
51	Let L-29 Delfin (491273)	Privately owned, Hawarden	
52	Yakovlev Yak-52 (LY-AKQ)	Privately owned, Little Gransden	
53	Curtiss P-40C Warhawk (41-13390)	The Fighter Collection, Duxford	
54	Sukhoi Su-17M (69004)	Privately owned, Hawarden	
56	Yakovlev Yak-52 (811504)	Privately owned, Strathallan	
69	Yakovlev Yak-50 (G-BTZB)	Privately owned, Duxford	
69	Yakovlev Yak-52 (LY-ALS)	Privately owned, Little Gransden	
71	Mikoyan MiG-27K (61912507006)	Privately owned, Hawarden	
73	Yakovlev Yak-52 (G-YAKK)	Privately owned, Wellesbourne Mountford	
74	Yakovlev Yak-52 (888802/LY-ALG)	Privately owned, Wellesbourne Mountford	
78	Yakovlev Yak-52 (811612/ RA-01337)	Privately owned, Wellesbourne Mountford	
100	Yakovlev Yak-52 (866904/G-YAKI)	Privately owned, Popham	
1342	Yakovlev Yak-1 (G-BTZD)	Privately owned, Audley End	
165221	WSK-Mielec An-2T (G-BTCU) [77]	Privately owned, Henstridge	
822303	Yakovlev Yak-50 (LY-ANJ/ G-YAKA)	Privately owned, Compton Abbas	
899404	Yakovlev Yak-52 (G-CCCP)	Privately owned, Gransden	
(RK858)	VS Spitfire LF.IX	The Fighter Collection, Duxford	

Singapore

305	BAC Strikemaster 84 (N2146S/ G-SARK)	Classic Jets, Biggin Hill	

Slovakia

7708	Mikoyan MiG-21MF	RAF Benevolent Fund, Boscombe Down	

South Africa

6130	Lockheed Ventura II	RAF Cosford Aerospace Museum (stored)	

Spain

C4E-88	Messerschmitt Bf-109E	Privately owned, Hungerford	
E3B-153	CASA 1.131E Jungmann (G-BPTS) [781-75]	Old Flying Machine Company, Duxford	
E3B-369	CASA 1.131E Jungmann (G-BPDM) [781-32]	Privately owned, Shoreham	
E3B-540	CASA 1.131E Jungmann (G-BRSH) [781-25]	Privately owned, Breighton	
EM-01	DH60G Moth (G-AAOR) [30-76]	Privately owned, Shoreham	
ES.1-16	CASA 1.133L Jungmeister	Privately owned, Stretton, Cheshire	

Sri Lanka

CM-192	Yakovlev Yak-50 (NX5224R)	Privately owned, Duxford	

Sweden

05108	DH.60 Moth	Privately owned, Langham	
29640	SAAB J-29F [20-08]	Midland Air Museum, Coventry	
32028	SAAB 32A Lansen (G-BMSG)	Privately owned, Cranfield	
35075	SAAB J-35J Draken [40]	Imperial War Museum, Duxford	

Switzerland

A-10	CASA 1.131E Jungmann (G-BECW)	Privately owned, Headcorn	
A-806	Pilatus P3-03 (G-BTLL)	Privately owned, Biggin Hill	
C-558	EKW C-3605	Privately owned, stored Gransden	
J-1008	DH Vampire FB6	Mosquito Aircraft Museum, London Colney	
J-1106	DH Vampire FB6 (G-BVPO)	RJAF Historic Flight, Bournemouth	
J-1121	DH Vampire FB6 <ff>	Jet Heritage, Bournemouth	
J-1149	DH Vampire FB6 (G-SWIS)	Jet Heritage, Bournemouth	
J-1172	DH Vampire FB6 (8487M)	Gtr Manchester Mus'm of Science & Industry	
J-1173	DH Vampire FB6 (G-DHXX)	Privately owned, Bournemouth	
J-1601	DH Venom FB50 (G-VIDI)	Privately owned, stored Bournemouth	
J-1605	DH Venom FB50 (G-BLID)	Privately owned, Charlwood, Surrey	
J-1614	DH Venom FB50 (G-BLIE)	Privately owned, Ipswich	
J-1632	DH Venom FB50 (G-VNOM)	Privately owned, Cranfield	
J-1704	DH Venom FB54	RAF Cosford Aerospace Museum	

Historic Aircraft

Notes	Serial	Type (other identity)	Owner/operator, location
	J-1758	DH Venom FB54 (N203DM)	Aces High Ltd, North Weald
	U-80	Bucker Bu.133D Jungmeister (G-BUKK)	Privately owned, White Waltham
	U-110	Pilatus P-2 (G-PTWO)	Privately owned, Earls Colne
	U-142	Pilatus P-2 (G-BONE)	Privately owned, Goudhurst
	U-1214	DH Vampire T55 (G-DHVV)	Privately owned, Bournemouth
	U-1219	DH Vampire T55 (G-DHWW)	Privately owned, Bournemouth
	U-1230	DH Vampire T55 (G-DHZZ)	Privately owned, Bournemouth
	U-1234	DH Vampire T55	Aces High Ltd, North Weald
	V-54	SE.3130 Alouette II (G-BVSD)	Privately owned, Ipswich
	USA		
	2	Boeing-Stearman N2S-5 Kaydet (G-AZLE)	Privately owned, Denham
	23	Fairchild PT-23 (N49272)	Privately owned, Halfpenny Green
	26	Boeing-Stearman A75N-1 Kaydet (G-BAVO)	Privately owned, Streethay, Lichfield
	27	NA SNJ-7 Texan (G-BRVG)	Intrepid Aviation, North Weald
	28	Boeing-Stearman PT-13D Kaydet (N8162G)	Privately owned, Swanton Morley
	33	Boeing-Stearman N2S-5 Kaydet (G-THEA)	Privately owned, Duxford
	41	NA T-6G Texan (G-DDMV) [BA]	Privately owned, Sywell
	44	Piper PA-18-95 Super Cub (G-BJLH) [33-K]	Privately owned, Felthorpe
	85	WAR P-47 Thunderbolt <R> (G-BTBI)	Privately owned, Manchester
	88	NA P-51D Mustang <R>	The Old Flying Machine Company, Duxford
	100	Grumman F8F-2P Bearcat (NX700HL) [S]	The Fighter Collection, Duxford
	112	Boeing-Stearman PT-13D Kaydet (G-BSWC)	Privately owned, Rendcomb
	118	Boeing-Stearman PT-13A Kaydet (G-BSDS)	Privately owned, Swanton Morley
	208	Boeing-Stearman N2S-5 Kaydet (N75664)	Privately owned, Spanhoe Lodge, Northants
	295	Ryan PT-22 (N56028)	Privately owned, Oaksey Park, Wilts
	379	Boeing-Stearman PT-13D Kaydet (G-ILLE)	Privately owned, Compton Abbas
	441	Boeing-Stearman N2S-4 Kaydet (G-BTFG)	Privately owned, Bryngwyn Bach, Clwyd
	442	Boeing-Stearman PT-17 Kaydet (G-BPTB)	Privately owned, Paddock Wood
	540	Piper L-4H Cub (G-BCNX)	Privately owned, Monewden
	796	Boeing-Stearman PT-13D Kaydet (N43SV)	Privately owned, Rendcomb
	854	Ryan PT-22 (G-BTBH)	Privately owned, Wellesbourne Mountford
	855	Ryan PT-22 (N56421)	Privately owned, Halfpenny Green
	897	Aeronca 11AC Chief (G-BJEV)	Privately owned, English Bicknor
	985	Boeing-Stearman PT-13D Kaydet (G-ERIX)	Privately owned, München
	1164	Beech D.18S (G-BKGL)	Classic Wings, Duxford
	1180	Boeing-Stearman N2S-3 Kaydet (G-BRSK)	Privately owned, Swanton Morley
	1411	Grumman G.44A Widgeon (N444M)	Privately owned, Biggin Hill
	2807	NA T-6G Texan (G-BHTH) [V-103]	Privately owned, Thruxton
	5547	Lockheed T-33A (19036)	Newark Air Museum, Winthorpe
	6771	Republic F-84F Thunderstreak (BAF FU-6)	Cosford Aerospace Museum, store
	7797	Aeronca L-16A (G-BFAF)	Privately owned, Finmere
	8178	NA F-86A Sabre (G-SABR) [FU-178]	Privately owned, Duxford
	01532	Northrop F-5E Tiger II <R>	RAF Alconbury on display
	14419	Lockheed T-33A	Midland Air Museum, Coventry
	14863	NA AT-6D Harvard <R> (G-BGOR)	Privately owned, Goudhurst, Kent
	15195	Fairchild PT-19A Cornell	RAF Museum, stored Cardington
	16443	Hughes OH-6A Cayuse (FY67)	IHM, Weston-super-Mare
	16579	Bell UH-1H Iroquois (FY66)	IHM, Weston-super-Mare
	17473	Lockheed T-33A	Midland Air Museum, Coventry
	17657	Douglas A-26K Invader <ff>	Booker Aircraft Museum
	O-17899	Convair VT-29B	Imperial War Museum, Duxford

Serial	Type (other identity)	Owner/operator, location	Notes
18010	Beech U-21A Ute (FY66)	Royal Armoured Corps Museum, Bovington	
19252	Lockheed T-33A	Privately owned, Bruntingthorpe	
24518	Kaman HH-43F Huskie (24535)	Midland Air Museum, Coventry	
28521	CCF Harvard IV (G-TVIJ) [TA-521]	Privately owned, Shoreham	
29963	Lockheed T-33A	Wales Aircraft Museum, Cardiff	
30861	NA TB-25J Mitchell (N9089Z)	Privately owned, North Weald	
31952	Aeronca O-58B Defender (G-BRPR)	Privately owned, Ross-on-Wye	
32947	Piper L-4H Cub (G-BGXA) [44-F]	Privately owned, Martley, Worcs	
34037	NA TB-25N Mitchell (N9115Z/ 8838M)	RAF Museum, Hendon	
37414	McD F-4C Phantom (FY63)	Midland Air Museum, Coventry	
37699	McD F-4C Phantom (FY63)	Midland Air Museum, Coventry	
38674	Thomas-Morse S4 Scout <R> (G-MTKM)	Privately owned, Rugby	
40467	Grumman F6F-5K Hellcat (G-BTCC) [19]	The Fighter Collection, Duxford	
40707	McD F-4C Phantom (FY64)	RAF Lakenheath, BDRT	
41386	Thomas-Morse S4 Scout <R> (G-MJTD)	Privately owned, Hitchin	
42157	NA F-100D Super Sabre	North-East Aviation Museum, Usworth	
42163	NA F-100D Super Sabre [HE]	Dumfries & Galloway Av'n Mus, Tinwald Downs	
42165	NA F-100D Super Sabre [VM]	Imperial War Museum, Duxford	
42174	NA F-100D Super Sabre [UH]	Midland Air Museum, Coventry	
42196	NA F-100D Super Sabre [LT]	Norfolk & Suffolk Aviation Museum, Flixton	
42223	NA F-100D Super Sabre	Newark Air Museum, Winthorpe	
42265	NA F-100D Super Sabre	RAF Lakenheath	
53319	Grumman TBM-3R Avenger (G-BTDP) [319-RB]	Privately owned, North Weald	
54137	CCF Harvard IV (G-CTKL) [69]	Privately owned, North Weald	
54433	Lockheed T-33A	Norfolk & Suffolk Av'n Museum, Flixton	
54439	Lockheed T-33A	North-East Aircraft Museum, Usworth	
60312	McDonnell F-101F Voodoo [AR]	Midland Air Museum, Coventry	
60689	Boeing B-52D Stratofortress	Imperial War Museum, Duxford	
63000	NA F-100D Super Sabre (42160) [FW-000]	Wales Aircraft Museum, Cardiff	
63000	NA F-100D Super Sabre (42212) [FW-000]	USAF Croughton, Oxon, at gate	
63319	NA F-100D Super Sabre (42269) [FW-319]	RAF Lakenheath, on display	
63428	Republic F-105G Thunderchief (24428)	USAF Croughton, Oxon, at gate	
66692	Lockheed U-2C	Imperial War Museum, Duxford	
70270	McDonnell F-101B Voodoo (fuselage)	Midland Air Museum, Coventry	
80260	McDonnell F-101B Voodoo	Midland Air Museum, Coventry	
82062	DHC U-6A Beaver	Midland Air Museum, Coventry	
88297	Goodyear FG-1D Corsair (G-FGID) [29]	The Fighter Collection, Duxford	
91007	Lockheed T-33A (G-NASA) [TR-007]	Privately owned, Bruntingthorpe	
93542	CCF Harvard IV (G-BRLV) [LTA-542]	Privately owned, North Weald	
111836	NA AT-6C Harvard IIA (G-TSIX) [JZ-6]	Privately owned, Breighton	
111989	Cessna L-19A Bird Dog (N33600)	Museum of Army Flying, Middle Wallop	
115042	NA T-6G Texan (G-BGHU) [TA-042]	Privately owned, Headcorn	
115302	Piper L-18C Super Cub (G-BJTP) [TP]	Privately owned, Winterbourne, Bristol	
122351	Beech C-45G (G-BKRG)	Aces High, North Weald	
124485	Boeing B-17G Fortress (G-BEDF) [DF-A]	B-17 Preservation Ltd., Duxford	
126922	Douglas AD-4NA Skyraider (G-RAID) [402-AK]	The Fighter Collection, Duxford	
140547	NA T-28C Trojan (N2800Q)	Privately owned, Duxford	
146289	NA T-28C Trojan (N99153) [2W]	Norfolk & Suffolk Aviation Museum, Flixton	
150225	Westland Wessex (G-AWOX) [123]	IHM, Weston-super-Mare	
151632	NA TB-25N Mitchell (NL9494Z)	Privately owned, Headcorn	
153008	McD F-4N Phantom	RAF Alconbury, BDRT	
155848	McD F-4S Phantom [WT-11]	FAA Museum stored, RNAS Yeovilton	

Historic Aircraft

| --- | --- | --- | --- |
	159233	McD AV-8A Harrier [CG-33]	FAA Museum, RNAS Yeovilton
	160810	Bell AH-1T Sea Cobra <ff>	GEC, Rochester
211072		Boeing-Stearman PT-27 Kaydet (N50755)	Privately owned, Swanton Morley
	217786	Boeing-Stearman PT-13 Kaydet (G-BRTK)[177]	Privately owned, Old Buckenham
	219993	Bell P-39Q Airacobra (N319DP)	The Fighter Collection, Duxford
	224211	Douglas C-47A Dakota (G-BPMP) [M2-Z]	Privately owned, Coventry
226671		Republic P-47M Thunderbolt (NX47DD) [MX-X]	The Fighter Collection, Duxford
231983		Boeing B-17G Fortress (F-BDRS) [IY-G]	Imperial War Museum, Duxford
236800		Piper L-4A Cub (G-BHPK) [44-A]	Privately owned, Tibenham
243809		Waco CG-4A Hadrian (BAPC 185)	Museum of Army Flying, Middle Wallop
	267543	Lockheed P-38J Lightning (NX3145X) [KI-S]	The Fighter Collection, Duxford
	269097	Bell P-63A Kingcobra (G-BTWR)	The Fighter Collection, Duxford
	314887	Fairchild Argus III (G-AJPI)	Privately owned, Liverpool
	315509	Douglas C-47A (G-BHUB) [W7-S]	Imperial War Museum, Duxford
329417		Piper L-4A Cub (G-BDHK)	Privately owned, Coleford
	329601	Piper L-4H Cub (G-AXHR) [44-D]	Privately owned, Nayland
	329854	Piper L-4H Cub (G-BMKC) [44-R]	Privately owned, St Just
	329934	Piper L-4H Cub (G-BCPH) [72-B]	Privately owned, White Waltham
	330238	Piper L-4H Cub (G-LIVH) [24-A]	Privately owned, Barton
	330485	Piper L-4H Cub (G-AJES) [44-C]	Privately owned, Saltash
343251		Boeing-Stearman N2S-5 Kaydet (G-NZSS)	Privately owned, Cumbernauld
413573		NA P-51D Mustang (9133M/ N6526D) [B6-V]	RAF Museum, Hendon
	430823	NA TB-25N Mitchell (N1042B) [69]	Aces High Ltd, North Weald
	431171	NA B-25J Mitchell (N7614C)	Imperial War Museum, Duxford
	435562	Douglas A-26 Invader (N7079G)	Privately owned, North Weald
	454467	Piper L-4J Cub (G-BILI) [44-J]	Privately owned, White Waltham
	454537	Piper L-4J Cub (G-BFDL) [04-J]	Privately owned, Breighton
	461748	Boeing B-29A Superfortress (G-BHDK) [Y]	Imperial War Museum, Duxford
463221		NA P-51D Mustang (G-BTCD) [G4-S]	The Fighter Collection, Duxford
	472216	NA P-51D Mustang (G-BIXL) [AJ-L]	Privately owned, North Weald
472258		NA P-51D Mustang (473979) [WZ-I]	Imperial War Museum, Lambeth
	472773	NA P-51D Mustang [AJ-C] (G-SUSY)	Privately owned, Sywell
	473877	NA P-51D Mustang (N167F) [B6-S]	Scandinavian Historic Flt., Duxford
	474008	NA P-51D Mustang (N51RR) [VF-R]	Privately owned, North Weald
	479766	Piper L-4H Cub (G-BKHG) [63-D]	Privately owned, Goldcliff, Gwent
	480015	Piper L-4H Cub (G-AKIB)	Privately owned, Bodmin
	480133	Piper L-4J Cub (G-BDCD) [44-B]	Privately owned, Slinfold
	480321	Piper L-4J Cub (G-FRAN) [44-H]	Privately owned, Rayne, Essex
	480480	Piper L-4J Cub (G-BECN) [44-E]	Privately owned, Kersey, Suffolk
	480636	Piper L-4J Cub (G-AXHP) [58-A]	Privately owned, Southend
	480752	Piper L-4J Cub (G-BCXJ) [39-E]	Privately owned, Old Sarum
	483868	Boeing B-17G Fortress (N5237V) [A-N]	RAF Museum, Hendon
	511701A	Beech C-45H (G-BSZC) [AF258]	Privately owned, Bryngwyn Bach
607327		Piper PA.18-95 Super Cub (G-ARAO) [09-L]	Privately owned, Lambley
2-134		NA T-6G Texan (114700)	Aces High Ltd, North Weald
	3-1923	Aeronca O-58B Defender (G-BRHP)	Privately owned, Chiseldon
18-2001		Piper L-18C Super Cub (G-BIZV)	Privately owned, Oxenhope
	40-1766	Boeing-Stearman PT-17 Kaydet	Privately owned, Swanton Morley
	41-33275	NA AT-6C Texan (G-BICE) [CE]	Privately owned, Ipswich
	42-12417	NA AT-16 Harvard IIB	Thameside Aviation Museum, East Tilbury
	42-58678	Taylorcraft DF-65 (G-BRIY) [IY]	Privately owned, North Weald
42-78044		Aeronca 11AC Chief (G-BRXL)	Privately owned, High Cross, Herts
	42-93510	Douglas C-47A Skytrain [CM] <ff>	Museum of Army Flying, Middle Wallop
	44-14574	NA P-51D Mustang (fuselage)	East Essex Aviation Museum, Clacton
	44-79609	Piper L-4H Cub (G-BHXY) [PR]	Privately owned, Aldergrove

Serial	Type (other identity)	Owner/operator, location	Notes
44-80594	Piper L-4J Cub (G-BEDJ)	Privately owned, Overton	
45-49192	Republic P-47D Thunderbolt (N47DD)	Imperial War Museum, Duxford	
45-49295	Republic P-47D Thunderbolt	RAF Museum/TFC, Duxford	
51-15227	NA T-6G Harvard (G-BKRA) [10]	Privately owned, Shoreham	
51-15673	Piper L-18C Super Cub (G-CUBI)	Privately owned, Felixkirk	
52-8521	CCF Harvard IV (G-TVIJ) [TA-521]	Privately owned, Shoreham	
52-8543	CCF Harvard IV (G-BUKY) [66]	Privately owned, Rochester	
54-2447	Piper L-21B Super Cub (G-SCUB)	Privately owned, Anwick	
54-2474	Piper L-21B Super Cub (G-PCUB)	Privately owned, Headcorn	
54-21261	Lockheed T-33A (N33VC)	Old Flying Machine Company, Duxford	
61-2414	Boeing CH-47A Chinook	RAF Odiham, instructional use	
63-419	McD F-4C Phantom (37419) [SA]	RAF Alconbury, BDRT	
63-471	McD F-4C Phantom (37471)	RAF Lakenheath, BDRT	
63-610	McD F-4C Phantom (37610)	RAF Lakenheath, BDRT	
67-120	GD F-111E (70120) [UH]	Imperial War Museum, Duxford	
68-011	GD F-111E (80011) [UH]	RAF Lakenheath	
68-060	GD F-111E (80060) <ff>	Dumfries & Galloway Av'n Mus, Tinwald Downs	
70-494	Republic F-105G Thunderchief (24434) [LN]	RAF Lakenheath, BDRT	
73-051	McD F-15A Eagle(30051)	RAF Lakenheath, BDRT	
74-131	McD F-15A Eagle (40131) [LN]	RAF Lakenheath, BDRT	
76-029	McD F-15A Eagle (60029)	RAF Lakenheath, BDRT	
76-124	McD F-15B Eagle (60124) [LN, 48 LSS]	RAF Lakenheath	
77-259	Fairchild A-10A Thunderbolt (70259) [AR]	Imperial War Museum, Duxford	
80-219	Fairchild GA-10A Thunderbolt (00219) [AR]	RAF Alconbury, on display	
88-9696	NA AT-6C Harvard IIA (G-TEAC) [688]	Privately owned, North Weald	
146-11042	Wolf WII <R> (G-BMZX) [7]	Privately owned, Haverfordwest	
146-11083	Wolf WII <R> (G-BNAI) [5]	Privately owned, Haverfordwest	
HL-6⁷/₈	Piper J-3C Cub (G-AKAZ)	Privately owned, Duxford	
TA-849	NA AT-6D Harvard (LN-AMY)	Old Flying Machine Company, Duxford	

Yugoslavia

Serial	Type (other identity)	Owner/operator, location	Notes
13064	Republic P-47D Thunderbolt (9212M/45-49295)	RAF Museum, Duxford	
30149	Soko P-2 Kraguj (G-SOKO) [149]	Privately owned, Liverpool	

Irish Air Corps Military Aircraft Markings

Notes	Serial	Type (other identity)	Owner/operator, location
	34	Miles Magister	Irish Aviation Museum Store, Dublin
	141	Avro Anson XIX	Irish Aviation Museum Store, Dublin
	157	VS Seafire III	Privately owned, Battle, East Sussex
	164	DH Chipmunk T20	Engineering Wing stored, Baldonnel
	168	DH Chipmunk T20	No 2 Support Wing, Gormanston
	172	DH Chipmunk T20	Training Wing stored, Gormanston
	173	DH Chipmunk T20	South East Aviation Enthusiasts, Waterford
	176	DH Dove 4 (VP-YKF)	South East Aviation Enthusiasts, Waterford
	177	Percival Provost T51 (G-BLIW)	Privately owned, Shoreham
	181	Percival Provost T51	Privately owned, Thatcham
	183	Percival Provost T51	Irish Aviation Museum Store, Dublin
	184	Percival Provost T51	South East Aviation Enthusiasts, Waterford
	187	DH Vampire T55	Av'n Society of Ireland, stored, Waterford
	189	Percival Provost T51	Baldonnel, Fire Section
	191	DH Vampire T55	Irish Aviation Museum Store, Dublin
	192	DH Vampire T55	South East Aviation Enthusiasts, Waterford
	193	DH Vampire T55 <ff>	Baldonnel Fire Section
	195	Sud Alouette III	No 3 Support Wing, Baldonnel
	196	Sud Alouette III	No 3 Support Wing, Baldonnel
	197	Sud Alouette III	No 3 Support Wing, Baldonnel
	198	DH Vampire T11	Engineering Wing, Baldonnel
	199	DH Chipmunk T22	Training Wing store, Gormanston (spares)
	202	Sud Alouette III	No 3 Support Wing, Baldonnel
	203	Cessna FR172H	No 2 Support Wing, Gormanston
	205	Cessna FR172H	No 2 Support Wing, Gormanston
	206	Cessna FR172H	No 1 Support Wing, Baldonnel, on rebuild
	207	Cessna FR172H	No 2 Support Wing, Gormanston
	208	Cessna FR172H	No 2 Support Wing, Gormanston
	209	Cessna FR172H	No 2 Support Wing, Gormanston
	210	Cessna FR172H	No 2 Support Wing, Gormanston
	211	Sud Alouette III	No 3 Support Wing, Baldonnel
	212	Sud Alouette III	No 3 Support Wing, Baldonnel
	213	Sud Alouette III	No 3 Support Wing, Baldonnel
	214	Sud Alouette III	No 3 Support Wing, Baldonnel
	215	Fouga Super Magister	No 1 Support Wing, Baldonnel
	216	Fouga Super Magister	No 1 Support Wing, Baldonnel
	217	Fouga Super Magister	No 1 Support Wing, Baldonnel
	218	Fouga Super Magister	No 1 Support Wing, Baldonnel
	219	Fouga Super Magister	No 1 Support Wing, Baldonnel
	220	Fouga Super Magister	No 1 Support Wing, Baldonnel
	221	Fouga Super Magister [79-KE]	Engineering Wing, Baldonnel
	222	SIAI SF-260WE Warrior	Training Wing, Baldonnel
	225	SIAI SF-260WE Warrior	Training Wing, Baldonnel
	226	SIAI SF-260WE Warrior	Training Wing, Baldonnel
	227	SIAI SF-260WE Warrior	Training Wing, Baldonnel
	229	SIAI SF-260WE Warrior	Training Wing, Baldonnel
	230	SIAI SF-260WE Warrior	Training Wing, Baldonnel
	231	SIAI SF-260WE Warrior	Training Wing, Baldonnel
	233	SIAI SF-260MC	Engineering Wing stored, Baldonnel
	237	Aérospatiale SA341F Gazelle	Advanced FTS, Baldonnel
	240	Beech King Air 200	Transport & Training Squadron, Baldonnel
	241	Aérospatiale SA341F Gazelle	Advanced FTS, Baldonnel
	243	Cessna FR172K	No 2 Support Wing, Gormanston
	244	SA365F Dauphin II	No 3 Support Wing, Baldonnel
	245	SA365F Dauphin II	No 3 Support Wing, Baldonnel
	246	SA365F Dauphin II	No 3 Support Wing, Baldonnel
	247	SA365F Dauphin II	No 3 Support Wing, Baldonnel
	248	SA365F Dauphin II	No 3 Support Wing, Baldonnel
	250	Airtech CN.235	Transport & Training Squadron, Baldonnel
	251	Grumman Gulfstream IV	Transport & Training Squadron, Baldonnel
	252	Airtech CN.235 MP	Transport & Training Squadron, Baldonnel
	253	Airtech CN.235 MP	Transport & Training Squadron, Baldonnel

Two-seat F-16B Fighting Falcon ET-206 of RDAF's Esk 730. *Daniel March*

French Army Aviation Cessna F406 Caravan II No 0010/AGT. *Daniel March*

German Navy Tornado IDSs 45+35 and 45+65 from MFG-2. *PRM*

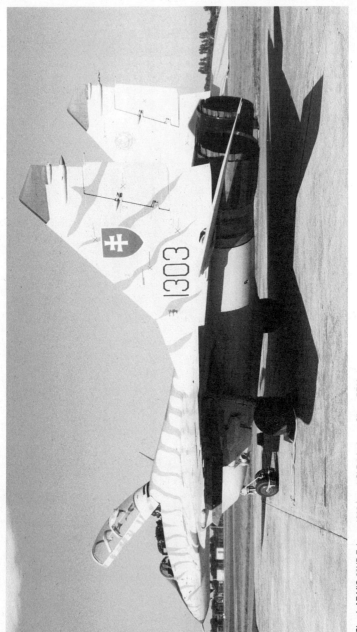

Slovak AF MiG-29UB Fulcrum 1303 from 1 SLP/1 Letka, at Sliac. *PRM*

Overseas Military Aircraft Markings

Aircraft included in this section are a selection of those likely to be seen visiting UK civil and military airfields on transport flights, exchange visits, exercises and for air shows. It is not a comprehensive list of *all* aircraft operated by the air arms concerned.

ALGERIA
Force Aérienne Algerienne
Lockheed C-130H Hercules

4911	(7T-WHT)
4912	(7T-WHS)
4913	(7T-WHY)
4914	(7T-WHZ)
4924	(7T-WHR)
4926	(7T-WHQ)
4928	(7T-WHJ)
4930	(7T-WHI)
4934	(7T-WHF)
4935	(7T-WHE)

Lockheed C-130H-30 Hercules

4987	(7T-WHO)
4989	(7T-WHL)
4997	(7T-WHA)
5224	(7T-WHB)

AUSTRALIA
Royal Australian Air Force
Boeing 707-338C
33 Sqn, Richmond, NSW
A20-623
A20-624
A20-627
A20-629

Boeing 707-368C
33 Sqn, Richmond, NSW
A20-261

Lockheed C-130H Hercules
36Sqn, Richmond, NSW
A97-001
A97-002
A97-003
A97-004
A97-005
A97-006
A97-007
A97-008
A97-009
A97-010
A97-011
A97-012

Lockheed C-130E Hercules
37 Sqn, Richmond, NSW
A97-159
A97-160
A97-167
A97-168
A97-171
A97-172
A97-177
A97-178
A97-180
A97-181
A97-189
A97-190

Lockheed P-3C Orion
10/11 Sqns, Edinburgh, NSW

A9-656	11Sqn
A9-657	11Sqn
A9-658	11Sqn
A9-659	11Sqn
A9-660	11Sqn
A9-661	11Sqn
A9-662	11Sqn
A9-663	11Sqn
A9-664	11Sqn
A9-665	11Sqn
A9-751	10Sqn
A9-752	10Sqn
A9-753	10Sqn
A9-755	10Sqn
A9-756	10Sqn
A9-757	10Sqn
A9-758	10Sqn
A9-759	10Sqn
A9-760	10Sqn

AUSTRIA
Oesterreichische Luftstreitkrafte
SAAB105ÖE
JbG, Linz;
1/Uberwg, Zeltweg;
2/Uberwg, Graz
(yellow)

1101/A	JbG
1102/B	JbG
1104/D	JbG
1105/E	JbG
1106/F	
1107/G	JbG
1108/H	
1109/I	
1110/J	JbG

(green)

1111/A	
1112/B	JbG
1114/D	JbG
1116/F	JbG
1117/G	JbG
1119/I	
1120/J	JbG

(red)

1122/B	1/Uberwg
1123/C	JbG
1124/D	1/Uberwg
1125/E	JbG
1126/F	1/Uberwg
1127/G	
1128/H	JbG
1129/I	1/Uberwg
1130/J	JbG

(blue)

1131/A	JbG
1132/B	JbG
1133/C	JbG
1134/D	JbG
1135/E	JbG
1136/F	
1137/G	JbG
1139/I	JbG
1140/J	1/Uberwg

Short SC7 Skyvan 3M
Flachenstaffel, Tulln
5S-TA
5S-TB

BELGIUM
Force Aérienne Belge/ Belgische Luchtmacht
D-BD Alpha Jet
7/11 Smaldeel
Brustem (9Wg)
AT01
AT02
AT03
AT05
AT06
AT08
AT09
AT10
AT11
AT12
AT13
AT14
AT15
AT16
AT17
AT18
AT19
AT20
AT21
AT22
AT23
AT24
AT25
AT26
AT27
AT28
AT29
AT30
AT31
AT32
AT33

Belgium

Boeing 727-29C
21 Smaldeel, Melsbroek
CB01
CB02

**Swearingen
Merlin IIIA**
21 Smaldeel, Melsbroek
CF01
CF02
CF04
CF05
CF06

**Lockheed
C-130H Hercules**
20 Smaldeel, Melsbroek
CH01
CH02
CH03
CH04
CH05
CH06
CH07
CH08
CH09
CH10
CH11
CH12

**Dassault
Falcon 20E**
21 Smaldeel, Melsbroek
CM01
CM02

**Hawker-Siddeley
HS748 Srs 2A**
21 Smaldeel, Melsbroek
CS01
CS02
CS03

General Dynamics F-16A
349,350 Smaldeel;
 Bevekom (1Wg);
1,2 Smaldeel, Florennes (2 Wg);
23,31 Smaldeel, Kleine-Brogel (10 Wg)

FA02	350 Sm
FA03	349 Sm
FA19	350 Sm
FA20	350 Sm
FA27	349 Sm
FA37	349 Sm
FA39	350 Sm
FA46	349 Sm
FA47	349 Sm
FA48	350 Sm
FA49	350 Sm
FA50	350 Sm
FA53	350 Sm
FA55	349 Sm
FA56	23 Sm
FA57	23 Sm
FA58	31 Sm
FA60	31 Sm
FA61	23 Sm
FA65	23 Sm
FA66	31 Sm
FA67	23 Sm
FA68	31 Sm
FA69	23 Sm
FA70	350 Sm
FA71	23 Sm
FA72	31 Sm
FA73	350 Sm
FA74	31 Sm
FA75	349 Sm
FA76	349 Sm
FA77	23 Sm
FA78	31 Sm
FA80	31 Sm
FA81	23 Sm
FA82	31 Sm
FA83	349 Sm
FA84	31 Sm
FA86	31 Sm
FA87	350 Sm
FA88	349 Sm
FA89	350 Sm
FA90	31 Sm
FA91	350 Sm
FA92	31 Sm
FA93	23 Sm
FA94	31 Sm
FA95	349 Sm
FA96	350 Sm
FA97	1 Sm
FA98	2 Sm
FA99	349 Sm
FA100	350 Sm
FA101	1 Sm
FA102	2 Sm
FA103	350 Sm
FA104	2 Sm
FA106	350 Sm
FA107	350 Sm
FA108	2 Sm
FA109	1 Sm
FA110	349 Sm
FA111	1 Sm
FA112	2 Sm
FA113	23 Sm
FA114	350 Sm
FA115	1 Sm
FA116	2 Sm
FA117	349 Sm
FA118	2 Sm
FA119	349 Sm
FA120	2 Sm
FA121	1 Sm
FA122	2 Sm
FA123	349 Sm
FA124	23 Sm
FA125	350 Sm
FA126	23 Sm
FA127	350 Sm
FA128	2 Sm
FA129	1 Sm
FA130	2 Sm
FA131	1 Sm
FA132	2 Sm
FA133	1 Sm
FA134	2 Sm
FA135	1 Sm
FA136 •	2 Sm

General Dynamics F-16B
349 Sm, 350 Sm, OCU, Bevekom (1Wg);
1 Sm, 2 Sm, Florennes (2 Wg);
23 Sm, 31 Sm, Kleine-Brogel (10Wg)

FB01	OCU
FB02	OCU
FB04	OCU
FB05	349 Sm
FB07	OCU
FB08	350 Sm
FB09	OCU
FB10	OCU
FB12	OCU
FB14	2Wg
FB15	OCU
FB17	10Wg
FB18	10Wg
FB19	350 Sm
FB20	10Wg
FB21	1 Sm
FB22	31 Sm
FB23	1 Sm
FB24	350 Sm

Fouga CM170 Magister
33 Sm (9Wg), Brustem
MT3
MT04
MT13
MT14
MT29
MT30
MT31
MT33
MT34
MT36
MT37
MT40
MT44
MT46
MT48
MT49

**Westland Sea
King Mk48**
40 Smaldeel, Koksijde
RS01
RS02
RS03
RS04
RS05

**SIAI Marchetti
SF.260MB/SF.260D***
Ecole de Pilotage
 Elementaire (5 Sm),
 Gossoncourt
ST01
ST03
ST04
ST05
ST06
ST08
ST09
ST10
ST12
ST13
ST15
ST16
ST17
ST18
ST19
ST20
ST21
ST22
ST23
ST24
ST25
ST26
ST27

ST28	
ST30	
ST31	
ST32	
ST33	
ST34	
ST35	
ST36	
ST40*	
ST41*	
ST42*	
ST43*	
ST44*	
ST45*	
ST46*	
ST47*	
ST48*	
ST49*	

Belgische Landmacht
Sud Alouette II
16 Batallion, Butzweilerhof, Germany;
17 Battalion, Bierset;
18 Battalion, Merzbrück, Germany;
SvHLV, Brasschaat

A04	16 Batt
A05	SvHLV
A12	17 Batt
A14	18 Batt
A15	17 Batt
A18	16 Batt
A22	16 Batt
A23	18 Batt
A24	18 Batt
A26	SvHLV
A31	SvHLV
A32	18 Batt
A34	17 Batt
A35	SvHLV
A37	18 Batt
A38	17 Batt
A40	SvHLV
A41	18 Batt
A42	SvHLV
A43	18 Batt
A44	SvHLV
A46	16 Batt
A47	SvHLV
A48	17 Batt
A49	16 Batt
A50	SvHLV
A53	18 Batt
A54	SvHLV
A55	SvHLV
A57	16 Batt
A61	SvHLV
A62	17 Batt
A64	16 Batt
A65	18 Batt
A66	17 Batt
A68	16 Batt
A69	SvHLV
A70	18 Batt
A72	SvHLV
A73	SvHLV
A74	SvHLV
A75	18 Batt
A76	SvHLV
A77	SvHLV
A78	16 Batt
A79	16 Batt
A80	16 Batt
A81	16 Batt

Britten-Norman BN-2A Islander
16 Battalion, Butzweilerhof, Germany;
SvHLV, Brasschaat

B01/LA	SvHLV
B02/LB	16 Batt
B03/LC	16 Batt
B04/LD	SvHLV
B07/LG	SvHLV
B08/LH	SvHLV
B09/LI	16 Batt
B10/LJ	SvHLV
B11/LK	SvHLV
B12/LL	SvHLV

Agusta A109HA/HO*
16 Battalion, Butzweilerhof, Germany;
17 Battalion, Bierset;
18 Battalion, Merzbrück, Germany;
SvHLV, Brasschaat

H01*	SvHLV
H02*	
H03*	SvHLV
H04*	
H05*	18 Batt
H06*	
H07*	
H08*	
H09*	
H10*	18 Batt
H11*	SvHLV
H12*	SvHLV
H13*	SvHLV
H14*	SvHLV
H15*	SvHLV
H16*	
H17*	SvHLV
H18*	SvHLV
H19	18 Batt
H20	18 Batt
H21	18 Batt
H22	18 Batt
H23	
H24	
H25	18 Batt
H26	18 Batt
H27	
H28	
H29	
H30	18 Batt
H31	
H32	
H33	18 Batt
H34	
H35	
H36	
H37	
H38	
H39	18 Batt
H40	
H41	
H42	
H43	
H44	
H45	
H46	

Force Navale Belge/Belgische Zeemacht

SA316B Alouette III
Koksijde Heli Flight

M1	(OT-ZPA)
M2	(OT-ZPB)
M3	(OT-ZPC)

Gendarmerie
Britten-Norman PBN-2T Islander
Base: Melsbroek

G05	(OT-GLA)

Cessna 182 Skylane
Base: Melsbroek
G01
G03
G04

Sud Alouette II
Base: Melsbroek
G90
G92
G93
G94
G95

BRAZIL
Forca Aerea Brazileira
Boeing KC-137
2GT 2 Esq, Afonsos
2401
2402
2403
2404

Lockheed
C-130E Hercules
1 GT, Afonsos

2451	C-130E
2453	C-130E
2454	C-130E
2455	C-130E
2456	C-130E
2458	SC-130E
2461	KC-130H
2462	KC-130H
2463	C-130H
2464	C-130H
2465	C-130H
2466	C-130H
2467	C-130H

Lockheed
RC-130E Hercules
6 GAV 1 Esq, Recife
2459

CANADA
CanadianForces
Lockheed
CC-130E/CC-130E(SAR)* Hercules
413 Sqn, Greenwood (SAR) (14 Wing);
418 Sqn, Edmonton (SAR) (18 Wing);
424 Sqn, Trenton (SAR) (8 Wing);
426 Sqn, Trenton (8 Wing);
429 Sqn, Trenton (8 Wing);
435 Sqn, Edmonton (18 Wing);
436 Sqn, Trenton (8 Wing)

130305*	8 Wing
130306*	18 Wing
130307*	8 Wing
130308	8 Wing
130310*	8 Wing
130311	8 Wing
130313	8 Wing
130314*	8 Wing
130315	18 Wing
130316	18 Wing
130317	8 Wing
130319	8 Wing
130320	8 Wing
130323	8 Wing
130324	18 Wing
130325	18 Wing
130326	8 Wing
130327	8 Wing
130328	8 Wing

**Lockheed
CC-130H/KCC-130H***
Hercules

130332	18 Wing
130333	8 Wing
130334	8 Wing
130335	
130336	8 Wing
130337	8 Wing
130338*	18 Wing
130339*	18 Wing
130340*	18 Wing
130341*	18 Wing
130342*	18 Wing

**Boeing CC-137
(B.707-374C)**
437 Sqn, Trenton (8 Wing)

13703	
13704	
13705	

**Lockheed
CP-140 Aurora**
404/405/415 Sqns,
Greenwood (14 Wing);
407 Sqn, Comox (19 Wing)

140101	
140102	14 Wing
140103	14 Wing
140104	
140105	407 Sqn
140106	407 Sqn
140107	407 Sqn
140108	14 Wing
140109	405 Sqn
140110	407 Sqn
140111	14 Wing
140112	
140113	
140114	14 Wing
140115	14 Wing
140116	407 Sqn
140117	
140118	14 Wing

**Lockheed
CP-140A Arcturus**

140119	
140120	
140121	

**Canadair CC-144/
CE-144A/CP-144
Challenger**
412 Sqn, Ottawa-Uplands
(7 Wing);
434 Sqn, Shearwater
(12 Wing)

144601	CC-144	434 Sqn
144602	CC-144	434 Sqn
144603	CE-144A	434 Sqn
144604	CP-144	
144605	CP-144	
144606	CC-144	
144607	CE-144A	434 Sqn
144608	CE-144A	434 Sqn
144609	CE-144A	434 Sqn
144610	CP-144	
144611	CE-144A	434 Sqn
144613	CC-144B	412 Sqn
144614	CC-144B	412 Sqn
144615	CC-144B	412 Sqn
144616	CC-144B	412 Sqn

**Airbus CC-150 Polaris
(A310-304)**
437 Sqn, Trenton (8 Wing)

15002	
15003	
15004	
15005	

**CHILE
Fuerza Aérea de Chile**
Boeing 707-321B/330/351C

902	351C
903	330B
904	321B

Extra EA-300
Los Halcones

021	[1]
022	[2]
023	[3]
024	[6]
025	[5]
027	[4]

**Lockheed
C-130B/H Hercules**
Grupo 10, Santiago

994	C-130H
995	C-130H
996	C-130H
997	C-130B

**CZECH REPUBLIC
Aero L.39/L.59 (L.39MS)
Albatros**
30 BILP, Pardubice;
1 LSP, Prerov;
1 SLP, Ceske Budejovice;
4 SSLT, Mosnov;
VU-030, Praha/Kbely

0001	L.39MS	VU-030
0004	L.39MS	1 LSP
0005	L.39MS	1 LSP
0006	L.39MS	1 LSP
0103	L.39C	1 LSP
0105	L.39C	1 SLP
0106	L.39C	1 SLP
0440	L.39C	1 LSP
0441	L.39C	1 LSP
0444	L.39C	1 LSP
0735	L.39V	1 SLP

2341	L.39ZA	1 SLP
2344	L.39ZA	4 SSLT
2347	L.39ZA	4 SSLT
2350	L.39ZA	1 SLP
2418	L.39ZA	4 SSLT
2430	L.39ZA	1 SLP
2433	L.39ZA	4 SSLT
2436	L.39ZA	1 SLP
3903	L.39ZA	30 BILP
5013	L.39ZA	30 BILP
5015	L.39ZA	30 BILP
5017	L.39ZA	30 BILP
5019	L.39ZA	30 BILP

Antonov An-24V
3 DLP, Praha/Kbely

2904	
5803	
7109	
7110	

Antonov An-26
3 DLP, Praha/Kbely;
VU-030, Praha/Kbely

2408	3 DLP
2409	3 DLP
2507	3 DLP
3209	VU-030
7110	3 DLP

Antonov An-30
10 SPOJZ, Pardubice

1107	

Let 410
3 DLP, Praha/Kbely;
36 SMDLP, Pardubice;
17 SPOJZ, Klecany

0402	L.410M	10SPOJZ
0403	L.410M	10SPOJZ
0501	L.410M	3 DLP
0503	L.410M	10 SPOJZ
0712	L.410UVP	3 DLP
0731	L.410UVP	3 DLP
0926	L.410T	3 DLP [4]
0928	L.410T	3 DLP [1]
0929	L.410T	3 DLP [2]
1132	L.410T	3 DLP [3]
1134	L.410T	17 SPOJZ
1504	L.410UVP	10 SPOJZ
1522	L.410FG	10 SPOJZ
1523	L.410FG	10 SPOJZ
1524	L.410FG	10 SPOJZ
1525	L.410FG	10 SPOJZ
1526	L.410FG	10 SPOJZ
2312	L.410UVP	3 DLP

Let 610
3 DLP, Praha/Kbely;
VU-030, Praha/Kbely

0003	3 DLP
0005	VU-030

**Sukhoi Su-22M-4K/
Su-22UM-3K***
20 SBOLP, Námest

2619	34	NA-2D
2620	35	NA-2D
3313	24	NA-2A
3315	39	NA-2B
3403	08	NA-1B
3405		
3406		
3701	02	NA-1A

124

3703	43	NA-1D
3704	44	NA-1D
3706	52	NA-1E
3803	27	NA-2B
4005	30	NA-2C
4006	31	NA-2E
4007	32	NA-2C
4010	28	NA-2B
4011	22	NA-2A
4208	53	NA-1E
4209	54	NA-1E
7103	03	NA-1A*
7104	40	NA-2C*
7309	41	NA-2D*
7310	25	NA-2A*

Sukhoi Su-25K/Su-25BK*
30 BILP, Námest
1002
1003
3348*
5003
5006
5007
5008
5039
5040
6020
8072
8076
8077
8078
9013
9014
9093
9094
9098
9099

Tupolev Tu-134A
3 DLP, Praha/Kbely
1407

Tupolev Tu-154B-2
3 DLP, Praha/Kbely
0601

DENMARK
**Kongelige Danske
Flyvevaabnet
Lockheed
C-130H Hercules**
Eskadrille 721, Vaerløse
B-678
B-679
B-680

General Dynamics F-16
Eskadrille 723, Aalborg;
Eskadrille 726, Aalborg;
Eskadrille 727, Skrydstrup;
Eskadrille 730, Skrydstrup

F-16A
E-004	Esk 726
E-005	Esk 726
E-006	Esk 726
E-007	Esk 726
E-008	Esk 726
E-016	Esk 726
E-017	Esk 726
E-018	Esk 726
E-024	
E-075	

E-107	
E-174	Esk 727
E-176	Esk 723
E-177	Esk 723
E-178	Esk 723
E-180	Esk 726
E-181	Esk 727
E-182	Esk 730
E-183	Esk 723
E-184	Esk 723
E-187	Esk 727
E-188	Esk 723
E-189	Esk 723
E-190	Esk 723
E-191	Esk 730
E-192	Esk 730
E-193	Esk 727
E-194	Esk 723
E-195	Esk 723
E-196	Esk 723
E-197	Esk 730
E-198	Esk 730
E-199	Esk 727
E-200	Esk 723
E-202	Esk 730
E-203	Esk 723
E-596	Esk 726
E-597	Esk 730
E-598	Esk 730
E-599	Esk 730
E-600	Esk 727
E-601	Esk 727
E-602	Esk 727
E-603	Esk 727
E-604	Esk 726
E-605	Esk 730
E-606	Esk 730
E-607	Esk 723
E-608	Esk 723
E-609	Esk 727
E-610	Esk 727
E-611	Esk 727

F-16B
ET-022	Esk 726
ET-197	Esk 726
ET-198	Esk 726
ET-199	Esk 726
ET-204	Esk 727
ET-205	Esk 730
ET-206	Esk 730
ET-207	Esk 727
ET-208	Esk 730
ET-210	Esk 726
ET-612	Esk 730
ET-613	Esk 727
ET-614	Esk 723
ET-615	Esk 727

**Grumman
Gulfstream III**
Eskadrille 721, Vaerløse
F-249
F-313
F-330

**SAAB T-17
Supporter**
Flyveskolen, Avnø (FLSK);
Haerens Flyvetjaeneste
(Danish Army), Vandel;
Eskadrille 721, Vaerløse
T-401	Karup Stn Flt
T-402	Skrydstrup Stn Flt

T-403	KarupStnFlt
T-404	Karup Stn Flt
T-405	Karup Stn Flt
T-407	Karup Stn Flt
T-408	FLSK
T-409	FLSK
T-410	Karup Stn Flt
T-411	FLSK
T-413	FLSK
T-414	Army
T-415	Army
T-417	Army
T-418	FLSK
T-419	FLSK
T-420	FLSK
T-421	FLSK
T-423	FLSK
T-425	Aalborg Stn Flt
T-426	FLSK
T-427	FLSK
T-428	FLSK
T-429	FLSK
T-430	FLSK
T-431	FLSK
T-432	FLSK

Sikorsky S-61A Sea King
Eskadrille 722, Vaerløse
Detachmentsat:
Aalborg, Ronne, Skrydstrup
U-240
U-275
U-276
U-277
U-278
U-279
U-280
U-481

**Sovaernets
Flyvetjaeneste (Navy)
Westland Lynx Mk 80/90***
Eskadrille 722, Vaerløse
S-035
S-134
S-142
S-170
S-175
S-181
S-191
S-249*
S-256*

**Haerens
Flyvetjaeneste (Army)
Hughes 500M**
Vandel
H-201
H-202
H-203
H-205
H-206
H-207
H-209
H-210
H-211
H-213
H-244
H-245
H-246

Aérospatiale AS550C-2
Fennec
P-090
P-234
P-254
P-275
P-276
P-287
P-288
P-319
P-320
P-352
P-369

ECUADOR
Fuerza Aérea Ecuatoriana
Lockheed
C-130H Hercules
FAE-812
FAE-893

EGYPT
Al Quwwat al-Jawwiya
Ilmisriya
Lockheed
C-130H/C-130H-30*
Hercules
16 Sqn, Cairo West
1271/SU-BAB
1272/SU-BAC
1273/SU-BAD
1274/SU-BAE
1275/SU-BAF
1277/SU-BAI
1278/SU-BAJ
1279/SU-BAK
1280/SU-BAL
1281/SU-BAM
1282/SU-BAN
1283/SU-BAP
1284/SU-BAQ
1285/SU-BAR
1286/SU-BAS
1287/SU-BAT
1288/SU-BAU
1289/SU-BAV
1290/SU-BEW
1291/SU-BEX
1292/SU-BEY
1293/SU-BKS*
1294/SU-BKT*
1295/SU-BKU*

FRANCE
Armée de l'Air
Aérospatiale SN601
Corvette
CEV, Bretigny

1	MV
2	MW
10	MX

Aérospatiale TB-30
Epsilon
GE.315, Cognac

1	315-UA	51	2-BD	99	315-XP
2	315-UB	52	315-VX	100	315-XQ
3	FZ	53	315-VY	101	315-XR
4	315-UC	54	315-VZ	102	315-XS
5	315-UD	56	315-WA	103	315-XT
6	315-UE	57	F-ZVLB	104	315-XU
7	315-UF	58	315-WB	105	315-XV
8	315-UG	60	315-WC	106	315-XW
9	315-UH	61	315-WD	107	315-XX
10	315-UI	62	315-WE	108	315-XY
11	315-UJ	63	315-WF	109	315-XZ
12	315-UK	64	315-WG	110	315-YA
13	315-UL	65	315-WH	111	315-YB
14	315-UM	66	315-WI	112	315-YC
15	315-UN	67	315-WJ	113	315-YD
16	315-UO	68	315-WK	114	315-YE
17	315-UP	69	315-WL	115	315-YF
18	315-UQ	70	315-WM	116	315-YG
19	315-UR	71	315-WN	117	315-YH
20	315-US	72	315-WO	118	315-YI
21	315-UT	73	315-WP	119	315-YJ
23	315-UV	74	315-WQ	120	315-YK
24	315-UW	75	315-WR	121	315-YL
25	315-UX	76	315-WS	122	315-YM
26	315-UY	77	315-WT	123	315-YN
27	315-UZ	78	315-WU	124	315-YO
28	315-VA	79	315-WV	125	315-YP
29	315-VB	80	315-WW	126	315-YQ
30	315-VC	81	315-WX	127	315-YR
31	315-VD	82	315-WY	128	315-YS
32	315-VE	83	315-WZ	129	315-YT
33	315-VF	84	315-XA	130	315-YU
34	315-VG	85	315-XB	131	315-YV
35	315-VH	86	315-XC	132	315-YW
36	315-VI	87	315-XD	133	315-YX
37	315-VJ	88	315-XE	134	315-YY
38	315-VK	89	315-XF	135	315-YZ
39	315-VL	90	315-XG	136	315-ZA
40	315-VM	91	315-XH	137	315-ZB
41	315-VN	92	315-XI	138	315-ZC
42	315-VO	93	315-XJ	139	315-ZD
43	315-VP	94	315-XK	140	315-ZE
44	315-VQ	95	315-XL	141	315-ZF
45	315-VR	96	315-XM	142	315-ZG
46	315-VS	97	315-XN	143	315-ZH
47	315-VT	98	315-XO	144	315-ZI
48	315-VU			145	315-ZJ
49	315-VV			146	315-ZK
50	315-VW			148	315-ZL
				149	315-ZM
				150	315-ZN
				152	315-ZO
				153	315-ZP
				154	315-ZQ
				155	315-ZR
				158	315-ZS
				159	315-ZT

Airbus A.310-304
ET.3/60, Charles de Gaulle
421   F-RADA
422   F-RADB

Airtech CN-235
ET.1/62, Creil

043	62-IA
045	62-IB
065	62-IC
066	62-ID
071	62-IE
072	62-IF

Boeing C-135FR
ERV.93, Istres,

470	93-CA
38471	93-CB
38472	93-CC
38474	93-CE
475	93-CF
735	93-CG
736	93-CH
737	93-CI
738	93-CJ
12739	93-CK
740	93-CL

Boeing KC-135R
ERV.93, Istres

38033	

Boeing E-3F Sentry
EDCA.00/036, Avord

201	36-CA
202	36-CB
203	36-CC
204	36-CD

CASA 212
CEV

377	MO
378	MP
386	MQ
387	MR
388	MS

Cessna 310
CEV, Bretigny & Istres

045	AU
046	AV
185	AU
187	BJ
188	BK
190	BL
192	BM
193	BG
194	BH
242	AW
244	AX
513	BE
693	BI
820	CL
981	BF

D-BD Alpha Jet
Patrouille de France (PDF), Salon de Provence;
EC.1/8, EC.2/8 Cazaux;
Gl.314, Tours;
CEAM (330), Mont-de-Marsan;
CEV, Bretigny

Serial	Code	Unit
01	F-ZJTS	CEV
02	F-ZWRU	
E1	CEV	
E3	8-NC	EC2/8
E4	CEV	
E5	8-NS	EC2/8
E7	8-MM	EC1/8
E8		
E9	314-TN	
E10	8-NM	EC2/8
E11	8-MW	EC1/8
E12	CEV	
E13	314-TK	
E14	314-LE	
E15	314-TT	
E17	8-NK	EC2/8
E18	8-MD	EC1/8
E19	314-TS	
E20	8-ML	EC1/8
E21	314-UD	
E22		
E23	F-TERO	PDF [1]
E24	314-TW	
E25	314-LL	
E26		
E27		
E28	8-MI	EC1/8
E29	8-MF	EC1/8
E30	330-AK	
E31	314-UA	
E32	8-NQ	EC2/8
E33	8-NN	EC2/8
E34	314-TC	
E35		
E36	314-LD	
E37		
E38		
E40		
E41	314-LC	
E42	314-LQ	
E43	314-TZ	
E44	CEV	
E45	330-AK	
E46	CEV	
E47		
E48	8-MO	EC1/8
E49	314-LP	
E51	314-UB	
E52	314-TX	
E53	314-LV	
E55	314-UN	
E58	314-TD	
E59		
E60		
E61	314-LJ	
E63		
E64	8-NH	EC2/8
E65		
E66	8-ME	EC1/8
E67	8-MR	EC1/8
E68	8-NA	EC2/8
E69	8-NX	EC2/8
E70		
E72	F-TERG	PDF [9]
E73		
E74	8-NO	EC2/8
E75	314-TU	
E76	314-TH	
E79	314-LN	
E80	CEV	
E81	314-LR	
E82	314-TE	
E83	8-NG	EC2/8
E84	8-MH	EC1/8
E85	330-AL	
E86	314-TJ	
E87	8-MP	EC1/8
E88	314-TF	
E89	F-TERE	PDF [4]
E90		
E91	8-NL	EC2/8
E92		
E93	8-NV	EC2/8
E94	314-TL	
E95	314-TP	
E96	8-MT	EC1/8
E97	F-TERL	PDF [0]
E98		
E99	314-LW	
E100	CEV	
E101	314-LX	
E102	8-MC	EC1/8
E103	314-LF	
E104	F-TERB	PDF
E105	F-TERF	PDF
E106	F-TERJ	PDF [8]
E107		
E108	8-NI	EC2/8
E109	8-MU	EC1/8
E110	8-ND	EC2/8
E112	314-LH	
E113	8-NY	EC2/8
E114	314-UC	
E115	8-MS	EC1/8
E116	8-NB	EC2/8
E117	314-UL	
E118	314-TB	
E119	314-TG	
E120	314-LM	
E121	F-TERK	PDF [2]
E122	314-UG	
E123	8-MQ	EC1/8
E124		
E125	F-TERH	PDF [3]
E126	F-TERA	PDF [7]
E127	8-MB	EC1/8
E128	314-LS	
E129	314-TO	
E130	314-TI	
E131	8-NE	EC2/8
E132	F-TERN	PDF [5]
E133		
E134		
E135	8-MJ	EC1/8
E136	314-LY	
E137	314-TG	
E138	314-UK	
E139	330-AH	
E140	F-TERD	PDF [6]
E141		
E142		
E143	314-UJ	
E144	8-NU	EC2/8
E145		
E146	8-MG	EC1/8
E147	8-NP	EC2/8
E148	8-NJ	EC2/8
E149	314-LI	
E150	8-NF	EC2/8
E151		
E152	314-TA	
E153	314-TM	
E154	8-MA	EC1/8
E155		
E156	314-LB	
E157	314-LG	
E158	8-NT	EC2/8
E159		
E160		
E161		
E162		
E163	314-TQ	
E164		
E165		

E166	8-MN	EC1/8
E167	8-MV	EC1/8
E168	8-MK	EC1/8
E169	314-LK	
E170		
E171		
E173	F-TERP	PDF
E174		
E175	314-LU	
E176		

Dassault
Falcon 20
CEV, Bretigny & Istres;
SIET.98/120, Cazaux;
ETEC.2/65, Villacoublay;
CITAC.339, Luxeuil

22	CS	CEV
49	120-FA	
79	CT	CEV
86	CG	CEV
93	(F-RAED)	ETEC
96	CB	CEV
104	CW	CEV
115	339-JG	
124	CC	CEV
131	CD	CEV
138	CR	CEV
145	CU	CEV
167	(F-RAEB)	ETEC
182	339-JA	
186	339-JE	
188	CX	CEV
238	F-RAEE	ETEC
252	CA	CEV
260	(F-RAEA)	CEV
263	CY	CEV
268	(F-RAEF)	ETEC
288	CVCEV	
291	(F-RAEG)	ETEC
342	(F-RAEC)	ETEC
375	CZ	CEV
422	65-EH	ETEC
451	339-JC	
483	339-JI	

Dassault Falcon 50
ET.60, Villacoublay

5	(F-RAFI)
27	(F-RAFK)
34	F-RAFL
78	(F-RAFJ)

Dassault Falcon 900
ET.60, Villacoublay

2	(F-RAFP)
4	F-RAFQ

Dassault Mirage IVA/IVP
EB.1/91, Mont-de-Marsan;
EB.2/91, Cazaux

2	AA	
5	AD	
8/01	AG	
11	AJ	1/91
12	AK	
13	AL	
15	AN	
20	AS	
23	AV	1/91
25	AX	2/91
26	AY	1/91
31	BD	1/91
37	BJ	

39	BL	
42	BO	
48	BU	1/91
49	BV	1/91
51	BX	
52	BY	2/91
54	CA	2/91
55	CB	1/91
57	CD	1/91
59	CF	1/91
61	CH	2/91
62	CI	1/91

Dassault
Mirage F.1C/F.1CT*
EC.12 Cambrai;
EC.13 Colmar;
EC.4/33 Djibouti;
EC.3/33 Reims;
CEAM (330) Mont-de-Marsan;
CEV, Bretigny & Istres

2		
3		
4	12-YE	CEV
5	12-ZP	2/12
6	30-SJ	
9	12-ZQ	2/12
10	12-ZD	2/12
14		
15	33-FD	3/33
16	30-SE	
17		
18		
19		
20	12-ZN	2/12
21		
22		
23		
24	12-ZM	2/12
25		
26		
27		
29		
30	12-ZO	2/12
31		
32	12-ZF	2/12
33	33-FS	3/33
35		
36		
37	30-MK	
38	12-ZC	2/12
39		
40	33-FM	3/33
41		
42	30-MC	
43		
44		
47	12-ZG	2/12
49		
50	12-YD	3/12
52	33-LP	4/33
54	30-MJ	
55	30-MN	
60	12-ZH	2/12
62	12-ZR	3/12
63	33-FJ	3/33
64	33-FC	3/33
67		
68		
69		
70	12-ZB	2/12
71		
72	12-ZA	2/12

73		
74		
75		
76	33-FF	3/33
77		
79		
80	33-LN	4/33
81		
82	33-LK	4/33
83	33-LB	4/33
84		
85		
87		
90		
100	33-FF	3/33
101		
103		
201	33-LA	4/33
202	33-LF	4/33
203	33-LG	4/33
205	33-FX	3/33
206	33-LR	4/33
207		
210	33-LD	4/33
211	33-LE	4/33
213	30-SR	
214	12-ZJ	2/12
216	33-FI	3/33
218	30-SK	
219		
220		
221	33-FO	3/33
223		
224	30-SS	
225*		
226*	13-QO	1/13
227*		CEV
228*		
229*	13-QI	1/13
230*	13-QM	1/13
231	30-SO	
232		
233*	13-QG	1/13
234*	13-QL	1/13
235*		
236	12-ZE	2/12
237*	13-SE	3/13
238*	13-QK	1/13
239*	13-QD	1/13
240		
241*	13-SI	3/13
242*	13-SG	3/13
243*	13-QN	1/13
244*	13-SD	3/13
245*	13-SA	3/13
246*		
248*		
249*		
251*		
252*	13-SK	3/13
253	30-MM	
254*	13-SF	3/13
255		
256*	13-SL	3/13
257	30-SX	
258	33-LA	4/33
259	30-SH	
260	30-SF	
261		
262*		
264*	13-QH	1/13
265		
267*	13-QB	1/13
268	33-LI	4/33

271	30-SN		**Dassault Mirage 2000-5**			37	2-EU	1/2
272	30-SA		AMD-BA			38	5-AR	3/5
273*	330-AI		BX1			39	5-OF	2/5
274*	330-AJ		BY1			40	5-OI	2/5
275	12-ZK	2/12				41		
277			**Dassault Mirage 2000B**			42	5-NM	1/5
278*	13-QA	1/13	CEV, Bretigny & Istres;			43		
279*	13-SC	3/13	EC.2, Dijon;			44	5-AQ	3/5
280*	13-QE	1/13	EC.5, Cambrai;			45	5-OM	2/5
281*			EC.12, Orange			46	5-AG	3/5
282*	13-QR	1/13	B01		CEV	47	5-AA	3/5
283*	13-SH	2/13	502	2-FA	2/2	48	5-AF	3/5
			504			49	5-OL	2/5
Dassault Mirage			505	2-FB	2/2	51	5-OG	2/5
F.1CR			506	2-FC	2/2	52	5-OC	2/5
ER.33, Reims;			507	2-FD	2/2	53	5-AJ	3/5
CEAM (330), Mont-de-			508	2-FE	2/2	54	5-AI	3/5
Marsan;			509	2-FF	2/2	55	5-OH	2/5
CEV, Istres;			510	2-FG	2/2	56	5-OA	2/5
601		CEV	511	2-FH	2/2	57		
602		CEV	512	2-FI	2/2	58	5-AM	3/5
603	33-CB	1/33	513	2-FJ	2/2	59	5-OB	2/5
604	33-CE	1/33	514	2-FK	2/2	61	5-OD	2/5
605	33-NF	2/33	515	2-FT	2/2	62	5-AL	3/5
606	33-NP	2/33	516	2-FM	2/2	63	5-OK	2/5
607	33-NM	2/33	518	2-FU	2/2	64	330-AQ	
608	33-NG	2/33	519	5-AM	3/5	65		
609			520	2-FW	2/2	66		
610	33-CH	1/33	521	2-FX	2/2	67	5-OQ	2/5
611	33-CO	1/33	522	5-NA	1/5	68	5-AP	3/5
612	33-NJ	2/33	523	5-OJ	2/5	69	5-OR	2/5
613	33-NK	2/33	524	12-YF	1/12	70	5-AO	3/5
614	33-TO		525	12-KN	3/12	71	5-AD	3/5
615	33-CU	1/33	526	12-KM	3/12	72	5-OE	2/5
616			527	5-NO	1/5	73	5-NB	1/5
617	33-CI	1/33				74	5-OP	2/5
619	33-CC	1/33	**Dassault Mirage 2000C**			76	5-NP	1/5
620	33-CT	1/33	CEAM (330), Mont-de-			77	12-KB	3/12
622	33-CR	1/33	Marsan;			78	5-NE	1/5
623	33-CM	1/33	CEV, Istres;			79	5-NF	1/5
624	33-NY	2/33	EC.2, Dijon;			80	330-AC	
625			EC.5, Orange;			81	330-AY	
627	33-NI	2/33	EC.12 Cambrai			82	5-NM	1/5
628	33-NN	2/33	01			83	5-NG	1/5
629	33-CG	1/33	04			84	5-NH	1/5
630	33-NL	2/33	1	2-EP	CEV	85	5-NI	1/5
631	33-CD	1/33	2		CEV	86	5-NJ	1/5
632	33-NE	2/33	3	2-FP	2/2	87	5-NK	1/5
634	33-CK	1/33	4	2-LB		88	5-NL	1/5
635	33-NS	2/33	5	2-FQ	2/2	89		
636	33-CS	1/33	8	2-EC	1/2	90	12-KO	3/12
637	33-CP	1/33	9	2-LO		91	12-YO	1/12
638	33-NU	2/33	11	2-EF	1/2	92	330-AW	
640	33-NV	2/33	12	2-FS	2/2	93	330-AR	
641	33-NT	2/33	13	2-EI	1/2	94	12-KA	3/12
642	33-NC	2/33	14	2-FO	1/2	95	12-YB	1/12
643			15	2-EK	1/2	96	12-KK	3/12
645	33-NO	2/33	16	2-EL	1/2	97	12-KP	3/12
646	33-NW	2/33	17	2-EM	1/2	98	12-YJ	1/12
647	33-TR		18	2-FL	2/2	99	12-YP	1/12
648	33-CF	1/33	19	2-EA	1/2	100	12-YH	1/12
649	33-TF		20	2-EQ	1/2	101	12-YQ	1/12
650	33-CJ	1/33	21	2-EG	1/2	102	12-YE	1/12
651	33-NB	2/33	22	2-LG		103	12-YN	1/12
653	33-CQ	1/33	25	2-EJ	1/2	104	12-YK	1/12
654	33-CL	1/33	27	2-EO	1/2	105	12-YL	1/12
655	33-NR	2/33	28	2-ER	1/2	106	12-KL	3/12
656	33-NH	2/33	29	2-ED	1/2	107	12-YR	1/12
657			30	2-FN	2/2	108	330-AT	
658	33-CW	1/33	32	2-EP	1/2	109	12-YI	1/12
659	33-CA	1/33	33	2-ES	1/2	110	12-KE	3/12
660	33-ND	2/33	34	2-ET	1/2	111	12-KI	3/12
661	33-CX	1/33	35	2-EE	1/2	112	5-NB	1/5
662			36	2-EN	1/2	113	5-NC	1/5

114	12-YG	1/12
115	12-KC	3/12
116	12-KG	3/12
117	12-YD	1/12
118	12-KH	3/12
119	12-KD	3/12
120	12-YM	1/12
121	12-KF	3/12
122		
123		
124		
125		
126		

Dassault Mirage 2000D
CEAM (330), Mont-de-Marsan;
EC.3, Nancy

D01	AMD-BA	
601	3-IA	1/3
602	3-IB	1/3
603	3-IC	1/3
604	3-ID	1/3
605	3-IE	1/3
606	3-IF	1/3
607		
608		
609	3-IH	1/3
610	3-II	1/3
611		
612	330-AX	
613		
614	3-IJ	1/3
615	3-IK	1/3
616	3-IL	1/3
617	3-XA	3/3
618	3-IG	1/3

Dassault Mirage 2000N
CEAM (330), Mont-de-Marsan;
EC.3, Nancy;
EC.1/4, EC.2/4 Luxeuil;
EC.3/4 Istres

301		
302	4-CA	3/4
303		
304	3-CB	3/4
305	4-BF	2/4
306	4-BE	2/4
307	4-BC	2/4
308	4-CD	3/4
309	4-BA	2/4
310	4-CE	3/4
311	4-BD	2/4
312	4-CF	3/4
313		
314	4-CG	3/4
315	4-BG	2/4
316	4-CH	3/4
317	4-BH	2/4
318	4-CI	3/4
319	4-BI	2/4
320		
322		
323	4-CJ	3/4
324	4-CL	3/4
325	4-BL	2/4
326	4-CM	3/4
327	4-BM	2/4
329	4-BN	2/4
330	4-CO	3/4
331	4-CP	3/4
332	3-JQ	2/3

333	330-AG	
334	330-AV	
335	4-BJ	2/4
336	4-BP	2/4
337		
338	4-AC	1/4
339	4-AD	1/4
340	4-AA	1/4
341	4-AF	1/4
342	4-AG	1/4
343	4-AH	1/4
344	4-AJ	1/4
345	4-AK	1/4
346	4-AL	1/4
347	4-BT	2/4
348	3-JA	2/3
349	4-AO	1/4
350	3-JR	2/3
351	4-AQ	1/4
353	3-JS	2/3
354	3-JC	2/3
355	3-JD	2/3
356	3-JE	2/3
357	3-JF	2/3
358	3-JG	2/3
359	3-JH	2/3
360	3-JI	2/3
361	3-JJ	2/3
362	3-JK	2/3
363	3-JL	2/3
364	3-JM	2/3
365	3-JN	2/3
366	3-JO	2/3
367	3-JP	2/3
368	4-AR	1/4
369	4-AS	1/4
370	4-AT	1/4
371	4-AV	1/4
372	4-BR	2/4
373	3-JV	2/3
374		
375	3-JB	2/3

Dassault Rafale-B

B01	AMD-BA

DassaultRafale-C

C01	CEV

DHC 6 Twin Otter
CEAM, Mont-de-Marsan;
GAM.56 Evreux;
ETEC.1/65 Villacoublay;
EdC.70 Chateaudun

292	CC	ETEC
298	CD	ETEC
300	OZ	GAM.56
603	MB	EdC.70
730	65-CA	ETEC
742	65-CB	ETEC
743	MA	EdC.70
745	IB	CEAM
786	CT	ETEC
790	65-CW	ETEC

Douglas DC-8F
EE.51 Evreux;
ET.3/60 Charles de Gaulle

45570	F-RAFE	EE.51
45819	F-RAFC	ET.3/60
46013	F-RAFG	ET.3/60
46043	F-RAFD	ET.3/60
46130	F-RAFF	ET.3/60

Embraer EMB.121 Xingu
CEAM, Mont-de-Marsan;
CITAC.339, Luxeuil;
ETE.43 Bordeaux;
ETE.44 Aix-en-Provence;
GE.319 Avord

054	YX	
064	YY	
072	YA	
073	YB	
075	YC	
076	YD	
078	YE	
080	YF	
082	YG	
084	YH	
086	YI	
089	YJ	
091	YK	
092	YL	
095	YM	
096	YN	
098	YO	
099	YP	
101	YR	
102	YS	
103	YT	ETE.44
105	YU	
107	YV	
108	YW	
111	YQ	

Embraer EMB.312F Tucano
CEAM (330), Mont-de-Marsan;
GI.312, Salon de Provence

438	330-DJ
439	330-DM
456	
457	
458	
459	
460	

Lockheed C-130H Hercules
*C-130H-30 Hercules
ET.2/61, Orleans

5114	61-PA
5116	61-PB
5119	61-PC
5140	61-PD
5142*	61-PE
5144*	61-PF
5150*	61-PG
5151*	61-PH
5152*	61-PI
5153*	61-PJ
5226*	61-PK
5227*	61-PL

Morane Saulnier 760 Paris
CEV, Bretigny & Istres;
ENOSA, Toulouse;
EC.4, Luxeuil;
EC.5, Orange;
EC.13, Colmar;
ETE.41, Metz;
ETE.44, Aix-en-Provence;
ETEC.1/65, Villacoublay;
GI.312, Salon de Provence;
GI.314, Tours;

CEAM (330), Mont-de-Marsan

1	330-DA	CEAM
19		
23	41-AL	ETE.41
24	65-LA	ETEC
25	41-AP	ETE.41
26	65-LN	ETEC
27	41-AR	ETE.41
29	4-WA	EC.4
30	65-LW	ETEC
34		
35	13-TB	EC.13
36	330-DO	CEAM
38	41-AS	ETE.41
44	5-ME	EC.5
45	DI	ENOSA
51	13-TA	EC.13
53		
54	330-DQ	CEAM
56	DJ	ENOSA
57	65-LK	ETEC
58	312-DG	Gl.312
59		
60	312-DE	Gl.312
61	312-DF	Gl.312
62	314-DD	Gl.314
65	330-DP	CEAM
68	NB	CEV
70	65-LF	ETEC
71	41-AC	ETE.41
73		
75	316-DK	ENOSA
78	65-LI	ETEC
81	DD	CEAM
83	NC	CEV
91	65-LU	ETEC
92	316-DL	ENOSA
93		
94		
97	DC	CEAM
100	NG	CEV
113	NI	CEV
114	NJ	CEV
115	OV	CEV
116	ON	CEV
117	AZ	CEV
118	NQ	CEV
119	NL	CEV

Nord 262 Fregate

CEV, Istres;
ENOSA, Toulouse;
ETE.41, Metz;
EL.43, Bordeaux;
ETE.44, Aix-en-Provence;
ETEC.1/65, Villacoublay;
EdC.070, Chateaudun;
CEAM (330), Mont-de-Marsan

01		CEV
3	OH	CEV
55	MH	CEV
58	MJ	CEV
64	AA	ETEC
66	AB	ETEC
67	MI	CEV
68	AC	ETEC
76	DA	ENOSA
77	AK	ETEC
78	AF	ETEC
80	AW	ETEC
81	AH	ETEC
83	DB	ENOSA
86	DD	ENOSA
87	DC	ENOSA
88	AL	ETEC
89	AZ	ETEC
91	AT	EL.43
92	DE	ENOSA
93	AP	ETEC
94	AU	ETE.44
95	AR	ETEC
105	AE	ETEC
106	AY	ETEC
107	AX	EL.43
108	AG	ETEC
109	AM	ETEC
110	AS	EL.43

SEPECAT
Jaguar A

EC.7, St Dizier;
EC.11, Toul;
CEAM (330), Mont-de-Marsan;
CITAC.339, Luxeuil;
CEV, Bretigny & Istres

A1		
A2	11-MC	2/11
A3		CEV
A5	7-PN	2/7
A7	7-PG	2/7
A8		
A9	7-PB	2/7
A11	7-PA	2/7
A13		
A14	11-MA	2/11
A15	7-IJ	3/7
A16		
A17		
A19		
A22		
A23	7-HK	1/7
A24		
A25	11-MO	2/11
A26	7-HM	1/7
A27	11-MQ	2/11
A28		
A29	11-MB	2/11
A31		
A32		
A33		
A34	7-ID	3/7
A35		
A36		
A37	7-HA	1/7
A38	11-EG	
A39	7-IT	3/7
A40	7-IQ	3/7
A41	7-HM	1/7
A43		
A44	11-MG	2/11
A46	7-HP	1/7
A47	7-IG	3/7
A48	7-PC	2/7
A49	11-RH	3/11
A50		
A53	11-RB	3/11
A54	11-RF	3/11
A55	7-HB	1/7
A58	7-HL	1/7
A59	7-IH	3/7
A60		
A61	11-RG	3/11
A64	11-	
A65		
A66	7-IB	3/7
A70	11-RL	3/11
A72	7-PD	2/7
A73	7-HH	1/7
A74		
A75		
A76	7-HI	1/7
A79		
A80	7-HN	1/7
A82		
A84	11-RQ	3/11
A86		
A87		
A88	7-II	3/7
A89	11-RE	3/11
A90		
A92	7-IO	3/7
A93	7-HP	1/7
A94	11-RN	3/11
A96		
A98	11-EC	
A99	11-EI	
A100	11-EE	
A101	1,1-MH	2/11
A103		
A104	7-IL	3/7
A107		
A108	11-MP	2/11
A112	11-ME	2/11
A113		
A115	7-HF	1/7
A117		
A118	7-IM	3/7
A119	7-IP	3/7
A120	11-MR	2/11
A121		
A122	7-HG	1/7
A123	11-RZ	3/11
A124		
A126		
A127	11-MM	2/11
A128	11-MD	2/11
A129		
A130	7-HJ	1/7
A131		
A133	11-MT	2/11
A135	11-RJ	3/11
A137	11-EM	
A138	11-RX	3/11
A139	11-RC	3/11
A140	11-MV	2/11
A141	11-EO	
A142		
A144	11-RW	3/11
A145	11-EP	
A148	11-MZ	2/11
A149	11-RK	3/11
A150	11-MF	2/11
A151	11-ER	
A152		
A153	11-RA	3/11
A154	11-RP	3/11
A157	11-MW	2/11
A158	11-RM	3/11
A159	11-RV	3/11
A160	11-RT	3/11

SEPECAT
Jaguar E

E1		CEV
E2	7-HD	1/7
E3	339-WI	
E4		
E5		
E6	11-EZ	

E7		
E8	339-WG	3/7
E9	7-PQ	2/7
E10	339-WF	
E11	7-PE	2/7
E12	7-PR	2/7
E13	11-RD	3/11
E15	7-PF	2/7
E16	7-HO	1/7
E18		
E19	11-MJ	2/11
E20		
E21		
E22	7-PI	2/7
E23		
E24	339-WK	
E25	7-PK	2/7
E27	11-RI	3/11
E28		
E29	7-PL	2/7
E30		
E32	7-PO	2/7
E33		
E35	7-PM	2/7
E36	7-PP	2/7
E37		
E39		
E40	7-PH	2/7

SOCATA TBM 700
EL.43, Bordeaux;
ETEC.2/65, Villacoublay

33	65-XA	ETEC
35	43-XB	EL.43
70	43-XC	EL.43
77	65-XD	ETEC
78	65-XE	ETEC
80	65-XF	ETEC
	65-XG	ETEC
	65-XH	ETEC

Transall C-160
Transall C-160H[1]
Transall C-160NG[2]
EET.54, Metz;
ETOM.55, Dakar;
EE.59, Evreux (C160H);
ET.61 Orleans (C160A/F);
ET.64 Evreux (C160NG);
CEAM (330), Mont-de-Marsan;
CEV, Bretigny

A02	61-MI	
A04		CEV
A06	61-ZB	
F1	61-MA	
F2	61-MB	
F3	61-MC	
F4	61-MD	
F5		
F11	61-MF	
F12	61-MG	
F13	61-MH	
R15	330-IR	
F16	61-MK	
F17		
F18	61-MM	
F42	61-MN	
F43	61-MO	
F44	61-MP	
F45	61-MQ	
F46	61-MR	
F48	61-MT	
F49	61-MU	

F51	61-MW
F52	61-MX
F53	61-MY
F54	61-MZ
F55	61-ZC
F86	61-ZD
F87	61-ZE
F88	61-ZF
F89	61-ZG
F90	61-ZH
F91	61-ZI
F92	61-ZJ
F93	61-ZK
F94	61-ZL
F95	61-ZM
F96	61-ZN
F97	61-ZO
F98	61-ZP
F99	61-ZQ
F100	61-ZR
F153	61-ZS
F154	61-ZT
F155	61-ZU
F157	61-ZW
F158	61-ZX
F159	61-ZY
F160	61-ZZ
F201[2]	64-GA
F202[2]	64-GB
R203[2]	330-IS
F204[2]	64-GD
F205[2]	64-GE
F206[2]	64-GF
F207[2]	64-GG
F208[2]	64-GH
F210[2]	64-GJ
F211[2]	64-GK
F212[2]	64-GL
F213[2]	64-GM
F214[2]	64-GN
F215[2]	64-GO
F216[2]	GT
F217[2]	64-GQ
F218[2]	64-GR
F221[2]	54-GS
F222[2]	64-GV
F223[2]	64-GW
F224[2]	64-GX
F225[2]	64-GY
F226[2]	64-GZ
F230[1]	F-ZJUA
F231[1]	F-ZJUB
F232[1]	
H01[1]	59-BA
H02[1]	59-BB
H03[1]	59-BC
H04[1]	59-BD

Aéronavale/Marine
Aérospatiale SA.321G
Super Frelon
32 Flotille, Lanveoc;
33 Flotille, San Mandrier

101	33F
2	32F
105	33F
106	32F
118	32F
120	32F
122	32F
134	32F
37	32F
141	32F
144	33F

148	33F
149	32F
60	32F
62	32F
163	32F
164	32F
165	33F

Breguet 1050
Alizé
4 Flotille, Lann Bihoué;
6 Flotille, Nimes-Garons;
ES59, Hyeres

11	6F
12	4F
17	4F
22	6F
24	6F
25	4F
26	6F
28	
30	6F
31	6F
33	4F
36	6F
41	4F
43	4F
47	4F
48	6F
49	6F
50	6F
51	4F
52	4F
53	4F
55	4F
56	4F
59	6F
60	6F
64	6F
65	6F
67	59S
68	6F
73	6F
76	6F
87	59S

Breguet Br 1150
Atlantic/Atlantique 2*
21 Flotille/22 Flotille, Nimes-Garons;
23 Flotille/24 Flotille, Lann Bihoué;
CEV, Bretigny & Istres

03	21F/22F
04	21F/22F
2	21F/22F
3	21F/22F
11	21F/22F
21	23F/24F
23	21F/22F
24	23F/24F
25	21F/22F
31	21F/22F
35	21F/22F
44	21F/22F
45	23F/24F
48	21F/22F
49	21F/22F
50	21F/22F
51	21F/22F
52	21F/22F
53	21F/22F
54	21F/22F
55	23F/24F

56	21F/22F
57	21F/22F
61	21F/22F
65	23F/24F
66	23F/24F
67	21F/22F
68	21F/22F
01*	21F/22F
02*	CEV
03*	CEV
04*	21F/22F
1*	23F/24F
2*	23F/24F
3*	23F/24F
4*	23F/24F
5*	23F/24F
6*	23F/24F
7*	23F/24F
8*	23F/24F
9*	23F/24F
10*	21F/22F
11*	23F/24F
12*	23F/24F
13*	21F/22F
14*	23F/24F
15*	
16*	
17*	23F/24F
18*	23F/24F
19*	21F/22F
20*	23F/24F
21*	
22*	
23*	
24*	
25*	
26*	
27*	
28*	
29*	
30*	

**Dassault Etendard
IVP/IVMP***
16 Flotille, Landivisiau

101	
107	
109	
114	
115	
118	
120	
153*	
162*	
163*	
166*	

Dassault Super Etendard
11 Flotille, Landivisiau;
17 Flotille, Landivisiau;
CEV, Bretigny & Istres;
ES59, Hyeres

1	11F
2	59S
3	11F
4	11F
6	59S
8	11F
10	11F
11	59S
12	11F
13	11F
14	59S
15	11F

16	11F
17	17F
18	59S
19	59S
21	
23	17F
24	17F
25	11F
26	11F
28	59S
29	
30	11F
31	11F
32	11F
33	17F
34	11F
35	17F
37	59S
38	11F
39	
41	11F
42	
43	11F
44	11F
45	11F
46	17F
47	17F
48	11F
49	59S
50	17F
51	
52	11F
53	
54	11F
55	17F
57	11F
59	17F
60	11F
61	11F
62	11F
63	11F
64	11F
65	17F
66	17F
68	CEV
69	11F
71	11F

**Dassault Falcon
10 (MER)**
ES3, Hyeres;
ES57, Landivisiau

32	3S
101	3S
129	57S
133	57S
143	3S
185	57S

**Dassault Falcon
Guardian**
ES9 Noumea;
ES12 Papeete;
CEPA, Istres

48	12S
65	9S
72	12S
77	9S
80	CEPA

Dassault Rafale-M

M01	AMD-BA
M02	AMD-BA

Embraer EMB.121 Xingu
ES2, Lann Bihoué;
ES11, Le Bourget;
ES52, Lann Bihoué;
ES57, Landivisiau

30	11S
47	11S
55	11S
65	11S
66	52S
67	2S
68	52S
69	2S
70	11S
71	2S
74	52S
77	52S
79	52S
81	57S
83	52S
85	52S
87	52S
90	52S

**LTV F-8P
Crusader**
12 Flotille, Landivisiau

3
4
5
7
8
10
11
17
19
22
23
27
29
31
32
34
35
37
39

**Morane Saulnier 760
Paris**
ES57, Landivisiau

32
33
40
41
46
85
87
88

Nord 262 Fregate
ES2, Lann Bihoué;
ES3, Hyeres;
ES11, Le Bourget;
ES56, Nimes-Garons;
ES57, Landivisiau

1	11S
16	3S
28	2S
43	11S
45	3S
46	56S
51	56S
52	56S

53	56S
59	3S
60	2S
61	2S
62	2S
63	3S
65	2S
69	56S
70	2S
71	2S
72	56S
73	56S
75	56S
79	56S
100	56S
102	11S
104	11S

Piper Navajo
ES3, Hyeres

227
906
916
925
927
931

Westland Lynx
HAS2 (FN);
HAS4 (FN)*
31 Flotille, San Mandrier;
34 Flotille, Lanvéoc;
ES20, St Raphael

260	20S
262	35F
263	34F
264	31F
265	34F
266	34F
267	
268	
269	34F
270	31F
271	35F
272	34F
273	34F
274	34F
275	31F
276	31F
278	34F
620	31F
621	34F
622	34F
623	34F
624	34F
625	34F
627	34F
801*	31F
802*	34F
803*	31F
804*	35F
806*	34F
807*	31F
808*	34F
809*	31F
810*	31F
811*	34F
812*	31F
813*	31F
814*	34F

Aviation Legére de l'Armée deTerre (ALAT)
Cessna F.406 Caravan
3 GHL, Rennes

0008	AGS
0010	AGT

GERMANY
Luftwaffe, Marineflieger
Boeing 707-307C
FBS, Köln-Bonn

10+01
10+02
10+03
10+04

Airbus A310-304
FBS, Köln-Bonn

10+21
10+22
10+23

Tupolev Tu-154M
FBS, Köln-Bonn

11+01
11+02

Canadair CL601-1A Challenger
FBS, Köln-Bonn

12+01
12+02
12+03
12+04
12+05
12+06
12+07

VFW-Fokker 614-100
FBS, Köln-Bonn

17+01
17+02
17+03

Mikoyan MiG-29
JG-73, Preschen;
WTD-61, Ingolstadt
MiG-29A

29+01	JG-73
29+02	JG-73
29+03	JG-73
29+04	JG-73
29+05	JG-73
29+07	JG-73
29+08	JG-73
29+09	JG-73
29+10	JG-73
29+11	JG-73
29+12	JG-73
29+14	JG-73
29+15	JG-73
29+16	JG-73
29+17	JG-73
29+18	JG-73
29+20	JG-73
98+06	WTD-61
98+08	WTD-61

MiG-29UB

29+22	JG-73
29+23	WTD-61
29+24	JG-73
29+25	JG-73

McDF-4F Phantom
JG-71, Wittmundhaven;
JG-72, Hopsten;
JG-73, Pferdsfeld;
JG-74, Neuburg/Donau;
TsLw-1, Kaufbeuren;
WTD-61, Ingolstadt

37+01	JG-72
37+03	JG-71
37+04	TsLw-1
37+05	JG-72
37+06	JG-73
37+07	JG-72
37+08	JG-74
37+09	JG-73
37+10	JG-73
37+11	JG-74
37+12	JG-73
37+13	JG-74
37+14	TsLw-1
37+15	WTD-61
37+16	WTD-61
37+17	JG-72
37+18	JG-72
37+19	JG-72
37+20	JG-73
37+21	JG-73
37+22	JG-72
37+23	JG-72
37+24	JG-72
37+25	JG-73
37+26	JG-72
37+28	JG-71
37+29	JG-73
37+30	JG-73
37+31	JG-74
37+32	JG-74
37+33	JG-73
37+34	JG-73
37+35	JG-73
37+36	JG-73
37+37	JG-72
37+38	JG-73
37+39	JG-71
37+40	JG-73
37+41	JG-73
37+42	JG-73
37+43	JG-73
37+44	JG-73
37+45	JG-73
37+47	JG-73
37+48	JG-74
37+49	JG-74
37+50	JG-73
37+52	JG-73
37+53	JG-74
37+54	JG-72
37+55	JG-74
37+56	JG-74
37+57	JG-73
37+58	JG-73
37+60	JG-74
37+61	JG-74
37+63	JG-74
37+64	JG-74
37+65	JG-74
37+66	JG-74
37+67	JG-74
37+69	JG-73
37+70	JG-74
37+71	JG-74
37+72	JG-74
37+73	JG-73
37+75	JG-73
37+76	JG-74

37+77	JG-74	38+62	JG-72	41+75	FLGFFB
37+78	JG-71	38+63	JG-71		
37+79	JG-74	38+64	JG-72	**Panavia Tornado**	
37+81	JG-72	38+66	JG-71	**Strike/Trainer[1]/ECR[2]**	
37+82	JG-71	38+67	JG-72	TTTE, RAF Cottesmore;	
37+83	JG-74	38+68	JG-72	AkG-51, Schleswig/Jagel;	
37+84	JG-74	38+69	JG-71	JbG-31, Nörvenich;	
37+85	JG-71	38+70	JG-71	JbG-32, Lechfeld;	
37+86	JG-71	38+72	JG-73	JbG-33, Böchel;	
37+88	JG-72	38+73	JG-72	JbG-34, Memmingen;	
37+89	JG-74	38+74	JG-71	JbG-38, Jever;	
37+90	JG-71	38+75	JG-71	MBB, Manching;	
37+91	WTD-61			MFG-2, Eggebek;	
37+92	JG-74	**D-BD Alpha Jet**		TsLw-1, Kaufbeuren;	
37+93	JG-72	FLGFFB, Fürstenfeldbruck;		WTD-61, Ingolstadt	
37+94	JG-71	WTD-61, Ingolstadt		43+01[1]	[G-20] TTTE
37+96	JG-74	40+01	FLGFFB	43+02[1]	[G-21] TTTE
37+97	JG-74	40+02	WTD-61	43+03[1]	[G-22] TTTE
37+98	JG-71	40+03	FLGFFB	43+04[1]	JbG-31
38+00	JG-74	40+05	FLGFFB	43+05[1]	[G-24] TTTE
38+01	JG-72	40+09	FLGFFB	43+06[1]	[G-25] TTTE
38+02	JG-71	40+11	FLGFFB	43+07[1]	[G-26] TTTE
38+03	JG-71	40+12	FLGFFB	43+08[1]	[G-27] TTTE
38+04	JG-71	40+15	WTD-61	43+09[1]	[G-28] TTTE
38+05	JG-74	40+18	FLGFFB	43+10[1]	[G-29] TTTE
38+06	JG-71	40+22	FLGFFB	43+11[1]	[G-30] TTTE
38+07	JG-72	40+26	FLGFFB	43+12[1]	[G-70] TTTE
38+08	JG-72	40+27	FLGFFB	43+13	[G-71] TTTE
38+09	JG-71	40+40	FLGFFB	43+14	[G-72] TTTE
38+10	JG-71	40+44	FLGFFB	43+15[1]	[G-31] TTTE
38+11	JG-71	40+49	FLGFFB	43+16[1]	[G-32] TTTE
38+12	JG-71	40+56	WTD-61	43+17[1]	[G-33] TTTE
38+13	WTD-61	40+59	TsLw-3	43+18	JbG-34
38+14	JG-71	40+61	FLGFFB	43+19	JbG-31
38+16	JG-71	40+65	WTD-61	43+20	JbG-38
38+17	JG-71	40+76	FLGFFB	43+22[1]	JbG-38
38+18	JG-71	40+78	TsLw-3	43+23[1]	JbG-38
38+20	JG-72	40+85	FLGFFB	43+25	[G-75] TTTE
38+21	JG-72	40+93	FLGFFB	43+26	JbG-38
38+24	JG-72	40+94	FLGFFB	43+27	AkG-51
38+25	JG-71	41+02	FLGFFB	43+28	JbG-38
38+26	JG-72	41+04	FLGFFB	43+29[1]	JbG-31
38+27	JG-71	41+09	FLGFFB	43+30	JbG-38
38+28	JG-71	41+14	FLGFFB	43+31[1]	JbG-31
38+29	JG-72	41+25	FLGFFB	43+32	[G-73] TTTE
38+30	JG-71	41+26	FLGFFB	43+33[1]	JbG-38
38+31	JG-72	41+29	FLGFFB	43+34	TsLw-1
38+32	JG-72	41+30	WTD-61	43+35[1]	JbG-38
38+33	JG-74	41+34	FLGFFB	43+36	JbG-32
38+34	JG-73	41+35	FLGFFB	43+37[1]	JbG-38
38+36	JG-71	41+36	FLGFFB	43+38	JbG-34
38+37	JG-72	41+37	FLGFFB	43+40	JbG-38
38+38	JG-73	41+38	FLGFFB	43+41	JbG-31
38+39	JG-72	41+39	WTD-61	43+42[1]	[G-39] TTTE
38+40	JG-71	41+42	FLGFFB	43+43[1]	AkG-51
38+42	JG-72	41+45	FLGFFB	43+44[1]	AkG-51
38+43	JG-72	41+49	FLGFFB	43+45[1]	AkG-51
38+44	JG-71	41+53	FLGFFB	43+46	AkG-51
38+45	JG-72	41+55	FLGFFB	43+47	AkG-51
38+46	JG-72	41+56	FLGFFB	43+48	AkG-51
38+47	JG-72	41+57	WTD-61	43+50	AkG-51
38+48	JG-71	41+58	FLGFFB	43+52	AkG-51
38+49	JG-72	41+59	FLGFFB	43+53	AkG-51
38+50	JG-72	41+61	FLGFFB	43+54	AkG-51
38+51	JG-73	41+62	FLGFFB	43+55	MFG-2
38+53	JG-72	41+63	FLGFFB	43+57	MFG-2
38+54	JG-72	41+64	FLGFFB	43+58	AkG-51
38+55	JG-71	41+66	FLGFFB	43+59	MFG-2
38+56	JG-72	41+67	FLGFFB	43+60	AkG-51
38+57	JG-72	41+68	FLGFFB	43+61	TsLw-1
38+58	JG-71	41+71	FLGFFB	43+62	AkG-51
38+59	JG-71	41+72	FLGFFB	43+63	AkG-51
38+60	JG-71	41+73	FLGFFB	43+64	AkG-51
38+61	JG-72	41+74	FLGFFB	43+65	AkG-51

Germany

Reg	Unit	Reg	Unit	Reg	Unit
43+67	AkG-51	44+46	JbG-34	45+25	JbG-33
43+68	AkG-51	44+48	JbG-31	45+26	MFG-2
43+69	AkG-51	44+50	JbG-38	45+27	MFG-2
43+70	AkG-51	44+51	JbG-38	45+28	MFG-2
43+71	AkG-51	44+52	JbG-31	45+29	WTD-61
43+72	AkG-51	44+53	JbG-38	45+30	MFG-2
43+73	AkG-51	44+54	JbG-33	45+31	MFG-2
43+74	AkG-51	44+55	JbG-38	45+32	MFG-2
43+75	[G-77] TTTE	44+56	JbG-34	45+33	MFG-2
43+76	AkG-51	44+57	JbG-31	45+34	MFG-2
43+77	AkG-51	44+58	JbG-38	45+35	MFG-2
43+78	AkG-51	44+59	JbG-31	45+36	MFG-2
43+79	[G-76] TTTE	44+60	JbG-31	45+37	MFG-2
43+80	AkG-51	44+61	JbG-34	45+38	MFG-2
43+81	JbG-32	44+62	JbG-33	45+39	MFG-2
43+82	AkG-51	44+63	JbG-33	45+40	MFG-2
43+83	AkG-51	44+64	JbG-38	45+41	MFG-2
43+85	AkG-51	44+65	JbG-34	45+42	MFG-2
43+86	AkG-51	44+66	JbG-31	45+43	MFG-2
43+87	MFG-2	44+67	JbG-33	45+44	MFG-2
43+88	AkG-51	44+68	JbG-32	45+45	MFG-2
43+90¹	JbG-38	44+69	JbG-38	45+46	MFG-2
43+91¹	JbG-32	44+70	JbG-38	45+47	MFG-2
43+92¹	JbG-31	44+71	JbG-31	45+48	MFG-2
43+94¹	JbG-31	44+72¹	JbG-33	45+49	MFG-2
43+95	JbG-31	44+73¹	JbG-33	45+50	MFG-2
43+96	JbG-31	44+75¹	JbG-33	45+51	MFG-2
43+97¹	JbG-31	44+76	JbG-34	45+52	MFG-2
43+98	JbG-31	44+77	JbG-38	45+53	MFG-2
43+99	JbG-31	44+78	JbG-38	45+54	MFG-2
44+00	JbG-31	44+79	JbG-33	45+55	MFG-2
44+01¹	JbG-32	44+80	JbG-33	45+56	MFG-2
44+02	JbG-31	44+81	JbG-34	45+57	MFG-2
44+03	JbG-31	44+82	JbG-31	45+59	MFG-2
44+04	JbG-38	44+83	JbG-38	45+60¹	JbG-38
44+05¹	JbG-38	44+84	JbG-33	45+61¹	JbG-34
44+06	JbG-31	44+85	JbG-38	45+62¹	JbG-38
44+07	JbG-31	44+86	JbG-38	45+64	TsLw-1
44+08	JbG-38	44+87	JbG-32	45+65	MFG-2
44+09	JbG-31	44+88	JbG-33	45+66	MFG-2
44+10¹	JbG-38	44+89	JbG-33	45+67	MFG-2
44+11	JbG-34	44+90	JbG-33	45+68	MFG-2
44+12	JbG-38	44+91	JbG-33	45+69	MFG-2
44+13	TsLw-1	44+92	JbG-33	45+70¹	JbG-33
44+14	JbG-34	44+94	JbG-33	45+71	MFG-2
44+15¹	JbG-38	44+95	JbG-33	45+72	MFG-2
44+16	JbG-31	44+96	JbG-32	45+73¹	JbG-31
44+17	JbG-32	44+97	JbG-33	45+74	MFG-2
44+19	JbG-31	44+98	JbG-33	45+76	JbG-38
44+20¹	JbG-32	45+00	JbG-33	45+77¹	JbG-38
44+21	JbG-31	45+01	JbG-33	45+78	JbG-34
44+22	JbG-31	45+02	JbG-33	45+79	JbG-32
44+23	JbG-31	45+03	JbG-33	45+80	JbG-34
44+24	JbG-38	45+04	JbG-33	45+81	JbG-34
44+25¹	JbG-38	45+05	JbG-33	45+82	JbG-34
44+26	JbG-31	45+06	JbG-33	45+83	JbG-34
44+27	JbG-31	45+07	JbG-33	45+84	JbG-34
44+28	JbG-31	45+08	JbG-33	45+85	JbG-34
44+29	JbG-31	45+09	JbG-34	45+86	JbG-34
44+30	JbG-31	45+10	JbG-33	45+87	JbG-34
44+31	JbG-31	45+11	JbG-33	45+88	JbG-34
44+32	JbG-38	45+12¹	MFG-2	45+89	JbG-34
44+33	JbG-31	45+13¹	MFG-2	45+90	JbG-34
44+34	JbG-32	45+14¹	MFG-2	45+91	JbG-32
44+35	JbG-31	45+15¹	MFG-2	45+92	JbG-34
44+36¹	JbG-38	45+16¹	MFG-2	45+93	JbG-34
44+37¹	JbG-38	45+17	JbG-33	45+94	JbG-34
44+38¹	JbG-32	45+18	JbG-34	45+95	JbG-34
44+39¹	JbG-33	45+19	JbG-33	45+96	JbG-34
44+40	JbG-33	45+20	JbG-38	45+97	JbG-34
44+41	JbG-31	45+21	JbG-33	45+98	JbG-34
44+42	JbG-32	45+22	JbG-33	45+99¹	JbG-34
44+43	JbG-34	45+23	JbG-33	46+00	JbG-34
44+44	JbG-31	45+24	JbG-33	46+01	JbG-34

46+02	JbG-34	50+34	LTG-62	51+11	LTG-62
46+03	JbG-34	50+35	LTG-62	51+12	LTG-63
46+04[1]	MFG-2	50+36	LTG-62	51+13	LTG-61
46+05[1]	MFG-2	50+37	LTG-62	51+14	LTG-61
46+06[1]	JbG-32	50+38	LTG-62	51+15	LTG-61
46+07	JbG-34	50+40	LTG-61		
46+08	JbG-34	50+41	LTG-63	**LET L.410**	
46+09	JbG-34	50+42	LTG-63	FBS, Köln-Bonn	
46+10	WTD-61	50+43	LTG-61	53+08	
46+11	MFG-2	50+44	LTG-61	53+09	
46+12	MFG-2	50+45	LTG-63	53+10	
46+13	MFG-2	50+46	LTG-62	53+11	
46+14	MFG-2	50+47	LTG-61	53+12	
46+15	MFG-2	50+48	LTG-61		
46+18	MFG-2	50+49	LTG-61	**Dornier Do.228**	
46+19	MFG-2	50+50	LTG-63	WTD-61, Ingolstadt;	
46+20	MFG-2	50+51	LTG-61	MFG-5, Kiel-Holtenau	
46+21	MFG-2	50+52	LTG-62	57+01	MFG-5
46+22	MFG-2	50+53	LTG-62	98+78	WTD-61
46+23[2]	JbG-32	50+54	LTG-61		
46+24[2]	JbG-32	50+55	LTG-62	**Breguet Br1151 Atlantic**	
46+25[2]	JbG-32	50+56	LTG-63	*Elint	
46+26[2]	JbG-32	50+57	LTG-61	MFG-3, Nordholz	
46+27[2]	JbG-32	50+58	LTG-63	61+01	
46+28[2]	JbG-32	50+59	LTG-63	61+02*	
46+29[2]	JbG-32	50+60	LTG-62	61+03*	
46+30[2]	JbG-32	50+61	LTG-63	61+04	
46+31[2]	JbG-32	50+62	LTG-61	61+05	
46+32[2]	JbG-32	50+64	LTG-61	61+06*	
46+33[2]	JbG-32	50+65	LTG-62	61+08	
46+34[2]	JbG-32	50+66	LTG-61	61+09	
46+35[2]	JbG-32	50+67	LTG-63	61+10	
46+36[2]	JbG-32	50+68	LTG-61	61+11	
46+37[2]	JbG-32	50+69	LTG-61	61+12	
46+38[2]	JbG-32	50+70	WTD-61	61+13	
46+39[2]	JbG-32	50+71	LTG-63	61+14	
46+40[2]	JbG-32	50+72	LTG-61	61+15	
46+41[2]	JbG-32	50+73	LTG-62	61+16	
46+42[2]	JbG-38	50+74	LTG-61	61+17	
46+43[2]	JbG-32	50+75	WTD-61	61+18	
46+44[2]	JbG-32	50+76	LTG-63	61+19*	
46+45[2]	JbG-32	50+77	LTG-63	61+20*	
46+46[2]	JbG-32	50+78	LTG-62		
46+47[2]	JbG-32	50+79	LTG-63	**Westland**	
46+48[2]	JbG-38	50+81	LTG-62	**Lynx Mk88**	
46+49[2]	JbG-32	50+82	LTG-63	MFG-3, Nordholz	
46+50[2]	JbG-32	50+83	LTG-62	83+02	
46+51[2]	JbG-32	50+84	LTG-61	83+03	
46+52[2]	JbG-32	50+85	LTG-63	83+04	
46+53[2]	JbG-32	50+86	LTG-61	83+05	
46+54[2]	JbG-32	50+87	LTG-63	83+06	
46+55[2]	JbG-32	50+88	LTG-61	83+07	
46+56[2]	JbG-32	50+89	LTG-62	83+08	
46+57[2]	JbG-38	50+90	LTG-62	83+09	
98+02	WTD-61	50+91	LTG-62	83+10	
98+03[2]	WTD-61	50+92	LTG-61	83+11	
98+59	WTD-61	50+93	LTG-61	83+12	
98+60	WTD-61	50+94	LTG-63	83+13	
98+79[2]	WTD-61	50+95	LTG-63	83+14	
98+97[2]	WTD-61	50+96	LTG-61	83+15	
		50+97	LTG-62	83+17	
Transall C-160D		50+98	LTG-61	83+18	
LTG-61, Landsberg;		50+99	LTG-61	83+19	
LTG-62, Wunstorf;		51+00	LTG-62		
LTG-63, Hohn;		51+01	LTG-62	**Westland Sea**	
WTD-61, Ingolstadt		51+02	LTG-63	**King HAS41**	
50+06	LTG-63	51+03	LTG-62	MFG-5, Kiel-Holtenau	
50+07	LTG-61	51+04	LTG-61	89+50	
50+08	LTG-61	51+05	LTG-62	89+51	
50+09	LTG-62	51+06	LTG-63	89+52	
50+10	LTG-62	51+07	LTG-62	89+53	
50+17	LTG-62	51+08	LTG-63	89+54	
50+29	LTG-62	51+09	LTG-63	89+55	
50+33	LTG-61	51+10	LTG-61	89+56	

89+57	
89+58	
89+59	
89+60	
89+61	
89+62	
89+63	
89+64	
89+65	
89+66	
89+67	
89+68	
89+69	
89+70	
89+71	

Eurofighter 2000
98+29   MBB   (ZH586)

English Electric
Canberra B2
WTD-61, Ingolstadt
99+34

Heeresfliegertruppe
Sikorsky/VFW CH-53G
HFlgRgt-15, Rheine-
Bentlage;
HFlgRgt-25, Laupheim;
HFlgRgt-35, Mendig;
HFWS, Bückeburg;
Tslw-3, Fassberg;
WTD-61, Ingolstadt

84+01	WTD-61
84+02	WTD-61
84+03	HFR-15
84+04	Tslw-3
84+05	HFR-35
84+06	HFR-35
84+07	HFWS
84+08	HFR-35
84+09	HFR-25
84+10	HFWS
84+11	HFWS
84+12	HFR-15
84+13	HFWS
84+14	HFWS
84+15	HFR-25
84+16	HFWS
84+17	HFR-25
84+18	HFWS
84+19	HFWS
84+20	HFR-35
84+21	HFWS
84+22	HFR-35
84+23	HFR-25
84+24	HFR-35
84+25	HFR-35
84+26	HFR-35
84+27	HFR-35
84+28	HFR-35
84+29	HFR-35
84+30	HFR-35
84+31	HFR-35
84+32	HFR-35
84+33	HFR-35
84+34	HFR-35
84+35	HFR-35
84+36	HFR-35
84+37	HFR-35

84+38	HFR-35
84+39	HFR-35
84+40	HFR-25
84+41	HFWS
84+42	HFR-25
84+43	HFR-25
84+44	HFR-25
84+45	HFR-25
84+46	HFR-25
84+47	HFR-25
84+48	HFR-25
84+49	HFWS
84+50	HFR-25
84+51	HFR-25
84+52	HFR-25
84+53	HFR-25
84+54	HFR-25
84+55	HFR-25
84+56	HFR-25
84+57	HFR-25
84+58	HFR-25
84+59	HFR-25
84+60	HFR-25
84+61	HFR-25
84+62	HFR-25
84+63	HFR-25
84+64	HFR-25
84+65	HFR-35
84+66	HFR-35
84+67	HFR-35
84+68	HFR-15
84+69	HFR-15
84+70	HFR-15
84+71	HFR-15
84+72	HFR-15
84+73	HFR-15
84+74	HFR-15
84+75	HFR-15
84+76	HFR-15
84+77	HFR-15
84+78	HFR-15
84+79	HFR-15
84+80	HFR-15
84+82	HFR-15
84+83	HFR-15
84+84	HFR-15
84+85	HFR-15
84+86	HFR-15
84+87	HFR-15
84+88	HFR-15
84+89	HFR-15
84+90	HFR-15
84+91	HFR-15
84+92	HFR-35
84+93	HFR-35
84+94	HFR-35
84+95	HFR-25
84+96	HFR-25
84+97	HFR-25
84+98	HFR-15
84+99	HFR-15
85+00	HFR-15
85+01	HFR-35
85+02	HFR-35
85+03	HFR-35
85+04	HFR-25
85+05	HFR-25
85+06	HFR-25
85+07	HFR-15
85+08	HFR-15
85+09	HFR-15
85+10	HFR-35
85+11	HFR-25
85+12	HFR-15

GHANA
Air Force
   Short SC7 Skyvan
   No 1 Transport Sqn,
      Takoradi
   G450 [A]
   G451 [B]
   G452 [C]
   G453 [D]
   G454 [E]
   G455 [F]

GREECE
Helliniki Aeroporia
   Lockheed
   C-130H Hercules
   356 Mira, Elefsis
   741
   742
   743
   744
   745
   746
   747
   749
   750
   751
   752

HUNGARY
Magyar Honvédseg Repülö
Csapatai
   Antonov An-26
   Szolnok Mixed Air Carrier
   Regiment

202	(02202)
203	(02203)
204	(02204)
208	(02208)
209	(02209)
405	(03405)
406	(03406)
407	(03407)
603	(03603)

ISRAEL
Heyl Ha'Avir
   Lockheed Hercules
   103 Sqn, 131 Sqn, Lod
   C-130E
   208
   301
   304/4X-FBE
   305/4X-FBJ
   307/4X-FBN
   310/4X-FBG
   311/4X-FBD
   313/4X-FBL
   314
   316/4X-FBM
   318

   C-130H
   102/4X-FBA
   106/4X-FBB
   309
   420
   427
   428/4X-FBX
   435/4X-FBT
   436/4X-FBW
   448/4X-FBU

KC-130H
545/4X-FBZ
622

ITALY
Aeronautica Militare Italiano
Aeritalia G222
46ª Brigata Aerea, Pisa;
14º Stormo, Pratica di Mare;
RSV, Pratica di Mare

MM62101	RS-45
MM62102	46-20
MM62104	46-91
MM62105	46-82
MM62108	46-30
MM62109	46-96
MM62110	46-81
MM62111	46-83
MM62112	46-85
MM62114	46-80
MM62115	46-22
MM62117	46-25
MM62118	46-24
MM62119	46-21
MM62120	46-90
MM62121	46-86
MM62122	46-23
MM62123	46-28
MM62124	46-88
MM62125	46-87
MM62126	46-26
MM62127	46-27
MM62130	RS-51
MM62132	46-32
MM62133	46-93
MM62134	46-33
MM62143	46-36
MM62144	46-98
MM62145	46-50
MM62146	46-51
MM62147	46-52

Aeritalia G222TCM

MM62103	46-37
MM62135	46-94
MM62136	46-97
MM62137	46-95
MM62152	
MM62153	46-99
MM62154	
MM62155	

Aeritalia G222RM

MM62107	
MM62138	
MM62139	14-20
MM62140	14-21
MM62141	14-22
MM62142	(14º Stormo)

Aeritalia-EMB AMX/AMX-T*
2º Stormo, Rivolto;
3º Stormo, Villafranca;
51º Stormo, Istrana;
RSV, Pratica di Mare

MMX595	Aeritalia
MMX596	Alenia
MMX597	Alenia
MMX599	Alenia
MM7089	3-34
MM7090	RS-12
MM7091	
MM7092	RS-14

MM7093	3-11
MM7094	3-42
MM7095	51-33
MM7096	51-62
MM7097	3-36
MM7098	3-35
MM7099	2-02
MM7100	51-63
MM7101	51-41
MM7102	2-03
MM7103	51-34
MM7104	51-31
MM7105	2-04
MM7106	51-37
MM7107	3-25
MM7109	51-45
MM7110	2-14
MM7111	51-50
MM7112	51-52
MM7114	2-07
MM7115	2-12
MM7116	
MM7117	3-41
MM7118	2-11
MM7119	3-24
MM7120	3-30
MM7121	3-31
MM7122	3-32
MM7123	3-13
MM7124	3-40
MM7125	3-15
MM7126	3-53
MM7127	3-22
MM7128	3-23
MM7129	3-30
MM7130	51-43
MM7131	RS-13
MM7132	
MM7133	51-57
MM7134	3-01
MM7135	51-32
MM7138	51-56
MM7139	3-02
MM7140	2-06
MM7141	51-55
MM7142	3-04
MM7143	3-05
MM7144	3-03
MM7145	3-06
MM7146	2-23
MM7147	2-20
MM7148	2-21
MM7149	51-53
MM7150	51-40
MM7151	51-42
MM7152	3-07
MM7153	2-16
MM7154	51-54
MM7155	2-24
MM7156	2-22
MM7157	51-51
MM7158	
MM7159	3-33
MM7160	51-30
MM55024*	Aeritalia
MM55025*	(RSV)
MM55026*	Aeritalia
MM55027*	
MM55028*	
MM55029*	

Aermacchi MB339
Frecce Tricolori
(313 Gruppo), Rivolto;

61ª Brigata Aerea, Lecce;
14º Stormo, Pratica di Mare;
RSV, Pratica di Mare

MM54438	61-93
MM54439	6*
MM54440	61-00
MM54442	61-95
MM54443	61-50
MM54445	8*
MM54446	61-01
MM54447	61-02
MM54448	61-03
MM54449	61-04
MM54450	61-94
MM54451	61-86
MM54452	61-41
MM54453	61-05
MM54454	61-06
MM54455	61-07
MM54456	RS-10
MM54457	61-11
MM54458	61-12
MM54459	61-13
MM54460	61-14
MM54461	61-15
MM54462	61-16
MM54463	61-17
MM54464	61-20
MM54465	61-21
MM54467	61-23
MM54468	61-24
MM54469	61-25
MM54470	61-26
MM54471	61-27
MM54472	61-30
MM54473	4*
MM54475	
MM54476	
MM54477	9*
MM54478	7*
MM54479	1*
MM54480	0*
MM54482	5*
MM54483	13*
MM54484	3*
MM54485	10*
MM54486	2*
MM54487	61-31
MM54488	61-32
MM54489	61-33
MM54490	61-34
MM54491	61-35
MM54492	61-36
MM54493	61-37
MM54494	61-40
MM54496	61-42
MM54497	61-43
MM54498	61-44
MM54499	61-45
MM54500	61-46
MM54503	61-51
MM54504	61-52
MM54505	61-53
MM54506	61-54
MM54507	61-55
MM54508	61-56
MM54509	61-57
MM54510	61-60
MM54511	(RSV)
MM54512	61-62
MM54513	61-63
MM54514	61-64
MM54515	61-65

MM54516	61-66
MM54517	61-67
MM54518	61-70
MM54532	61-71
MM54533	61-72
MM54534	61-73
MM54535	61-74
MM54536	9*
MM54537	
MM54538	61-75
MM54539	61-76
MM54540	61-77
MM54541	61-80
MM54542	61-81
MM54543	61-82
MM54544	61-83
MM54545	61-84
MM54546	61-85
MM54547	61-87
MM54548	61-90
MM54549	61-91
MM54550	61-92
MM54551	
MM54553	
MM54554	61-95

Boeing 707-328B/-3F5C*
14° Stormo, Pratica di Mare;
31° Stormo, Roma-Ciampino

MM62148	14-01
MM62149	(14)
MM62150*	(31)
MM62151*	14-02

Breguet Br1150 Atlantic
30° Stormo, Cagliari;
41° Stormo, Catania

MM40108	41-70
MM40109	30-71
MM40110	41-72
MM40111	41-73
MM40112	30-74
MM40113	30-75
MM40114	41-76
MM40115	41-77
MM40116	30-01
MM40117	41-02
MM40118	30-03
MM40119	30-04
MM40120	41-05
MM40121	41-06
MM40122	30-07
MM40123	30-10
MM40124	41-11
MM40125	30-12

Dassault Falcon 50
31° Stormo, Roma-Ciampino

MM62020	
MM62021	
MM62026	
MM62029	

Grumman Gulfstream III
31° Stormo, Roma-Ciampino

MM62022	
MM62025	

Lockheed F-104 Starfighter
4° Stormo, Grosseto;
5° Stormo, Rimini;
9° Stormo, Grazzanise;
36° Stormo, Gioia del Colle;
37° Stormo, Trapani;
51° Stormo, Istrana;
53° Stormo, Cameri

F-104S

MM6701	36-13
MM6703	51-23
MM6704	5-42
MM6705	
MM6710	
MM6713	53-05
MM6714	
MM6716	53-21
MM6717	9-32
MM6719	51-06
MM6720	9-40
MM6721	9-42
MM6722	5-45
MM6726	4-21
MM6727	9-45
MM6730	9-33
MM6731	4-10
MM6732	36-02
MM6733	36-10
MM6734	9-43
MM6735	51-22
MM6736	
MM6737	5-43
MM6739	51-01
MM6740	9-35
MM6741	37-21
MM6742	36-
MM6744	5-07
MM6747	37-24
MM6748	
MM6749	9-41
MM6750	37-04
MM6756	37-10
MM6758	
MM6759	37-26
MM6760	4-50
MM6761	4-3
MM6762	5-37
MM6763	53-12
MM6764	
MM6767	51-05
MM6768	36-05
MM6769	53-06
MM6770	5-30
MM6771	5-31
MM6772	9-52
MM6773	
MM6774	36-21
MM6775	9-50
MM6776	
MM6778	4-4
MM6780	
MM6781	
MM6782	37-15
MM6784	37-27
MM6785	5-25
MM6786	37-21
MM6787	4-7
MM6788	5-01
MM6789	37-02
MM6791	36-14
MM6792	5-21
MM6794	37-20
MM6795	5-46
MM6796	
MM6797	
MM6798	4-5
MM6800	
MM6802	4-1

MM6804	51-07
MM6805	36-06
MM6807	5-41
MM6808	9-30
MM6809	36-03
MM6810	9-31
MM6812	5-36
MM6814	53-16
MM6815	
MM6816	53-14
MM6817	
MM6818	36-22
MM6819	9-31
MM6821	5-16
MM6822	
MM6823	
MM6824	53-02
MM6825	36-11
MM6826	53-03
MM6827	5-27
MM6828	36-07
MM6830	5-27
MM6831	4-22
MM6833	5-22
MM6835	36-12
MM6836	5-10
MM6838	
MM6839	4-6
MM6840	37-25
MM6841	
MM6842	
MM6843	
MM6844	
MM6845	5-11
MM6847	37-11
MM6848	53-04
MM6849	5-33
MM6850	
MM6870	51-04
MM6872	53-15
MM6873	
MM6875	5-32
MM6876	5-40
MM6878	53-10
MM6879	51-02
MM6880	4-12
MM6881	
MM6886	5-02
MM6887	9-51
MM6890	
MM6908	36-16
MM6909	
MM6910	37-12
MM6912	53-03
MM6913	51-10
MM6914	5-13
MM6915	5-15
MM6916	37-03
MM6918	37-22
MM6920	5-35
MM6921	
MM6922	5-04
MM6923	
MM6924	
MM6925	53-01
MM6926	
MM6929	
MM6930	4-20
MM6932	
MM6934	51-14
MM6935	
MM6936	
MM6937	51-16
MM6938	4-16

MM6939	53-11		MM7016		MM55006[1]	
MM6940	4-11		MM7017	50-04	MM55007[1]	50-51
MM6941	51-20		MM7018		MM55008[1]	6-40
MM6942	53-13		MM7019	19	MM55009[1]	
MM6943	36-20		MM7020	50-12	MM55010[1]	50-50
MM6944	5-24		MM7021	6-21	MM55011[1]	36-55
MM6946	37-06		MM7022	6-02		

TF-104G

MM54226	4-23		MM7023	50-03	
MM54228	4-26		MM7024	24	

Piaggio RP-180 Avanti
RSV, Pratica di Mare

MM54232	4-29		MM7025		
MM54233	4-30		MM7026	50-06	MM62159	RSV
MM54237	4-32		MM7027	6-47	MM62160	54 RSV
MM54250	4-33		MM7028		MM62161	RSV
MM54251	4-34		MM7029	6-25	MM62162	
MM54253	4-35		MM7030	6-14	MM62163	
MM54254	4-36		MM7031	50-01	MM62164	RSV
MM54255	4-37		MM7033	6-03	
MM54256	4-38		MM7034	6-04	

Piaggio-Douglas PD-808/
[1]PD-808-GE/[2]PD-808-RM/
[3]PD-808-TA
14º Stormo, Pratica di Mare;
31º Stormo, Roma-
Ciampino;
RSV, Pratica di Mare

MM54257	4-39		MM7035	35	
MM54258	4-40		MM7036	6-43	
MM54260	4-41		MM7037	6-15	
MM54261	4-42		MM7038	36-33	
MM54552			MM7039	50-30	
MM54553	4-44		MM7040	36-35	MM577[3]	RS-48
MM54554	4-48		MM7041	50-42	MM578[3]	RS-49
MM54555	4-45		MM7042		MM61948	(14)
MM54556	4-47		MM7043	43	MM61949	(14)
MM54557			MM7044		MM61950	14-50
MM54558	4-46		MM7046	50-36	MM61951	(31)

Lockheed
C-130H Hercules
46ª Brigata Aerea, Pisa

			MM7047	36-36	MM61952[1]	(14)
			MM7048	36-54 (Alenia)	MM61953[3]	(31)
			MM7049	50-44	MM61954[3]	(31)
MM61988	46-02		MM7050	50	MM61955[1]	(14)
MM61989	46-03		MM7051	36-32	MM61956[2]	(14)
MM61990	46-04		MM7052	6-32	MM61957[3]	(14)
MM61991	46-05		MM7053	53	MM61958[1]	(14)
MM61992	46-06		MM7054	6-54	MM61959[1]	(14)
MM61993	46-07		MM7055	6-55	MM61960[1]	(14)
MM61994	46-08		MM7056	36-52	MM61961[1]	(14)
MM61995	46-09		MM7057	36-54	MM61962[1]	(14)
MM61997	46-11		MM7058	36-57	MM62014[2]	(14)
MM61998	46-12		MM7059	36-50	MM62015[2]	(14)
MM61999	46-13		MM7060		MM62016[2]	(14)
MM62001	46-15		MM7061	36-41	MM62017[2]	(14)
			MM7062	36-53	
			MM7063	36-43	

McDonnell Douglas
DC-9-32
31º Stormo, Roma-Ciampino

			MM7064	50-43
			MM7065	
MM62012			MM7066	6-44
MM62013			MM7067	36-45

Marina Militare Italiano
McDonnell AV-8B/TAV-8B
Harrier II+
6º Reparto Aeromobili,
Taranto

AV-8B

			MM7068	6-26	
			MM7069	6-07	

Panavia Tornado
Strike/Trainer[1]/ECR[2]
TTTE, RAF Cottesmore;
6º Stormo, Ghedi;
36º Stormo, Gioia del Colle;
50º Stormo, Piacenza;
RSV, Pratica di Mare

			MM7070	6-07	
			MM7071	6-42	MM7199	1-03
			MM7072	6-36	MM7200	1-04
			MM7073	6-45	MM7201	1-05
			MM7074	6-12	MM7202	1-06
MM586			MM7075	36-31	MM7203	1-07
MM7002	I-92 TTTE		MM7078	50-32	MM7204	1-08
MM7003	I-93 TTTE		MM7079[2]	(Alenia)	MM7205	1-09
MM7004	36-37		MM7080	6-31	MM7206	1-10
MM7005			MM7081	RS-01	MM7207	1-11
MM7006	6-16		MM7082	RS-02	MM7208	1-12
MM7007	50-31		MM7083	36-30	MM7209	1-13
MM7008			MM7084	36-42	MM7210	1-14
MM7009	50-44		MM7085	36-50 (Alenia)	MM7211	1-15
MM7010			MM7086	36-40	MM7212	1-16
MM7011	6-11		MM7087	50-37	MM7213	1-17
MM7013	6-13		MM7088	6-27	MM7214	1-18
MM7014			MM55000[1]	I-42 TTTE	**TAV-8B**	
MM7015	50-05		MM55001[1]	I-40 TTTE	MM55032	1-01
			MM55002[1]	I-41 TTTE	MM55033	1-02
			MM55003[1]	I-43 TTTE	
			MM55004[1]	I-44 TTTE	
			MM55005[1]	I-45 TTTE	

Jordan – Netherlands

JORDAN
Al Quwwatal-Jawwiya
al Malakiya al-Urduniya
    Lockheed C-130H
    Hercules
    3 Sqn, Amman
    344
    345
    346
    347

KUWAIT
Kuwait Air Force
    McDonnell Douglas
    DC9-32
    42 Sqn, Ali Al Salem
    KAF321

    McDonnell Douglas
    DC9-83
    42 Sqn, Ali Al Salem
    KAF26

    Lockheed
    L100-30 Hercules
    41 Sqn, Kuwait International
    KAF323
    KAF324
    KAF325

LUXEMBOURG
NATO
    Boeing E-3A
    NAEWF, Geilenkirchen
    LX-N90442
    LX-N90443
    LX-N90444
    LX-N90445
    LX-N90446
    LX-N90447
    LX-N90448
    LX-N90449
    LX-N90450
    LX-N90451
    LX-N90452
    LX-N90453
    LX-N90454
    LX-N90455
    LX-N90456
    LX-N90457
    LX-N90458
    LX-N90459

    Boeing 707-329C
    NAEWF, Geilenkirchen
    LX-N19996
    LX-N20198
    LX-N20199

MOROCCO
Force Aerienne Royaume
    Marocaine
    CAP-230
    Green March
    04   CN-ABD
    05   CN-ABF
    06   CN-ABI
    07   CN-ABJ
    08   CN-ABK
    09   CN-ABL

Lockheed C-130H
Hercules

4535	CN-AOA
4551	CN-AOC
4575	CN-AOD
4581	CN-AOE
4583	CN-AOF
4713	CN-AOG
4717	CN-AOH
4733	CN-AOI
4738	CN-AOJ
4739	CN-AOK
4742	CN-AOL
4875	CN-AOM
4876	CN-AON
4877	CN-AOO
4888	CN-AOP
4892	CN-AOQ
4907	CN-AOR
4909	CN-AOS
4940	CN-AOT

NETHERLANDS
Koninklijke Luchtmacht
    Agusta-Bell AB.412
    SAR Flight, Leeuwarden
    R-01
    R-02
    R-03

    Fokker F-27-100
    Friendship
    334 Sqn, Eindhoven
    C-1
    C-2
    C-3

    Fokker F-27-300M
    Troopship
    334 Sqn, Eindhoven
    C-4
    C-5
    C-6
    C-7
    C-8
    C-9
    C-11

    Fokker 60
    334 Sqn, Eindhoven
    U-01
    U-02
    U-03
    U-04

    General Dynamics
    F-16A/F-16B*
    TGp/306/311/312Sqns,
      Volkel;
    313/315 Sqns, Twente;
    314 Sqn, Gilze-Rijen;
    322/323 Sqns, Leeuwarden

J-001	311 Sqn
J-002	315 Sqn
J-003	315 Sqn
J-004	311 Sqn
J-005	313 Sqn
J-006	311/312 Sqn
J-008	311/312 Sqn
J-009	311 Sqn
J-010	312 Sqn
J-011	311/312 Sqn
J-012	311/312 Sqn
J-013	311 Sqn

J-014	315 Sqn
J-015	311 Sqn
J-016	311 Sqn
J-017	315 Sqn
J-018	312 Sqn
J-019	311 Sqn
J-020	315 Sqn
J-021	311 Sqn
J-055	315 Sqn
J-057	313 Sqn
J-058	312 Sqn
J-059	311 Sqn
J-060	311 Sqn
J-061	311/312 Sqn
J-062	311 Sqn
J-063	311 Sqn
J-064*	311/312 Sqn
J-065*	306 Sqn
J-066*	311 Sqn
J-067*	311 Sqn
J-068*	311 Sqn
J-135	314 Sqn
J-136	314 Sqn
J-137	314 Sqn
J-138	312 Sqn
J-139	314 Sqn
J-140	322 Sqn
J-141	322 Sqn
J-142	314 Sqn
J-143	314 Sqn
J-144	314 Sqn
J-145	314 Sqn
J-146	314 Sqn
J-192	322 Sqn
J-193	322 Sqn
J-194	322 Sqn
J-196	322 Sqn
J-197	322 Sqn
J-198	322 Sqn
J-199	322 Sqn
J-201	314 Sqn
J-202	322 Sqn
J-203	322 Sqn
J-204	322 Sqn
J-205	322 Sqn
J-206	314 Sqn
J-207	315 Sqn
J-208*	322 Sqn
J-209*	322 Sqn
J-210*	314 Sqn
J-211*	322 Sqn
J-212	312 Sqn
J-213	312 Sqn
J-214	312 Sqn
J-215	312 Sqn
J-218	315 Sqn
J-220	312 Sqn
J-223	312 Sqn
J-226	323 Sqn
J-228	315 Sqn
J-230	315 Sqn
J-231	315 Sqn
J-232	312 Sqn
J-234	314 Sqn
J-235	312 Sqn
J-236	314 Sqn
J-239	315 Sqn
J-240	315 Sqn
J-241	315 Sqn
J-243	315 Sqn
J-246	315 Sqn
J-248	315 Sqn
J-249	315 Sqn
J-250	312 Sqn

J-251	313 Sqn
J-253	313 Sqn
J-254	312 Sqn
J-255	313 Sqn
J-256	312 Sqn
J-259*	313 Sqn
J-261*	313 Sqn
J-262*	313 Sqn
J-264*	313 Sqn
J-265*	313 Sqn
J-266*	313 Sqn
J-267*	315 Sqn
J-270*	315 Sqn
J-360	314 Sqn
J-361	314 Sqn
J-362	323 Sqn
J-363	323 Sqn
J-365	323 Sqn
J-366	323 Sqn
J-367	314 Sqn
J-368*	314 Sqn
J-369*	315 Sqn
J-508	311 Sqn
J-509	311/312 Sqn
J-510	314 Sqn
J-511	311/312 Sqn
J-512	311 Sqn
J-513	315 Sqn
J-514	311/312 Sqn
J-515*	311/312 Sqn
J-516*	315 Sqn
J-616	322 Sqn
J-617	322 Sqn
J-619	322 Sqn
J-620	322 Sqn
J-622	311 Sqn
J-623	322 Sqn
J-624	322 Sqn
J-627	306 Sqn
J-628	306 Sqn
J-630	306 Sqn
J-631	306 Sqn
J-632	306 Sqn
J-633	306 Sqn
J-635	306 Sqn
J-636	306 Sqn
J-637	306 Sqn
J-638	306 Sqn
J-640	306 Sqn
J-641	306 Sqn
J-642	306 Sqn
J-643	306 Sqn
J-644	306 Sqn
J-646	306 Sqn
J-647	306 Sqn
J-648	306 Sqn
J-649*	323 Sqn
J-650*	Lockheed
J-651*	306 Sqn
J-652*	313 Sqn
J-653*	TGp
J-654*	323 Sqn
J-655*	322 Sqn
J-656*	322 Sqn
J-657*	323 Sqn
J-864	306 Sqn
J-866	323 Sqn
J-867	306 Sqn
J-868	323 Sqn
J-869	323 Sqn
J-871	323 Sqn
J-872	323 Sqn
J-873	323 Sqn
J-874	323 Sqn

J-875	323 Sqn
J-876	323 Sqn
J-877	323 Sqn
J-878	323 Sqn
J-879	323 Sqn
J-881	323 Sqn
J-882*	323 Sqn
J-884*	314 Sqn
J-885*	313 Sqn

Lockheed C-130H-30 Hercules
334 Sqn, Eindhoven
G-273
G-275

MBB Bo.105CB/ Bo.105CD[1]
299 Sqn, Deelen
B-37
B-38
B-39
B-40
B-42
B-43
B-44
B-47
B-48
B-63
B-64
B-66
B-67
B-68
B-69
B-70
B-71
B-72
B-74
B-75
B-76
B-77
B-78
B-79
B-80
B-83[1]

McDonnell-Douglas KDC-10
334 Sqn, Eindhoven
T-235
T-264

Pilatus PC-7
EMVO, Woensdrecht
L-01
L-02
L-03
L-04
L-05
L-06
L-07
L-08
L-09
L-10

Sud Alouette III
*Grasshoppers**
298 Sqn, Soesterberg;
300 Sqn, Deelen;
302 Sqn, Deelen
A-177
A-208
A-209
A-217

A-218
A-226
A-227
A-235
A-246
A-247
A-253
A-261
A-266
A-267
A-275
A-292
A-293
A-301
A-302
A-307
A-324*
A-336
A-342
A-343
A-350*
A-366
A-374
A-390*
A-398*
A-399
A-407
A-414
A-451
A-452
A-453*
A-464
A-465*
A-471
A-482
A-483
A-488
A-489
A-494
A-495
A-499
A-500
A-514
A-515
A-521
A-522
A-528
A-529
A-535
A-536
A-542
A-549
A-550

Marine Luchtvaart Dienst Fokker F-27-200MPA
336 Sqn, Hato, Antilles
M-1
M-2

Lockheed P-3C Orion
MARPAT, Valkenburg,
Sigonella and Keflavik
300
301
302
303
304
305
306
307
308
309

310
311
312

Westland SH-14D Lynx
7 Sqn & 860 Sqn, De Kooij
260	860 Sqn
261	860 Sqn
262	860 Sqn
264	860 Sqn
265	860 Sqn
266	860 Sqn
267	860 Sqn
268	860 Sqn
269	860 Sqn
270	860 Sqn
271	860 Sqn
272	7 Sqn
273	860 Sqn
274	860 Sqn
276	860 Sqn
277	860 Sqn
278	860 Sqn
279	860 Sqn
280	860 Sqn
281	860 Sqn
282	860 Sqn
283	7 Sqn

NEW ZEALAND
Royal New Zealand Air Force
Boeing 727-22C
40 Sqn, Whenuapai
NZ7271
NZ7272

Lockheed
C-130H Hercules
40 Sqn, Whenuapai
NZ7001
NZ7002
NZ7003
NZ7004
NZ7005

Lockheed
P-3K Orion
5 Sqn, Whenuapai
NZ4201
NZ4202
NZ4203
NZ4204
NZ4205
NZ4206

NIGERIA
Federal Nigerian Air Force
Lockheed
C-130H Hercules
Lagos
NAF-910
NAF-912
NAF-913
NAF-914
NAF-915
NAF-917
NAF-918
NAF-918 (NAF916)

NORWAY
Kongelige Norske
Luftforsvaret
Dassault
Falcon 20 ECM
335 Skv, Gardermoen

041
053
0125

DHC-6 Twin Otter
719 Skv, Bodø
184
7057
7062

General Dynamics
F-16A/*F-16B
331 Skv, Bodø (*r/w/bl*);
334 Skv, Bodø;
332 Skv, Rygge (*y/bk*);
338 Skv, Ørland
272	332 Skv
273	332 Skv
274	332 Skv
275	332 Skv
276	332 Skv
277	332 Skv
278	332 Skv
279	332 Skv
281	332 Skv
282	332 Skv
284	332 Skv
285	332 Skv
288	338 Skv
289	338 Skv
291	338 Skv
292	338 Skv
293	338 Skv
295	338 Skv
297	338 Skv
298	338 Skv
299	338 Skv
302*	332 Skv
304*	332 Skv
305*	332 Skv
306*	332 Skv
307*	332 Skv
658	334 Skv
659	334 Skv
660	334 Skv
661	334 Skv
662	334 Skv
663	334 Skv
664	334 Skv
665	334 Skv
666	334 Skv
667	334 Skv
668	334 Skv
669	334 Skv
670	334 Skv
671	335 Skv
672	331 Skv
673	331 Skv
674	331 Skv
675	331 Skv
677	331 Skv
678	331 Skv
680	331 Skv
681	331 Skv
682	331 Skv
683	331 Skv
686	331 Skv
687	331 Skv
688	331 Skv
689*	338 Skv
690*	338 Skv
691*	334 Skv
692*	334 Skv
693*	338 Skv
711*	331 Skv
712*	331 Skv

Lockheed
C-130H Hercules
335 Skv, Gardermoen
952
953
954
955
956
957

Lockheed P-3C Orion
333 Skv, Andøya
3296
3297
3298
3299

Lockheed P-3N Orion
333 Skv Andøya
4576
6603

Northrop F-5A
336 Skv, Rygge
128
130
131
132
133
134
208
210
215
225
895
896
898
902

Northrop F-5B
336 Skv, Rygge
136
241
243
244
387
594
595
906
907
908
909

Westland Sea King Mk43/
Mk43A^A/Mk43B^B
330 Skv, Bodø
060^A
062
066^A
069
070^A
071^B
072^A
073^A
074^A
189
322^B

Kystvakt (Coast Guard)
Westland Lynx Mk86
337 Skv, Bardufoss
207
216
228
232
237
350

OMAN
Royal Air Force of Oman
BAC 1-11/485GD
4 Sqn, Seeb
551
552
553

Lockheed
C-130H Hercules
4 Sqn, Seeb
501
502
503

Short Skyvan 3M
2 Sqn, Seeb
901
902
903
904
905
906
907
908
910
911
912
913
914
915
916

PAKISTAN
Air Force
Boeing 707-340C

68-19866	12 Sqn
69-19635	12 Sqn

PORTUGAL
Forca Aerea Portuguesa
CASA212A/212ECM*
Aviocar
401 Esq, Sintra;
502 Esq, Sintra;
503 Esq, Lajes;
552 Esq, Sintra

16501	502 Esq
16502*	401 Esq
16503	502 Esq
16504	502 Esq
16505	502 Esq
16506	502 Esq
16507	502 Esq
16508	502 Esq
16509	401 Esq
16510	401 Esq
16511	502 Esq
16512	401 Esq
16513	503 Esq
16514	503 Esq
16515	503 Esq
16517	503 Esq
16519	401 Esq
16520	503 Esq
16521*	401 Esq
16522*	401 Esq
16523*	401 Esq
16524*	401 Esq

D-BD Alpha Jet
103 Esq, Beja;
301 Esq, Beja
15201
15202
15203
15204
15205
15206
15207
15208
15209
15210
15211
15212
15213
15214
15215
15216
15217
15218
15219
15220
15221
15222
15223
15224
15225
15226
15227
15228
15229
15230
15231
15232
15233
15234
15235
15236
15237
15238
15239
15240
15241
15242
15243
15244
15245
15246
15247
15248
15249
15250

Dassault
Falcon 20C
504 Esq, Lisbon/Montijo
17101
17102
17103

Dassault
Falcon 50
504 Esq, Lisbon/Montijo
17401
17402
17403

Lockheed
C-130H/C-130H-30*
Hercules
501 Esq, Lisbon/Montijo
16801
16802
16803
16804
16805
16806*

Lockheed (GD)
F-16A/F-16B*
201 Esq, Monte Real
15101
15102
15103
15104
15105
15106
15107
15108
15109
15110
15111
15112
15113
15114
15115
15116
15117
15118*
15119*
15120*

Lockheed P-3P Orion
601 Esq, Lisbon/Montijo
14801
14802
14804
14805
14806

RUSSIA
Voenno-Vozdushniye Sily
Rossioki Federatsii (Russian
Air Force)
Sukhoi Su-27
TsAGI, Zhukhovsky

595	(27595)	Su-27P
597	(27597)	Su-30
598	(27598)	Su-27SK

SAUDI ARABIA
Al Quwwatal-Jawwiya
as Sa'udiya
Boeing E-3A/KE3A*
18 Sqn, Riyadh
1801
1802
1803
1804
1805
1811*
1812*
1813*
1814*
1815*
1816*
1817*
1818*

Saudi Arabia – Spain

Lockheed C-130 Hercules
1 Sqn, Riyadh;
4 Sqn, Jeddah;
16 Sqn, Jeddah;

112	VC-130H	1 Sqn
451	C-130H	4 Sqn
452	C-130H	4 Sqn
455	C-130E	4 Sqn
456	KC-130H	4 Sqn
457	KC-130H	4 Sqn
458	KC-130H	4 Sqn
459	KC-130H	4 Sqn
461	C-130H	4 Sqn
462	C-130H	4 Sqn
463	C-130H	4 Sqn
464	C-130H	4 Sqn
465	C-130H	4 Sqn
466	C-130H	4 Sqn
467	C-130H	4 Sqn
468	C-130H	4 Sqn
470	C-130H	4 Sqn
471	C-130H-30	4 Sqn
472	C-130H	4 Sqn
473	C-130H	4 Sqn
474	C-130H	4 Sqn
475	C-130H	4 Sqn
1601	C-130H	16 Sqn
1602	C-130H	16 Sqn
1603	C-130H	16 Sqn
1604	C-130H	16 Sqn
1605	C-130H	16 Sqn
1606	C-130E	16 Sqn
1607	C-130E	16 Sqn
1608	C-130E	16 Sqn
1609	C-130E	16 Sqn
1610	C-130E	16 Sqn
1611	C-130E	16 Sqn
1612	C-130H	16 Sqn
1613	C-130H	16 Sqn
1614	C-130H	16 Sqn
1615	C-130H	16 Sqn
1616	KC-130H	16 Sqn
1617	KC-130H	16 Sqn
1618	C-130H	16 Sqn
1619	C-130H	16 Sqn
1620	KC-130H	16 Sqn
1621	KC-130H	16 Sqn
1622	C-130H-30	16 Sqn
1623	C-130H-30	16 Sqn
1624	C-130H	16 Sqn
1625	C-130H	16 Sqn
1626	C-130H	16 Sqn
1627	C-130H	16 Sqn
1628	C-130H	16 Sqn

SINGAPORE
Republic of Singapore Air Force
122 Sqn, Changi
Lockheed Hercules
C-130B
720
721
724
725
C-130H
730
731
732
733
KC-130H
734
735

SLOVAKIA
Aero L.39/L.59 (L.39MS)
Albatros
5 LSP/1 Letka & 2 Letka, Kosice
1 SLP/2 Letka & 3 Letka, Sliac;
2 ZDLP/1 Letka, Trencin;
White Albatros, Kosice (WA)

0002	L.39MS	5 LSP
0003	L.39MS	5 LSP
0101	L.39C	WA
0102	L.39C	WA
0103	L.39C	5 LSP
0111	L.39C	WA
0112	L.39C	WA
0442	L.39C	WA
0443	L.39C	WA
0730	L.39V	5 LSP
1725	L.39ZA	2 ZDLP
3905	L.39ZA	2 ZDLP
4355	L.39C	WA
4357	L.39C	WA
4701	L.39ZA	5 LSP
4703	L.39ZA	1 SLP
4705	L.39ZA	1 SLP
4707	L.39ZA	1 SLP
4711	L.39ZA	1 SLP

Antonov An-12BP
2 ZDLP/2 Letka, Piestany
2209

Antonov An-24V
2 ZDLP/2 Letka, Piestany
2903
5605

Antonov An-26
2 ZDLP/2 Letka, Piestany
2506
3208

Let 410
5 LSP/3 Letka, Kosice;
2 ZDLP/2 Letka, Piestany

0404	L.410M	2 ZDLP
0405	L.410M	2 ZDLP
0730	L.410UVP	2 ZDLP
0927	L.410T	5 LSP
0930	L.410T	5 LSP
1133	L.410T	5 LSP
1203	L.410FG	2 ZDLP
1504	L.410UVP	
1511	L.410UVP	2 ZDLP
1810	L.410UVP-E	
2006	L.410UVP-E	2 ZDLP
2311	L.410UVP	2 ZDLP

Mikoyan MiG-29/UB*
1 SLP/1 Letka, Sliac
0619
0820
0921
1903*
2022
2123
3709
3911
4401*
5113
5515

5817
7501
8003
8605
9207
9308

Sukhoi Su-25K/BK*
2 ZDLP/1 Letka, Trencin
1006
1007
1008
1027
3237*
5036
6017
6018
8073
8074
8075

Tupolev Tu-154B-2
2 ZDLP/4 Letka, Bratislava
0420

SPAIN
Ejercito del Aire
Airtech CN235
Ala 35, Getafe

T-19A-01	35-60
T-19A-02	35-61
T.19B-03	35-21
T.19B-04	35-22
T.19B-05	35-23
T.19B-06	35-24
T.19B-07	35-25
T.19B-08	35-26
T.19B-09	35-27
T.19B-10	35-28
T.19B-11	35-29
T.19B-12	35-30
T.19B-13	35-31
T.19B-14	35-32
T.19B-15	35-33
T.19B-16	35-34
T.19B-17	35-35
T.19B-18	35-36
T.19B-19	35-37
T.19B-20	35-38

Boeing 707-381B/368C*
Grupo 45, Torrejon

T.17-1	45-10
TK.17-2	45-11
T.17-3*	45-12

CASA 101 Aviojet
Grupo 21, Moron;
Grupo 54, Torrejon;
Grupode Escuelas de Matacan (74);
AGA, San Javier (79)
Patrulla Aguila, San Javier*

E.25-01	79-01 [1]*
E.25-02	793-02
E.25-03	79-03
E.25-04	79-04
E.25-05	79-05
E.25-06	79-06 [6]*
E.25-07	79-07 [7]*
E.25-08	79-08 [8]*
E.25-09	79-09
E.25-10	79-10
E.25-11	79-11

E.25-12	79-12	**CASA 212 Aviocar**			T.12B-51	74-78
E.25-13	79-13 [3]*	**212 (XT.12)/212A (T.12B)/**			T.12B-52	72-07
E.25-14	79-14 [4]*	**212B (TR.12A)/212D**			T.12B-53	46-37
E.25-15	79-15	**(TE.12B)/212DE (TR.12D)/**			T.12B-54	37-54
E.25-16	79-16	**212E (T.12C)/212S**			T.12B-55	46-38
E.25-17	21-01	**(D.3A)/212S1 (D.3B)**			T.12B-56	74-79
E.25-18	21-02	Ala 22, Moron;			T.12B-57	72-08
E.25-19	21-03	Ala 35, Getafe;			T.12B-58	46-39
E.25-20	79-20	Ala 37, Villanubla;			T.12C-59	37-51
E.25-21	79-21 [9]*	Ala 46, Gando, Las Palmas;			T.12C-60	37-52
E.25-22	79-22 [13]*	Grupo 72, Alcantarilla;			T.12C-61	37-53
E.25-23	79-23 [10]*	Grupo Esc, Matacan (74);			T.12B-63	37-14
E.25-24	79-24	AGA (Ala 79), San Javier;			T.12B-64	46-40
E.25-25	79-25 [5]*	403 Esc, Cuatro Vientos;			T.12B-65	74-80
E.25-26	79-26 [2]*	408 Esc, Torrejon;			T.12B-66	72-09
E.25-27	79-27 [11]*	721 Esc, Alcantarilla;			T.12B-67	74-81
E.25-28	79-28 [12]*	801 Esc, Palma/Son San			T.12B-68	37-15
E.25-29	79-29	Juan;			T.12B-69	37-16
E.25-30	79-30	803 Esc, Cuatro Vientos			T.12B-70	37-17
E.25-31	79-31	D.3A-01	801 Esc		T.12B-71	37-18
E.25-32	74-01	D.3A-02	803-11		TR.12D-72	408-01
E.25-33	74-02	D.3B-03	803 Esc		TR.12D-73	408-02
E.25-34	21-04	D.3B-04	801 Esc		TR.12D-74	408-03
E.25-35	21-05	D.3B-05	801 Esc			
E.25-36	79-36	D.3B-06	803-12		**Cessna 560 Citation VI**	
E.25-37	21-06	D.3B-07	803-13		403 Esc, Cuatro Vientos	
E.25-38	79-38	D.3B-08	22-92		TR.20-01	403-11
E.25-40	74-06	D.3B-09	803 Esc		TR.20-02	403-12
E.25-41	21-07	XT.12A-1	54-10			
E.25-42	793-32	TR.12A-3	403-01		**Dassault Falcon 20**	
E.25-43	21-08	TR.12A-4	403-02		Grupo 45, Torrejon;	
E.25-44	79-44	TR.12A-5	403-03		408 Esc, Torrejon	
E.25-45	79-45	TR.12A-6	403-04		T.11-1	45-02
E.25-46	79-46	TR.12A-7	403-05		TM.11-2	45-03
E.25-47	79-47	TR.12A-8	403-06		TM.11-3	408-11
E.25-48	79-48	TE.12B-9	79-91		TM.11-4	45-01
E.25-49	79-49	TE.12B-10	79-92		T.11-5	45-05
E.25-50	79-40	T.12B-12	74-82			
E.25-51	74-07	T.12B-13	74-70		**Dassault Falcon 50**	
E.25-52	74-08	T.12B-14	46-30		Grupo 45, Torrejon	
E.25-53	411-07	T.12B-15	37-02		T.16-1	45-20
E.25-54	74-10	T.12B-16	74-71			
E.25-55	44-05	T.12B-17	37-03		**Dassault Falcon 900**	
E.25-56	21-09	T.12B-18	46-31		Grupo 45, Torrejon	
E.25-57	74-12	T.12B-19	46-32		T.18-1	45-40
E.25-58	54-06	T.12B-20	37-04		T.18-2	45-41
E.25-59	21-10	T.12B-21	35-05			
E.25-60	74-14	T.12B-22	37-06		**Fokker F.27M**	
E.25-61	21-11	T.12B-23	72-01		**Friendship 400MPA**	
E.25-62	74-16	T.12B-24	37-07		802 Esc, Gando	
E.25-63	74-17	T.12B-25	74-72		D.2-01	802-10
E.25-64	74-18	T.12B-26	72-02		D.2-02	802-11
E.25-65	74-19	T.12B-27	46-33		D.2-03	802-12
E.25-66	21-13	T.12B-28	72-03			
E.25-67	21-13	T.12B-29	35-08		**Lockheed P-3A/P-3B***	
E.25-68	79-95	T.12B-30	74-73		**Orion**	
E.25-69	79-97	T.12B-31	46-34		Grupo 22, Moron	
E.25-71	21-14	T.12B-33	72-04		P.3-01	22-21
E.25-72	21-14	T.12B-34	74-74		P.3-03	22-22
E.25-73	79-98	T.12B-35	46-35		P.3-08	22-31*
E.25-74	74-28	T.12B-36	37-09		P.3-09	22-32*
E.25-75	21-16	T.12B-37	72-05		P.3-10	22-33*
E.25-76	21-17	T.12B-38	35-10		P.3-11	22-34*
E.25-78	79-02	T.12B-39	74-75		P.3-12	22-35*
E.25-79	74-32	TE.12B-40	79-93			
E.25-80	74-33	TE.12B-41	79-94		**Lockheed Hercules**	
E.25-81	74-34	TE.12B-42	744-42		**C-130H/C-130H-30**[1]	
E.25-83	21-18	T.12C-43	46-50		311 Esc/312 Esc (Ala 31),	
E.25-84	79-04	T.12C-44	35-50		Zaragoza	
E.25-85	74-36	T.12B-46	74-46		TL.10-1	31-01[1]
E.25-86	74-37	T.12B-47	72-06		T.10-2	31-02
E.25-87	74-38	T.12B-48	37-11		T.10-3	31-03
E.25-88	74-39	T.12B-49	46-36		T.10-4	31-04
		T.12B-50	74-77		T.10-08	31-05

T.10-9	31-06
T.10-10	31-07

KC-130H
312 Esc (Ala 31), Zaragosa

TK.10-5	31-50
TK.10-6	31-51
TK.10-7	31-52
TK.10-11	31-53
TK.10-12	31-54

**McDonnell Douglas
EF-18A/EF-18B* Hornet**
Ala 12, Torrejon;
Grupo 15, Zaragoza

CE.15-1	15-70*
CE.15-2	15-71*
CE.15-3	15-72*
CE.15-4	15-73*
CE.15-5	15-74*
CE.15-6	15-75*
CE.15-7	12-70*
CE.15-8	12-71*
CE.15-9	12-72*
CE.15-10	12-73*
CE.15-11	12-74*
CE.15-12	12-75*
C.15-13	12-01
C.15-14	15-01
C.15-15	15-02
C.15-16	15-03
C.15-18	15-05
C.15-20	15-07
C.15-21	15-08
C.15-22	15-09
C.15-23	15-10
C.15-24	15-11
C.15-25	15-12
C.15-26	15-13
C.15-27	15-14
C.15-28	15-15
C.15-29	15-16
C.15-30	15-17
C.15-31	15-18
C.15-32	15-19
C.15-33	15-20
C.15-34	15-21
C.15-35	15-22
C.15-36	15-23
C.15-37	15-24
C.15-38	15-25
C.15-39	15-26
C.15-40	15-27
C.15-41	15-28
C.15-42	15-29
C.15-43	15-30
C.15-44	12-02
C.15-45	12-03
C.15-46	12-04
C.15-47	12-05
C.15-48	12-06
C.15-49	12-07
C.15-50	12-08
C.15-51	12-09
C.15-52	12-10
C.15-53	12-11
C.15-54	12-12
C.15-55	12-13
C.15-56	12-14
C.15-57	12-15
C.15-58	12-16
C.15-59	12-17
C.15-60	12-18
C.15-61	12-19
C.15-62	12-20
C.15-63	12-21
C.15-64	12-22
C.15-65	12-23
C.15-66	12-24
C.15-67	12-25
C.15-68	12-26
C.15-69	12-27
C.15-70	12-28
C.15-72	12-30

**Arma Aéreade
l'Arma da Espanola
BAe/McDonnell-Douglas
AV-8
EAV-8B Harrier II**
Esc 009, Rota

VA.2-1	01-901
VA.2-2	01-902
VA.2-3	01-903
VA.2-4	01-904
VA.2-5	01-905
VA.2-6	01-906
VA.2-7	01-907
VA.2-8	01-908
VA.2-9	01-909
VA.2-10	01-910
VA.2-11	01-911
VA.2-12	01-912

AV-8S Matador
Esc 008, Rota

VA.1-2	01-803
VA.1-3	01-804
VA.1-4	01-805
VA.1-5	01-806
VA.1-6	01-809
VA.1-8	01-811
VA.1-10	01-814

TAV-8S Matador
Esc 008, Rota

VAE.1-1	01-807
VAE.1-2	01-808

Cessna 550 Citation 2
Esc 004, Rota

U.20-1	01-405
U.20-2	01-406
U.20-3	01-407

SUDAN
**Silakh Al Jawwiya as Sudaniya
Lockheed
C-130H Hercules**

1100
1101
1102
1103
1104
1105

SWEDEN
**Kungliga Svenska Flygvapnet
Aerospatiale AS.332M-1
Super Puma (Hkp.10)**
F7, Såtenäs;
F15, Söderhamn;
F17, Ronneby/Kallinge;
F21, Luleå/Kallax

10401	91	F17
10402	92	F17
10403	93	F21
10404	94	F21
10405	95	F15
10406	96	F17
10407	97	F17
10408	98	F15
10409	99	F17
10410	90	F17
10411	81	F7
10412	82	F7

**Beechcraft Super King Air
(Tp.101)**
F7, Satenäs;
F17, Ronneby;
F21, Lulea

101002	012	F21
101003	013	F17
101004	014	F7

**Grumman G.1159C
Gulfstream 4 (Tp.102)**
F16, Uppsala

102001	021

**Lockheed
C-130E Hercules (Tp.84)**
F7, Satenäs

84001	841
84002	842

**Lockheed
C-130H Hercules (Tp.84)**
F7, Satenäs

84003	843
84004	844
84005	845
84006	846
84007	847
84008	848

**SAAB SF.340B/
SF.340AEW&C* (Tp.100)**
F16, Uppsala

100001	001	F16
100002	002*	

**Swearingen
Metro III (Tp.88)**
F16, Uppsala

88003	883

**Marine Flygtjanst
Vertol 107-II-5 (Hkp.4C)**
1 Hkp Div, Berga

04061	61
04063	63
04064	64

**Kawasaki-Vertol
KV-107-II (Hkp.4C)**
1 Hkp Div, Berga;
2 Hkp Div, Säve;
3 Hkp Div, Ronneby;
FC, Malmslatt

04065	65	2 Hkp Div
04067	67	2 Hkp Div
04068	68	2 Hkp Div
04069	69	1 Hkp Div
04070	70	1 Hkp Div
04071	71	1 Hkp Div
04072	72	FC
04073	73	1 Hkp Div
04074	74	3 Hkp Div
04075	75	3 Hkp Div

Armen
MBB Bo.105CB (Hkp.9B)
Armeflyget 1 (AF1), Boden;
Armeflyget 2 (AF2), Malmslatt;
FC, Malmslatt;
F6, Karlsborg (Air Force)

09201	01	AF2
09202	02	AF1
09203	03	AF2
09204	04	AF2
09205	05	AF1
09206	06	AF1
09207	07	AF1
09208	08	AF1
09209		
09210	10	AF1
09211	11	AF1
09212	12	AF2
09213	13	AF2
09214	14	AF2
09215	15	AF2
09216	16	AF2
09217	17	AF2
09218		
09219	19	AF1
09220	20	AF2
09221	90	FC
09411	91	
09412	92	
09414	94	F6

SWITZERLAND
Schweizerische Flugwaffe
Aérospatiale AS.532
Super Puma
Leichte Fliegerstaffeln 5 (LtSt 5), Mollis;
Leichte Fliegerstaffeln 6 (LtSt 6), Mollis;
Leichte Fliegerstaffeln 8 (LtSt 8), Mollis
Detachments at Interlaken, Meiringen, Payerne & Sion
T-311
T-312
T-313
T-314
T-315
T-316
T-317
T-318
T-319
T-320
T-321
T-322
T-323
T-324
T-325

Gates Learjet 35A
Swiss Air Force, Dubendorf
T-781
T-782

Northrop F-5 Tiger II
Flieger Staffel 1 (FlSt 1), Turtman;
Flieger Staffel 6 (FlSt 6), Sion;
Flieger Staffel 8 (FlSt 8), Meiringen;
Flieger Staffel 11 (FlSt 11),

Alpnach;
Flieger Staffel 13 (FlSt 13), Meiringen;
Flieger Staffel 18 (FlSt 18), Payerne;
Flieger Staffel 19 (FlSt 19), Alpnach;
Gruppe fur Rustunggdienste (GRD), Emmen;
Instrumentation Flieger Staffel 14 (InstruFlSt 14), Dübendorf;
Patrouille Suisse
F-5E

J-3001	GRD
J-3002	FlSt11
J-3003	FlSt18
J-3004	FlSt11
J-3005	FlSt11
J-3006	FlSt11
J-3007	FlSt11
J-3008	InstruFlSt 14
J-3009	FlSt11
J-3010	FlSt 18
J-3011	FlSt 18
J-3012	FlSt 11
J-3014	FlSt 11
J-3015	FlSt 11
J-3016	FlSt 11
J-3019	FlSt 11
J-3020	FlSt 11
J-3021	FlSt 18
J-3022	FlSt 19
J-3023	FlSt 11
J-3023	FlSt 11
J-3025	FlSt 13
J-3026	FlSt 18
J-3027	FlSt 13
J-3028	FlSt 13
J-3029	FlSt 19
J-3030	FlSt 13
J-3031	FlSt 13
J-3032	FlSt 13
J-3033	FlSt 19
J-3034	FlSt 13
J-3035	FlSt 19
J-3036	FlSt 1
J-3037	FlSt 13
J-3038	FlSt 18
J-3039	FlSt 13
J-3040	
J-3041	FlSt 19
J-3043	FlSt 13
J-3044	FlSt 1
J-3045	FlSt 19
J-3046	FlSt 13
J-3047	FlSt 13
J-3049	FlSt 1
J-3050	FlSt 19
J-3051	FlSt 1
J-3052	FlSt 13
J-3053	FlSt 13
J-3054	FlSt 18
J-3055	
J-3056	FlSt 13
J-3057	
J-3058	FlSt 13
J-3060	FlSt 1
J-3061	FlSt 18
J-3062	FlSt 18
J-3063	FlSt 1
J-3064	FlSt 13
J-3065	FlSt 13
J-3066	
J-3067	FlSt 1
J-3068	FlSt 19
J-3069	FlSt 13
J-3070	FlSt 8
J-3072	FlSt 19
J-3073	FlSt 13
J-3074	FlSt 13
J-3075	FlSt 13
J-3076	FlSt 13
J-3077	FlSt 8
J-3078	
J-3079	FlSt 1
J-3080	FlSt 1
J-3081	FlSt 13
J-3082	FlSt 11
J-3083	FlSt 13
J-3084	FlSt 11
J-3085	FlSt 13
J-3086	
J-3087	FlSt 19
J-3088	FlSt 8
J-3089	FlSt 1
J-3090	
J-3091	FlSt 11
J-3092	FlSt 13
J-3093	
J-3094	FlSt 1
J-3095	
J-3096	FlSt 1
J-3097	GRD
J-3098	FlSt 1

F-5F

J-3201	FlSt 1
J-3202	FlSt 1
J-3203	FlSt 1
J-3204	GRD
J-3205	InstruFlSt 14
J-3206	
J-3207	FlSt 1
J-3208	FlSt 11
J-3209	FlSt 1
J-3210	FlSt 11
J-3211	
J-3212	

TURKEY
Turk Hava Kuvvetleri
Cessna 650 Citation VII
224 Filo, Etimesgut
93-7024 ETI-024
93-7026 ETI-026

Grumman G.1159C
Gulfstream 4
224 Filo, Etimesgut
003

Transall C.160D
221 Filo, Erkilet

019	
020	12-020
021	
022	12-022
023	12-023
024	12-024
025	12-025
026	12-026
027	12-027
028	12-028
029	
030	12-030
031	12-031
032	12-032
033	12-033

034	12-034
035	12-035
036	12-036
037	12-037
038	12-038
039	12-039
040	12-040

Lockheed
C-130B Hercules
222 Filo, Erkilet
10960
10963
23496
70527
80736
91527

Lockheed
C-130E Hercules
222 Filo, Erkilet

00991	12-991
01468	12-468
01947	12-947
13186	12-186
13187	12-187
13188	12-188
13189	12-189
17949	12-949

UNITED ARAB EMIRATES
United Arab Emirates Air Force
Abu Dhabi
  Lockheed
  C-130H Hercules
  1211
  1212
  1213
  1214

Dubai
  Lockheed
  L.100-30 Hercules
  311
  312

US Military Aircraft Markings

All USAF aircraft have been allocated a fiscal year (FY) number since 1921. Individual aircraft are given a serial according to the fiscal year in which they are ordered. The numbers commence at 0001 and are prefixed with the year of allocation. For example F-15C Eagle 40001 (84-001) was the first aircraft ordered in 1984. The fiscal year (FY) serial is carried on the technical data block which is usually stencilled on the left-hand side of the aircraft just below the cockpit. The number displayed on the fin is a corruption of the FY serial. Most tactical aircraft carry the fiscal year in small figures followed by the last three or four digits of the serial in large figures. For example Lakenheath-based F-15E Eagle 10311 carries 91-0311/LN on its tail. Large transport and tanker aircraft such as C-130s and KC-135s sometimes display a five-figure number commencing with the last digit of the appropriate fiscal year and four figures of the production number. An example of this is KC-135R 58-0128 which displays 80128 on its fin.

USN serials follow a straightforward numerical sequence which commenced, for the present series, with the allocation of 00001 to an SB2C Helldiver by the Bureau of Aeronautics in 1940. Numbers in the 165000 series are presently being issued. They are usually carried in full on the rear fuselage of the aircraft.

UK based USAF Aircraft

The following aircraft are normally based in the UK. They are listed in numerical order of type with individual aircraft in serial number order, as depicted on the aircraft. The number in brackets is either the alternative presentation of the five-figure number commencing with the last digit of the fiscal year, or the fiscal year where a five-figure serial is presented on the aircraft. Where it is possible to identify the allocation of aircraft to individual squadrons by means of colours carried on fin or cockpit edge, this is also provided.

Lockheed U-2R	86-0172 (60172) F-15C y	91-0307 (10307) F-15E bl
9RW,RAFAlconbury [BB]	86-0173 (60173) F-15C y	91-0308 (10308) F-15E bl
01066 (FY80)	86-0174 (60174) F-15C y	91-0309 (10309) F-15E bl
01080 (FY80)	86-0175 (60175) F-15C y	91-0310 (10310) F-15E bl
01092 (FY80)	86-0176 (60176) F-15C y	91-0311 (10311) F-15E bl
	86-0178 (60178) F-15C y	91-0312 (10312) F-15E bl
McDonnellDouglas	86-0180 (60180) F-15C y	91-0313 (10313) F-15E r [3rdAF]
F-15C Eagle/F-15D Eagle/	86-0182 (60182) F-15D y	91-0314 (10314) F-15E r [494FS]
F-15E Strike Eagle	90-0248 (00248) F-15E m	91-0315 (10315) F-15E r
48 FW, RAF Lakenheath [LN]	[48FW]	91-0316 (10316) F-15E r
492 FS blue/white	90-0251 (00251) F-15E bl	91-0317 (10317) F-15E r
493 FS black/yellow	[492FS]	91-0318 (10318) F-15E r
494 FS red/white	90-0255 (00255) F-15E bl	91-0319 (10319) F-15E r
86-0147 (60147) F-15C y	90-0256 (00256) F-15E bl	91-0320 (10320) F-15E r
86-0154 (60154) F-15C y	90-0257 (00257) F-15E bl	91-0321 (10321) F-15E r
86-0156 (60156) F-15C y	90-0258 (00258) F-15E bl	91-0322 (10322) F-15E r
86-0159 (60159) F-15C y	90-0259 (00259) F-15E bl	91-0323 (10323) F-15E r
86-0160 (60160) F-15C y	90-0260 (00260) F-15E bl	91-0324 (10324) F-15E r
86-0163 (60163) F-15C y	90-0261 (00261) F-15E bl	91-0325 (10325) F-15E bl
86-0164 (60164) F-15C y	90-0262 (00262) F-15E bl	91-0326 (10326) F-15E bl
[493 FS]	91-0300 (10300) F-15E bl	91-0327 (10327) F-15E r
86-0165 (60165) F-15C y	91-0301 (10301) F-15E bl	91-0328 (10328) F-15E r
86-0166 (60166) F-15C y [48OG]	91-0302 (10302) F-15E bl	91-0329 (10329) F-15E bl
86-0167 (60167) F-15C y	91-0303 (10303) F-15E bl	91-0330 (10330) F-15E r
86-0169 (60169) F-15C y	91-0304 (10304) F-15E bl	91-0331 (10331) F-15E r
86-0170 (60170) F-15C y	91-0305 (10305) F-15E bl	91-0332 (10332) F-15E bl
86-0171 (60171) F-15C y	91-0306 (10306) F-15E r	91-0333 (10333) F-15E r

USAF/USN UK

91-0334 (10334) F-15E *r*	88284 (FY68)	95823 (FY69) HC-130N
91-0335 (10335) F-15E *r*	95785 (FY69)	95826 (FY69) HC-130N
91-0601 (10601) F-15E *r*	95791 (FY69)	95827 (FY69) HC-130N
91-0602 (10602) F-15E *r*	95794 (FY69)	
91-0603 (10603) F-15E *r*	95795 (FY69)	**Boeing KC-135R**
91-0604 (10604) F-15E *r*		**Stratotanker**
91-0605 (10605) F-15E *r*	**Lockheed C-130 Hercules**	351 ARS, 100 ARW [D]
92-0364 (20364) F-15E *r*	7 SOS*	RAF Mildenhall (*r/w/bl*)
	67 SOS, 352 SOG	10313 (FY61)
Sikorsky MH-53J	RAF Mildenhall	10321 (FY61)
21 SOS, 352 SOG	37814 (FY63) C-130E	23561 (FY62)
RAF Alconbury	40476 (FY84) MC-130H*	23577 (FY62)
01629 (FY70)	60223 (FY66) HC-130P	38003 (FY63)
10357 (FY68)	61699 (FY86) MC-130H*	38008 (FY63)
10930 (FY68)	70023 (FY87) MC-130H*	38875 (FY63)
14993 (FY67)	80193 (FY88) MC-130H*	71486 (FY57)
31648 (FY73)	80194 (FY88) MC-130H*	
31652 (FY73)	95820 (FY69) HC-130N	

Using its serial 91-0313 to indicate a 3rd AF operating unit, F-15E Strike Eagle from Lakenheath (48th FW/494th FS). *PRM*

UK based US Navy Aircraft

Beech UC-12M
Super King Air
Naval Air Facility, Mildenhall [8G]
3837 (163837)
3840 (163840)
3843 (163843)

European based USAF Aircraft

These aircraft are normally based in Western Europe with the USAFE. They are shown in numerical order of type designation, with individual aircraft in serial number order as carried on the aircraft. An alternative five-figure presentation of the serial is shown in brackets where appropriate. Fiscal year (FY) details are also provided if necessary. The unit allocation and operating bases are given for most aircraft.

McDonnell Douglas C-9A Nightingale
75 AAS, 86 AW Ramstein, Germany
SHAPE, Chievres, Belgium[1]
FY71

10876[1]	(VIP)
10879	
10880	
10881	
10882	

Fairchild A-10A/OA-10A* Thunderbolt II
SP: 52 FW Spangdahlem, Germany
81FS black

81-951	(10951)	bk
81-952	(10952)*	m [52 FW]
81-954	(10954)*	bk
81-956	(10956)*	bk
81-962	(10962)	bk
81-963	(10963)	bk
81-966	(10966)	bk
81-976	(10976)	bk
81-978	(10978)*	bk
81-980	(10980)	bk [81FS]
81-983	(10983)	bk
81-984	(10984)	bk
81-985	(10985)*	bk
81-988	(10988)	bk
81-991	(10991)*	bk
81-992	(10992)	bk
82-649	(20649)*	bk
82-650	(20650)	bk
82-654	(20654)	bk
82-655	(20655)	bk
82-656	(20656)	bk

Beech C-12C
[1]JUSMG, Ankara, Turkey
[2]US Embassy Flight, Athens

31216	(FY73)[1]
31218	(FY73)[2]
60173	(FY76)[1]

McDonnell Douglas F-15C/F-15D* Eagle
IS: 35 Wg Keflavik,Iceland
57 FS black/white
SP: 52 FW Spangdahlem, Germany
53 FS yellow/black

79-012	(90012)*	SP	y
79-021	(90021)	IS	bk
79-025	(90025)	SP	y
79-057	(90057)	SP	y
79-064	(90064)	SP	y
79-068	(90068)	SP	y
80-004	(00004)	SP	y
80-012	(00012)	SP-y	
80-021	(00021)	IS	
80-027	(00027)	IS	bk
80-029	(00029)	IS	bk
80-035	(00035)	IS	bk [35 Wg]
80-038	(00038)	IS	bk
80-039	(00039)	IS	bk
80-041	(00041)	IS	bk
80-042	(00042)	IS	bk
80-047	(00047)	IS	bk
80-048	(00048)	IS	bk
80-050	(00050)	IS	bk
80-052	(00052)	IS	bk
80-056	(00056)*	IS	bk
81-047	(10047)	IS	bk
81-061	(10061)*	IS	bk
84-001	(40001)	SP	y [53 FS]
84-003	(40003)	SP	y
84-005	(40005)	SP	y
84-008	(40008)	SP	y
84-009	(40009)	SP	m [52 FW]
84-010	(40010)	SP	y
84-014	(40014)	SP	y
84-015	(40015)	SP	y
84-019	(40019)	SP	y
84-023	(40023)	SP	y
84-024	(40024)	SP	y
84-025	(40025)	SP	y
84-027	(40027)	SP	y [53 FS]
84-044	(40044)*	SP	y

Lockheed (GD) F-16C/F-16D*
AV: 31 FW Aviano, Italy
510 FS purple/white
555 FS blue/yellow
SP: 52 FW Spangdahlem, Germany
22 FS red/white
23 FS blue/white

87-355	(70355)	AV	pr
87-359	(70359)	AV	bl
88-174	(80174)*	AV	pr
88-413	(80413)	AV	pr
			[510 FS]
88-425	(80425)	AV	bl
88-443	(80443)	AV	pr
88-444	(80444)	AV	pr
88-446	(80446)	AV	pr
88-491	(80491)	AV	pr
88-525	(80525)	AV	pr
88-526	(80526)	AV	bl
88-529	(80529)	AV	bl
88-532	(80532)	AV	bl
88-535	(80535)	AV	bl
88-541	(80541)	AV	pr
88-550	(80550)	AV	bl
			[555 FS]
89-001	(92001)	AV	bl [31 FW]
89-009	(92009)	AV	bl
89-011	(92011)	AV	pr
89-016	(92016)	AV	bl
89-023	(92023)	AV	bl
89-024	(92024)	AV	bl
89-026	(92026)	AV	pr
89-029	(92029)	AV	bl
89-030	(92030)	AV	bl
89-032	(92032)	AV	bl
89-035	(92035)	AV	bl
89-036	(92036)	AV	pr
89-038	(92038)	AV	bl
89-039	(92039)	AV	bl
89-044	(92044)	AV	pr
89-046	(92046)	AV	pr
89-047	(92047)	AV	bl
89-049	(92049)	AV	bl
89-050	(92050)	AV	bl
89-137	(92137)	AV	bl
89-178	(92178)*	AV	pr
90-709	(00709)	AV	bl
90-795	(00795)*	AV	pr
90-796	(00796)*	AV	pr
90-800	(00800)*	AV	bl
90-813	(00813)	SP	r
90-818	(00818)	SP	r
90-827	(00827)	SP	r
90-828	(00828)	SP	r
90-829	(00829)	SP	r
90-831	(00831)	SP	r
90-833	(00833)	SP	r
90-843	(00843)*	SP	r
90-846	(00846)*	SP	r
90-849	(00849)*	SP	r
91-336	(10336)	SP	r [22 FS]
91-337	(10337)	SP	m [52 FW]
91-338	(10338)	SP	r
91-339	(10339)	SP	r
91-340	(10340)	SP	r
91-341	(10341)	SP	r
91-342	(10342)	SP	r
91-343	(10343)	SP	r
91-344	(10344)	SP	r [22 FS]
91-351	(10351)	SP	r
91-352	(10352)	SP	m [52 FW]
91-402	(10402)	SP	bl
91-403	(10403)	SP	bl [23 FS]
91-405	(10405)	SP	bl
91-406	(10406)	SP	bl
91-407	(10407)	SP	bl
91-408	(10408)	SP	bl
91-409	(10409)	SP	bl
91-410	(10410)	SP	bl
91-412	(10412)	SP	m [52 FW]
91-414	(10414)	SP	bl
91-415	(10415)	SP	bl
91-416	(10416)	SP	bl
91-417	(10417)	SP	bl
91-418	(10418)	SP	bl
91-419	(10419)	SP	bl
91-420	(10420)	SP	bl
91-421	(10421)	SP	bl
91-464	(10464)*	SP	bl
91-472	(10472)*	SP	bl
91-474	(10474)*	SP	bl

USAF/USN Europe

Grumman C-20A
Gulfstream III
76 ALS, 86 AW Ramstein,
  Germany
FY83
30500
30501
30502

Gates C-21A
Learjet
76 ALS, 86 AW Ramstein,
  Germany
*7005 ABS/HQUSEUCOM,-
  Stuttgart, Germany
FY84
40068*
40081*
40082*
40083*
40084
40085
40086

40087
40108
40109
40110
40111
40112

Boeing CT-43A
76 ALS, 86 AW Ramstein,
  Germany
31149   (FY73)

Sikorsky HH-60G
Blackhawk
56 RQS, 35 Wg Keflavik,
  Iceland [IS]
26205   (FY89)
26206   (FY89)
26208   (FY89)
26212   (FY89)
26461   (FY92)

Lockheed C-130E
Hercules
37 ALS, 86 AW Ramstein,
  Germany [RS]
01260   (FY70)
01264   (FY70)
01271   (FY70)
01274   (FY70)
10935   (FY68)
10938   (FY68)
10943   (FY68)
10947   (FY68)
17681   (FY64)
18240   (FY64)
37885   (FY63)
37887   (FY63)
40502   (FY64)
40527   (FY64)
40533   (FY64)
40550   (FY64)
96566   (FY69)
96582   (FY69)
96583   (FY69)

European based US Navy Aircraft

Lockheed P-3 Orion
CINCAFSE, NAF Sigonella, Italy
CinCLANT, NAS Norfolk, Virginia
VQ-2, NAF Rota, Spain
149668   EP-3E   [21]
150495   UP-3A   NAF Keflavik
150496   VP-3A   CinCLANT
150505   EP-3E   [24]
150515   VP-3A   CinCAFSE
152740   UP-3B   VQ-2
157320   EP-3E   VQ-2
157325   EP-3E   VQ-2
160770   P-3C   [32]
161125   P-3C   [30]

Beech UC-12M
Super King Air
[1]NAF Sigonella, Italy
[2]NAF Rota, Spain
3838 (163838)[1]
3839 (163839)[2]
3841 (163841)[1]
3842 (163842)[2]
3844 (163844)[1]

NA CT-39G
Sabreliner
NAF Sigonella, Italy
159361 [31]
159362 [32]
159363 [33]

Sikorsky CH-53E
Sea Stallion
HC-4, NAF Sigonella, Italy
161532 [HC-532]
161536 [HC-536]
161537 [HC-537]
161542 [HC-542]

European based US Army Aircraft

Beech C-12 Super King Air
7th ATC, Grafenwohr;
207 AvCo, Heidelberg;
HQ/USEUCOM, Stuttgart;
6th Avn Det, Vicenza, Italy;
'A' Co, 5 Batt, 158 Avn Reg't, Wiesbaden;
1 MIB, Wiesbaden

FY73		
22253	C-12C	HQ/USEUCOM
22254	C-12C	207 AvCo
22255	C-12C	6 Avn Det
22260	C-12C	7th ATC
22261	C-12C	5-158 ACo
FY76		
22549	C-12C	HQ/USEUCOM
22550	C-12C	HQ/USEUCOM
22556	C-12C	6 Avn Det
22557	C-12C	207 AvCo
22564	C-12C	207 AvCo
FY77		
22932	C-12C	6 Avn Det
22944	C-12C	207 AvCo
22950	C-12C	207 AvCo
FY78		
23126	C-12C	207 AvCo
23127	C-12C	207 AvCo
23128	C-12C	207 AvCo
FY84		
24380	C-12D	207 AvCo
FY85		
50147	RC-12K	1 MIB
50148	RC-12K	1 MIB
50150	RC-12K	1 MIB
50151	RC-12K	1 MIB
50152	RC-12K	1 MIB
50153	RC-12K	1 MIB
50154	RC-12K	1 MIB
50155	RC-12K	1 MIB

Boeing-Vertol CH-47D Chinook
'A' Co, 5 Batt, 159 Avn Reg't Giebelstadt;
'E' Co, 502 Avn Reg't, Aviano

FY87	
70072	5/159 ACo
70073	5/159 ACo
70079	5/159 ACo
70081	5/159 ACo
70082	5/159 ACo
70083	5/159 ACo
70085	5/159 ACo
70086	5/159 ACo
70088	5/159 ACo
70089	5/159 ACo
70091	5/159 ACo
70092	5/159 ACo
70094	5/159 ACo
70096	5/159 ACo
70112	5/159 ACo
FY88	
80098	502 ECo
80099	502 ECo
80100	502 ECo
80101	502 ECo
80102	502 ECo
80103	502 ECo
80104	502 ECo
80106	502 ECo
FY89	
90138	502 ECo
90139	502 ECo
90140	502 ECo
90141	502 ECo
92142	502 ECo
90143	502 ECo
90144	502 ECo
90145	502 ECo

Sikorsky UH-60A Black Hawk
2-1 Avn, Ansbach;
3-1 Avn, Ansbach;
7-1 Avn, Ansbach;
45 Med Co, Ansbach;
1-1 Cav, Budingen;
357th Avn Det/SHAPE, Chievres;
'C' Co, 7th Btn, 158 Avn Reg't, Giebelstadt;
8-158 Avn, Giebelstadt;
'C' Co, 6th Btn, 159 Avn Reg't, Giebelstadt;
2-227 Avn, Hanau;
3-227 Avn, Hanau;
'A' Co, 7th Btn, 227 Avn Reg't, Hanau;
207th Aviation Co, Heidelberg;
2-6 Cavalry, Illesheim;
6-6 Cavalry, Illesheim;
4-229 Avn, Illesheim;
236th Med Co (HA), Landstuhl;
'A' Co, 5th Btn, 158 Avn Reg't, Wiesbaden;
159th Med Co, Wiesbaden

FY78	
22996	236 Med Co
FY80	
23425	7/158 CCo
23427	
23434	45 Med Co
23439	7-1Avn
23440	
23442	
23489	
23490	6/159 CCo
23496	7-1 Avn
FY81	
23551	236 Med Co
23568	8-158 Avn
23571	7/227 ACo
23572	
23573	159 Med Co
23582	3-227 Avn
23583	
23584	
23586	159 Med Co
23589	7-1 Avn
23590	7/227 ACo
23592	236 Med Co
23594	7-1 Avn
23596	236 Med Co
23597	159 Med Co
23598	5/158 ACo
23602	
23603	
23605	7/158 CCo
23606	7/158 CCo
23608	159 Med Co
23609	7/227 ACo
23610	
23613	159 Med Co
23615	236 Med Co
23616	7-1 Avn
23617	
23622	
23623	7-158 CCo
23626	
FY82	
2364	7 1 HCo
2366	0 7/158 CCo
2366	145 Med Co
23662	
23663	7-1 Avn
23664	236 Med Co
23665	
23667	
23668	
23669	
23672	236 Med Co
23673	6/159 CCo
23675	45 Med Co
23676	236 Med Co
23682	7/227 ACo
23684	6-159 CCo
23685	236 Med Co
23686	159 Med Co
23689	207 Av Co
23690	7/158 CCo
23691	
23692	
23693	236 Med Co
23695	45 Med Co
23699	6/159 CCo
23702	7-1 Avn
23703	
23704	
23722	159 Med Co
23723	159 Med Co
23726	45 Med Co
23727	236 Med Co
23728	236 Med Co
23729	45 Med Co
23730	236 Med Co
23731	45 Med Co
23733	7-1 Avn
23734	7/227 ACo
23735	236 Med Co
23736	159 Med Co
23737	159 Med Co
23738	159 Med Co
23739	45 Med Co
23741	
23743	45 Med Co
23744	5/158 ACo
23745	45 Med Co
23746	159 Med Co
23748	7-1 Avn
23750	159 Med Co
23751	45 Med Co
23753	159 Med Co
23754	45 Med Co
23755	45 Med Co
23756	159 Med Co
23757	45 Med Co
23761	7/227 ACo

US Army

Serial	Unit
FY83	
23854	7/158 CCo
23855	
23869	
FY86	
24498	1-1 Cav
24506	7/227 ACo
24530	7-1 Avn
24531	2-6 Cav
24532	6/159 CCo
24533	
24538	207 AvCo
24547	7-1 Avn
24550	236 Med Co
24551	235 Med Co
24552	7-1 Avn
24553	6/158 BCo
24554	7/227 ACo
24555	6/159 CCo
FY87	
24579	5/158 ACo
24581	236 Med Co
24583	357 Av Det
24584	357 Av Det
24589	207Av Co
24621	3-1 Avn
24628	7-1 Avn
24634	6/159 CCo
24642	
24643	7-1 Avn
24644	6/159 CCo
24645	6/159 CCo
24647	7-1 Avn
24656	
26001	
26002	159 Med Co
26003	7/227 ACo
26004	7-1 Avn
FY88	
26019	7/227 ACo
26020	4-229 Avn
26021	6/159 CCo
26023	6-6 Cav
26024	7/158 CCo
26025	7/158 CCo
26026	7/158 CCo
26027	7/158 CCo
26028	7/158 CCo
26031	7-1 Avn
26034	7/227 ACo
26037	4-229 Avn
26038	5/158 ACo
26039	6/159 CCo
26040	7-1 Avn
26041	5/158 ACo
26042	6/159 CCo
26045	6/159 CCo
26050	7-227 Avn
26051	5/158 ACo
26052	7/227 ACo
26053	7-227 Avn
26054	236 Med Co
26055	6-6 Cav
26056	5/158 ACo
26058	6-6 Cav
26061	
26063	
26067	7/227 ACo
26068	7/227 ACo
26070	
26071	7/227 ACo
26072	7/227 ACo
26073	
26074	
26075	2-227 Avn
26077	3-227 Avn
26080	3-1 Avn
26083	7/158 CCo
26085	2-227 Avn
26086	3-227 Avn
FY89	
26138	2-6 Cav
26142	2-227 Avn
26145	3-227 Avn
26146	3-227 Avn
26151	2-1 Avn
26153	3-1 Avn
26155	7/227 ACo
26164	2-1 Avn
26165	2-1 Avn

McD AH-64A Apache

2-1 Avn, Ansbach;
3-1 Avn, Ansbach;
2-227 Avn, 3-227 Avn, Hanau;
2-6 Cav, 6-6 Cav, Illesheim;
7/159 ACo, 4-229 Avn, Illesheim

Serial	Unit
FY84	
24204	3-227 Avn
24207	2-6 Cav
24218	2-6 Cav
24244	6-6 Cav
24247	
24250	3-227 Avn
24257	4-229 Avn
24260	2-6 Cav
24262	2-6 Cav
24266	2-6 Cav
24277	2-6 Cav
24290	2-6 Cav
24293	2-6 Cav
24296	2-6 Cav
24297	2-6 Cav
24299	
24303	2-6 Cav
24304	2-6 Cav
FY85	
25352	3-1 Avn
25357	2-6 Cav
25397	
25424	
25430	2-6 Cav
25460	3-1 Avn
25465	2-6 Cav
25469	7/159 ACo
25470	2-227 Avn
25471	2-227 Avn
25472	2-227 Avn
25473	3-1 Avn
25474	2-227 Avn
25475	2-6 Cav
25476	
25478	3-1 Avn
25479	3-1 Avn
25480	2-227 Avn
25482	2-227 Avn
25485	2-227 Avn
FY86	
8940	2-6 Cav
8941	4-229 Avn
8942	2-6 Cav
8943	2-6 Cav
8946	2-6 Cav
8947	4-229 Avn
8948	2-6 Cav
8949	2-6 Cav
8950	4-229 Avn
8951	2-6 Cav
8952	2-6 Cav
8955	4-229 Avn
8956	3-1 Avn
8957	2-6 Cav
8959	4-229 Avn
8960	2-6 Cav
8961	2-6 Cav
8970	3-227 Avn
8981	2-6 Cav
8983	3-227 Avn
9010	2-1 Avn
9011	2-1 Avn
9019	3-1 Avn
9026	2-6 Cav
9029	2-227 Avn
9030	
9032	2-1 Avn
9033	3-227 Avn
9037	2-6 Cav
9039	3-1 Avn
9041	2-227 Avn
9048	2-1 Avn
FY87	
408	3-1 Avn
409	3-1 Avn
410	3-227 Avn
412	2-1 Avn
413	
415	3-227 Avn
417	2-1 Avn
418	3-227 Avn
419	2-1 Avn
420	3-1 Avn
423	3-1 Avn
428	3-1 Avn
432	2-1 Avn
433	3-227 Avn
434	3-227 Avn
435	3-227 Avn
436	3-1 Avn
437	
438	3-227 Avn
439	3-1 Avn
440	3-227 Avn
441	3-227 Avn
442	3-1 Avn
443	2-6 Cav
444	2-227 Avn
445	3-227 Avn
446	3-227 Avn
447	3-227 Avn
449	3-227 Avn
451	2-227 Avn
455	2-227 Avn
457	2-6 Cav
459	2-1 Avn
465	1 Avn
467	
470	2-1 Avn
471	2-1 Avn
473	2-1 Avn
474	2-1 Avn
475	3-227 Avn
476	2-1 Avn
477	2-1 Avn
478	2-1 Avn
479	2-1 Avn
481	2-1 Avn
482	2-1 Avn
487	2-227 Avn
496	3-227 Avn
498	
503	2-227 Avn
504	2-227 Avn

505	3-227 Avn	213	6-6 Cav	229	6-6 Cav
506	2-227 Avn	214	6-6 Cav	232	6-6 Cav
507	3-227 Avn	215	6-6 Cav	233	6-6 Cav
FY88		216	6-6 Cav	234	6-6 Cav
197	2-227 Avn	217	6-6 Cav	236	6-6 Cav
198	2-227 Avn	218	6-6 Cav	238	6-6 Cav
199	2-227 Avn	219	6-6 Cav	243	6-6 Cav
203	6-6 Cav	222	6-6 Cav	246	6-6 Cav
204	6-6 Cav	225	6-6 Cav	250	6-6 Cav
212	6-6 Cav	228	6-6 Cav		

US based USAF Aircraft

The following aircraft are normally based in the USA but are likely to be seen visiting the UK from time to time. The presentation is in numerical order of the type, commencing with the B-1B and concluding with the C-141. The aircraft are listed in numerical progression by the serial actually carried externally. Fiscal year information is provided, together with details of mark variations and in some cases operating units. Where base-code letter information is carried on the aircrafts' tails, this is detailed with the squadron/base data; for example the 7th Wing's B-1B 30069 carries the letters DY on its tail, thus identifying the Wing's home base as Dyess AFB, Texas.

Rockwell B-1B Lancer
7 Wg Dyess AFB, Texas [DY]
28 BW Ellsworth AFB, South Dakota [EL]
127 BS/184 BG, Kansas ANG, McConnell AFB, Kansas
319 BG Grand Forks AFB, North Dakota [GF]
366 Wg Ellsworth AFB, South Dakota [MO]
384 BG McConnell AFB, Kansas [OZ]
410 TS Edwards AFB, California

Serial	Unit
FY83	
30065	7 Wg
30066	7 Wg
30067	7 Wg
30068	7 Wg
30069	7 Wg
30070	7 Wg
30071	7 Wg
FY84	
40049	410 TS
40050	7 Wg
40051	7 Wg
40053	7 Wg
40054	7 Wg
40055	7 Wg
40056	7 Wg
40057	7 Wg
40058	7 Wg
FY85	
50059	7 Wg
50060	28 BW
50061	28 BW
50062	7 Wg
50064	28 BW
50065	7 Wg
50066	28 BW
50067	7 Wg
50068	410 TS
50069	7 Wg
50070	7 Wg
50071	7 Wg
50072	7 Wg
50073	7 Wg
50074	7 Wg
50075	28 BW
50077	28 BW
50078	28 BW
50079	28 BW
50080	384 BG
50081	127 BS
50082	7 Wg
50083	28 BW
50084	28 BW
50085	28 BW
50086	28 BW
50087	28 BW
50088	127 BS
50089	28 BW
50090	28 BW
50091	28 BW
50092	28 BW
FY86	
60093	28 BW
60094	28 BW
60095	127 BS
60096	28 BW
60097	319 BG
60098	28 BW
60099	28 BW
60100	7 Wg
60101	384 BG
60102	28 BW
60103	7 Wg
60104	28 BW
60105	7 Wg
60107	319 BG
60108	28 BW
60109	7 Wg
60110	366 Wg
60111	319 BG
60112	7 Wg
60113	28 BW
60114	28 BW
60115	127 BS
60116	319 BG
60117	7 Wg
60118	319 BG
60119	7 Wg
60120	7 Wg
60121	319 BG
60122	7 Wg
60123	319 BG
60124	127 BS
60125	384 BG
60126	384 BG
60127	384 BG
60128	384 BG
60129	384 BG
60130	384 BG
60131	319 BG
60132	7 Wg
60133	28 BW
60134	384 BG
60135	384 BG
60136	384 BG
60137	384 BG
60138	384 BG
60139	366 Wg
60140	384 BG

Northrop B-2A Spirit
412 TW Edwards AFB, California [ED]
509 BW Whiteman AFB, Missouri [WM]

Serial	Unit
FY82	
21066	Northrop
21067	412 TW
21068	412 TW
21069	412 TW
21070	412 TW
21071	412 TW
FY88	
80328	509 BW
80329	509 BW
80330	509 BW
80331	509 BW
80332	509 BW

Boeing E-3 Sentry
552 ACW
961 AW&CS/18 Wg (*or*) Kadena AB, Japan [ZZ]
962 AW&CS (*gn*) Elmendorf AFB, Alaska [AK]
963 AW&CS (*bk*)
964 AW&CS (*r*)
965 AW&CS (*y*)
966 AW&CS (TS) (*bl*) Tinker AFB, Oklahoma [OK]

Serial	Mark	Code
FY80		
00137	E-3C	*r*
00138	E-3C	*y*
00139	E-3C	*bk*
FY81		
10004	E-3C	*bk*
10005	E-3C	*m*
FY71		
11407	E-3B	*bl*
11408	E-3B	*y*
FY82		
20006	E-3C	*y*
20007	E-3C	*y*
FY83		
30008	E-3C	*or*
30009	E-3C	*bk*
FY73		
31674	E-3C	
31675	E-3B	*r*
FY75		
50556	E-3B	*bk*
50557	E-3B	*r*
50558	E-3B	*y*
50559	E-3B	*r*
50560	E-3B	*r*

FY76		
61604	E-3B	y
61605	E-3B	bl
61606	E-3B	m
61607	E-3B	m
FY77		
70351	E-3B	bk
70352	E-3B	r
70353	E-3B	bl
70354	E-3B	gn
70355	E-3B	r
70356	E-3B	y
FY78		
80576	E-3B	bk
80577	E-3B	or
80578	E-3B	y
FY79		
90001	E-3B	bk
90002	E-3B	gn
90003	E-3B	bk

Boeing E-4B
1ACCS/55 Wg
Offutt AFB, Nebraska [OF]

31676	(FY73)
31677	(FY73)
40787	(FY74)
50125	(FY75)

Lockheed C-5 Galaxy
60 AMW Travis AFB, California
97 AMW Altus AFB, Oklahoma
137 ALS/105 AG
  Stewart AFB, New York (bl)
433 AW/68 ALS Kelly, AFB, Texas★
436 AW Dover AFB, Delaware
439 AW/337 ALS Westover ARB, Massachusetts★
(★=AFRES: Air Force Reserve)

FY70		
00445	C-5A	433 AW★
00446	C-5A	433 AW★
00447	C-5A	436 AW
00448	C-5A	439 AW★
00449	C-5A	97 AMW
00450	C-5A	433 AW★
00451	C-5A	97 AMW
00452	C-5A	436 AW
00453	C-5A	97 AMW
00454	C-5A	97 AMW
00455	C-5A	97 AMW
00456	C-5A	97 AMW
00457	C-5A	60 AMW
00458	C-5A	97 AMW
00459	C-5A	60 AMW
00460	C-5A	436 AW
00461	C-5A	433 AW★
00462	C-5A	97 AMW
00463	C-5A	436 AW
00464	C-5A	97 AMW
00466	C-5A	436 AW
00465	C-5A	436 AW
00467	C-5A	436 AW
FY83		
31285	C-5B	436 AW
FY84		
40059	C-5B	436 AW
40060	C-5B	60 AMW
40061	C-5B	436 AW
40062	C-5B	60 AMW
FY85		
50001	C-5B	436 AW
50002	C-5B	60 AMW

50003	C-5B	436 AW
50004	C-5B	60 AMW
50005	C-5B	436 AW
50006	C-5B	60 AMW
50007	C-5B	436 AW
50008	C-5B	60 AMW
50009	C-5B	436 AW
50010	C-5B	60 AMW
FY86		
60011	C-5B	436 AW
60012	C-5B	60 AMW
60013	C-5B	436 AW
60014	C-5B	60 AMW
60015	C-5B	436 AW
60016	C-5B	60 AMW
60017	C-5B	436 AW
60018	C-5B	60 AMW
60019	C-5B	436 AW
60020	C-5B	436 AW
60021	C-5B	60 AMW
60022	C-5B	60 AMW
60023	C-5B	436 AW
60024	C-5B	60 AMW
60025	C-5B	436 AW
60026	C-5B	60 AMW
FY66		
68304	C-5A	439 AW★
68305	C-5A	433 AW★
68306	C-5A	433 AW★
68307	C-5A	433 AW★
FY87		
70027	C-5B	436 AW
70028	C-5B	60 AMW
70029	C-5B	436 AW
70030	C-5B	60 AMW
70031	C-5B	436 AW
70032	C-5B	60 AMW
70033	C-5B	436 AW
70034	C-5B	60 AMW
70035	C-5B	436 AW
70036	C-5B	60 AMW
70037	C-5B	436 AW
70038	C-5B	60 AMW
70039	C-5B	436 AW
70040	C-5B	60 AMW
70041	C-5B	436 AW
70042	C-5B	60 AMW
70043	C-5B	436 AW
70044	C-5B	60 AMW
70045	C-5B	436 AW
FY67		
70167	C-5A	439 AW★
70168	C-5A	433 AW
70169	C-5A	137 ALS
70170	C-5A	137 ALS
70171	C-5A	433 AW★
70173	C-5A	137 ALS
70174	C-5A	137 ALS
FY68		
80211	C-5A	439 AW★
80212	C-5A	137 ALS
80213	C-5C	60 AMW
80214	C-5A	436 AW
80215	C-5A	439 AW★
80216	C-5C	60 AMW
80217	C-5A	436 AW
80219	C-5A	439 AW★
80220	C-5A	433 AW★
80221	C-5A	433 AW★
80222	C-5A	439 AW★
80223	C-5A	433 AW★
80224	C-5A	137 ALS
80225	C-5A	439 AW★
80226	C-5A	137 ALS

FY69		
90001	C-5A	60 AMW
90002	C-5A	433 AW★
90003	C-5A	439 AW★
90004	C-5A	433 AW★
90005	C-5A	439 AW★
90006	C-5A	137 ALS
90007	C-5A	433 AW★
90008	C-5A	137 ALS
90009	C-5A	137 ALS
90010	C-5A	60 AMW
90011	C-5A	439 AW★
90012	C-5A	137 ALS
90013	C-5A	439 AW★
90014	C-5A	60 AMW
90015	C-5A	137 ALS
90016	C-5A	433 AW★
90017	C-5A	439 AW★
90018	C-5A	60 AMW
90019	C-5A	439 AW★
90020	C-5A	439 AW★
90021	C-5A	137 ALS
90022	C-5A	439 AW★
90023	C-5A	60 AMW
90024	C-5A	60 AMW
90025	C-5A	60 AMW
90026	C-5A	60 AMW
90027	C-5A	436 AW

Boeing E-8 J-STARS
Grumman, Melbourne, Florida

FY90		
00175	(N526SJ)	E-8C
FY86		
60416	(N770JS)	E-8A
60417	(N8411)	E-8A

McDonnell-Douglas KC-10A Extender
4 Wg Seymour-Johnson AFB, North Carolina [SJ]
305 AMW McGuire AFB, New Jersey
380 ARW Plattsburgh AFB, New York
722 ARW March AFB, California (bl/y)

FY82		
20191	722 ARW	
20192	4 Wg	r/bk
20193	722 ARW	
FY83		
30075		
30076	722 ARW	
30077	4 Wg	r
30078	722 ARW	
30079	305 AMW	
30080	722 ARW	
30081	305 AMW	
30082	305 AMW	
FY84		
40185	722 ARW	
40186	380 ARW	
40187	722 ARW	
40188	305 AMW	
40189	722 ARW	
40190	305 AMW	
40191	722 ARW	
40192	305 AMW	
FY85		
50027	722 ARW	
50028		
50029	4 Wg	bk
50030	4 Wg	r

KC-10A (continued)

50031	4 Wg	bk
50032		
50033		
50034	305 AMW	
FY86		
60027	305 AMW	
60028	4 Wg	bk
60029	4 Wg	r
60030	4 Wg	r
60031	4 Wg	bk
60032	4 Wg	bk
60033	4 Wg	r
60034	4 Wg	bk
60035	4 Wg	bk
60036	4 Wg	r
60037	4 Wg	bk
60038	4 Wg	r
FY87		
70117	722 ARW	
70118	722 ARW	
70119	722 ARW	
70120	722 ARW	
70121	4 Wg	bk
70122	4 Wg	r
70123	4 Wg	r
70124	4 Wg	bk
FY79		
90433		
90434	305 AMW	
91710	305 AMW	
91711		
91712		
91713		
91946	722 ARW	
91947	722 ARW	
91948	722 ARW	
91949	722 ARW	
91950	722 ARW	
91951	722 ARW	

McDonnell-Douglas C-17 Globemaster III

417 TS Edwards AFB, California [ED]
437 AW Charleston AFB, South Carolina

FY90		
00532	C-17A	437 AW
00533	C-17A	437 AW
00534	C-17A	437 AW
00535	C-17A	437 AW
FY92		
23291	C-17A	437 AW
23292	C-17A	437 AW
23293	C-17A	437 AW
23294	C-17A	437 AW
FY93		
30599	C-17A	437 AW
30600	C-17A	
30601	C-17A	
30602	C-17A	
30603	C-17A	
30604	C-17A	
FY87		
70025	YC-17A	417 TS
FY88		
80265	C-17A	417 TS
80266	C-17A	417 TS
80267	C-17A	
FY89		
91189	C-17A	417 TS
91190	C-17A	417 TS
91191	C-17A	437 AW
91192	C-17A	437 AW

Boeing C-18

452 TS/452 TS Edwards AFB, California;
966 AW&CS (TS) /552ACW (bl) Tinker AFB, Oklahoma [OK]

FY81		
10891	EC-18B	452 TS
10892	EC-18B	452 TS
10893	EC-18D	452 TS
10894	EC-18B	452 TS
10895	EC-18D	452 TS
10896	EC-18B	452 TS
10898	C-18A	452 TS
FY84		
41398	TC-18E	966 AW&CS
41399	TC-18E	966 AW&CS

Grumman C-20 Gulfstream II/III/IV

89 AW Andrews AFB, Maryland
US Army Andrews AFB, Maryland

C-20B Gulfstream III

FY86	
60200	89 AW
60201	89 AW
60202	89 AW
60203	89 AW
60204	89 AW
60205	89 AW
60206	89 AW
60403	89 AW

C-20C Gulfstream III

FY85	
50049	89 AW
50050	89 AW

C-20E Gulfstream III

FY87	
70139	US Army
70140	US Army

C-20F Gulfstream IV

FY91	
10108	US Army

C-20J Gulfstream II

FY89	
90266	US Army

Boeing C-22B/C-22C[1]

24 AW Howard AFB, Panama [HW]
201 ALS Andrews AFB, Maryland

FY83	
34610	201 ALS
34612	201 ALS
34615	201 ALS
34616	201 ALS
34618[1]	24 AW

Boeing VC-25A

89 AW Andrews AFB, Maryland

FY82	
28000	
FY92	
29000	

Boeing CT-43A

12 FTW Randolph AFB, Texas [RA] (bk/y)
24 Wg Howard AFB, Panama [HW]
200 ALS Buckley ANGB, Colorado

FY71	
11403	12 FTW
11404	12 FTW
11405	12 FTW
11406	12 FTW
FY72	
20283	24 AW
20288	200 ALS
FY73	
31150	12 FTW
31151	12 FTW
31152	12 FTW
31153	12 FTW
31154	200 ALS
31155	12 FTW
31156	12 FTW

Boeing B-52G Stratofortress

2 BW Barksdale AFB, Louisiana [LA]
93 BW Castle AFB, California [CA]
419 TS Edwards AFB, California [ED]

FY57	
76476	93 BW
FY58	
80191	93 BW
80213	93 BW
80221	93 BW
80234	
80258	93 BW
FY59	
92565	93 BW
92572	93 BW
92577	2 BW
92586	419 TS

Boeing B-52H Stratofortress

2 BW Barksdale AFB, Louisiana [LA]
5 BW Minot AFB, North Dakota [MT]
410 BW KI Sawyer AFB, Michigan [KI]
416 BW Griffiss AFB, New York [GR]
419 TS Edwards AFB, California [ED]
*AFRES, Air Force Reserve:
917 Wg Barksdale AFB, Louisiana [BD]

FY60	
00001	5 BW
00002	410 BW
00003	5 BW
00004	
00005	410 BW
00007	2 BW
00008	2 BW
00009	2 BW
00010	2 BW
00011	410 BW
00012	416 BW
00013	410 BW
00014	2 BW
00015	
00016	2 BW
00017	2 BW
00018	2 BW
00019	2 BW
00020	2 BW
00021	416 BW
00022	5 BW

00023	5 BW
00024	416 BW
00025	2 BW
00026	410 BW
00028	416 BW
00029	
00030	416 BW
00031	2 BW
00032	2 BW
00033	416 BW
00034	416 BW
00035	2 BW
00036	410 BW
00037	2 BW
00038	410 BW
00041	2 BW
00042	2 BW
00043	2 BW
00044	
00045	917 Wg★
00046	5 BW
00047	410 BW
00048	416 BW
00049	2 BW
00050	419 TS
00051	
00052	5 BW
00053	2 BW
00054	410 BW
00055	5 BW
00056	410 BW
00057	5 BW
00058	917 Wg
00059	2 BW
00060	416 BW
00061	5 BW
00062	2 BW
FY61	
10001	
10002	2 BW
10003	
10004	2 BW
10005	
10006	5 BW
10007	5 BW
10008	917 Wg
10009	
10010	5 BW
10011	2 BW
10012	416 BW
10013	5 BW
10014	416 BW
10015	416 BW
10016	
10017	917 Wg
10018	2 BW
10019	2 BW
10020	416 BW
10021	416 BW
10022	917 Wg
10023	5 BW
10024	410 BW
10025	416 BW
10027	2 BW
10028	2 BW
10029	2 BW
10031	5 BW
10032	2 BW
10034	5 BW
10035	
10036	5 BW
10038	2 BW
10039	
10040	5 BW

Lockheed C-130 Hercules
1 SOS Kadena AB, Japan
3 Wg Elmendorf AFB, Alaska [AK]
7 SOS RAF Alconbury, UK
7 Wg Dyess AFB, Texas [DY]
8 SOS Hurlburt Field, Florida
9 SOS Eglin AFB, Florida
15 SOS Hurlburt Field, Florida
16 SOS Hurlburt Field, Florida
16 SOW Hurlburt Field, Florida
17 SOS Kadena AB, Japan
23 Wg Pope AFB, North Carolina [FT]
41 ECS Davis-Monthan AFB, Arizona [DM] (bl)
42 ACCS Davis-Monthan AFB, Arizona [DM] (w)
43 ECS Davis-Monthan AFB, Arizona [DM] (r)
52 ALS Moody AFB, Georgia [MY]
53 WRS Keesler AFB, Missouri [KT]★
58 SOW Kirtland AFB, New Mexico
64 ALS Chicago O'Hare, Illinois [VO]★
67 SOS RAF Alconbury, UK
71 RQS Patrick AFB, Florida [FF]
86 AW Ramstein AB, Germany [RS]
95 ALS Milwaukee, Wisconsin [MK]★
96 ALS St Paul, Minnesota [MS] (pr)★
102 RQS New York ANG
105 ALS Tennessee ANG
109 ALS Minnesota ANG [MN]
115 ALS California ANG [CI]
129 RQS California ANG
130 ALS West Virginia ANG
135 ALS Maryland ANG
139 ALS New York ANG
142 ALS Delaware ANG
143 ALS RhodeIsland ANG [RI]
144 ALS Alaska ANG
154 ALS Arkansas ANG
156 ALS North Carolina ANG
158 ALS Georgia ANG
164 ALS Ohio ANG
165 ALS Kentucky ANG
167 ALS West Virginia ANG
171 ALS Michigan ANG
180 ALS Missouri ANG
181 ALS Texas ANG
185 ALS Oklahoma ANG
187 ALS Wyoming ANG
193 SOS Pennsylvania ANG
204 ALS Hawaii ANG
210 RQS Alaska ANG
301 RQS Patrick AFB, Florida [FL]★
303 ALS March AFB, California★
304 RQS Portland, Oregon [PD]★
310 ALS, Howard AFB, Canal Zone [HW]
314 AW Little Rock AFB, Arkansas [LK]
327 ALS NAS Willow Grove, Pennsylvania [WG]★
328 ALS Niagara Falls, New York [NF]★

357 ALS Maxwell AFB, AL [MX]★
374 AW Yokota AB, Japan [YJ]
418 TS Edwards AFB, California [ED]
514 TS Hill AFB, Utah
700 ALS Dobbins AFB, Georgia [DB]★
711 ALS Duke Field, Florida★
731 ALS Peterson AFB, Colorado [PP]★
757 ALS Youngstown, Ohio [YO]★
758 ALS Pittsburgh, Pennsylvania [PI]★
815 ALS Keesler, Missouri [KT]★
(★=AFRES: Air Force Reserve)

FY90		
00161	MC-130H	15 SOS
00162	MC-130H	AFSC
00163	AC-130U	16 SOW
00164	AC-130U	16 SOW
00165	AC-130U	16 SOW
00166	AC-130U	16 SOS
00167	AC-130U	AFSC

FY60		
00294	C-130B	731 ALS★
00310	C-130B	731 ALS★

FY80		
00320	C-130H	158 ALS
00321	C-130H	158 ALS
00322	C-130H	158 ALS
00323	C-130H	158 ALS
00324	C-130H	158 ALS
00325	C-130H	158 ALS
00326	C-130H	158 ALS
00331	C-130H	158 ALS
00332	C-130H	158 ALS

FY90		
01057	C-130H	105 ALS
01058	C-130H	105 ALS

FY70		
01259	C-130E	23 Wg
01260	C-130E	80 AW
01261	C-130E	23 Wg
01262	C-130E	23 Wg
01263	C-130E	23 Wg
01264	C-130E	86 AW
01265	C-130E	23 Wg
01266	C-130E	23 Wg
01267	C-130E	23 Wg
01268	C-130E	23 Wg
01269	C-130E	23 Wg
01270	C-130E	23 Wg
01271	C-130E	86 AW
01272	C-130E	23 Wg
01273	C-130E	23 Wg
01274	C-130E	86 AW
01275	C-130E	23 Wg
01276	C-130E	23 Wg

FY90		
01791	C-130H	164 ALS
01792	C-130H	164 ALS
01793	C-130H	164 ALS
01794	C-130H	164 ALS
01795	C-130H	164 ALS
01796	C-130H	164 ALS
01797	C-130H	164 ALS

01798	C-130H	164 ALS	14854	HC-130P	58 SOW	FY62		
02103	HC-130H	210 RQS	14855	HC-130P	304 RQS★	21784	C-130E	154 ALS
09107	C-130H	757 ALS★	14856	HC-130P	304 RQS★	21786	C-130E	109 ALS
09108	C-130H	757 ALS★	14857	HC-130H	514 TS	21787	C-130E	154 ALS
			14858	HC-130P	17 SOS	21788	C-130E	154 ALS
FY81			14859	C-130H	711 SOS	21789	C-130E	731 ALS★
10626	C-130H	700 ALS★	14860	HC-130P	304 RQS★	21790	C-130E	154 ALS
10627	C-130H	700 ALS★	14861	WC-130H	53 WRS★	21791	EC-130E	42 ACCS
10628	C-130H	700 ALS★	14862	EC-130H	41 ECS	21792	C-130E	115 ALS
10629	C-130H	700 ALS★	14863	HC-130P	71 RQS	21793	C-130E	115 ALS
10630	C-130H	700 ALS★	14864	HC-130P	304 RQS★	21794	C-130E	731 ALS★
10631	C-130H	700 ALS★	14865	HC-130P	304 RQS★	21795	C-130E	154 ALS
			14866	WC-130H	53 WRS★	21798	C-130E	154 ALS★
FY68			17680	C-130E	314 AW	21801	C-130E	115 ALS
10934	C-130E	23 Wg	17681	C-130E	86 AW	21803	C-130E	96 ALS★
10935	C-130E	86 AW	18240	C-130E	86 AW	21804	C-130E	154 ALS
10937	C-130E	23 Wg				21806	C-130E	96 ALS★
10938	C-130E	86 AW	FY91			21807	C-130E	327 ALS★
10939	C-130E	23 Wg	19141	C-130H	64 ALS★	21808	C-130E	731 ALS★
10940	C-130E	23 Wg	19142	C-130H	95 ALS★	21810	C-130E	731 ALS★
10941	C-130E	23 Wg	19143	C-130H	328 ALS	21811	C-130E	115 ALS
10942	C-130E	23 Wg	19144	C-130H	700 ALS★	21812	C-130E	109 ALS
10943	C-130E	86 AW				21816	C-130E	96 ALS★
10947	C-130E	86 AW	FY82			21817	C-130E	109 ALS
10948	C-130E	314 AW	20054	C-130H	144 ALS	21818	EC-130E	42 ACCS
10949	C-130E	314 AW	20055	C-130H	144 ALS	21819	C-130E	310 ALS
10950	C-130E	314 AW	20056	C-130H	144 ALS	21820	C-130E	731 ALS★
			20057	C-130H	144 ALS	21821	C-130E	314 AW
FY61			20058	C-130H	144 ALS	21822	C-130E	310 ALS
10949	C-130B	156 ALS	20059	C-130H	144 ALS	21823	C-130E	731 ALS★
10950	C-130B	156 ALS	20060	C-130H	144 ALS	21824	C-130E	154 ALS
10956	C-130B	303 ALS★	20061	C-130H	144 ALS	21825	EC-130E	42 ACCS
10957	C-130B	303 ALS★				21826	C-130E	115 ALS
10959	C-130B	731 ALS★	FY92			21827	C-130E	314 AW
10967	C-130B	303 ALS★	20547	C-130H	314 AW	21828	C-130E	310 ALS
10968	C-130B	303 ALS★	20548	C-130H	314 AW	21829	C-130E	109 ALS
			20549	C-130H	314 AW	21830	C-130E	731 ALS★
FY91			20550	C-130H	314 AW	21832	EC-130E	42 ACCS
11231	C-130H	165 ALS	20551	C-130H	314 AW	21833	C-130E	115 ALS
11232	C-130H	123 ALS	20552	C-130H	314 AW	21834	C-130E	96 ALS★
11233	C-130H	123 ALS	20553	C-130H	314 AW	21835	C-130E	96 ALS★
11234	C-130H	123 ALS	20554	C-130H	314 AW	21836	EC-130E	42 ACCS
11235	C-130H	123 ALS				21837	C-130E	109 ALS
11236	C-130H	123 ALS	FY72			21838	C-130E	731 ALS★
11237	C-130H	123 ALS	21288	C-130E	374 AW	21839	C-130E	96 ALS★
11238	C-130H	123 ALS	21289	C-130E	374 AW	21842	C-130E	171 ALS
11239	C-130H	123 ALS	21290	C-130E	374 AW	21843	C-130E	
11651	C-130H	165 ALS	21291	C-130E	374 AW	21844	C-130E	96 ALS★
11652	C-130H	165 ALS	21292	C-130E	314 AW	21846	C-130E	109 ALS
11653	C-130H	165 ALS	21293	C-130E	314 AW	21847	C-130E	96 ALS★
			21294	C-130E	314 AW	21848	C-130E	96 ALS★
FY61			21295	C-130E	314 AW	21849	C-130E	815 ALS★
12358	C-130E	171 ALS	21296	C-130E	314 AW	21850	C-130E	327 ALS★
12359	C-130E	115 ALS	21298	C-130E	314 AW	21851	C-130E	115 ALS
12361	C-130E	109 ALS	21299	C-130E	374 AW	21852	C-130E	96 ALS★
12362	C-130E	314 AW	21302	HC-130H		21855	MC-130E	8 SOS
12363	C-130E	314 AW				21856	C-130E	109 ALS
12367	C-130E	115 ALS	FY92			21857	EC-130E	42 ACCS
12368	C-130E	96 ALS	21394	LC-130H	109 ALS	21858	C-130E	731 ALS★
12369	C-130E	314 AW	21395	LC-130H	109 ALS	21859	C-130E	167 ALS
12370	C-130E	171 ALS	21451	C-130H	156 ALS	21860	C-130E	731 ALS★
12371	C-130E	143 ALS	21452	C-130H	156 ALS	21862	C-130E	115 ALS
12372	C-130E	115 ALS	21453	C-130H	156 ALS	21863	EC-130E	42 ACCS
12636	C-130B	156 ALS	21454	C-130H	156 ALS	21864	C-130E	109 ALS
12638	C-130B	156 ALS	21531	C-130H	187 ALS	21866	C-130E	731 ALS★
12639	C-130B		21532	C-130H	187 ALS			
12640	C-130B	156 ALS	21533	C-130H	187 ALS	FY92		
12647	C-130B	303 ALS★	21534	C-130H	187 ALS	23021	C-130H	328 ALS★
			21535	C-130H	187 ALS	23022	C-130H	757 ALS★
FY64			21536	C-130H	187 ALS	23023	C-130H	328 ALS★
14852	HC-130P	71 RQS	21537	C-130H	187 ALS	23024	C-130H	328 ALS★
14853	HC-130P	71 RQS	21538	C-130H	187 ALS	23281	C-130H	328 ALS★
						23282	C-130H	328 ALS★

Serial	Type	Unit
23283	C-130H	328 ALS★
23284	C-130H	328 ALS★
23285	C-130H	328 ALS★
23286	C-130H	328 ALS★
23287	C-130H	328 ALS★
23288	C-130H	328 ALS★
FY62		
23487	C-130B	757 ALS★
23493	C-130B	303 ALS★
FY83		
30486	C-130H	139 ALS
30487	C-130H	139 ALS
30488	C-130H	139 ALS
30489	C-130H	139 ALS
30490	LC-130H	139 ALS
30491	LC-130H	139 ALS
30492	LC-130H	139 ALS
30493	LC-130H	139 ALS
FY93		
31036	C-130H	
31037	C-130H	
31038	C-130H	
31039	C-130H	
31040	C-130H	
31041	C-130H	
31042	C-130H	
31043	C-130H	
FY83		
31212	MC-130H	16 SOW
FY93		
31455	C-130H	156 ALS
31456	C-130H	156 ALS
31457	C-130H	156 ALS
31458	C-130H	156 ALS
31459	C-130H	156 ALS
31460	C-130H	156 ALS
31461	C-130H	156 ALS
31462	C-130H	156 ALS
31463	C-130H	156 ALS
FY73		
31580	EC-130H	43 ECS
31581	EC-130H	43 ECS
31582	C-130H	374 AW
31583	EC-130H	43 ECS
31584	EC-130H	41 ECS
31585	EC-130H	41 ECS
31586	EC-130H	41 ECS
31587	EC-130H	41 ECS
31588	EC-130H	41 ECS
31590	EC-130H	43 ECS
31592	EC-130H	43 ECS
31594	EC-130H	41 ECS
31595	EC-130H	43 ECS
31597	C-130H	374 AW
31598	C-130H	374 AW
FY93		
32041	C-130H	204 ALS
32042	C-130H	204 ALS
32043	C-130H	204 ALS
32044	C-130H	204 ALS
32045	C-130H	204 ALS
32046	C-130H	204 ALS
32047	C-130H	204 ALS
32048	C-130H	204 ALS
FY53		
33129	AC-130A	711 SOS★
FY93		
37311	C-130H	731 ALS★
37312	C-130H	731 ALS★
37313	C-130H	731 ALS★
37314	C-130H	731 ALS★
FY63		
37764	C-130E	815 ALS★
37765	C-130E	314 AW
37767	C-130E	314 AW
37768	C-130E	314 AW
37769	C-130E	96 ALS★
37770	C-130E	815 ALS★
37771	C-130E	71 RQS
37773	EC-130E	193 SOS
37776	C-130E	327 ALS★
37777	C-130E	167 ALS
37778	C-130E	314 AW
37781	C-130E	314 AW
37782	C-130E	143 ALS
37783	EC-130E	193 SOS
37784	C-130E	52 ALS
37785	MC-130E	1 SOS
37786	C-130E	314 AW
37788	C-130E	143 ALS
37790	C-130E	314 AW
37791	C-130E	314 AW
37792	C-130E	167 ALS
37793	C-130E	314 AW
37794	C-130E	314 AW
37795	C-130E	314 AW
37796	C-130E	314 AW
37799	C-130E	314 AW
37800	C-130E	167 ALS
37803	C-130E	374 AW
37804	C-130E	314 AW
37805	C-130E	815 ALS★
37806	C-130E	314 AW
37807	C-130E	314 AW
37808	C-130E	314 AW
37809	C-130E	23 Wg
37811	C-130E	143 ALS
37812	C-130E	167 ALS
37813	C-130E	23 Wg
37814	C-130E	67 SOS
37815	C-130E	193 SOS
37816	C-130E	193 SOS
37817	C-130E	815 ALS★
37818	C-130E	167 ALS
37819	C-130E	374 AW
37820	C-130E	314 AW
37821	C-130E	23 Wg
37822	C-130E	815 ALS★
37823	C-130E	327 ALS★
37824	C-130E	143 ALS
37825	C-130E	135 ALS
37826	C-130E	327 ALS★
37828	C-130E	193 SOS
37829	C-130E	314 AW
37830	C-130E	314 AW
37831	C-130E	314 AW
37832	C-130E	327 ALS★
37833	C-130E	327 ALS★
37834	C-130E	327 ALS★
37835	C-130E	314 AW
37836	C-130E	314 AW
37837	C-130E	374 AW
37838	C-130E	314 AW
37839	C-130E	314 AW
37840	C-130E	143 ALS
37841	C-130E	314 AW
37842	C-130E	8 SOS
37845	C-130E	314 AW
37846	C-130E	23 Wg
37847	C-130E	154 ALS
37848	C-130E	327 ALS★
37849	C-130E	314 AW
37850	C-130E	52 ALS
37851	C-130E	167 ALS
37852	C-130E	328 ALS★
37853	C-130E	327 ALS★
37854	C-130E	314 AW
37856	C-130E	815 ALS★
37857	C-130E	374 AW
37858	C-130E	167 ALS
37859	C-130E	143 ALS
37860	C-130E	314 AW
37861	C-130E	314 AW
37863	C-130E	328 ALS★
37864	C-130E	314 AW
37865	C-130E	374 AW
37866	C-130E	314 AW
37867	C-130E	327 ALS★
37868	C-130E	143 ALS
37869	EC-130E	193 SOS
37871	C-130E	23 Wg
37872	C-130E	167 ALS
37874	C-130E	314 AW
37876	C-130E	314 AW
37877	C-130E	167 ALS
37879	C-130E	374 AW
37880	C-130E	314 AW
37881	C-130E	314 AW
37882	C-130E	314 AW
37883	C-130E	327 ALS★
37884	C-130E	23 Wg
37885	C-130E	86 AW
37887	C-130E	86 AW
37888	C-130E	314 AW
37889	C-130E	143 ALS
37890	C-130E	314 AW
37891	C-130E	314 AW
37892	C-130E	327 ALS★
37893	C-130E	314 AW
37894	C-130E	314 AW
37895	C-130E	135 ALS
37896	C-130E	314 AW
37897	C-130E	167 ALS
37898	C-130E	8 SOS
37899	C-130E	314 AW
39810	C-130E	52 ALS
39811	C-130E	314 AW
39812	C-130E	314 AW
39813	C-130E	193 SOS
39814	C-130E	314 AW
39815	C-130E	193 SOS
39816	EC-130E	193 SOS
39817	EC-130E	193 SOS
FY84		
40204	C-130H	700 ALS★
40205	C-130H	700 ALS★
40206	C-130H	142 ALS
40207	C-130H	142 ALS
40208	C-130H	142 ALS
40209	C-130H	142 ALS
40210	C-130H	142 ALS
40211	C-130H	142 ALS
40212	C-130H	142 ALS
40213	C-130H	142 ALS
40475	MC-130H	418 TS
40476	MC-130H	7 SOS
FY64		
40495	C-130E	23 Wg
40496	MC-130E	23 Wg

C-130

40498	C-130E	23 Wg		41676	C-130H	3 Wg		50986	C-130H	71 RQS
40499	C-130E	23 Wg		41677	C-130H	7 Wg		50987	HC-130P	71 RQS
40500	C-130E	AFLC		41679	C-130H	7 Wg		50988	HC-130P	102 RQS
40502	C-130E	86 AW		41680	C-130H	7 Wg		50989	EC-130H	41 ECS
40504	C-130E	23 Wg		41682	C-130H	374 AW		50991	HC-130P	9 SOS
40510	C-130E	135 ALS		41684	C-130H	374 AW		50992	HC-130P	17 SOS
40512	C-130E	154 ALS		41685	C-130H	374 AW		50993	HC-130P	9 SOS
40513	C-130E	314 AW		41687	C-130H	7 Wg		50994	HC-13OP	9 SOS
40514	C-130E	135 ALS		41688	C-130H	7 Wg				
40515	C-130E	135 ALS		41689	C-130H	7 Wg		*FY85*		
40517	C-130E	23 Wg		41690	C-130H	3 Wg		51361	C-130H	181 ALS
40518	C-130E	314 AW		41691	C-130H	7 Wg		51362	C-130H	181 ALS
40519	C-130E	314 AW		41692	C-130H	3 Wg		51363	C-130H	181 ALS
40520	C-130E	135 ALS		42061	C-130H	7 Wg		51364	C-130H	181 ALS
40521	C-130E	135 ALS		42062	C-130H	3 Wg		51365	C-130H	181 ALS
40523	MC-130E	8 SOS		42063	C-130H	7 Wg		51366	C-130H	181 ALS
40524	C-130E	314 AW		42065	C-130H	7 Wg		51367	C-130H	181 ALS
40525	C-130E	23 Wg		42066	C-130H	3 Wg		51368	C-130H	181 ALS
40526	C-130E	135 ALS		42067	C-130H	7 Wg				
40527	C-130E	86 AW		42069	C-130H	7 Wg		*FY66*		
40529	C-130E	23 Wg		42070	C-130H	3 Wg		60212	HC-130P	58 SOW
40530	C-130E	314 AW		42071	C-130H	3 Wg		60213	HC-130P	9 SOS
40531	C-130E	86 AW		42072	C-130H	7 Wg		60215	HC-130P	9 SOS
40533	C-130E	314 AW		42130	C-130H	7 Wg		60216	HC-130P	9 SOS
40535	C-130E	23 Wg		42131	C-130H	3 Wg		60217	HC-130P	9 SOS
40537	C-130E	314 AW		42132	C-130H	7 Wg		60219	HC-130P	58 SOW
40538	C-130E	314 AW		42133	C-130H	374 AW		60220	HC-130P	9 SOS
40539	C-130E	23 Wg		42134	C-130H	7 Wg		60221	HC-130P	129 RQS
40540	C-130E	23 Wg						60222	HC-130P	102 RQS
40541	C-130E	314 AW		*FY55*				60223	HC-130P	67 SOS
40542	C-130E	314 AW		50011	AC-130A	711 SOS*		60224	HC-130P	129 RQS
40544	C-130E	135 ALS		50014	AC-130A	711 SOS*		60225	HC-130P	9 SOS
40550	C-130E	86 AW		50022	C-130A					
40551	MC-130E	8 SOS		50029	AC-130A	711 SOS*		*FY86*		
40555	MC-130E			50036	C-130A			60410	C-130H	758 ALS*
40557	C-130E	314 AW		50046	AC-130A	711 SOS*		60411	C-130H	758 ALS*
40559	MC-130E	8 SOS						60412	C-130H	758 ALS*
40560	C-130E	314 AW		*FY85*				60413	C-130H	758 ALS*
40561	MC-130E	8 SOS		50011	MC-130H	8 SOS		60414	C-130H	758 ALS*
40562	MC-130E	8 SOS		50012	MC-130H	15 SOS		60415	C-130H	758 ALS*
40565	MC-130E	1 SOS		50035	C-130H	357 ALS*		60418	C-130H	758 ALS*
40566	MC-130E	8 SOS		50036	C-130H	357 ALS*		60419	C-130H	758 ALS*
40567	MC-130E	8 SOS		50037	C-130H	357 ALS*				
40568	MC-130E	8 SOS		50038	C-130H	357 ALS*		*FY56*		
40569	C-130E	314 AW		50039	C-130H	357 ALS*		60469	AC-130A	711 SOS*
40570	C-130E	23 Wg		50040	C-130H	357 ALS*		60498	C-130A	155 ALS
40571	MC-130E	1 SOS		50041	C-130H	357 ALS*		60509	AC-130A	711 SOS*
40572	MC-130E	8 SOS		50042	C-130H	357 ALS*		60522	C-130A	711 SOS*
								60524	C-130A	155 ALS
FY54				*FY65*				60525	C-130A	155 ALS*
41623	AC-130A	711 SOS*		50962	EC-130H	42 ACCS		60547	C-130A	155 ALS
41628	AC-130A	711 SOS*		50963	WC-130H	53 WRS*				
41630	AC-130A	711 SOS*		50964	C-130E	815 ALS*		*FY86*		
41637	C-130A	155 ALS		50966	WC-130H	53 WRS*		61391	C-130H	180 ALS
				50967	WC-130H	53 WRS*		61392	C-130H	180 ALS
FY74				50968	WC-130H	53 WRS*		61393	C-130H	180 ALS
41658	C-130H	3 Wg		50969	C-130E	711 SOS*		61394	C-130H	180 ALS
41659	C-130H	3 Wg		50970	HC-130P	304 RQS*		61395	C-130H	180 ALS
41660	C-130H	374 AW		50971	HC-130P	58 SOW		61396	C-130H	180 ALS
41661	C-130H	374 AW		50972	C-130E	711 SOS*		61397	C-130H	180 ALS
41662	C-130H	7 Wg		50973	HC-130P	71 RQS		61398	C-130H	180 ALS
41663	C-130H	7 Wg		50974	HC-130P	102 RQS		61699	MC-130H	7 SOS
41664	C-130H	7 Wg		50975	HC-130P	58 SOW				
41665	C-130H	7 Wg		50976	HC-130P	304 RQS*		*FY87*		
41666	C-130H	7 Wg		50977	WC-130H	53 WRS*		70023	MC-130H	7 SOS
41667	C-130H	7 Wg		50978	HC-130P	102 RQS		70024	MC-130H	15 SOS
41668	C-130H	3 Wg		50979	NC-130H	514 TS		70125	MC-130H	58 SOW
41669	C-130H	7 Wg		50980	WC-130H	53 WRS*		70126	MC-130H	58 SOW
41670	C-130H	7 Wg		50981	HC-130P	129 RQS		70127	MC-130H	58 SOW
41671	C-130H	7 Wg		50982	HC-130P	71 RQS		70128	AC-130U	418 TS
41673	C-130H	7 Wg		50983	HC-130P	129 RQS				
41674	C-130H	7 Wg		50984	WC-130H	53 WRS*		*FY57*		
41675	C-130H	7 Wg		50985	WC-130H	53 WRS*		70465	C-130A	155 ALS
								70526	C-130B	412 TW

FY67		
77184	C-130H	310 ALS
FY87		
79281	C-130H	64 ALS★
79282	C-130H	64 ALS★
79283	C-130H	64 ALS★
79284	C-130H	64 ALS★
79285	C-130H	64 ALS★
79286	C-130H	64 ALS★
79287	C-130H	64 ALS★
79288	C-130H	64 ALS★
FY88		
80191	MC-130H	58 SOW
80192	MC-130H	58 SOW
80193	MC-130H	7 SOS
80194	MC-130H	7 SOS
80195	MC-130H	15 SOS
80264	MC-130H	15 SOS
FY58		
80711	C-130B	187 ALS
80716	C-130B	514 TS
80728	C-130B	156 ALS
80729	C-130B	156 ALS
80734	C-130B	187 ALS
80738	C-130B	731 ALS★
FY78		
80806	C-130H	185 ALS
80807	C-130H	185 ALS
80808	C-130H	185 ALS
80809	C-130H	185 ALS
80810	C-130H	185 ALS
80811	C-130H	185 ALS
80812	C-130H	185 ALS
80813	C-130H	185 ALS
81301	C-130H	130 ALS
81302	C-130H	130 ALS
81303	C-130H	130 ALS
81304	C-130H	130 ALS
81305	C-130H	130 ALS
81306	C-130H	130 ALS
81307	C-130H	130 ALS
81308	C-130H	130 ALS
81803	MC-130H	16 SOW
82101	HC-130H	210 RQS
82102	HC-130H	210 RQS
84401	C-130H	95 ALS★
84402	C-130H	95 ALS★
84403	C-130H	95 ALS★
84404	C-130H	95 ALS★
84405	C-130H	95 ALS★
84406	C-130H	95 ALS★
84407	C-130H	95 ALS★
84408	C-130H	95 ALS★
FY89		
90280	MC-130H	15 SOS
90281	MC-130H	15 SOS
90282	MC-130H	15 SOS
90283	MC-130H	AFSC
FY79		
90473	C-130H	144 ALS
90474	C-130H	
90475	C-130H	159 FS
90476	C-130H	157 FS
90477	C-130H	158 ALS
90478	C-130H	199 FS
90479	C-130H	185 ALS
90480	C-130H	122 FS
FY89		
90509	AC-130U	AFSC
90510	AC-130U	418 TS
90511	AC-130U	418 TS
90512	AC-130U	
90513	AC-130U	
90514	AC-130U	
91051	C-130H	105 ALS
91052	C-130H	105 ALS
91053	C-130H	105 ALS
91054	C-130H	105 ALS
91055	C-130H	105 ALS
91056	C-130H	105 ALS
91181	C-130H	155 ALS
91182	C-130H	155 ALS
91183	C-130H	155 ALS
91184	C-130H	155 ALS
91185	C-130H	155 ALS
91186	C-130H	155 ALS
91187	C-130H	155 ALS
91188	C-130H	155 ALS
FY59		
91524	C-130B	757 ALS★
91528	C-130B	156 ALS
91531	C-130B	731 ALS★
91532	C-130B	757 ALS★
91535	C-130B	757 ALS★
91537	C-130B	303 ALS★
FY69		
95819	HC-130N	9 SOS
95820	HC-130N	67 SOS
95821	HC-130N	17 SOS
95822	HC-130N	17 SOS
95823	HC-130N	67 SOS
95824	HC-130N	301 RQS★
95825	HC-130N	17 SOS
95826	HC-130N	67 SOS
95827	HC-130N	67 SOS
95828	HC-130N	9 SOS
95829	HC-130N	301 RQS★
95830	HC-130N	301 RQS★
95831	HC-130N	9 SOS
95832	HC-130N	9 SOS
95833	HC-130N	301 RQS★
96566	C-130E	86 AW
96568	AC-130H	16 SOS
96569	AC-130H	16 SOS
96570	AC-130H	16 SOS
96572	AC-130H	16 SOS
96573	AC-130H	16 SOS
96574	AC-130H	16 SOS
96575	AC-130H	16 SOS
96577	AC-130H	16 SOS
96579	C-130E	314 AW
96580	C-130E	23 Wg
96582	C-130E	86 AW
96583	C-130E	86 AW
FY89		
99101	C-130H	757 ALS★
99102	C-130H	757 ALS★
99103	C-130H	757 ALS★
99104	C-130H	757 ALS★
99105	C-130H	757 ALS★
99106	C-130H	757 ALS★

BoeingC-135/C-137

6 Wg Eielson AFB, Alaska
8 ADCS/552 ACW, Tinker AFB, Oklahoma [OK]
18 Wg Kadena AB, Japan [ZZ]
19 ARW Robins AFB, Georgia (*bl* & *w*)
22 ARW McConnell AFB, Kansas
43 ARG Malmstrom AFB,-Montana (*y/bk*)
55 Wg Offutt AFB, Nebraska [OF]
63 ARS/927 ARW, Selfridge ANGB, Michigan (*gn*)★
65 ALS, Hickam AFB, H awaii
71 ARS Barksdale AFB, Louisiana [LA]
72 ARS/434 ARW, Grissom AFB, Indiana (*bl*)★
74 ARS/434 ARW, Grissom AFB, Indiana (*r*)★
89 AW Andrews AFB, Maryland
92 ARW Fairchild AFB, Washington
100 ARW RAF Mildenhall, UK [D] (*r/w/bl*)
106 ARS Alabama ANG
108 ARS Illinois ANG (*wh/bl*)
116 ARS Washington ANG (*bl*)
117 ARS Kansas ANG (*bl/y*)
126 ARS Wisconsin ANG (*w/bk*)
132 ARS Maine ANG (*gn*)
133 ARS New Hampshire ANG
136 ARS New York ANG (*bl*)
141 ARS New Jersey ANG (*y*)
145 ARS Ohio ANG (*r/w*)
146 ARS Pennsylvania ANG (*y/bk*)
147 ARS Pennsylvania ANG (*bk/y*)
150 ARS New Jersey ANG (*bl*)
151 ARS Tennessee ANG (*or*)
153 ARS Mississippi ANG (*bl/y*)
166 ARS Ohio ANG (*bl/w*)
168 ARS Alaska ANG (*bl*)
173 ARS Nebraska ANG (*r/w*)
191 ARS Utah ANG
196 ARS California ANG (*bl/w*)
197 ARS Arizona ANG (*gd*)
203 ARS Hawaii ANG
314 ARS/940 ARW, Beale AFB, California (*r*)★
319 ARW Grand Forks AFB, North Dakota
336 ARS/452 AMW, March AFB, California (*y*)★
366 Wg Mountain Home AFB, Idaho [MO] (*y/gn*)
398 OG/97 AMW Castle AFB, California
452 TS/412TW, Edwards AFB, California
457 OG/19 ARW, Altus AFB, Oklahoma (*y/gn*)
465 ARS/507 ARW, Tinker AFB, Oklahoma★
507 ARG, Tinker AFB, Oklahoma★
(★=AFRES: Air Force Reserve)

FY60		
00313	KC-135R	18 Wg
00314	KC-135R	74 ARS★
00315	KC-135R	126 ARS
00316	KC-135E	116 ARS
00318	KC-135R	457 OG
00319	KC-135R	19 ARW
00320	KC-135R	18 Wg
00321	KC-135R	319 ARW

Serial	Type	Unit
00322	KC-135R	72 ARS★
00323	KC-135R	
00324	KC-135R	319 ARW
00327	KC-135E	191 ARS
00328	KC-135R	92 ARW
00329	KC-135R	203 ARS
00331	KC-135R	97 AMW
00332	KC-135R	457 OG
00333	KC-135R	398 OG
00334	KC-135R	126 ARS
00335	KC-135Q	71 ARS
00336	KC-135Q	
00337	KC-135T	92 ARW
00339	KC-135Q	
00341	KC-135R	145 ARS
00342	KC-135R	350 ARS
00343	KC-135T	380 ARW
00344	KC-135T	380 ARW
00345	KC-135Q	22 ARW
00346	KC-135Q	71 ARS
00347	KC-135R	166 ARS
00348	KC-135R	43 ARG
00349	KC-135R	398 OG
00350	KC-135R	43 ARG
00351	KC-135R	43 ARG
00353	KC-135R	319 ARW
00355	KC-135R	43 ARG
00356	KC-135R	22 ARW
00357	KC-135R	22 ARW
00358	KC-135R	43 ARG
00359	KC-135R	74 ARS★
00360	KC-135R	18 Wg
00362	KC-135R	22 ARW
00363	KC-135R	72 ARS★
00364	KC-135R	74 ARS★
00365	KC-135R	366 Wg
00366	KC-135R	18 Wg
00367	KC-135R	136 ARS
00372	C-135E	452 TS
00374	EC-135E	452 TS
00375	C-135E	452 TS
00377	C-135A	452 TS

FY61

Serial	Type	Unit
10264	KC-135R	145 ARS
10266	KC-135R	173 ARS
10267	KC-135R	19 ARW
10268	KC-135E	314 ARS★
10270	KC-135E	63 ARS★
10271	KC-135E	63 ARS★
10272	KC-135E	74 ARS★
10275	KC-135R	18 Wg
10276	KC-135R	22 ARW
10277	KC-135R	366 Wg
10280	KC-135E	336 ARS★
10281	KC-135E	197 ARS
10284	KC-135R	92 ARW
10288	KC-135R	28 ARS
10290	KC-135R	203 ARS
10292	KC-135R	22 ARW
10293	KC-135R	22 ARW
10294	KC-135R	
10295	KC-135R	457 OG
10298	KC-135R	126 ARS
10299	KC-135R	92 ARW
10300	KC-135R	457 OG
10302	KC-135R	92 ARW
10303	KC-135E	336 ARS★
10304	KC-135R	18 Wg
10305	KC-135R	92 ARW
10306	KC-135R	43 ARG
10307	KC-135R	74 ARS★
10308	KC-135R	398 OG
10309	KC-135R	126 ARS
10310	KC-135R	133 ARS
10311	KC-135R	398 OG
10312	KC-135R	28 ARS
10313	KC-135R	100 ARW
10314	KC-135R	18 Wg
10315	KC-135R	18 Wg
10317	KC-135R	319 ARW
10318	KC-135R	319 ARW
10320	KC-135R	18 Wg
10321	KC-135R	100 ARW
10323	KC-135R	18 Wg
10324	KC-135R	22 ARW
10326	EC-135E	452 TS
10327	EC-135N	CinC CC
10329	EC-135E	452 TS
10330	EC-135E	452 TS
12662	RC-135S	55 Wg
12663	RC-135S	55 Wg
12665	WC-135B	55 Wg
12666	WC-135B	
12667	TC-135B	55 Wg
12668	C-135C	65 ALS
12669	C-135C	452 TS
12670	WC-135B	55 Wg
12672	OC-135B	55 Wg
12674	OC-135B	55 Wg

FY64

Serial	Type	Unit
14828	KC-135R	22 ARW
14829	KC-135R	
14830	KC-135R	906 ARS
14831	KC-135R	92 ARW
14832	KC-135R	203 ARS
14833	KC-135R	
14834	KC-135R	92 ARW
14835	KC-135R	22 ARW
14836	KC-135R	43 ARG
14837	KC-135R	319 ARW
14838	KC-135R	380 ARW
14839	KC-135R	136 ARS
14840	KC-135R	166 ARS
14841	RC-135V	55 Wg
14842	RC-135V	55 Wg
14843	RC-135V	55 Wg
14844	RC-135V	55 Wg
14845	RC-135V	55 Wg
14846	RC-135V	55 Wg
14847	RC-135U	55 Wg
14848	RC-135V	55 Wg
14849	RC-135U	55 Wg

FY67

Serial	Type	Unit
19417	EC-137D	19 Wg

FY62

Serial	Type	Unit
23498	KC-135R	92 ARW
23499	KC-135R	398 OG
23500	KC-135R	126 ARS
23502	KC-135R	398 OG
23503	KC-135R	18 Wg
23504	KC-135R	319 ARW
23505	KC-135R	319 ARW
23506	KC-135R	19 ARW
23507	KC-135R	398 OG
23508	KC-135R	19 ARW
23509	KC-135R	319 ARW
23510	KC-135R	74 ARS★
23511	KC-135R	145 ARS
23512	KC-135R	136 ARS
23513	KC-135R	366 Wg
23514	KC-135R	203 ARS
23515	KC-135R	22 ARW
23516	KC-135R	
23517	KC-135R	380 ARW
23518	KC-135R	72 ARS★
23519	KC-135R	18 Wg
23520	KC-135R	19 ARW
23521	KC-135R	72 ARS★
23523	KC-135R	19 ARW
23524	KC-135A	457 OG
23526	KC-135R	457 OG
23527	KC-135E	150 ARS
23528	KC-135R	906 ARS
23529	KC-135R	92 ARW
23530	KC-135R	72 ARS★
23531	KC-135R	145 ARS
23533	KC-135R	43 ARG
23534	KC-135R	19 ARW
23537	KC-135R	43 ARG
23538	KC-135R	43 ARG
23540	KC-135R	92 ARW
23541	KC-135R	398 OG
23542	KC-135R	92 ARW
23543	KC-135R	72 ARS★
23544	KC-135R	19 ARW
23545	KC-135R	19 ARW
23546	KC-135R	43 ARG
23547	KC-135R	133 ARS
23548	KC-135R	398 OG
23549	KC-135R	43 ARG
23550	KC-135R	398 OG
23551	KC-135R	
23552	KC-135R	19 ARW
23553	KC-135R	319 ARW
23554	KC-135R	19 ARW
23556	KC-135R	457 OG
23557	KC-135R	319 ARW
23558	KC-135R	
23559	KC-135R	398 OG
23561	KC-135R	100 ARW
23562	KC-135R	380 ARW
23564	KC-135R	28 ARS
23565	KC-135R	398 OG
23566	KC-135E	168 ARS
23568	KC-135R	457 OG
23569	KC-135R	19 ARW
23571	KC-135R	145 ARS
23572	KC-135R	366 Wg
23573	KC-135R	
23575	KC-135R	43A RG
23576	KC-135R	133 ARS
23577	KC-135R	100 ARW
23578	KC-135R	92 ARW
23580	KC-135R	398 OG
23581	EC-135C	55 Wg
23582	EC-135C	55 Wg
23585	EC-135C	55 Wg
24125	C-135B	65 ALS
24126	C-135B	141 ARS
24127	C-135B	65 ALS
24129	TC-135W	55 Wg
24130	C-135B	55 Wg
24131	RC-135W	55 Wg
24132	RC-135W	55 Wg
24133	TC-135S	6 Wg
24134	RC-135W	55 Wg
24135	RC-135W	55 Wg
24138	RC-135W	55 Wg
24139	RC-135W	55 Wg
26000	C-137C	89 AW

FY72

Serial	Type	Unit
27000	C-137C	89 AW

FY63

Serial	Type	Unit
37976	KC-135R	319 ARW
37977	KC-135R	18 Wg

37978	KC-135R	906 ARS		38879	KC-135R	92 ARW		71441	KC-135E	108 ARS
37979	KC-135R	457 OG		38880	KC-135R	457 OG		71443	KC-135E	132 ARS
37980	KC-135R	43 ARS		38881	KC-135R	319 ARW		71445	KC-135E	141 ARS
37981	KC-135R	136 ARS		38883	KC-135R	18 Wg		71447	KC-135E	146 ARS
37982	KC-135R	43 ARS		38884	KC-135R	457 OG		71448	KC-135E	168 ARS
37984	KC-135R	19 ARW		38885	KC-135R	906 ARS		71450	KC-135E	132 ARS
37985	KC-135R	380 ARW		38886	KC-135R	18 Wg		71451	KC-135E	168 ARS
37987	KC-135R	319 ARW		38887	KC-135R	380 ARW		71452	KC-135E	197 ARS
37988	KC-135R	173 ARS		38888	KC-135R	906 ARS		71453	KC-135R	509 ARS
37991	KC-135R	173 ARS		39792	RC-135V	55 Wg		71454	KC-135R	43 ARG
37992	KC-135R	166 ARS						71455	KC-135R	151 ARS
37993	KC-135R	166 ARS		*FY55*				71456	KC-135R	92 ARW
37995	KC-135R	19 ARW		53118	EC-135K	8 ADCS		71458	KC-135E	108 ARS
37996	KC-135R	72 ARS★		53125	EC-135Y	CinC CC		71459	KC-135E	196 ARS
37997	KC-135R	19 ARW		53128	NKC-135A	452 TS		71460	KC-135E	117 ARS
37999	KC-135R	319 ARW		53132	NKC-135E	452 TS		71461	KC-135R	457 OG
38000	KC-135R	22 ARW		53134	NKC-135A	USN/FTRG		71462	KC-135E	145 ARS
38002	KC-135R	19 ARW		53135	NKC-135E	452 TS		71463	KC-135E	117 ARS
38003	KC-135R	100 ARW		53141	KC-135E	196 ARS		71464	KC-135E	141 ARS
38004	KC-135R	366 ARS		53143	KC-135E	197 ARS		71465	KC-135E	168 ARS
38005	KC-135R	398 OG		53145	KC-135E	314 ARS★		71468	KC-135R	336 ARS★
38006	KC-135R	18 Wg		53146	KC-135E	141 ARS		71469	KC-135E	166 ARS
38007	KC-135R	457 OG						71471	KC-135E	132 ARS
38008	KC-135R	100 ARW		*FY85*				71472	KC-135R	72 ARS★
38011	KC-135R	319 ARW		56973	C-137C	89 AW		71473	KC-135R	
38012	KC-135R	906 ARS		56974	C-137C	89 AW		71474	KC-135E	398 OG
38013	KC-135R	166 ARS						71475	KC-135E	197 ARS
38014	KC-135R	380 ARW		*FY56*				71478	KC-135E	151 ARS
38015	KC-135R	173 ARS		63593	KC-135E	141 ARS		71479	KC-135E	336 ARS★
38017	KC-135R	92 ARW		63596	NKC-135A	USN/FTRG		71480	KC-135E	108 ARS
38018	KC-135R	173 ARS		63604	KC-135E	117 ARS		71482	KC-135E	117 ARS
38019	KC-135R	380 ARW		63606	KC-135E	132 ARS		71483	KC-135R	22 ARW
38020	KC-135R	457 OG		63607	KC-135E	151 ARS		71484	KC-135E	197 ARS
38021	KC-135R	319 ARW		63609	KC-135E	151 ARS		71485	KC-135E	151 ARS
38022	KC-135R	22 ARW		63611	KC-135E	146 ARS		71486	KC-135R	100 ARW
38023	KC-135R	92 ARW		63612	KC-135E	146 ARS		71487	KC-135R	72 ARS★
38024	KC-135R	74 ARS★		63622	KC-135E	132 ARS		71488	KC-135R	457 OG
38025	KC-135R	319 ARW		63623	KC-135E	336 ARS★		71491	KC-135E	132 ARS
38026	KC-135R	319 ARW		63626	KC-135E	133 ARS		71492	KC-135E	151 ARS
38027	KC-135R	92 ARW		63630	KC-135E	146 ARS		71493	KC-135R	43 ARG
38028	KC-135R	133 ARS		63631	KC-135E	117 ARS		71494	KC-135E	168 ARS
38029	KC-135R	126 ARS		63638	KC-135E	197 ARS		71495	KC-135E	197 ARS
38030	KC-135R	203 ARS		63640	KC-135E	132 ARS		71496	KC-135E	197 ARS
38031	KC-135R	22 ARW		63641	KC-135E	117 ARS		71497	KC-135E	191 ARS
38032	KC-135R	72 ARS★		63643	KC-135E	151 ARS		71499	KC-135R	92 ARW
38034	KC-135R	380 ARW		63645	KC-135E	314 ARS★		71501	KC-135R	116 ARS
38035	KC-135R			63648	KC-135E	146 ARS		71502	KC-135R	319 ARW
38036	KC-135R	19 ARW		63650	KC-135E	116 ARS		71503	KC-135E	151 ARS
38037	KC-135R	398 OG		63654	KC-135E	132 ARS		71504	KC-135E	63 ARS★
38038	KC-135R	133 ARS		63658	KC-135E	117 ARS		71505	KC-135E	132 ARS
38039	KC-135R	43 ARG						71506	KC-135R	
38040	KC-135R	319 ARW		*FY57*				71507	KC-135E	141 ARS
38041	KC-135R	72 ARS★		71418	KC-135R	153 ARS		71508	KC-135E	203 ARS
38043	KC-135R	166 ARS		71419	KC-135R	319 ARW		71509	KC-135E	147 ARS
38044	KC-135R	906 ARS		71421	KC-135R	116 ARS		71510	KC-135E	196 ARS
38045	KC-135R	319 ARW		71422	KC-135E	63 ARS★		71511	KC-135E	314 ARS★
38046	EC-135C	55 Wg		71423	KC-135E	147 ARS		71512	KC-135E	336 ARS★
38048	EC-135C	55 Wg		71425	KC-135E	151 ARS		71514	KC-135R	126 ARS
38050	EC-135C	55 Wg		71426	KC-135E	168 ARS		72589	KC-135E	55 Wg
38052	EC-135C	55 Wg		71427	KC-135R	145 ARS		72593	KC-135R	166 ARS
38053	EC-135C	55 Wg		71428	KC-135E	196 ARS		72594	KC-135E	108 ARS
38054	EC-135C	55 Wg		71429	KC-135E	117 ARS		72595	KC-135R	147 ARS
38058	KC-135D	168 ARS		71430	KC-135R	92 ARW		72597	KC-135R	153 ARS
38060	KC-135D	168 ARS		71431	KC-135E	141 ARS		72598	KC-135E	336 ARS★
38061	KC-135D	168 ARS		71432	KC-135R	380 ARW		72599	KC-135R	92 ARW
38871	KC-135R	398 OG		71433	KC-135E	197 ARS		72600	KC-135E	116 ARS
38872	KC-135R	136 ARS		71434	KC-135R	116 ARS		72601	KC-135E	151 ARS
38873	KC-135R	380 ARW		71435	KC-135R	398 OG		72602	KC-135E	150 ARS
38874	KC-135R	18 Wg		71436	KC-135E	196 ARS		72603	KC-135E	336 ARS★
38875	KC-135R	100 ARW		71437	KC-135R	457 OG		72604	KC-135E	146 ARS
38876	KC-135R	173 ARS		71438	KC-135E	63 ARS★		72605	KC-135R	22 ARW
38877	KC-135R	319 ARW		71439	KC-135E			72606	KC-135E	150 ARS
38878	KC-135R	457 OG		71440	KC-135R	319 ARW		72607	KC-135E	147 ARS
								72608	KC-135E	147 ARS

FY58		
80001	KC-135R	457 OG
80003	KC-135R	108 ARS
80004	KC-135R	153 ARS
80005	KC-135R	117 ARS
80006	KC-135E	191 ARS
80008	KC-135E	196 ARS
80009	KC-135R	126 ARS
80010	KC-135R	153 ARS
80011	KC-135R	19 ARW
80012	KC-135E	191 ARS
80013	KC-135E	63 ARS★
80014	KC-135E	108 ARS
80015	KC-135R	74 ARS★
80016	KC-135R	92 ARW
80017	KC-135E	146 ARS
80018	KC-135R	22 ARW
80020	KC-135E	116 ARS
80021	KC-135R	126 ARS
80023	KC-135R	92 ARW
80024	KC-135E	146 ARS
80027	KC-135R	92 ARW
80030	KC-135R	
80032	KC-135E	150 ARS
80034	KC-135R	380 ARW
80035	KC-135R	22 ARW
80036	KC-135R	22 ARW
80037	KC-135E	147 ARS
80038	KC-135R	92 ARW
80040	KC-135E	150 ARS
80041	KC-135E	63 ARS★
80042	KC-135T	
80043	KC-135E	191 ARS
80044	KC-135E	141 ARS
80045	KC-135Q	71 ARS
80046	KC-135Q	350 ARS
80047	KC-135Q	
80049	KC-135Q	
80050	KC-135Q	
80051	KC-135R	398 OG
80052	KC-135E	336 ARS★
80053	KC-135E	314 ARS★
80054	KC-135Q	71 ARS
80055	KC-135Q	350 ARS
80056	KC-135R	153 ARS
80057	KC-135R	108 ARS
80058	KC-135E	314 ARS★
80059	KC-135R	153 ARS
80060	KC-135Q	71 ARS
80061	KC-135T	380 ARW
80062	KC-135Q	
80063	KC-135R	
80064	KC-135E	314 ARS★
80065	KC-135T	380 ARW
80066	KC-135R	19 ARW
80067	KC-135E	108 ARS
80068	KC-135E	108 ARS
80069	KC-135Q	
80071	KC-135Q	350 ARS
80072	KC-135Q	350 ARS
80073	KC-135R	
80074	KC-135Q	350 ARS
80075	KC-135R	72 ARS★
80076	KC-135R	74 ARS★
80077	KC-135T	22 ARW
80078	KC-135E	150 ARS
80079	KC-135R	906 ARS
80080	KC-135E	191 ARS
80082	KC-135E	116 ARS
80083	KC-135R	166 ARS
80084	KC-135Q	350 ARS
80085	KC-135E	336 ARS★
80086	KC-135Q	22 ARW
80087	KC-135E	150 ARS
80088	KC-135T	22 ARW
80089	KC-135T	380 ARW
80090	KC-135E	314 ARS★
80092	KC-135R	
80093	KC-135R	
80094	KC-135T	92 ARW
80095	KC-135Q	22 ARW
80096	KC-135E	314 ARS★
80098	KC-135R	133 ARS
80099	KC-135Q	350 ARS
80100	KC-135R	43 ARG
80102	KC-135R	74 ARS★
80103	KC-135Q	350 ARS
80104	KC-135R	
80106	KC-135R	380 ARW
80107	KC-135E	191 ARS
80108	KC-135E	314 ARS★
80109	KC-135R	153 ARS
80111	KC-135E	141 ARS
80112	KC-135Q	22 ARW
80113	KC-135R	19 ARW
80114	KC-135R	398 OG
80115	KC-135E	150 ARS
80116	KC-135E	197 ARS
80117	KC-135Q	350 ARS
80118	KC-135R	22 ARW
80119	KC-135R	28 ARS
80120	KC-135R	457 OG
80121	KC-135R	92 ARW
80122	KC-135R	136 ARS
80123	KC-135R	19 ARW
80124	KC-135R	22 ARW
80125	KC-135Q	350 ARS
80126	KC-135R	19 ARW
80128	KC-135R	
80129	KC-135Q	350 ARS
80130	KC-135R	126 ARS
86970	C-137B	89 AW
86971	C-137B	89 AW
86972	C-137B	89 AW

FY59		
91444	KC-135R	145 ARS
91445	KC-135E	116 ARS
91446	KC-135R	153 ARS
91447	KC-135E	63 ARS★
91448	KC-135E	196 ARS
91450	KC-135E	196 ARS
91451	KC-135E	63 ARS★
91452	KC-135E	116 ARS
91453	KC-135R	145 ARS
91455	KC-135R	153 ARS
91456	KC-135E	141 ARS
91457	KC-135E	147 ARS
91458	KC-135R	145 ARS
91459	KC-135R	457 OG
91460	KC-135Q	22 ARW
91461	KC-135R	153 ARS
91462	KC-135Q	22 ARW
91463	KC-135R	173 ARS
91464	KC-135Q	
91466	KC-135R	319 ARW
91467	KC-135T	380 ARW
91468	KC-135R	
91469	KC-135R	92 ARW
91470	KC-135Q	22 ARW
91471	KC-135Q	71 ARS
91472	KC-135R	457 OG
91473	KC-135E	191 ARS
91474	KC-135Q	
91475	KC-135R	43 ARG
91476	KC-135R	457 OG
91477	KC-135E	63 ARS★
91478	KC-135R	153 ARS
91479	KC-135E	146 ARS
91480	KC-135Q	350 ARS
91482	KC-135R	22 ARW
91483	KC-135R	166 ARS
91484	KC-135E	147 ARS
91485	KC-135R	150 ARS
91486	KC-135R	380 ARW
91487	KC-135E	108 ARS
91488	KC-135R	19 ARW
91489	KC-135E	191 ARS
91490	KC-135Q	71 ARS
91492	KC-135R	92 ARW
91493	KC-135E	132 ARS
91495	KC-135R	173 ARS
91496	KC-135E	146 ARS
91497	KC-135R	150 ARS
91498	KC-135R	366 Wg
91499	KC-135E	196 ARS
91500	KC-135R	380 ARW
91501	KC-135R	398 OG
91502	KC-135R	380 ARW
91503	KC-135E	141 ARS
91504	KC-135Q	22 ARW
91505	KC-135R	196 ARS
91506	KC-135E	147 ARS
91507	KC-135R	28 ARS
91508	KC-135R	380 ARW
91509	KC-135E	196 ARS
91510	KC-135Q	
91511	KC-135R	19 ARW
91512	KC-135Q	22 ARW
91513	KC-135Q	71 ARS
91514	KC-135E	55 Wg
91515	KC-135R	22 ARW
91516	KC-135E	196 ARS
91517	KC-135R	380 ARW
91518	EC-135K	8 ADCS
91519	KC-135E	146 ARS
91520	KC-135Q	350 ARS
91521	KC-135R	133 ARS
91522	KC-135R	136 ARS
91523	KC-135Q	350 ARS

Lockheed C-141B Starlifter
60 AMW Travis AFB, California
62 AW McChord AFB, Washington
63 AW Norton AFB, California
97 AMW Altus AFB, Oklahoma (r/y)
155 ALS/164 AG Memphis, Tennessee ANG (r)
183 ALS/172 AG Jackson Field AFB, Mississippi ANG (bl)
305 AMW McGuire AFB, New Jersey (bl/w)
356 ALS/445 AW, Wright-Patterson AFB, Ohio★
437 AW Charleston AFB, South Carolina (bl/y)
452 AMW March AFB, California (r/y)★
756 ALS/459 AW Andrews AFB, Maryland (bk)
(★=AFRES, Air Force Reserve)

FY61		
12778		155 ALS

FY63		
38075		60 AMW
38076		305 AMW
38080		155 ALS
38081		62 AW

38082	62 AW	50241	62 AW	60153	756 ALS★
38083	305 AMW	50242	60 AMW	60154	97 AMW
38084	452 AMW★	50243	60 AMW	60155	305 AMW
38085	452 AMW★	50244	62 AW	60156	62 AW
38086	62 AW	50245	60 AMW	60157	155 ALS
38087	62 AW	50247	60 AMW	60158	62 AW
38088	97 AMW	50248	452 AMW★	60159	62 AW
38089	62 AW	50249	356 ALS★	60160	60 AMW
38090	305 AMW	50250	60 AMW	60161	62 AW
		50251	60 AMW	60162	305 AMW
FY64		50252	60 AMW	60163	305 AMW
40609	97 AMW	50254	60 AMW	60164	183 ALS
40610	437 AW	50256	60 AMW	60165	62 AW
40611	437 AW	50257	60 AMW	60166	60 AMW
40612	437 AW	50258	62 AW	60167	437 AW
40613	305 AMW	50259	60 AMW	60168	437 AW
40614	183 ALS	50260	60 AMW	60169	356 ALS★
40615	437 AW	50261	356 ALS★	60171	97 AMW
40616	305 AMW	50263	62 AW	60172	62 AW
40617	97 AMW	50265	60 AMW	60174	756 ALS★
40618	437 AW	50266	437 AW	60175	62 AW
40619	437 AW	50267	62 AW	60177	356 ALS★
40620	183 ALS	50268	60 AMW	60178	305 AMW
40621	305 AMW	50269	437 AW	60179	62 AW
40622	183 ALS	50270	437 AW	60180	155 ALS
40623	305 AMW	50271	756 ALS★	60181	452 AMW★
40625	305 AMW	50272	305 AMW	60182	452 AMW★
40626	305 AMW	50273	437 AW	60183	60 AMW
40627	305 AMW	50275	437 AW	60184	62 AW
40628	305 AMW	50276	305 AMW	60185	183 ALS
40629	437 AW	50277	62 AW	60186	183 ALS
40630	305 AMW	50278	63 AW	60187	437 AW
40631	437 AW	50279	437 AW	60190	183 ALS
40632	183 ALS	50280	305 AMW	60191	60 AMW
40633	305 AMW	59397	62 AW	60192	62 AW
40634	97 AMW	59399	62 AW	60193	452 AMW★
40635	62 AW	59400	97 AMW	60194	437 AW
40637	459 AW★	59401	437 AW	60195	305 AMW
40638	305 AMW	59402	97 AMW	60196	437 AW
40639	183 ALS	59403	60 AMW	60197	62 AW
40640	183 ALS	59404	62 AW	60198	62 AW
40642	452 AMW★	59405	305 AMW	60199	305 AMW
40643	60 AMW	59406	63 AW	60200	62 AW
40644	437 AW	59408	437 AW	60201	452 AMW★
40645	756 ALS★	59409	445 AW	60202	437 AW
40646	305 AMW	59411	305 AMW	60203	97 AMW
40649	437 AW	59412	356 ALS★	60204	305 AMW
40650	305 AMW	59413	305 AMW	60205	62 AW
40651	305 AMW	59414	452 AMW★	60206	62 AW
40653	62 AW			60207	305 AMW
		FY66		60208	62 AW
FY65		60128	62 AW	60209	437 AW
50216	756 ALS★	60129	62 AW	67944	60 AMW
50217	305 AMW	60130	183 ALS	67945	437 AW
50218	62 AW	60131	437 AW	67946	62 AW
50219	60 AMW	60132	305 AMW	67947	305 AMW
50220	305 AMW	60133	305 AMW	67948	305 AMW
50221	305 AMW	60134	356 ALS★	67949	62 AW
50222	155 ALS	60135	437 AW	67950	305 AMW
50223	305 AMW	60136	452 AMW★	67951	62 AW
50224	305 AMW	60137	62 AW	67952	452 AMW★
50225	452 AMW★	60138	97 AMW	67953	356 ALS★
50226	756 ALS★	60139	155 ALS	67954	356 ALS★
50227	97 AMW	60140	305 AMW	67955	437 AW
50229	452 AMW★	60141	62 AW	67956	305 AMW
50230	60 AMW	60144	437 AW	67957	452 AMW★
50231	60 AMW	60145	305 AMW	67958	62 AW
50232	63 AW	60146	305 AMW	67959	452 AMW★
50234	60 AMW	60147	60 AMW		
50235	62 AW	60148	60 AMW	*FY67*	
50237	60 AMW	60149	437 AW	70001	62 AW
50238	60 AMW	60151	452 AMW★	70002	437 AW
50239	60 AMW	60152	452 AMW★	70003	62 AW
50240	62 AW				

70004	437 AW	70015	452 AMW★	70025	305 AMW
70005	62 AW	70016	437 AW	70026	437 AW
70007	305 AMW	70018	62 AW	70027	305 AMW
70009	62 AW	70019	305 AMW	70028	62 AW
70010	437 AW	70020	305 AMW	70029	155 ALS
70011	437 AW	70021	155 ALS	70031	356 ALS★
70012	437 AW	70022	60 AMW	70164	60 AMW
70013	305 AMW	70023	356 ALS★	70165	305 AMW
70014	305 AMW	70024	155 ALS	70166	305 AMW (VIP)

First-time visitor to the UK, 437 AW McDonnell Douglas C-17A 23291 visited Mildenhall in May 1994. *PRM*

US based USN/USMC Aircraft

Boeing E-6A Mercury
Sea Control Wing 1 (SCW-1), Tinker AFB, Oklahoma

162782	SCW-1
162783	SCW-1
162784	SCW-1
163918	SCW-1
163919	SCW-1
163920	SCW-1
164386	SCW-1
164387	SCW-1
164388	SCW-1
164404	SCW-1
164405	SCW-1
164406	SCW-1
164407	SCW-1
164408	SCW-1
164409	SCW-1
164410	SCW-1

**McDonnell Douglas
C-9B Skytrain II**
VR-46 Atlanta, Georgia [JS];
VR-51 Glenview NAS, Illinois [RV];
VR-52 Willow Grove NAS, Pennsylvania [JT];
VR-56 Norfolk NAS, Virginia [JU];
VR-57 North Island NAS, California [RX];
VR-58 Jacksonville NAS, Florida [JV];
VR-59 Dallas, Texas [RY];
VR-60 Memphis NAS, Tennessee [RT];
VR-61 Whidbey Island NAS, Washington [RS];
VR-62 Detroit, Michigan [JW];
SOES Cherry Point MCAS, North Carolina

159113 [JS]	VR-46
159114 [RX]	VR-57
159115 [RX]	VR-57
159116 [RX]	VR-57
159117 [JU]	VR-56
159118 [JU]	VR-56
159119 [JU]	VR-56
159120 [JT]	VR-52
160046	SOES
160047	SOES
160048 [JV]	VR-58
160049 [JV]	VR-58
160050 [JV]	VR-58
160051 [RS]	VR-61
161266 [RY]	VR-59
161529 [RY]	VR-59
161530 [RY]	VR-59
162753 [RV]	VR-51
162754 [JT]	VR-52
163036 [JT]	VR-52
163037 [JT]	VR-52
163208 [JS]	VR-46
163511 [JS]	VR-46
163512 [JS]	VR-46
163513 [JW]	VR-62
164605 [RT]	VR-60
164606 [RT]	VR-60
164607 [RS]	VR-61
164608 [RS]	VR-61

**Grumman C-20D Gulfstream III/
C-20G Gulfstream IV***
CFLSW, NAF Washington;
VR-48, NAF Washington [JR]

163691	CFLSW
163692	CFLSW
165093* [JR]	VR-48
165094* [JR]	VR-48
165151* [JR]	VR-48
165152* [JR]	VR-48
165153* [JR]	VR-48

Lockheed C-130 Hercules
VRC-50 North Island NAS, California [RG];
VR-53 Martinsburg, West Virginia [WV];
VR-54 New Orleans NAS, Louisiana [CW];
VR-55 Moffett Field NAS, California [RU];
VMGR-152 Futenma MCAS, Japan [QD];
VMGR-234 NAS Fort Worth, Texas [QH];
VMGR-252 Cherry Point MCAS, North Carolina [BH];
VMGRT-253 Cherry Point MCAS, North Carolina [GR];
VMGR-352 El Toro MCAS, California [QB];
VMGR-452 Stewart Field, New York [NY]

147572 [QB]	KC-130F	VMGR-352
147573 [QD]	KC-130F	VMGR-152
148246 [GR]	KC-130F	VMGRT-253
148247 [QD]	KC-130F	VMGR-152
148248 [QD]	KC-130F	VMGR-152
148249 [GR]	KC-130F	VMGRT-253
148890 [GR]	KC-130F	VMGRT-253
148891 [BH]	KC-130F	VMGR-252
148892 [GR]	KC-130F	VMGRT-253
148893 [QH]	KC-130F	VMGR-234
148894 [GR]	KC-130F	VMGRT-253
148895 [BH]	KC-130F	VMGR-252
148896 [BH]	KC-130F	VMGR-252
148897 [BH]	KC-130F	VMGR-252
148898 [BH]	KC-130F	VMGR-252
148899 [BH]	KC-130F	VMGR-252
149787 [RG]	KC-130F	VRC-50
149788 [BH]	KC-130F	VMGR-252
149789 [BH]	KC-130F	VMGR-252
149790	C-130F	
149791 [QB]	KC-130F	VMGR-352
149792 [QB]	KC-130F	VMGR-352
149793 [RG]	KC-130F	VRC-50
149794	C-130F	
149795 [QB]	KC-130F	VMGR-352
149796 [QB]	KC-130F	VMGR-352
149797	C-130F	
149798 [QB]	KC-130F	VMGR-352
149799 [QD]	KC-130F	VMGR-152
149800 [QB]	KC-130F	VMGR-352
149803 [GR]	KC-130F	VMGRT-253
149804 [GR]	KC-130F	VMGRT-253
149805 [RG]	C-130F	VRC-50
149806 [GR]	KC-130F	VMGRT-253
149807 [QD]	KC-130F	VMGR-152
149808 [BH]	KC-130F	VMGR-252
149811 [GR]	KC-130F	VMGRT-253
149812 [QD]	KC-130F	VMGR-152
149815 [QB]	KC-130F	VMGR-352
149816 [QD]	KC-130F	VMGR-152
150684 [GR]	KC-130F	VMGRT-253
150686 [BH]	KC-130F	VMGR-252
150687 [GR]	KC-130F	VMGRT-253
150688 [GR]	KC-130F	VMGRT-253
150689 [QB]	KC-130F	VMGR-352
150690 [QD]	KC-130F	VMGR-152
151891	TC-130G	*BlueAngels*
160013 [QB]	KC-130R	VMGR-352
160014 [QB]	KC-130R	VMGR-352
160015 [QB]	KC-130R	VMGR-352
160016 [QB]	KC-130R	VMGR-352
160017 [QB]	KC-130R	VMGR-352

USN/USMC

160018 [QB]	KC-130R	VMGR-352	164441 [QH]	KC-130T	VMGR-234
160019 [QB]	KC-130R	VMGR-352	164442 [QH]	KC-130T	VMGR-234
160020 [QB]	KC-130R	VMGR-352	164597 [NY]	KC-130T-30	VMGR-452
160021 [QB]	KC-130R	VMGR-352	164598 [QH]	KC-130T-30	VMGR-234
160022 [QB]	KC-130R	VMGR-352	164759 [NY]	KC-130T	VMGR-452
160240 [QB]	KC-130R	VMGR-352	164760 [QH]	KC-130T	VMGR-234
160625 [BH]	KC-130R	VMGR-252	164762 [CW]	C-130T	VR-54
160626 [BH]	KC-130R	VMGR-252	164763 [CW]	C-130T	VR-54
160627 [BH]	KC-130R	VMGR-252	164993 [CW]	C-130T	VR-54
160628 [BH]	KC-130R	VMGR-252	164994 [WV]	C-130T	VR-53
162308 [QH]	KC-130T	VMGR-234	164995 [CW]	C-130T	VR-54
162309 [QH]	KC-130T	VMGR-234	164996 [WV]	C-130T	VR-53
162310 [QH]	KC-130T	VMGR-234	164997 [WV]	C-130T	VR-53
162311 [QH]	KC-130T	VMGR-234	164998 [WV]	C-130T	VR-53
162785 [QH]	KC-130T	VMGR-234	164999 [NY]	KC-130T	VMGR-452
162786 [QH]	KC-130T	VMGR-234	165000 [QH]	KC-130T	VMGR-234
163022 [QH]	KC-130T	VMGR-234	165158		C-130T	VR-55
163023 [QH]	KC-130T	VMGR-234	165159		C-130T	VR-55
163310 [NY]	KC-130T	VMGR-452	165160		C-130T	VR-55
163311 [NY]	KC-130T	VMGR-452	165161		C-130T	VR-55
163591 [NY]	KC-130T	VMGR-452	165162 [NY]	KC-130T	VMGR-452
163592 [NY]	KC-130T	VMGR-452	165163 [NY]	KC-130T	VMGR-452
164105 [NY]	KC-130T	VMGR-452	165313		C-130T	
164106 [NY]	KC-130T	VMGR-452	165314		C-130T	
164180 [NY]	KC-130T	VMGR-452	165315		KC-130T	
164181 [NY]	KC-130T	VMGR-452	165316		KC-130T	

AIRBAND LISTENERS

Turn your airband radio into a monitoring station with the amazing AUTO-VOX. Connect to any radio with a squelch control and the AUTO-VOX will automatically turn your recorder on and off as transmissions are detected.
"A must for all Scanner Owners"

Kit £15.00	AUTO - VOX	Built £25

"Return to a neatly compressed tape of all the action"

Available as an easy assemble kit with full instructions or ready built and tested. Or send SAE or IRC for full details of this and all our scanner upgrades.

Radio Research (MAM) P.O. Box 555 Stoke-on-Trent ST6 5BF

Addendum

Serial	Type (other identity) [code]	Owner/operator, location or fate	Notes
WB711	DHC1 Chipmunk T10 (G-APPM)	Privately owned, Duxford	
WD374	DHC1 Chipmunk T10 [903]	Sold to Tasmania, November 1994	
WH953	EE Canberra B6(mod)	Scrapped at Farnborough, January 1995	
WJ607	EE Canberra T17A (G-BVWU) [EB]	Privately owned, Exeter	
WJ874	EE Canberra T4 [AS]	RAF No 39(1 PRU) Sqn, Marham	
WK163	EE Canberra B6(mod) (G-BVWC)	Privately owned, Bruntingthorpe	
WM994	Hawker Sea Hawk FB5 (G-SEAH)	Sold to the USA, December 1994	
WP180	Hawker Hunter F5 (WP190/7582M/8473M) [K]	Gloucestershire Aviation Collection, Hucclecote	
WP856	DHC1 Chipmunk T10 (G-BVWP) [904]	Privately owned, Cuckfield	
WT333	EE Canberra B6(mod) (G-BVXC)	Privately owned, Bruntingthorpe	
WT744	Hawker Hunter GA11 [868/VL]	Privately owned, Eaglescott	
XE685	Hawker Hunter GA11 (G-GAII) [861/VL]	Lightning Flying Club, Exeter	
XG691	DH112 Sea Venom FAW22 [93/J]	Gloucestershire Aviation Collection, Hucclecote	
XH980	Gloster Javelin FAW8 (7867M) <ff>	Privately owned, Stock, Essex	
XJ639	Hawker Hunter F6A (8687M) [H]	Privately owned, Ipswich	
XL598	Hawker Hunter T8C (G-BVWG) [880/VL]	Privately owned, Exeter	
XL739	Saro Skeeter AOP12	AAC Wattisham, for display	
XM370	Hunting Jet Provost T3A (G-BVSP) [10]	Privately owned, Bruntingthorpe	
XM376	Hunting Jet Provost T3A [27]	Privately owned, Binbrook	
XM378	Hunting Jet Provost T3A [34]	Privately owned, Binbrook	
XM386	Hunting Jet Provost T3 (8076M) [08]	To Stanford PTA, 1994	
XM412	Hunting Jet Provost T3A (9011M) [41]	Privately owned, Binbrook	
XM424	Hunting Jet Provost T3A	Privately owned, Binbrook	
XM455	Hunting Jet Provost T3A (8960M) [K]	Privately owned, Binbrook	
XM479	Hunting Jet Provost T3A (G-BVEZ)	Privately owned, Binbrook	
XN185	Slingsby T21B Sedbergh TX1 (8942M)	Sold as BGA 4077, 1994	
XN510	Hunting Jet Provost T3A [40]	Privately owned, Binbrook	
XN692	DH110 Sea Vixen FAW2 [125/E]	Privately owned, Stock, Essex	
XN769	EE Lightning F2 (8402M) <ff>	Privately owned, Stock, Essex	
XP547	Hunting Jet Provost T4 (8992M) [N,03]	Privately owned, Binbrook	
XR980	HS Gnat T1 (8622M) [70]	Sold to the USA as N936FC, October 1994	
XS597	HS Andover C1	Sold as 3D-ATS, November 1994	
XS868	WS58 Wessex HAS1	RNAS Lee-on-Solent, BDRT	
XT443	WS Wasp HAS1 [422/AU]	IHM, Weston-super-Mare	
XT752	Fairey Gannet T5 (WN365/G-APYO)	Sold to the USA, November 1994	
XV660	WS61 Sea King HAS6 [698/CL]	RN No 810 Sqn, Culdrose	
XV672	WS61 Sea King AEW2A	RN No 849 Sqn, Culdrose	
XW236	WS Puma HC1 [BZ]	RAF No 18 Sqn, Laarbruch	
XW264	HS Harrier T2 <ff>	Gloucestershire Aviation Collection, Hucclecote	
XW271	HS Harrier T4 [X]	SAH, RNAS Culdrose	
XW289	BAC Jet Provost T5A [73]	Privately owned, Cranfield	
XW313	BAC Jet Provost T5A (G-BVTB) [85]	Privately owned, Ipswich	
XW319	BAC Jet Provost T5A [76]	Sold to the USA, 1994	
XW322	BAC Jet Provost T5B [D]	Sold to the USA, 1994	
XW336	BAC Jet Provost T5A [67]	Sold to the USA, 1994	
XW412	BAC Jet Provost T5A [74]	Sold to the USA, 1994	
XW437	BAC Jet Provost T5A [71]	Privately owned, Binbrook	
XW903	WS Gazelle AH1	AAC No 3 (TA) Flt, Turnhouse	
XW913	WS Gazelle AH1 [U]	AAC No 663 Sqn, Wattisham	
XX187	HS Hawk T1A	RAF No 6 FTS, Finningley	
XX254	HS Hawk T1A	MoD(PE), BAe Brough	
XX381	WS Gazelle AH1	AAC No 657 Sqn, Dishforth	
XX416	WS Gazelle AH1	AAC No 657 Sqn, Dishforth	
XX435	WS Gazelle AH1	AAC No 662 Sqn, Gütersloh	
XX445	WS Gazelle AH1	AAC No 664 Sqn, Dishforth	
XX456	WS Gazelle AH1	AAC No 3(TA) Flt, Turnhouse	
XZ171	WS Lynx AH7	AAC No 664 Sqn, Wattisham	
XZ173	WS Lynx AH7 [W]	AAC No 663 Sqn, Wattisham	
XZ197	WS Lynx AH7	AAC No 669 Sqn, Dishforth	
XZ199	WS Lynx AH7	AAC No 657 Sqn, Dishforth	
XZ208	WS Lynx AH7	AAC No 664 Sqn, Dishforth	
XZ210	WS Lynx AH7 [X]	AAC No 663 Sqn, Wattisham	

Addendum

Notes	Serial	Type (other identity) [code]	Owner/operator, location or fate
	XZ239	WS Lynx HAS3 [307]	RN No 815 Sqn, Portland
	XZ301	WS Gazelle AH1	AAC No 663 Sqn, Wattisham
	XZ331	WS Gazelle AH1	AAC No 663 Sqn, Wattisham
	XZ581	WS61 Sea King HAS6 [503]	RN No 810 Sqn, Culdrose
	XZ594	WS61 Sea King HAR3	RAF SAREW, St Mawgan
	XZ596	WS61 Sea King HAR3	MoD(PE), Westland Yeovil
	XZ611	WS Lynx AH7 [Y]	AAC No 663 Sqn, Wattisham
	XZ651	WS Lynx AH7	AAC No 657 Sqn, Dishforth
	XZ668	WS Lynx AH7 [T]	AAC No 663 Sqn, Wattisham
	XZ998	BAe Harrier GR3 (9161M) [D]	To RAF Brüggen for BDRT, October 1994
	ZA128	WS61 Sea King HAS6 [598/CU]	RN No 706 Sqn, Culdrose
	ZA297	WS61 Sea King HC4 [C]	RN No 845 Sqn, Yeovilton
	ZA712	B-V Chinook HC2	RAF No 78 Sqn, Mount Pleasant, FI
	ZB500	WS Lynx 800 (G-LYNX)	IHM, Weston-super-Mare
	ZB605	BAe Harrier T8	RN No 899 Sqn OEU, Boscombe Down
	ZD277	WS Lynx AH7	AAC No 662 Sqn, Wattisham
	ZD435	BAe Harrier GR7 [AK]	RAF No 3 Sqn, Laarbruch
	ZD463	BAe Harrier GR7 [AL]	RAF No 3 Sqn, Laarbruch
	ZD579	BAe Sea Harrier F/A2 [002]	RN No 801 Sqn, Yeovilton
	ZD611	BAe Sea Harrier F/A2 [716]	RN No 899 Sqn, Yeovilton
	ZD709	Panavia Tornado GR1 [DG]	RAF No 31 Sqn, Brüggen
	ZE339	Panavia Tornado F3 [AQ]	RAF F3 OCU/No 56(R) Sqn, Coningsby
	ZE428	WS61 Sea King HC4	RN No 846 Sqn, Yeovilton
	ZE697	BAe Sea Harrier F/A2 [004]	RN No 801 Sqn, Yeovilton
	ZE732	Panavia Tornado F3 [AS]	RAF No 56(R) Sqn, Coningsby
	ZF121	WS61 Sea King HC4 [21]	RN No 772 Sqn, Portland
	ZF161	Shorts Tucano T1	RAF No 1 FTS, Linton-on-Ouse
	ZF375	Shorts Tucano T1	RAF No 1 FTS, Linton-on-Ouse
	ZF414	Shorts Tucano T1	RAF No 1 FTS, Linton-on-Ouse
	ZG507	BAe Harrier GR7 [AC]	RAF No 3 Sqn, Laarbruch
	ZG511	BAe Harrier GR7	RAF No 4 Sqn, Laarbruch
	ZG858	BAe Harrier GR7 [AG]	RAF No 3 Sqn, Laarbruch
	ZG916	WS Lynx AH9 [8]	AAC No 653 Sqn, Wattisham
	ZG989	PBN 2T Islander Astor (G-DLRA)	MoD(PE), A&AEE Boscombe Down
	ZH654	BAe Harrier T10	MoD(PE), A&AEE Boscombe Down
	ZH670	BAe Hawk 103	For RAF of Oman as 102
	ZH791	BAe Hawk 208	For R Malaysian AF as M40-34
	ZH792	BAe Hawk 208	For R Malaysian AF as M40-35

AIR SUPPLY

OPENING HOURS: 10-5pm DAILY
CLOSED WEDNESDAY & SUNDAY

FRIENDLY ADVICE AND HELP AVAILABLE.
RADIO TRADE-INS WELCOME.

Supplying the Aviation Industry:

Airlines, Aviators, Enthusiasts and Listeners

Specialists in Airband Scanners, Monitors, Aerials & Accessories

PHONE KEN COTHLIFF ON:

0113 250 9581

OR SEND £1.50 INC. P&P FOR **NEW** CATALOGUE, REFUNDABLE WITH FIRST ORDER.

AGENTS FOR: AIRTOURS - AFE - DAVE CLARK & ICOM - YUPITERU - AOR - LOWE RADIOS AND WOOSTER - SHABAK MODELS

83B, HIGH STREET, YEADON, LEEDS LS19 7TA. Fax: 0532 500119

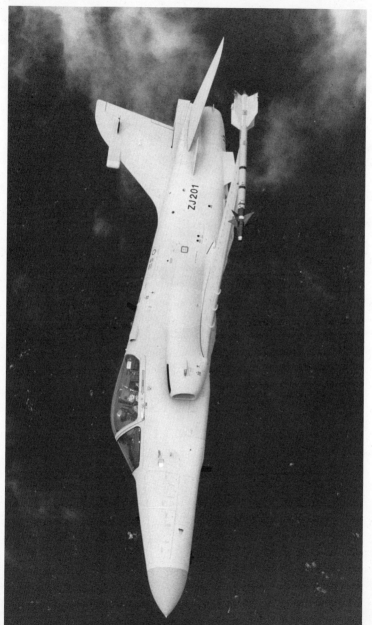

BAe Hawk 200RDA. *BAe Defence*

GK For a Personal & Friendly Service

GK Professional Advice & the BEST PRICE

THE PHOTOGRAPHIC & OPTICAL EQUIPMENT SPECIALIST FOR THE AVIATION ENTHUSIAST

We believe that, with over 30 years combined experience as aviation enthusiasts and in photographic retail, we are in a unique position to offer the very best advice to the aviation hobbyist.

EXPERT OPINIONS
PERSONAL SERVICE
QUALITY EQUIPMENT
FRIENDLY ADVICE
THE BEST PRICE

BINOCULARS & SCOPES

Viking
MINOLTA
PRAKTICA SPORT
STEINER GERMANY
SWIFT
ROSS LONDON
PYSIS Night Vision
Kowa
HERTEL & REUSS

CAMERAS

Canon CONTAX
MINOLTA Nikon
PRAKTICA RICOH
SIGMA YASHICA

LENSES

Canon CONTAX
MINOLTA Nikon
SIGMA TAMRON
Tokina Vivitar

☆ TRIPODS ☆ MONOPODS ☆ GADGET BAGS ☆ FILMS ☆

EXCLUSIVE
MAM95
CAM95
5% DISCOUNT VOUCHER
Excludes goods at SALE prices

GK PHOTOGRAPHIC LTD
324 Regent Street
London W1R 5AA.
Tel: 0171 637 1237 /
0171 636 5677 (24hr)

Access   Access

MasterCard   MasterCard

VISA   VISA

MAIL ORDER A SPECIALITY